T0073230

Membrane Computing Models:
Implementations

Gexiang Zhang • Mario J. Pérez-Jiménez •
Agustín Riscos-Núñez • Sergey Verlan •
Savas Konur • Thomas Hinze •
Marian Gheorghe

Membrane Computing Models: Implementations

 Springer

Gexiang Zhang 🆔
School of Control Engineering
Chengdu University of Information
Technology
Chengdu, China

Mario J. Pérez-Jiménez 🆔
Department of Computer Science
and Artificial Intelligence
University of Seville
Sevilla, Spain

Agustín Riscos-Núñez 🆔
Department of Computer Science
and Artificial Intelligence
University of Seville
Sevilla, Spain

Sergey Verlan 🆔
Département Informatique, LACL
Université Paris Est Créteil
Creteil cedex, France

Savas Konur 🆔
Department of Computer Science
University of Bradford
Bradford, West Yorkshire, UK

Thomas Hinze
Department of Bioinformatics
Friedrich Schiller University Jena
Jena, Thüringen, Germany

Marian Gheorghe 🆔
Department of Computer Science
University of Bradford
Bradford, West Yorkshire, UK

ISBN 978-981-16-1565-8   ISBN 978-981-16-1566-5 (eBook)
https://doi.org/10.1007/978-981-16-1566-5

This Springer imprint is published by the registered company Springer Nature Singapore Pte Ltd.
The registered company address is: 152 Beach Road, #21-01/04 Gateway East, Singapore 189721,
Singapore

Dedicated to Academician Gheorghe Păun's 70th Anniversary.

Foreword

An Interlaced Triad: Theory, Applications and Implementations

The present book nicely completes and illustrates the triad mentioned in the title above for the *membrane computing* research area.

Membrane computing (a more suggestive name could be *cellular computing*) is a branch of natural computing aiming to abstract computing models from the structure and the functioning of biological cells, considered alone or cooperating in populations of cells, tissues, and organs, neuronal nets included. The obtained models form a rather diverse-versatile *modeling framework*, characterized by a series of features which are attractive from a theoretical computer science point of view (especially in what concerns imagining new computing devices, involving new ideas concerning the computer architecture, data structures, operations with these structures, ways to organize/control the computations, and so on, with a direct and promising influence on the computing power and on the computational complexity/efficiency), but also very important from the point of view of applications (the models are distributed and parallel, involving discrete mathematics—which is adequate to a large variety of processes, from biology to economics, from linguistics to engineering, where traditional tools based on continuous mathematics, typically, differential equations, cannot be applied). From the applications point of view, the membrane computing models have also other attractive features—I only mention some of them: easy scalability/extensibility, non-linear complex behavior, easy programmability, and understandability/transparency.

In more than two decades since membrane computing research was initiated, a large bibliography was accumulated (see, e.g., the information provided by http://ppage.psystems.eu/ and by http://imcs.org.cn/—the latter one is the web page of the International Membrane Computing Society). As expected, initially mainly theoretical computer science investigations were carried out: variations of models (shortly called *P systems* in the community), trying to capture more and more biological features or motivated by "classic" computer science, results concerning the computing power, in comparison with usual computing hierarchies, of Turing, Chomsky types and related, computational complexity results. The results are somewhat expected for a natural computing model: Turing universality, reached sometimes with unexpectedly "simple" models; speed-up of computations, until theoretically solving intractable problems (typically, **NP**-complete problems) in feasible time (typically, polynomial); and so on.

Soon (actually, already in the first years of developing this research area) applications were explored, initially in biology—which is rather natural: the model is abstracted from the cell biology and the biologists need new (computational, discrete, understandable) models for investigating the cell. In time, the range of applications got wider and wider, while the applications became more and more sophisticated, hence more relevant for the users.

I recall here only three books (two are collective volumes) reporting applications of P systems, also suggestive in what concerns the areas of applications (rather general/diverse for the first volume: cell biology, computer graphics, cryptography, linguistics, sorting):

> Gabriel Ciobanu, Gheorghe Păun, Mario J. Pérez-Jiménez (Eds.), *Applications of Membrane Computing*, Springer-Verlag, 2006.
> Pierluigi Frisco, Marian Gheorghe, Mario J. Pérez-Jiménez (Eds.), *Applications of Membrane Computing in Systems and Synthetic Biology*, Springer-Verlag, 2014.
> Gexiang Zhang, Mario J. Pérez-Jiménez, Marian Gheorghe, *Real-Life Applications with Membrane Computing*, Springer-Verlag, 2017.

Many other similar volumes can be found in the bibliographies indicated above.

Especially for the applications, but also for theory (towards the application edge, e.g., of computational complexity), of a direct interest are the *simulators* and the *implementations* of membrane systems. A "standard" application in biology consists of writing a (mathematical) model, then simulating its evolution on a computer; this means writing a program, a software support, then making experiments (tuning parameters, checking the evolution in time, modifying certain features of the model, checking the evolution in time, and repeating these steps in a dialogue between biologist and computer scientist and between user and software producer), until adequately covering the modeled reality and until obtaining relevant insights about it.

The importance of having at hand an efficient, reliable, and easy to use computer support—both software and hardware—is obvious in this framework. This means the importance of *simulation* and of *implementation* of membrane systems.

The difference between the two is apparent—and we have to mention from the very beginning that at this moment there is no real bio-implementation of a P system, no lab "wet" simulation (unlike, for instance, the case of *DNA computing*, which started in 1987 by a theoretical model, the so-called splicing operation, introduced by Tom Head, but got an essential impulse in 1994, by the Leonard Adleman lab experiment of computing in a test tube, using DNA molecules). There are, however, many programs for simulating various types of P systems, using a large variety of programming languages and programming techniques—on the top of all these, there also exists a dedicated programming language, *P-lingua*, elaborated by the membrane computing research group at Seville University, Spain.

In several research groups, a series of attempts were made to implement P systems on a dedicated hardware (the big challenges are related to the implementation of the distribution and, mainly, of the parallelism of the model), one specially designed for this purpose or adapted to that (such as existing parallel hardware, like GPUs—graphic processing units).

The present book provides details about all these directions of investigation—and still more, as it starts with general considerations about the difficulties encountered when trying to simulate or implement (the borderline/difference between the two are not always sharp) a P system. It also describes the possibility of automatic designing of a P system, proposes a workbench for verifying the obtained models, and discusses a series of applications.

This is a really necessary and timely book, written by a team of professionals, among the most active and highly knowledgeable experts in membrane computing, from all three points of view mentioned in the title—theory, applications, implementations. The reader interested in modeling real-life processes, especially of a discrete, compartmental/distributed type, or in developing tools for that, software or hardware alike, will surely benefit from exploring this book.

Bucharest, Romania   Gheorghe Păun
November 25, 2020

Preface

Membrane computing is a branch of natural computing, investigating computational models, called *membrane systems* or *P systems*, inspired by the structure and functioning of the biological cell. This computing paradigm was initiated by Gheorghe Păun in 1998. The membrane computing community has succeeded to achieve during its more than 20 years' history a set of landmark successes: the establishment of the *International Membrane Computing Society* (IMCS); the organisation of four regular conference/workshop events, namely *European Branch of International Conference on Membrane Computing* (ECMC), *Asian Branch of International Conference on Membrane Computing* (ACMC), *Brainstorming Week on Membrane Computing* (BWMC), and *Chinese Workshop on Membrane Computing* (CWMC); and the gestation and birth of two periodic publications, *Journal of Membrane Computing* (JMC)—four issues per year—and IMCS Bulletin—two issues per year. IMCS awards three yearly IMCS Prizes: The PhD Thesis of the Year, The Theoretical Result of the Year and The Application of the Year.

This book presents for the first time to the international community a set of robust, efficient, reliable and easy-to-use tools supporting membrane computing models. As numerous theoretical results and a wide range of applications have been published in several comprehensive monographs or collective books

> G. Ciobanu, M.J. Pérez-Jiménez, Gh. Păun (eds.), *Applications of Membrane Computing*, in Natural Computing Series, Springer, 2006.
> P. Frisco, M. Gheorghe, M.J. Pérez-Jiménez (eds.), *Applications of Membrane Computing in Systems and Synthetic Biology*, in Emergence, Complexity and Computation Series, Springer, 2014.
> Gh. Păun, *Membrane Computing—An Introduction*, Springer, 2002.
> Gh. Păun, G. Rozenberg, A. Salomaa (eds.), *The Oxford Handbook of Membrane Computing*, Oxford University Press, 2010.
> G. Zhang, M.J. Pérez-Jiménez, M. Gheorghe. *Real-life applications with membrane computing*, Springer, 2017.
> G. Zhang, J. Cheng, T. Wang, X. Wang, J. Zhu. *Membrane Computing: Theory and Applications*, Science China Press, 2015.

this book aims to present the most recent and significant implementation models, algorithms and platforms of membrane computing models on a variety of software and hardware platforms, and to describe the most relevant applications, facilitating a better and deep understanding on how the tools are used in building, experimenting with and analysing membrane computing models of complex problems arising in robotics, automatic design of P systems, ecosystem modelling, systems and synthetic biology, and bioinformatics.

The chapters covered in this monograph provide a clear image of the depth and breadth of the software and hardware implementations of membrane systems.

- In Chap. 1, *Introduction*: An overview of membrane computing is provided. Software and hardware implementation development of P systems are presented. The challenging problems of P systems implementation are discussed.
- In Chap. 2, *P Systems Implementation on P-Lingua Framework*: P-Lingua framework, the most widely used product for the specification and simulation of different types of P systems, is described. A high-level tool for virtual experiments, membrane computing simulator (MeCoSim) is also presented.
- In Chap. 3, *Applications of Software Implementations of P Systems*: Automatic design of cell-like P systems and spiking neural P systems are discussed to address the programmability issue of membrane computing models. The methodologies for modelling real ecosystems and mobile robots motion planning are also presented.
- In Chap. 4, *Infobiotics Workbench: An In Silico Software Suite for Computational Systems Biology*: The Infobiotics Workbench, an integrated software suite developed for computational systems biology, is presented. The tool is built upon stochastic P systems, a probabilistic extension of P systems, as modelling framework. The platform utilises computer-aided modelling and analysis of biological systems through simulation, verification and optimisation.
- In Chap. 5, *Molecular Physics and Chemistry in Membranes: the Java Environment for Nature-Inspired Approaches (JENA)*: The JENA is described as a modular, configurable and extendable platform towards a *virtual laboratory* and a *virtual cell* complementing more abstract and more idealised approaches in membrane computing. An introduction to JENA with its features and capabilities from the user's perspective and from a technical point of view is given. Four illustrative case studies are used to demonstrate JENA's practicability and descriptive capacity.
- In Chap. 6, *P Systems Implementation on Graphics Processing Units (GPUs)*: The concepts behind GPU computing and a taxonomy of GPU-based simulators, generic, specific and adaptive simulation, are introduced.
- In Chap. 7, *P Systems Implementation on Field-Programmable Gate Arrays (FPGA)*: Different existing implementations of P systems using FPGA hardware are presented. The strong and the weak points of each implementation is given. A particular attention is given to the latest implementation of generalised numerical P systems that considers many advanced techniques. A discussion about the challenges and the necessity of an FPGA implementation is finally performed.

- In Chap. 8, *Applications of Hardware Implementation of P Systems*: Enzymatic numerical P system (ENPS) based robot controllers and path planning algorithm are implemented in FPGA, achieving a speedup of 10^5 and 10^4 order of magnitude compared to software simulation. FPGA-hardened (E)NPS in this research can be regarded as a heterogeneous multicore processor since membranes inside work as processing units which possess different functions.

This book provides comprehensive descriptions of software and hardware tools, making it a valuable resource for anyone interested in membrane computing models, and it will be of particular interest to researchers looking for implementation methodology of membrane systems and also a variety of computing models in natural computing. The readers can get benefits from this book in the aspects of software or hardware implementation ideas of parallel distributed computing models, software/hardware development ideas and skills, the link procedure between computing models with applications.

Chengdu, China   Gexiang Zhang
Sevilla, Spain   Mario J. Pérez-Jiménez
Sevilla, Spain   Agustín Riscos-Núñez
Paris, France   Sergey Verlan
Bradford, UK   Savas Konur
Jena, Germany   Thomas Hinze
Bradford, UK   Marian Gheorghe

Acknowledgments

The first thank is given to the father of membrane computing, Gheorghe Păun, for his persistently strong support and perfect foreword, especially on the occasion of his 70th birthday.

The conception of this book originates from the friendly and fruitful collaborations of our five teams (Chengdu, Sevilla, Paris, Bradford and Jena) in the past more than 10 years. Many contributors could not be included in the author list and are therefore acknowledged below.

The authors gratefully acknowledge the excellent work and outstanding contributions of Ignacio Pérez-Hurtado, David Orellana-Martín, Miguel Ángel Martínez-del-Amor, and Luis Valencia-Cabrera to the Sevilla team; Prithwineel Paul, Zeyi Shang, Jianping Dong, Zhu Ou, and Xiaoli Huang to the Chengdu team; Jonathan Blakes, Jamie Twycross, Natalio Krasnogor, Francisco Jose Romero-Campero, and Laurenţiu Mierlă to Infobiotics Workbench; 35 students up till now to the JENA software system implementation presented in Chap. 5; Anthony Aguillon, Benjamin Förster, Gerd Grünert, Hendrik Happe, Florian Höch, Sinan Kaya, Korcan Kirkici, Alexander Melcher, Daniel Noelpp, Jonas Pilot, and Lea Weber who claim the greatest share to turn the project into major success.

The work of Gexiang Zhang and Sergey Verlan is supported by the National Natural Science Foundation of China (61972324, 61672437, 61702428, 61373047, 61170016), Sichuan Science and Technology Program (2018GZ0185, 2018GZ0086), Beijing Advanced Innovation Center for Intelligent Robots and Systems (2019IRS14), New Generation Artificial Intelligence Science and Technology Major Project of Sichuan Province (2018GZDZX0043), and Artificial Intelligence Key Laboratory of Sichuan Province (2019RYJ06). The work of Savas Konur is supported by EPSRC research grant EP/R043787/1. The work of Mario Pérez-Jiménez, Agustín Riscos-Núñez and the rest of the Sevilla team is supported by research project TIN2017-89842-P (MABICAP), co-financed by Ministerio de Ciencia e Innovación of Spain, through the *Agencia Estatal de Investigación* (AEI), and by *Fondo Europeo de Desarrollo Regional* (FEDER) of the European Union.

Contents

Acronyms

3-COL	3-CoLor (problem)
AC	Alternating Current
AG	Average Generation
BBB	Binomial Block Based (algorithm)
CLBs	Configurable Logic Blocks
CPU	Central Processing Unit
CUDA	Compute Unified Device Architecture
DC	Direct Current
DCBA	Direct Distribution Based on Consistent Blocks Algorithm
DNA	Deoxyribonucleic Acid
DND	Direct Non-Deterministic Distribution
DNDP	Direct Non-Deterministic Algorithm with Probabilities
DSL	Domain Specific Language
DSP	Digital Signal Processing
ENPS	Enzymatic Numerical P Systems
FFs	Flip-Flops
FPGA	Field Programmable Gate Array
GAPE	Genetic Algorithm with the Permutation Encoding Technique
GNPS	Generalized Numerical P Systems
GPU	Graphics Processing Unit
HAM-CYCLE	Hamiltonian CYCLE
HDL	Hardware Description Language
HPC	High Performance Computing
IBL	Infobiotics Language
IBW	Infobiotics Workbench
ILA	Integrated Logic Analyzer
JENA	Java Environment for Nature-Inspired Approaches
JGAP	Java Genetic Algorithm Package
KP	Kernel P (Systems)
LC	Logic Cell
LFSR	Linear Feedback Shift Register
LHS	Left-Hand Side
LPP	Lattice Population P (Systems)
LUTs	Look-Up Tables

MC	Membrane Computing
MCSS	Multi-compartmental Stochastic Simulation
MeCoSim	Membrane Computing Simulator
MX	Multiplexers
NoFE	Number of Function Evaluations
NP problem	Nondeterministic Polynomial Time Problem
NPS	Numerical P systems
PDP	Population Dynamics P (System)
PID	Proportional Integral Derivative Controller
PPGA	Permutation Penalty Genetic Algorithm
PRNG	Pseudo Random Number Generator
PSNP	SNP Systems with Polarization
PSPACE	Polynomial Space (complete)
QIEA	Quantum-Inspired Evolutionary Algorithm
RHS	Right-Hand Side
RNA	RiboNucleic Acid
RRTs	Rapidly Exploring Random Trees
RTL	Register-Transfer Level
SAT	Satisfiability (problem)
SBML	Systems Biology Markup Language
SIMD	Single Instruction Multiple Data
SN	Spiking Neural (P system)
SNP	Spiking Neural P (System)
SP	Stochastic P (Systems)
SR	Success Rate
SRSim	Spatial Rules Simulator
SSA	Stochastic Simulation Algorithm
SNUPS	Simulator of Numerical P Systems
TRNG	True Random Number Generator
UART	Universal Asynchronous Receiver Transmitter
VHDL	VHSIC Hardware Description Language
VHSIC	Very High Speed Integrated Circuit

Introduction

1

1.1   Membrane Computing Overview

Membrane computing (MC for short) is a branch of *natural computing* investigating computational models called *membrane systems* or *P systems*, inspired by the structure and functionality of the *living cell*. This computing paradigm was introduced by Gh. Păun, initially in a technical report [26] and then in a journal paper [27]. The MC research has initially developed mostly as a theoretical investigation looking at various models and bringing inspiration from a multitude of living cell concepts, topics, and phenomena. All these models have in common a set of compartments separated by membranes and organized according to a certain structure (tree, graph) that can be fixed or dynamic. Each of these compartments contains biochemical entities, called *objects*, which evolve according to local rules by transforming multisets of objects and/or moving them from a compartment to a neighboring one. This common framework uses various bioinspired features such as *activators* and *inhibitors*, *membrane electrical charges*, *catalysts*, *membrane thickness*, and cross-membrane movement of objects (*symport*, *antiport*) in order to generate various types of models, all fine-tuned by a rigorous way of selecting them in a consistent and coherent manner. The main characteristic of these models is their distributed and parallel behavior, that is, the computation takes place in each compartment and multiple transformations and/or cross-membrane movement of objects may take place in parallel. Well-defined topics for many classes of (natural computing) computational models, such as *computational power*, *complexity*, and connections with other computational models, have been investigated, revealing a wealth of new and exciting results. A first research monograph [28] included some of these initial theoretical aspects of this field.

These theoretical investigations have paved the way for applications in biology, computer science, computer graphics, and linguistics. Some tools have been also produced, supporting these research developments. All these have been published in another Springer monograph [11]. The key theoretical developments and applications of membrane computing, at the level of 2010, have been presented in a handbook [29]. More recently, some more specific MC applications have been reported [16]. With the exploration of MC models with real-life background, more and more real-life complex and challenging applications have been investigated [14, 43].

From this very brief MC overview, it is clear that the theoretical investigations and MC applications have had a very consistent and steady development. With a multitude of models requesting, in certain circumstances, tools to verify various hypotheses and numerous applications involving the simulation, verification, and analysis of complex systems, a new type of research activity has been launched, the design and development of adequate software and hardware tools. Thus, this book will systematically report the results and applications on software and hardware implementations of a variety of MC models.

The rest of this chapter is organized as follows: Sect. 1.2 introduces software implementation of P systems. Section 1.3 introduces hardware implementation of P systems. Section 1.4 discusses challenging problems of P systems implementation. Concluding remarks, other implementations of P systems, and a brief presentation of the chapters of this book will be discussed in Sect. 1.5.

1.2   Software Implementation of P Systems

When conducting research in MC, the design of *computational models* (P systems) can be guided by a broad spectrum of questions, ranging from solving *hard* problems (i.e., problems having a high computational complexity) to modelling complex systems. The desired answer can be extracted from the analysis of the corresponding computations of the designed P system over initial scenarios of interest. Obviously, in order for the designs to be reliable, it is important to verify their correctness, that is, making sure that the described system actually reflects its expected behavior. In this context, the need for software implementations able to manipulate P systems and recreate their behavior naturally arose. Such automatic tools provide not only an invaluable help for the verification process (especially when dealing with large and complicated designs and/or long computations) but also the possibility to run virtual experiments and to process the data associated to the simulated computations (especially in the case of computational modelling of complex systems). A very brief overview of existing P systems simulators is provided in what follows. For a more detailed history and bibliography, we refer the reader to [11, 29, 33, 40].

First software implementations were written in `LISP` [38] and `Prolog` [19], followed closely by `Scheme` [2] and `Haskell` [1] simulators. Note that the term *implementation* is used in a software engineering sense (i.e., developing code that somehow captures the specification of an abstract theoretical model), but it does not correspond to a faithful and precise materialization of the semantics of the model. In particular, the inherent parallelism concerning rule applications in <u>one</u> step of a membrane system cannot be implemented *as is* in the sequential Central Processing

Unit (CPU) of a standard computer although it can be "imitated" or "emulated" by means of loops of intermediate auxiliary steps. Nevertheless, there were also several early attempts to get closer to such an ideal implementation by using parallel techniques of different programming languages, such as MPI for communicating threads in C++ [9, 10] or RMI for the communication among processes in different computers in Java [39].

From that point on, new simulators kept coming out on a regular basis as the field grew and different research groups started to investigate new types of membrane systems. However, at that time, software tools were mostly considered as auxiliary by-products, typically featuring an *ad hoc* design oriented to a specific type of P system, and they were not meant to be extended.

In this situation, P-Lingua project was created [12, 13], pursuing a standard formalization that could be used by software implementations independently of the underlying programming language used to develop the simulator. The initial goal was to cover as many types of P systems as possible and to define a syntax specification, which was similar to the notation used in the MC literature. Chapter 3 offers more details about P-Lingua project, as well as about MeCoSim, a general purpose tool for virtual experimentation in membrane computing built on top of P-Lingua.

It is also worth pointing out that there exist some specialized integrated simulation tools that offer modelization services to users, which are not required to have a strong membrane computing training (mostly dealing with biochemical processes). Some of the most relevant works in this direction are *Cyto-Sim* [34], *MetaPlab / MpTheory* [6], *BioSimWare* [3], *Infobiotics Workbench* [4] (see Chap. 4), and *The Java Environment for Nature-inspired Approaches (JENA)* [17] (see Chap. 5).

1.3   Hardware Implementation of P Systems

Software simulations of P systems face difficulties in expressing in an efficient way the parallel and distributed nature of the model as current-day computers are based on a different, mostly sequential, paradigm. So from the very beginning, a research aiming to accelerate the execution of P system simulators using different types of hardware platforms was proposed. Two main research directions have been developed in this respect, depending on the underlying hardware utilized: *Graphics Processing Unit* (GPU) *Compute Unified Device Architecture* (CUDA)-based and Field Programmable Gate Array (FPGA)-based implementations. We refer to Chaps. 6 and 7 for the presentation of the corresponding hardware.

The development cycle for a GPU CUDA-based implementation is very similar to a traditional software development cycle and allows a relatively quick prototyping and implementation of corresponding algorithms. The major difficulty is to handle the data parallelism provided by these devices. In the FPGA case, a unique circuit design is created for each concrete system and its initial data. This allows to optimize the circuit for the corresponding computation and to achieve important speedups of several orders of magnitude. In order to accommodate more designs, a software generator is used that provides a hardware description corresponding to the system description and its initial configuration.

First, FPGA-based implementation of a P systems model was proposed in 2003 by Petreska and Teuscher [30], for transitional P systems and using a variant of sequential rule application strategy. Then, in 2008–2010, Nguyen et al. presented a series of implementations of transitional P systems with maximal parallelism evolution strategy [22–25]. These implementations featured up to 500 times speedup with respect to a reference software implementation. In 2012, Quiros and Verlan proposed a first truly nondeterministic implementation of a variant of network of cells (a generic P systems model; see [15]) [31, 32, 42]. This is also the first implementation achieving a speedup of order 10^4. In 2019–2020, Shang et al. proposed an implementation of numerical P systems [35–37] with several applications in robotics and achieving a speedup of order 10^5. More details about these implementations can be found in Chap. 7.

The first GPU simulators came relatively late, in 2010 [7]. However, due to a lower development effort with respect to FPGA-based designs, their number is bigger. Besides P systems with active membranes [7, 8], population dynamics P (PDP) systems [21], spiking neural P systems [5], enzymatic numerical P systems, and evolution-communication P systems with energy [20] were targeted for simulation. The obtained speedups range from 1.6 to 100 with respect to a reference software implementation.

In conclusion, we would like to remark that the development of hardware implementations is very promising as it allows to achieve important speedups. Unfortunately, the development time for these implementations, especially for FPGA-based ones, is much larger than for an ordinary software one. So there is a kind of a trade-off between the efficiency of an implementation and the development speed. Hence, for a hardware implementation to be cost-effective, it should target a problem with significant further development, such as like mobile robot controller, in order to compensate for the high development effort.

We also refer to a recent paper [44] that gives a detailed overview of different hardware implementations of P systems.

1.4   Challenges of P Systems Implementation

We mention here some of the most significant challenges of P systems implementation that are discussed in the next chapters: inherent parallelism of the MC models, a broad spectrum of models, combining in different ways various features associated with the generic framework, the usability of the tools, and nondeterminism implementation on computers with von Neumann architecture. These challenges require new algorithms, adequate software and/or hardware platforms, generic or specific solutions, and an effort, in some cases, to produce tools that might appeal to researchers outside the MC community—we have in mind those complex systems requesting models that have to be simulated and analyzed with specific tools. More details can refer to [41, 44]. Some of these challenges are explained as follows:

- *Parallelism*: How to realize a P system with inherent parallelism is one of the main challenging problem in P systems software and/or hardware tools. The challenge results from both model design and simulator implementation or hardware constraints. Simulating P systems is a memory-demanding task, given that the execution of rules requires several accesses to memory for just one conditional operation [41]. The design of P system variants of high computational intensity and with memory-bandwidth bounded is a challenging task. The rule competition for objects in the selection phases and finding ways to extend the idea of adaptive simulators represent significant bottlenecks.
- *Nondeterminism*: Simulating a P system with nondeterminism on the inherently deterministic computers or hardware with von Neumann architecture is another main challenge. Pseudorandom numbers, instead pf actual random numbers, are used in the present simulators.
- *Universality and flexibility*: There are numerous P system models with their own syntactical elements, such as initial structures, initial multisets of objects and initial set of rules, and specific semantics of the execution strategy. Thus, it is a challenging task in the development of a software simulator or selection of a hardware platform that is flexible enough to support all the P system variants.

1.5   Concluding Remarks

As each of the following chapters has an abstract summarizing its content, we will not present here a summary of each chapter but will discuss instead the main problems pointing to where they appear in this book.

Three software platforms, P-Lingua (Chap. 2), Infobiotics Workbench (Chap. 4), and JENA Environment (Chap. 5), are described, pointing to their key features and usage. *P-Lingua* framework, probably the most widely used software tool, allows for the specification and simulation of a large spectrum of types of P systems. Algorithms describing the semantics of these classes of P systems and a higher level tool, called *MeCoSim*, providing a visual representation of the simulation environment, are presented. *Infobiotics Workbench* is an integrated software suite developed for computational systems biology and relying upon stochastic P systems. Its components providing computer-aided modelling and analysis of biological systems through simulation, verification, and optimization are described, and their usage illustrated with some case studies. *JENA* is a modular, configurable, and extendable platform conceived as a virtual laboratory and a virtual cell. Biological information processing is based on natural laws at a molecular level. Resulting principles make use of dedicated chemical reactions, mechanisms for transportation of biomolecules, and forces among molecules and their environment mainly induced by electric charges and by movement in local space. An introduction to JENA is presented, including its features and capabilities from the user's perspective and from a technical point of view. Four illustrative case studies are described.

Tools supporting the automatic design of various types of MC models (cell-like P systems and spiking neural P systems), by using various classes of genetic algorithms, are described in Chap. 3. The performance of the tools is proved through a set of examples. In the same chapter are illustrated the capabilities of the MeCoSim tool for modelling a complex ecosystem and issues related to the parallelization of a robot motion problem when modelled with a special class of numerical P systems.

As mentioned above, the parallelization of various processes occurring in the simulation of certain classes of MC models is a challenging aspect in building efficient tools. In this respect, implementations relying on specific hardware, namely, GPU and FPGA, are investigated in Chaps. 6 and 7, respectively. Concepts related to GPU computing and its applications are introduced. Three types of simulators are identified and presented: those developed for very specific P systems or family of P systems (specific simulators), others developed for a wide range of P systems inside a variant (generic simulators), and a hybrid simulator that receives high-level information to be better adapted (adaptive simulators). Some guidelines on how to develop new simulators for P systems on GPUs are presented.

The other hardware option for implementing parallel computation, FPGA, is discussed in the context of implementing generalized numerical P systems by considering many advanced techniques. A discussion related to the challenges posed by FPGA implementations is presented. Enzymatic numerical P systems-based robot controllers and path planning algorithm are implemented in FPGA, achieving a speedup of 10^5 and 10^4 order of magnitude compared to software simulation.

Also, there are other software tools, such as kPWorkbench [18] or MetaPlab [6], dedicated to the simulation and analysis of two specific classes of P systems, kernel P systems and Metabolic P systems, respectively, which are not presented in this book as they target topics that are not within its scope.

The gain obtained by reading this book is twofold: On the one hand, the tools presented are introduced together with a thorough investigation of various algorithms, methods, and guidelines regarding the implementation strategies, and on the other hand, a consistent description of the usage of the tools and a set of illustrative examples are presented.

We hope that the readers will find this book interesting, useful, and helpful in their own investigations and research and will open the desire to make use of these tools in modelling, analyzing, and better understanding of complex systems modelled with different types of membrane systems.

References

1. F. Arroyo, C. Luengo, A.V. Baranda, L. Mingo, A software simulation of transition P systems in Haskell, in *Membrane Computing (WMC 2002)*, ed. by Gh. Păun, G. Rozenberg, A. Salomaa, C. Zandron. Lecture Notes in Computer Science, vol. 2597 (2003), pp. 19–32. https://doi.org/10.1007/3-540-36490-0_2

2. D. Balbontín-Noval, M.J. Pérez-Jiménez, F. Sancho-Caparrini, A MzScheme implementation of transition P systems, in *Membrane Computing (WMC 2002)*, ed. by Gh. Păun, G. Rozenberg, A. Salomaa, C. Zandron. Lecture Notes in Computer Science, vol. 2597 (2003), pp. 58–73. https://doi.org/10.1007/3-540-36490-0_5

3. D. Besozzi, P. Cazzaniga, G. Mauri, D. Pescini, BioSimWare: a software for the modeling, simulation and analysis of biological systems, in *Membrane Computing (CMC 2010)*, ed. by M. Gheorghe, T. Hinze, Gh. Păun, G. Rozenberg, A. Salomaa. Lecture Notes in Computer Science, vol. 6501 (2010), pp. 119–143. https://doi.org/10.1007/978-3-642-18123-8_12

4. J. Blakes, J. Twycross, F.J. Romero-Campero, N. Krasnogor, The Infobiotics Workbench: an integrated in silico modelling platform for systems and synthetic biology. Bioinformatics **27**(23), 3323–3324 (2011). https://doi.org/10.1093/bioinformatics/btr571

5. J.P.A. Carandang, J.M.B. Villaflores, F.G.C. Cabarle, H.N. Adorna, M.A. Martínez-del-Amor, CuSNP: spiking neural P systems simulators in CUDA. Rom. J. Inf. Sci. Technol. **20**(1), 57–70 (2017)

6. A. Castellini, V. Manca, MetaPlab: a computational framework for metabolic P systems, in *Membrane Computing (WMC 2008)*, ed. by D.W. Corne, P. Frisco, Gh. Păun, G. Rozenberg, A. Salomaa. Lecture Notes in Computer Science, vol. 5391 (2008), pp. 157–168. https://doi.org/10.1007/978-3-540-95885-7_12

7. J.M. Cecilia, J.M. García, G.D. Guerrero, M.A. Martínez-del-Amor, I. Pérez-Hurtado, M.J. Pérez-Jiménez, Simulation of P systems with active membranes on CUDA. Briefings Bioinf. **11**(3), 313–322 (2010). https://doi.org/10.1093/bib/bbp064

8. J.M. Cecilia, J.M. García, G.D. Guerrero, M.A. Martínez-del-Amor, M.J. Pérez-Jiménez, M. Ujaldón, The GPU on the simulation of cellular computing models. Soft Comput. **16**(2), 231–246 (2012). https://doi.org/10.1007/s00500-011-0716-1

9. G. Ciobanu, G. Wenyuan, A parallel implementation of transition P systems, in *Pre-Proceedings of the Workshop on Membrane Computing, Tarragona, Spain, 2003*, ed. by A. Alhazov, C. Martín-Vide, Gh. Păun. Report RGML 28/03 (2003), pp. 169–184

10. G. Ciobanu, G. Wenyuan, P systems running on a cluster of computers, in *Membrane Computing (WMC 2003)*, ed. by C. Martín-Vide, G. Mauri, Gh. Păun, G. Rozenberg, A. Salomaa. Lecture Notes in Computer Science, vol.2933 (2004), pp. 123–139. https://doi.org/10.1007/978-3-540-24619-0_9

11. G. Ciobanu, M.J. Pérez-Jiménez, Gh. Păun, *Applications of Membrane Computing* (Springer, Berlin, 2005)

12. D. Díaz-Pernil, I. Pérez-Hurtado, M.J. Pérez-Jiménez, A. Riscos-Núñez, P-Lingua: a programming language for membrane computing, in *Proceedings of the Sixth Brainstorming Week on Membrane Computing*, ed. by D. Díaz-Pernil, C. Graciani, M.A. Gutiérrez-Naranjo, Gh. Păun, I. Pérez-Hurtado, A. Riscos-Núñez, Fénix Editora (2008), pp. 135–155

13. D. Díaz-Pernil, I. Pérez-Hurtado, M.J. Pérez-Jiménez, A. Riscos-Núñez, A P-Lingua programming environment for Membrane Computing, in *Membrane Computing (WMC 2008)*, ed. by D.W. Corne, P. Frisco, Gh. Păun, G. Rozenberg, A. Salomaa. Lecture Notes in Computer Science, vol. 5391 (2009), pp. 187–203. https://doi.org/10.1007/978-3-540-95885-7_14

14. S. Fan, P. Paul, T. Wu, H. Rong, G. Zhang, On applications of spiking neural P systems. Appl. Sci. **10**(20), 7011 (2020). https://doi.org/10.3390/app10207011

15. R. Freund, S. Verlan, A formal framework for static (tissue) P systems, in *Membrane Computing (WMC 2007)*, ed. by G. Eleftherakis, P. Kefalas, Gh. Păun, G. Rozenberg, A. Salomaa. Lecture Notes in Computer Science, vol. 4860 (2007), pp. 271–284. https://doi.org/10.1007/978-3-540-77312-2_17

16. P. Frisco, M. Gheorghe, M.J. Pérez-Jiménez, *Applications of Membrane Computing in Systems and Synthetic Biology* (Springer, Berlin, 2014)

17. T. Hinze, The Java Environment for Nature-inspired Approaches (JENA): A workbench for bioComputing and bioModelling enthusiasts, in *Enjoying Natural Computing, Series Lecture Notes in Computer Science*, ed. by C. Graciani, A. Riscos-Núñez, Gh. Păun, G. Rozenberg, A. Salomaa, vol. 11270 (2018), pp. 155–169. https://doi.org/10.1007/978-3-030-00265-7_13

18. S. Konur, L. Mierlă, F. Ipate, M. Gheorghe, kP-Workbench: a software suite for membrane systems. SoftwareX **11**, Article No. 100407 (2020)
19. M. Malita, Membrane computing in Prolog, in *Pre-Proceedings of the Workshop on Multiset Processing, Curtea de Arges, Romania, TR 140, CDMTCS*, ed. by C.S. Calude, M.J. Dinneen, Gh. Păun (University of Auckland, Auckland, 2000), pp. 159–175
20. M.A. Martínez-del-Amor, M. García-Quismondo, L.F. Macías-Ramos, L. Valencia-Cabrera, A. Riscos-Núñez, M.J. Pérez-Jiménez, Simulating P systems on GPU devices: a survey. Fundam. Inform. **136**(3), 269–284 (2015). https://doi.org/10.3233/FI-2015-1157
21. M.A. Martínez-del-Amor, L.F. Macías-Ramos, L. Valencia-Cabrera, M.J. Pérez-Jiménez, Parallel simulation of population dynamics P systems: updates and roadmap. Nat. Comput. **15**(4), 565–573 (2016). https://doi.org/10.1007/s11047-016-9566-1
22. V.T.T. Nguyen, *An Implementation of the Parallelism, Distribution and Nondeterminism of Membrane Computing Models on Reconfigurable Hardware* (University of South Australia, Australia, 2010)
23. V.T.T. Nguyen, D. Kearney, G. Gioiosa, An algorithm for non-deterministic object distribution in P systems and its implementation in hardware, in *Membrane Computing (WMC 2008)*, ed. by D.W. Corne, P. Frisco, Gh. Păun, G. Rozenberg, A. Salomaa. Lecture Notes in Computer Science, vol.5391 (2008), pp. 325–354. https://doi.org/10.1007/978-3-540-95885-7_24
24. V.T.T. Nguyen, D. Kearney, G. Gioiosa, An implementation of membrane computing using reconfigurable hardware. Comput. Inf. **27**(3+), 551–569 (2008)
25. V.T.T. Nguyen, D. Kearney, G. Gioiosa, A region-oriented hardware implementation for Membrane Computing applications, in *Membrane Computing (WMC 2009)*, ed. by Gh. Păun, M.J. Pérez-Jiménez, A. Riscos, G. Rozenberg, A. Salomaa. Lecture Notes in Computer Science, vol. 5957 (2010), pp. 385–409. https://doi.org/10.1007/978-3-642-11467-0_27
26. Gh. Păun, Computing with membranes, in *Technical Report* (Turku Centre for Computer Science, Turku, 1998)
27. Gh. Păun, Computing with membranes. J. Comput. Syst. Sci. **61**(1), 108–143 (2000). https://doi.org/10.1006/jcss.1999.1693
28. Gh. Păun, *Membrane Computing, An Introduction* (Springer, Berlin, 2002)
29. Gh. Păun, G. Rozenberg, A. Salomaa, *The Oxford Handbook of Membrane Computing* (Oxford University, Oxford, 2010)
30. B. Petreska, C. Teuscher, A reconfigurable hardware membrane system, in *Membrane Computing (WMC 2003)*, ed. by C. Martín-Vide, G. Mauri, Gh. Păun, G. Rozenberg, A. Salomaa. Lecture Notes in Computer Science, vol. 2933 (2003), pp. 269–285. https://doi.org/10.1007/978-3-540-24619-0_20
31. J. Quirós, *Implementación Sobre Hardware Reconfigurable de una Arquitectura no Determinista, Paralela y Distribuida de Alto Rendimiento, Basada en Modelos de Computación con Membranas*, Ph.D. thesis (Universidad de Sevilla, Sevilla, 2015, in Spanish). http://hdl.handle.net/11441/39088
32. J. Quirós, S. Verlan, J. Viejo, A. Millán, M.J. Bellido, Fast hardware implementations of static P systems. Comput. Inf. **35**(3), 687–718 (2016)
33. S. Raghavan, K. Chandrasekaran, Tools and simulators for membrane computing: a literature review, in *Bio-inspired Computing–Theories and Applications (BIC-TA 2016)*, ed. by M. Gong, L. Pan, T. Song, G. Zhang. Communications in Computer and Information Science, vol. 681 (Springer, Singapore, 2016), pp. 249–277. https://doi.org/10.1007/978-981-10-3611-8_23
34. S. Sedwards, T. Mazza, Cyto-Sim: a formal language model and stochastic simulator of membrane-enclosed biochemical processes. Bioinformatics **23**(20), 2800–2802 (2007). https://doi.org/10.1093/bioinformatics/btm416
35. Z. Shang, *Hardware Implementation of Cell-inspired Computational Models*. Ph.D. Thesis (University Paris-Est Créteil Val de Marne, Paris, 2020)
36. Z. Shang, S. Verlan, G. Zhang, Hardware implementation of numerical P systems, in *Proceedings of the 20th International Conference on Membrane Computing, CMC20, August 5–8, 2019*, ed. by Gh. Păun (Curtea de Arges, Romania, 2019), pp. 463–474

37. Z. Shang, S. Verlan, G. Zhang, H. Rong, FPGA implementation of numerical P systems. Int. J. Unconv. Comput. **16**(2–3), 279–302 (2021)
38. Y. Suzuki, H. Tanaka. On a LISP implementation of a class of P systems. Rom. J. Inf. Sci. Technol. **3**(2), 173–186 (2000)
39. A. Syropoulos, E.G. Mamatas, P.C. Allilomes, K.T. Sotiriades, A distributed simulation of transition P systems, in *Membrane Computing (WMC 2003)*, ed. by C. Martín-Vide, G. Mauri, Gh. Păun, G. Rozenberg, A. Salomaa. Lecture Notes in Computer Science, vol. 2933 (2004), pp. 357–368. https://doi.org/10.1007/978-3-540-24619-0_25
40. L. Valencia-Cabrera, D. Orellana-Martín, M.A. Martínez-del-Amor, M.J. Pérez-Jiménez, An interactive timeline of simulators in Membrane Computing. J. Membr. Comput. **1**, 209–222 (2019). https://doi.org/10.1007/s41965-019-00016-z
41. L. Valencia-Cabrera, I. Pérez-Hurtado, M.A. Martínez-del-Amor, Simulation challenges in membrane computing. J. Membr. Comput. **2**(4), 392–402 (2020). https://doi.org/10.1007/s41965-020-00056-w
42. S. Verlan, J. Quirós, Fast hardware implementations of P systems, in *Membrane Computing (CMC 2012)*, ed. by E. Csuhaj-Varjú, M. Gheorghe, G. Rozenberg, A. Salomaa, G. Vaszil. Lecture Notes in Computer Science, vol. 7762 (2012), pp. 404–423. https://doi.org/10.1007/978-3-642-36751-9_27
43. G. Zhang, M.J. Pérez-Jiménez, M. Gheorghe, *Real-life Applications with Membrane Computing* (Springer, Berlin, 2017)
44. G. Zhang, Z. Shang, S. Verlan, M.A. Martínez-del-Amor, C. Yuan, L. Valencia-Cabrera, M.J. Pérez-Jiménez, An overview of hardware implementation of Membrane Computing models. ACM Comput. Surv. **53**(4), Article No. 90, 1–38 (2020). https://doi.org/10.1145/3402456

P Systems Implementation on P-Lingua Framework

2

2.1 Introduction

As previously mentioned, from the early days of the discipline, different approaches have been followed to provide software tools assisting the P systems designers in their design and verification tasks for a number of membrane system types and variants. However, at the beginning, the most common case was the development of specific-purpose tools devoted to the solution of a particular model based on a P system or P systems family. While these early initiatives constituted relevant achievements for membrane computing, their usefulness for the general community was significant mostly in the context of the specific paper or scientific result they were developed around. Surveys on the first generation of software tools related to membrane computing can be found in [5, 49].

In order to move a step forward in this sense, aiming to provide some solution for the P systems community in the form of a set of general tools for the software implementation of P systems, P-Lingua framework emerged more than a decade ago. As a first crucial element in the framework, a specification language, the so-called P-Lingua language, was defined, aiming to be a standard for the community to speak the same language when defining P systems. One of the advantages of having such a standard is to avoid ambiguities, and moreover to foster collaboration, facilitating that researchers share their designs, even if they use different simulation software—similarly as the Systems Biology Markup Language (SBML) format works for the systems biology community.

The language started with some very general elements common to most P system types, such as the membrane structure, objects, membrane labels, or rewriting rules. Along with such general elements, each P system type or variant would admit specific rules, and the framework would provide parsing tools to detect syntactic or semantic errors. Along with the specification language, P-Lingua framework provided from the beginning a number of built-in simulators, capturing the semantic and dynamic aspects of each P system type. Such simulators were included for the sake of completeness of the tool, but they were not intended to compete against existing software. Actually, the framework included the functionality to compile P-Lingua code into something else so that one could provide such compiled result as an input for an external simulator. Software implementation of P systems is further explored in Chap. 3.

The chapter elaborates on some of the main capabilities of the framework and is structured as follows. The main elements involved in P-Lingua language will be introduced in Sect. 2.2, along with a classification of the main types and variants of P systems supported by the framework, including the main references related with them. Then, several simulation algorithms will be presented in Sect. 2.3, capturing the dynamics of some especially relevant types of P systems used in the solution of real-life problems. Finally, in Sect. 2.4, a higher-level tool will be presented, MeCoSim, as a step forward to provide a visual virtual research environment.

2.2 P-Lingua Language

P-Lingua is a domain-specific language started in 2008 [4] that has been continuously evolving since then (technical details on the foundations can be found in [6, 9, 36] and a survey together with some recent developments in [40]). The approach is to keep the definitions as simple as possible, being a sort of "LaTeX-like" pseudocode, in such a way that P systems designers can use similar notation to the one used in the literature. A P system can thus be defined in a (plain text) .pli file, where the designer indicates the *model*, *structure*, *initial multisets*, *variables* (if any), etc. The elements of the definition will be further explained in what follows.

2.2.1 P System Models

When designing a membrane system in P-Lingua, the instruction @model must be present at the beginning of the .pli file, followed by a keyword identifying the model used. Through the development of P-Lingua, several classes of P systems have been included within the framework, while others have been discarded due to the lack of their use. The latest stable version, pLinguaCore 4.0, was released in 2013, covering only 10 model types. The P-Lingua framework has been continuously expanding since then although the development efforts have been focusing in the core distributed within MeCoSim. Tables 2.1, 2.2, 2.3 and 2.4 illustrate the diversity of variants considered in the current version, with the corresponding keywords and a reference introducing the model. For more details about the exact pLinguaCore release where some models were included or discarded, we refer the reader to [39].

In the case of neural-like P systems, the model keyword spiking_psystems is slightly overloaded since it covers multiple subclasses. Each time the model has been extended, special symbols and tokens were used so that the parser and the

Table 2.1 Cell-like membrane systems implemented in P-Lingua

Variant of membrane systems	Model specification keyword	Ref.
P systems with active membranes and membrane creation	`membrane_creation`	[25]
P systems with active membranes and membrane division	`membrane_division` / `dam`	[33]
P systems with symport/antiport rules	`symport_antiport` / `infEnv_symport_antiport`	[18]
Polarizationless P systems with active membranes with minimal cooperation and membrane division	`dam_wp`	[48]
Polarizationless P systems with active membranes with minimal cooperation, membrane division, and without dissolution	`dam_wp_wd`	[48]
Polarizationless P systems with active membranes with minimal cooperation and membrane division only for elementary membranes and without dissolution	`dam_wp_wd_wn`	[48]
P systems with active membranes with minimal cooperation and membrane separation	`sam`	[47]
Polarizationless P systems with active membranes with minimal cooperation and membrane separation	`sam_wp`	[47]
Polarizationless P systems with active membranes with minimal cooperation and membrane separation and without dissolution	`sam_wp_wd`	[47]
Polarizationless P systems with active membranes with minimal cooperation and membrane separation only for elementary membranes and without dissolution	`sam_wp_wd_wn`	[47]
Transition P systems	`transition` / `rewriting`	[32]

Table 2.2 Tissue-like membrane systems implemented in P-Lingua

Variant of membrane systems	Model specification keyword	Ref.
Tissue P systems with cell division	`tissue_psystems` / `tpdc`	[20, 34]
Tissue P systems with cell division and antiport rules	`tpda`	[34]
Tissue P systems with cell division and symport rules	`tpds`	[34]
Tissue P systems with cell separation	`TSCS`	[27, 38]
Tissue P systems with evolutional communication rules with cell division	`evolution_communication` / `ev_symport_antiport`	[31]
Tissue P systems with evolutional communication rules with cell separation	`tsec`	[31]
Tissue P systems with promoters	`tpdc` / `tpda` / `tpds`	[45]

Table 2.3 Neural-like membrane systems implemented in P-Lingua

Variant of membrane systems	Model specification keyword	Ref.
Asynchronous SN P systems	`spiking_psystems`	[3]
Asynchronous SN P systems with local synchronization	`spiking_psystems`	[41]
Cell-like spiking neural P systems	`cell_like_snp`	[46, 50]
Dendrite P systems	`dendrite`	[26]
Fuzzy reasoning spiking neural P systems	`fuzzy_psystems`	[13, 17]
Limited asynchronous SN P systems	`spiking_psystems`	[29]
Spiking neural P systems	`spiking_psystems`	[13, 15, 16]
Spiking neural P systems with anti-spikes	`spiking_psystems`	[28]
Spiking neural P systems with hybrid astrocytes	`spiking_psystems`	[30]
Spiking neural P systems with structural plasticity	`spiking_psystems`	[1]

Table 2.4 Other variants of membrane systems implemented in P-Lingua

Variant of membrane systems	Model specification keyword	Ref.
Enzymatic numerical P systems	`enps`	[35]
Population dynamics P systems	`probabilistic`	[2]
Probabilistic guarded P systems	`probabilistic_guarded_` `_psystems`	[8, 10]
Regenerative P systems	`regenerative_psystems`	[11]
Simple kernel P systems	`simple_kernel_psystems`	[12, 14]
Simple regenerative P systems	`simple_regenerative_` `_psystems`	[11]
Stochastic P systems* *(discontinued)	`stochastic`	[42]

simulator are capable to identify which type of rules are being used and how they should be interpreted.

2.2.2 Membrane Structure

The topology of the membrane system to be simulated will depend on the model selected in the file. If an invalid structure with respect to the model is defined, the *parser* will show a message notifying it. The instruction @mu[1] is used to define the architecture of the system. The syntax is similar to the one used in the literature. For example, for cell-like membrane systems, the definition

$$@\texttt{mu} = [[[]'4]'2[]'3]'1$$

---

[1]The usual notation for the structure of P systems is the Greek letter μ.

would lead to a P system with a skin membrane labelled by 1 and 2 internal membranes: an elementary membrane labelled by 3, and a membrane labelled by 2 which contains an elementary membrane labelled by 4 inside.

In the case of tissue P systems, membranes (called *cells*) are not hierarchically arranged, but they can be connected by means of an arbitrary graph, which is not required to be explicitly given in the definition. Typically, the set of directed arcs connecting cells can be reconstructed from the implicit information provided by the set of rules. However, in P-Lingua format, it is necessary to indicate the initial cells in the system, formally considering them as elementary membranes located within an external compartment labelled by 0, that will act as the environment of the system.

Spiking neural P systems need both the initial neurons and the *synapses* defined in order to work. The former is defined as previously with the @mu instruction and the later with @marcs indicating with pairs of labels which arcs will be present in the underlying graph of the SNP system.

Note that not all the definitions of @mu must be in the same line, but instead of the = symbol, it is possible to add more compartments to a specific region. For instance, in cell-like membrane systems, it is possible to use

$$@mu = [[]'2]'1; \ @mu(1)+ = []'3;$$

in order to generate a structure identical to the one defined above. Note that a semicolon indicates the end of an instruction.

2.2.3 Initial Multisets

In order to describe the initial multisets of the different compartments, the command @ms is used in a similar way to the literature, with braces {} as the delimiters of the multisets. Like before, the + = symbols can be used to add new objects to a predefined multiset. The multiplicity of a symbol is indicated by the * symbol as in a multiplication (e.g., c*5 indicates 5 copies of object c).

2.2.4 P System Rules

Rules, like the structure of the P system, depend on the model of membrane system being simulated. The P-Lingua parser was defined in such a way that P systems researchers can use a very close language to the one used in literature, putting special emphasis in the definition of rules. Therefore, brackets [] are used in P-Lingua files as in the definition of rules in research papers. An evolution rule is defined in the following way: +[a1 - -> b,c]'1. Note the differences between the P-Lingua and the formal definitions: The subscripts are between braces, the arrow is replaced by an ASCII version of an arrow, the label is preceded by a ' symbol instead of being a subscript, and the polarization precedes the rule instead of being a superscript. For tissue P systems, instead of using parentheses, a similar brackets notation is used with a double arrow as follows: `[a]'1 <- -> [b]'2` to denote the rule $(1, a/b, 2)$.

Usually, several rules with the same structure but with different subindexes are defined in P systems, and it can be translated into a P-Lingua file with the colon: symbol, followed by the corresponding limits. Let $r \equiv [a_i \rightarrow a_{i+1}]_1$ for $0 \le i \le n$ be a set of rules of a P system with active membranes that can be defined in a P-Lingua file as follows: `[ a{i} - -> a{i+1} ]'1 : 0 <= i <= n`. If two or more variables have to be defined, they will be declared from the right to the left; that is, if a variable j is limited by i, then the range of i must be written "before" (to the right), for example, `[ a{i,j} - -> a{i,j+1}]'1 : 0 <= j < i, 0 <= i <= n`.

The user must define all these parameters (except the model type) in a `main` function. A `function` in the P-Lingua language is defined with the keyword `def` followed by the name of the function. A function can have parameters whose names will be indicated between parentheses and separated by commas. More than one function can be defined in a single P-Lingua file, and they are widely used, for instance, to construct the membrane system in a modular way. An example of this would be the following code:

```
@model<membrane_division>


n = 3 /* A parameter n is defined to be used later */
m = 1000 /* A parameter m is defined to be used later */

def main() {
   define_structure();
   define_initial_multisets(m);
   define_rules(n);
}
def define_structure() {
   @mu = []'1;
}
define_initial_multisets(number_objects) {
   @ms(1) += a{0}*{number_objects};
}
define_rules(number_steps) {
   [a{i} - -> a{i+1}]'1 : 0 <= i < {number_steps};
}
```

Note that it is allowed to insert comments in P-Lingua files, surrounded by the symbols /* and */. As indicated above, several examples of the different types of P systems implemented in P-Lingua can be found in the websites of the P-Lingua project [43] and MeCoSim [24].

2.3 Simulation Algorithms

P systems are bioinspired devices that work in a massively parallel and nondeterministic way. While there are preliminary studies analyzing the problems related to implementations in biological means, there is still a long way to reach this ultimate goal. That is why developing hardware/software implementations of P systems becomes a vital necessity for the advancement of scientific activities in membrane computing.

The P-Lingua framework includes a Java library called *pLinguaCore* that provides at least one simulation algorithm for each P system variant. A simulation algorithm for membrane computing can be described as an algorithm which is able to reproduce P system computations on conventional software/hardware architectures. Usually, only one branch of computation is considered, and it is expected to display the sequence of configurations, including information on the executed rules for each step of computation. Concerning the hardware used, the simulation algorithms can be designed to run on sequential machines (single-thread CPU) or parallel architectures (multi-thread CPU, GPU, FPGA, etc.). The simulation algorithms in pLinguaCore are designed for single-thread CPU, but it is possible to parse a P-Lingua file and compile it into an appropriate input for an external simulator.

All simulation algorithms in pLinguaCore share the same underlying implementation of a computation step as a loop divided into two stages: selection stage and execution stage. The selection stage consists in searching for applicable rules and selecting which ones will actually be executed in each membrane of a given configuration, taking into account the restrictions dictated by the system semantics. Then, the execution stage actually implements the changes on the configuration caused by the execution of the selected rules, and this completes the simulation of the computation step. The input data for the selection stage contains the description of the membranes with their multisets (strings over the working alphabet of objects, labels associated with the membrane, etc.) and the set of defined rules. The output data of this stage are the multisets of selected rules. Only the execution stage changes the information of the configuration. It is the reason why execution stage needs synchronization when accessing to the membrane structure and the multisets. At the end of the execution stage, the simulation process restarts the selection stage in an iterative way until a halting configuration is reached (i.e., none of the rules is applicable). Alternatively, a maximum number of iterations can be set at the beginning of the simulation to avoid getting stuck on too long (or even infinite) computations.

With the general design explained above, the pLinguaCore library includes simulation algorithms for the cell-like, tissue-like, and neural-like P systems enumerated in Sect. 2.2. For more information, see the corresponding references in Tables 2.1, 2.2, and 2.3, respectively. There exist in the literature other P system variants whose computations are not synchronized by a global clock in a step-by-step fashion (e.g., asynchronous, time-free, or stochastic models). Such variants are not currently supported under the P-Lingua framework, but there exist fully functional alternative implementations available (see Chaps. 4 and 5).

Other variants are also contemplated [2, 8, 10, 11]. A special mention should be given to the simulation algorithms for population dynamics P systems (PDP systems) which is a variant widely used for simulation of ecosystem dynamics (see Chap. 6) in which each rule has a probability associated. The first description of probabilistic semantics was quite ambiguous: "Rules should be applied in a maximally parallel way, according to their probabilities." There are many ways of interpreting this sentence, and each one could lead to different behaviors. While all of them might be "correct" from a formal point of view, not all simulation algorithms are acceptable when the goal is to reproduce the behavior of a complex system. Since P-Lingua is a general-purpose framework, indicating which is the appropriate choice should be a decision of the model designer.

Three simulation algorithms have been designed for PDP systems and implemented in pLinguaCore [19]:

- DNDP algorithm [21].
- BBB algorithm [19].
- DCBA algorithm [22, 23].

In the algorithm DNDP, the rules are selected individually according to its probabilities. On the other hand, algorithms BBB and DCBA work by grouping rules in blocks by analyzing the left-hand side, each block has the same left-hand side, and all the rule probabilities must sum 1. DCBA uses a refined definition of block in which the charges of the right-hand side must be consistent. More about simulation algorithms for PDP systems will be explained in Chap. 6 since this kind of algorithms requires a large amount of computational power being suitable for high-performance computing platforms such as CUDA.

As it was mentioned before, there are various approaches in the literature where the standard semantics of P systems (namely, nondeterministic behavior and maximally parallel application of the rules) is modified by adding different regulation elements, which need to be carefully described in order to explain how the system evolves. In particular, it is worth highlighting that the concept of "simulation algorithm" is used in this section in a theoretical sense, that is, a formalization that translates the specification of the semantics into a pseudocode capturing precisely the routine that the system follows when deciding what rules to apply. It should not be confused with an implementation of such algorithm in a programming language. Some attempts trying to bring semantic elements explicitly into the description of a P system in P-Lingua language have been already initiated, and it is being considered for upcoming release of P-Lingua 5.0.

2.4   Membrane Computing Simulator (MeCoSim)

The previous sections have presented the essential elements of P-Lingua framework: the standard specification language and the simulation engines to run the computations of the given P systems. These elements constitute the core features, the chassis of our car. However, in order for this vehicle to move smoothly, several additional pieces (as the external body but also others as the steering wheel, the pedals, or the dashboard icons, among others) are needed to provide the users with the desired driving experience, in order for them to sit down and enjoy while conducting their virtual experiments with models based on P systems.

With the metaphor introduced, we aim to present the main idea behind MeCoSim (membrane computing simulator) [24, 37], conceived in a search for the generalization of certain high-level visual applications to manage population dynamics models, known as EcoSim product family [36, 44]. Built on top of P-Lingua core, this visual environment provides a higher level of abstraction, transforming the solid set of tools of our internal chassis and engine given by P-Lingua core into a whole car, complementing the previous elements with an external layer allowing the drivers conduct their experiments through the proper sensors and actuators.

Thus, MeCoSim was devised with a manifold purpose, assisting in the design of the heart of the cars (P system-based models), delivering the final cars (custom apps based on the models), and helping users drive their vehicles (through the tools coming with the apps). Firstly, the visual interface provides the expert users (P system designers) with an interface where they can specify, debug, and run (*step-by-step* or entire) computations of their P systems in a smoother way; this is made easier with the tools provided by a friendly environment, aiding in the task of designing and verifying the core part of our cars: the P systems modelling certain case studies. Secondly, the environment provides certain tools to make the technical pieces constituting the model become a final product, *that is*, bridging the gaps to convert the engine, car axles, controls, or wheels into the final car. To this purpose, MeCoSim provides some tools to define, through configuration files, a final visual application using the core elements of the framework, plus the P system (or P system family) specified, and the inputs and outputs to control and monitor, respectively, each trip made with the car (i.e., each computation of the system, each virtual experiment conducted). Finally, end users receive their car: the customized application satisfying their needs. Probably, they will have no idea about the internal specifications of the car, they are not car mechanics/technicians, but they will be able to drive their specific car. In such car, the custom app, they will be able to sit, introduce the details about each particular trip (experiment) they want to make (run), decide about the speed, and control the steering wheel and pedals, enjoying the drive and finally getting to their destiny (the end of the computation) while obtaining all the desired additional information through the monitoring system provided by the dashboard.

In this context, everything starts with the identification of a certain need, such as solving a certain NP-complete problem or modelling a real-life system in economy, ecology, medicine, or any other field. In this context, a P system (or P system family) must be defined to satisfy such need. Thus, the definition of the system requires the translation of the P system into a file using P-Lingua standard specification language. Then, an iterative process of design, debug, and verification starts, progressing with the problem until the model has been properly validated according to the experts in the problem domain.

Then, the central problem has been solved, but only the technicians could use the tools to run computations of the system. Then, a new effort can be made by such P system designers to set in a spreadsheet configuration file the specific elements of the final car and the application where the end users (ecologists, economists, etc.) will be able to conduct their visual experiments. The custom elements will include the hierarchical structure arranging all the visual blocks of the final app, the tables allowing the introduction of specific input data by the end user, and the outputs to monitor the activity and the final results of the trip. Now, everything is ready for the end user to drive, to analyze each particular scenario of interest (each trip), introducing in the tables the specific parameter values and input data for each scenario of interest and run each virtual experiments, getting the desired results in their dashboard given by the custom output tables and charts defined in the configuration file set by the P system designers during the building of the car (the custom app).

The description above has been probably illustrative at a general level, but people not familiarized with MeCoSim might find it difficult to figure out how this approach look like at a deeper level. The following subsections will try to clarify those aspects only outlined before, detailing the main goals achieved (Sect. 2.4.1) and the software components involved (Sect. 2.4.2). In Ref. [44], a methodology is proposed based for the solution of a problem through membrane-based systems making use of P-Lingua framework and MeCoSim, where the corresponding tools described are employed in a systematic way.

2.4.1   Primary goals

As it has just been depicted, MeCoSim's main intent is the provision of a high-level visual interface to handle P system-based models. This is right, but what should we exactly expect from this environment? Let us try to clarify this by analyzing the origin and initial view of the tools involved.

To start with this overview, it is worth recalling that we are studying a paradigm, membrane computing, where many computing models have been defined along the years. As specifically addressed by this book, the implementation of these computational devices is crucial in order to take advantage of all the theoretical properties, the strengths, of such machines. However, our biologically inspired models present certain features that are not easy to implement in certain biological or artificial substrate, and even if it can be done, it implies major efforts to apply these machines to each particular problem. Nevertheless, there is a faster convenient approach that can be applied in order to make this process more manageable in

(a) the study of theoretical aspects of the different types of devices (such as their computational power, efficiency, etc.) or the practical use of models based on these devices (its tasks such as the design, verification, or validation of properties and virtual experimentation) and (b) the simulation of the computations for the given models.

This volume is devoted to implementations of membrane computing models. Consequently, we actually expect real devices that can capture all the features of the theoretical machines. Some of the solutions provided by later chapters will succeed, addressing aspects such as capturing the inherent parallelism of such ideal machines. However, those real machines will need to take many things into account at a very technical level, it will be a very tough process, and this will make it very challenging to validate the proper functioning of these devices according to all the properties of the types of P systems used, along with all the properties of the models built for a particular problem, based on such types of P systems.

In order to avoid attacking all the problems at once, a different approach can be followed: first facing the "soft" implementation of the theoretical devices, the intended type of P systems, through sequential software simulators, not addressing all the technical aspects required by the actual implementations but properly simulating the computations of the theoretical systems, conducting to the very same results. This allows us to validate a simpler implementation at a functional level, in terms of the results of the computations, permitting a first step toward more complex high-performance hardware, hybrid, or biological implementations. These initial simulators could handle any solution or model solving a certain problem (from SAT, 3-COL, or HAM-CYCLE to the population dynamics of an ecosystem or an economy system, among others) by means of the types of P systems implemented in the corresponding simulators. Such handling will involve helping in the design, debug, and verification tasks, but of course also the computation of the given model or solution according to the semantic and dynamic rules of the theoretical devices. Naturally, for any problem of certain size, analyzing a manual trace of the computation in a paper would be too tedious or practically unfeasible for significantly big instances. Therefore, even if a real implementation with the desirable parallelism is not available, it would be necessary to have at disposal a machine where one could simulate computations to validate the model or analyze the evolution of the system under certain scenarios. That would be the approach followed by P-Lingua framework and MeCoSim so that we can focus on aspects such as reliability or feasibility (to preserve the same evolution and results of the theoretical systems), along with user-friendliness, over the efficiency of other later implementations.

We have clarified the first goal of MeCoSim approach: providing an environment for the design, verification, and simulation of the models based on P systems in a reliable and user-friendly way, albeit not prioritizing efficiency. However, there are more aspects to analyze in our approach. A major one is the search for the generalization, *that is*, a definite purpose of providing general-purpose tools to be applied to each particular membrane system type and each particular solution for a problem based on them. Thus, the development of *ad hoc* simulators (for a specific solution for a problem, a single instance/scenario, or different instances of that problem) is definitely different from the development of a general-purpose simulator for certain types of P systems, capturing the ingredients of the theoretical model of computation so that this machine allows the provision of any P system and scenario and performs its corresponding intended computations.

Many software developments in scientific research are focused on the first approach, providing simulators for certain problems or even specific instances of the problem only. Other studies address the development of tools for the analysis or verification of a specific type or variant of membrane system, such that they can handle any P system of the type. However, the approach of P-Lingua framework and MeCoSim has been more ambitious from its origin: providing tools being as general as possible, for as many types of P systems as possible (including many variants of cell-like, tissue-like, and neuron-like P systems, among others), while preserving the strict deep analysis of the syntactic, semantic, and dynamic aspects of each P system variant, in order to control that the corresponding constraints are met. The wide range of variants covered include computing models with different global structures (hierarchical, plain graph, or graph with nodes containing trees— as in multienvironment, PDP systems), a variety of ingredients in terms of rules or other elements (dissolution, division, charges, stopping objects, etc.), and different handling of semantic aspects (related with sequentiality, nondeterminism, priorities, maximality, probabilistic or stochastic behaviors, among others).

As described above and in Sects. 2.2 and 2.3, many types and variants of P systems have been covered by the tools developed within the framework. Moreover, as detailed in Sect. 2.2, along with the specification language and its corresponding parsers for each computing models, many simulators were developed inside P-Lingua project. This infrastructure provided from the beginning [36] a complete programming environment for *membrane computing* and has kept incorporating new elements along the years, staying as an alive project, including a living version inside MeCoSim.

In Sect. 3.4, the basic steps of the approach followed with these tools are depicted, illustrating their use for real applications.

2.4.2   Main Functional Components

As previously mentioned, a clear separation of the roles involved in modeling and simulation process is stated (apart from the software developers in charge of P-Lingua and MeCoSim development): (a) P systems designer and (b) end users of a simulation app. What does MeCoSim provide within this scope?

As shown in Fig. 2.1, the software developer releases different versions of MeCoSim (and certain plug-ins) available for any potential users. In contrast, P systems designer, possibly unrelated with software development, defines a simulation app based on MeCoSim, customized for its particular problem. Then, he can debug its solution and analyze the underlying P system. Finally, the end user

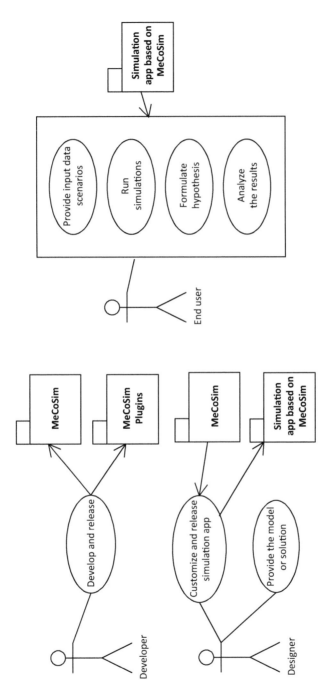

Fig. 2.1 Roles and uses of MeCoSim

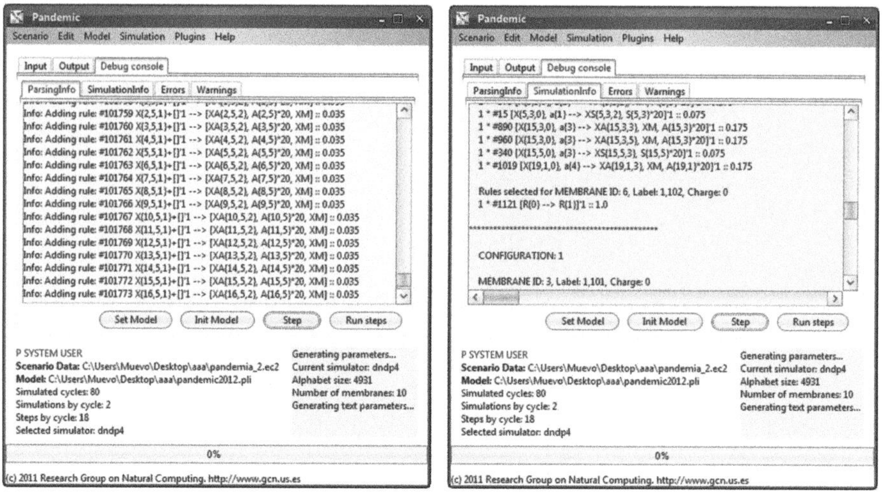

Fig. 2.2 Model debugging

employs the custom simulation app to study different scenarios of interest involving specific instances of the problem.

In summary, the main functionalities of MeCoSim are the following:

- *General environment to simulate computations of P systems*
  With the default custom application, any P-Lingua file not requiring additional inputs can be edited, while detecting aspects to modify; parsed and debugged (see Fig. 2.2), to find possible warnings or errors, both at a syntactic and a semantic level, alerting the P systems designer if some rules of the intended model type are violated; and simulated (through the algorithm selected in the interface, as shown in Fig. 2.3), generating the initial structure and multisets of the system and then running the computation either step-by-step or until its end (after a fixed number of steps or when a halting configuration is reached, where no rules can be applied). Besides, the default output is given in the form of a flat table (with a row for each object symbol present in each computation step inside each region, with a certain multiplicity), and also some of the main internal elements of the P system can be visualized at any moment (membrane structure, multisets, and alphabet).
- *Mechanism for the definition of custom simulation apps*
  Any custom app consists of:
  – A hierarchical structure for the visual arrangement of the information (inputs and outputs) in the app for the end user, according to the setting introduced by the designer in an .xls spreadsheet file, as illustrated by the first table in Fig. 2.4.
  – A definition of input tables, and output tables and charts, to respectively introduce data and visualize results. More details about the definition of such

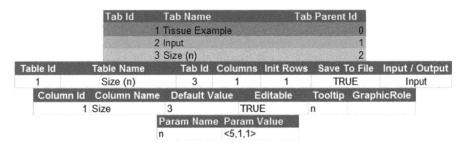

Fig. 2.3 Available simulators for a loaded P systems variant

Tab Id	Tab Name	Tab Parent Id
1	Tissue Example	0
2	Input	1
3	Size (n)	2

Table Id	Table Name	Tab Id	Columns	Init Rows	Save To File	Input / Output
1	Size (n)	3	1	1	TRUE	Input

Column Id	Column Name	Default Value	Editable	Tooltip	GraphicRole
1	Size	3	TRUE	n	

Param Name	Param Value
n	<5,1,1>

Fig. 2.4 Custom app definition—input

components can be found at Refs. [24, 37, 44], and a basic example of tables
(header and columns) configuration is given by the second and third tables
present in Fig. 2.4.

- The configuration of parameters, establishing which parameters and input data
  for the model, should be generated from the input tables, either directly taking
  the value from the table at the beginning of the simulation or applying some
  processing from the input data to generate calculated derived values. To this
  purpose, a specific parameters generation language was defined, as described
  in detail in [37, 44]. The generation of a basic parameter n from the first row

and column of a table with $id = 5$ is illustrated in the last table of Fig. 2.4. Much more complex parameters can be generated, as described in [37, 44].

- Results: In order for the output tables and charts to show some information about the simulation, the custom configuration must define which elements from the computation should be taken into account when extracting information from all the computation trace data. An additional language is used in the *.xls* spreadsheet file to provide a flexible mechanism to express the retrieval of information from the computation. Internally, for every simulation performed, from the previous definition, a database query is generated, being executed against the given *on-memory* database containing the flat structure with the computation.

Apart from this core functionalities, additional features and abilities are provided in the form of MeCoSim plug-ins following a certain architecture proposed [24, 37, 44]. These *add-ons* can be given either as Java-based packages (as a graph viewer [see Fig. 2.5], a window for the introduction and encoding of logical formulas or a tool to define and detect invariants in the models based on Daikon [7]) or as external programs being called from MeCoSim and properly connected (using the so-called *processes plug-in*). A detailed description of the underlying mechanisms and the plug-ins developed is given in [44].

Additionally to the features of MeCoSim software and its plug-ins, a system of repositories was made available, manageable from MeCoSim environment, having access to repositories of four types: apps (*.xls*), models (*.pli*), scenarios (*.ec2*), and plug-ins (*.jar*). Besides the official repositories, any user can provide additional ones (through the definition of the corresponding *.xml* file for the desired type of repository), providing the corresponding URL to the resource.

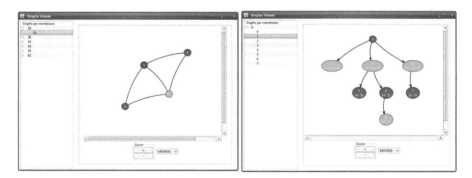

Fig. 2.5 GraphsPlugin—trees of graphs

2.5 Conclusion

This chapter presented the very representative and widely used P-Lingua language for a variety of P systems such as cell-like P systems, tissue-like P systems, spiking neural P systems, and kernel P systems. The description of P-Lingua language with pLinguaCore consists of P systems models, membrane structure, initial multisets, and P system rules. The simulation algorithms in P-Lingua and MeCoSim on top of pLinguaCore with primary goals and main functional components were also discussed.

References

1. F.G.C. Cabarle, H.N. Adorna, N. Ibo, Spiking neural P systems with structural plasticity, in *Pre-proceedings of 2nd Asian Conference on Membrane Computing, Chengdu, China* (2013), pp. 13–26
2. M. Cardona, M.A. Colomer, A. Margalida, A. Palau, I. Pérez-Hurtado, M.J. Pérez-Jiménez, D. Sanuy, A computational modeling for real ecosystems based on P systems. Nat. Comput. **10**(1), 39–53 (2011). https://doi.org/10.1007/s11047-010-9191-3
3. M. Cavaliere, O. Egecioglu, O.H. Ibarra, M. Ionescu, Gh. Păun, S. Woodworth, Asynchronous spiking neural P systems: decidability and undecidability, in *DNA Computing. Lecture Notes in Computer Science*, ed. by M. Garzon, H. Yan, vol. 4848 (2008), 246–255. https://doi.org/10.1007/978-3-540-77962-9_26
4. D. Díaz-Pernil, I. Pérez-Hurtado, M.J. Pérez-Jiménez, A. Riscos-Núñez, P-Lingua: a programming language for Membrane Computing, in *Proceedings of the Sixth Brainstorming Week on Membrane Computing*, Fénix Editora, D. Díaz-Pernil, C. Graciani, M.A. Gutiérrez-Naranjo, Gh. Păun, I. Pérez-Hurtado, A. Riscos-Núñez (2008), pp. 135–155
5. D. Díaz-Pernil, C. Graciani, M.A. Gutiérrez-Naranjo, I. Pérez-Hurtado, M.J. Pérez-Jiménez, Software for P systems, in *The Oxford Handbook of Membrane Computing*, ed. by Gh. Păun, G. Rozenberg, A. Salomaa (Oxford University, Oxford, 2009), pp. 437–454. Chapter 17
6. D. Díaz-Pernil, I. Pérez-Hurtado, M.J. Pérez-Jiménez, A. Riscos-Núñez, A P-Lingua programming environment for Membrane Computing, in *Membrane Computing (WMC 2008)*, ed. by D.W. Corne, P. Frisco, Gh. Păun, G. Rozenberg, A. Salomaa. Lecture Notes in Computer Science, vol. 5391 (2009), pp. 187–203. https://doi.org/10.1007/978-3-540-95885-7_14
7. M.D. Ernst, J.H. Perkins, P.J. Guo, S. McCamant, C. Pacheco, M.S. Tschantz, C. Xiao, The Daikon system for dynamic detection of likely invariants. Sci. Comput. Program. **69**(1–3), 35–45 (2007). https://doi.org/10.1016/j.scico.2007.01.015
8. M. García-Quismondo, *Modelling and Simulation of Real-life Phenomena in Membrane Computing*. Ph.D. Thesis (Universidad de Sevilla, Sevilla, 2014). http://hdl.handle.net/11441/66147
9. M. García-Quismondo, R. Gutiérrez-Escudero, I. Pérez-Hurtado, M.J. Pérez-Jiménez, A. Riscos-Núñez, An overview of P-Lingua 2.0, in *Membrane Computing. WMC 2009. Lecture Notes in Computer Science*, vol. 5957, ed. by Gh. Păun, M.J. Pérez-Jiménez, A. Riscos, G. Rozenberg, A. Salomaa (2010), pp. 264–288. https://doi.org/10.1007/978-3-642-11467-0_20
10. M. García-Quismondo, M.A. Martínez-del-Amor, M.J. Pérez-Jiménez, Probabilistic guarded P systems: a formal definition, in *Proceedings of the Twelfth Brainstorming Week on Membrane Computing*, Fénix Editora, ed. by L.F. Macías-Ramos, M.A. Martínez-del-Amor, Gh. Păun, A. Riscos-Núñez, L. Valencia-Cabrera (2014), pp. 183–206
11. M. García-Quismondo, M. Levin, D. Lobo, Modeling regenerative processes with membrane computing. Inf. Sci. **381**, 229–249 (2017). https://doi.org/10.1016/j.ins.2016.11.017

12. M. Gheorghe, F. Ipate, R. Lefticaru, M.J. Pérez-Jiménez, A. Turcanu, L. Valencia, M. García-Quismondo, F. Mierla, 3-COL problem modelling using simple kernel P systems. Int. J. Comput. Math. **90**(4), 816–830 (2013). https://doi.org/10.1080/00207160.2012.743712
13. M. Ionescu, Gh. Păun, T. Yokomori, Spiking Neural P systems. Fundam. Inform., **71**(2–3), 279–308 (2006)
14. F. Ipate, R. Lefticaru, L. Mierla, L. Valencia, H. Hang, G. Zhang, C. Dragomir, M.J. Pérez-Jiménez, M. Gheorghe, Kernel P systems: applications and implementations. Adv. Intell. Syst. Comput. **212**, 1081–1089 (2013). https://doi.org/10.1007/978-3-642-37502-6_126
15. L.F. Macías-Ramos, *Developing Efficient Simulators for Cell Machines*. Ph.D. Thesis (Universidad de Sevilla, Seville, 2016). http://hdl.handle.net/11441/36828
16. L.F. Macías-Ramos, I. Pérez-Hurtado, M. García-Quismondo, L. Valencia-Cabrera, M.J. Pérez-Jiménez, A. Riscos-Núñez, A P-Lingua based simulator for Spiking Neural P systems, in *Membrane Computing (CMC 2011)*, ed. by M. Gheorghe, Gh. Păun, G. Rozenberg, A. Salomaa, S. Verlan. Lecture Notes in Computer Science, vol. 7184 (2012), pp. 257–281. https://doi.org/10.1007/978-3-642-28024-5_18
17. L.F. Macías-Ramos, M.A. Martínez-del-Amor, M.J. Pérez-Jiménez, Simulating FRSN P systems with real numbers in P-Lingua on sequential and CUDA platforms, in *Membrane Computing (CMC 2015)*, ed. by G. Rozenberg, A. Salomaa, J.M. Sempere, C. Zandron. Lecture Notes in Computer Science, vol. 9504, pp. 262–276 (2015). https://doi.org/10.1007/978-3-319-28475-0_18
18. L.F. Macías-Ramos, L. Valencia-Cabrera, B. Song, T. Song, L. Pan, M.J. Pérez-Jiménez, A P-lingua based simulator for P systems with symport/antiport rules. Fundam. Inform. **139**(2), 211–227 (2015). https://doi.org/10.3233/FI-2015-1232
19. M.A. Martínez-del-Amor, *Accelerating Membrane Systems Simulators using High Performance Computing with GPU*. Ph.D. Thesis (Universidad de Sevilla, Sevilla, 2013). http://hdl.handle.net/11441/15644
20. M.A. Martínez-del-Amor, I. Pérez-Hurtado, M.J. Pérez-Jiménez, A. Riscos-Núñez, A P-Lingua based simulator for Tissue P systems. J. Logic Algebraic Program. **79**(6), 374–382 (2010). https://doi.org/10.1016/j.jlap.2010.03.009
21. M.A. Martínez-del-Amor, I. Pérez-Hurtado, M.J. Pérez-Jiménez, A. Riscos-Núñez, M.A. Colomer, A new simulation algorithm for multienvironment probabilistic P systems, in *2010 IEEE Fifth International Conference on Bio-Inspired Computing: Theories and Applications (BIC-TA)*, Changsha, 2010, vol. 1 (2010), pp. 59–68. https://doi.org/10.1109/BICTA.2010.5645352
22. M.A. Martínez-del-Amor, I. Pérez-Hurtado, M. García-Quismondo, L.F. Macías-Ramos, L. Valencia-Cabrera, A. Romero-Jiménez, C. Graciani-Díaz, A. Riscos-Núñez., M.A. Colomer, M.J. Pérez-Jiménez, DCBA: simulating Population Dynamics P Systems with proportional object distribution, in *Membrane Computing. CMC 2012*, ed. by E. Csuhaj-Varjú, M. Gheorghe, G. Rozenberg, A. Salomaa, G. Vaszil. Lecture Notes in Computer Science, vol. 7762 (2012), pp. 291–310. https://doi.org/10.1007/978-3-642-36751-9_18
23. M.A. Martínez-del-Amor, I. Pérez-Hurtado, M. García-Quismondo, L.F. Macías-Ramos, L. Valencia-Cabrera, A. Romero-Jiménez, C. Graciani, A. Riscos-Núñez, M.A. Colomer, M.J. Pérez-Jiménez, DCBA: simulating population dynamics P systems with proportional objects distribution, in *Membrane Computing (CMC 2012)*, ed. by E. Csuhaj-Varjú, M. Gheorghe, G. Rozenberg, A. Salomaa, G. Vaszil. Lecture Notes in Computer Science, vol. 7762 (2013), pp. 257–276. https://doi.org/10.1007/978-3-642-36751-9_18
24. MeCoSim website. http://www.p-lingua.org/mecosim
25. M. Mutyam, K. Krithivasan, P systems with membrane creation: universality and efficiency, in *Machines, Computations, and Universality (MCU 2001)*, ed. by M. Margenstern, Y. Rogozhin. Lecture Notes in Computer Science, vol. 2055 (2001), pp. 276–287. https://doi.org/10.1007/3-540-45132-3_19

26. D. Orellana-Martín, M.A. Martínez-del-Amor, L. Valencia-Cabrera, I. Pérez-Hurtado, Agustín Riscos-Núñez, M.J. Pérez-Jiménez, Dendrite P Systems toolbox: representation, algorithms and simulators. Int. J. Neural Syst.. Available online 30 September 2020. https://doi.org/10.1142/S0129065720500719

27. L. Pan, T.-O. Ishdorj, P systems with active membranes and separation rules. J. Universal Comput. Sci. **10**(5), 630–64 (2004). https://doi.org/10.3217/jucs-010-05-0630

28. L. Pan, Gh. Păun, Spiking neural P systems with anti-spikes. Int. J. Comput. Commun. Control **4**(3), 273–282 (2009). https://doi.org/10.15837/ijccc.2009.3.2435

29. L. Pan, J. Wang, H.J. Hoogeboom, Limited asynchronous spiking neural P systems. Fundam. Inform. **110**(1–4), 271–293 (2011). https://doi.org/10.3233/FI-2011-543

30. L. Pan, J. Wang, H.J. Hoogeboom, Asynchronous extended spiking neural Psystems with astrocytes, in *Membrane Computing (CMC 2011)*, ed. by M. Gheorghe, Gh. Păun, G. Rozenberg, A. Salomaa, S. Verlan. Lecture Notes in Computer Science, vol. 7184 (2012), pp. 243–256. https://doi.org/10.1007/978-3-642-28024-5_17

31. L. Pan, B. Song, L. Valencia-Cabrera, M.J. Pérez-Jiménez, The computational complexity of tissue P systems with evolutional symport/antiport rules. Complexity **2018**, Article ID 3745210, 21 (2018). https://doi.org/10.1155/2018/3745210

32. Gh. Păun, Computing with membranes. J. Comput. Syst. Sci. **61**(1), 108–143 (2000). https://doi.org/10.1006/jcss.1999.1693. First circulated at TUCS Research Report No. 208, November 1998. http://www.tucs.fi

33. Gh. Păun, P systems with active membranes: attacking NP complete problems. J. Autom. Lang. Comb. **6**(1), 75–90 (2000). Auckland University, CDMTCS Report No 102 (1999)

34. Gh. Păun, M.J. Pérez-Jiménez, A. Riscos-Núñez, Tissue P systems with cell division. Int. J. Comput. Commun. Control **3**(3), 295–303 (2008). https://doi.org/10.15837/ijccc.2008.3.2397

35. A.B. Pavel, O. Arsene, C. Buiu, Enzymatic numerical P systems: a new class of Membrane Computing systems, in *Proceedings of the 2010 IEEE Fifth International Conference on Bio-Inspired Computing: Theories and Applications (BIC-TA 2010), Changsha, China, September 23–26* (2010), pp. 1331–1336. https://doi.org/10.1109/BICTA.2010.5645071

36. I. Pérez-Hurtado, *Desarrollo y Aplicaciones de un Entorno de Programación para Computación Celular: P-Lingua*. Ph.D. Thesis (Universidad de Sevilla, Sevilla, 2010, in Spanish). http://hdl.handle.net/11441/66241

37. I. Pérez-Hurtado, L. Valencia-Cabrera, M.J. Pérez-Jiménez, M.A. Colomer, A. Riscos-Núñez, MeCoSim: a general purpose software tool for simulating biological phenomena by means of P systems, in *Proceedings of the IEEE Fifth International Conference on Bio-inspired Computing: Theories and Applications (BIC-TA 2010)*, vol. I, ed. by K. Li, Z. Tang, R. Li, A.K. Nagar, R. Thamburaj (2010), pp. 637–643. https://doi.org/10.1109/BICTA.2010.5645199

38. I. Pérez-Hurtado, L. Valencia-Cabrera, J.M. Chacón, A. Riscos-Núñez, M.J. Pérez-Jiménez, A P-lingua based simulator for tissue P systems with cell separation. Rom. J. Inf. Sci. Technol. **17**(1), 89–102 (2014)

39. I. Pérez-Hurtado, D. Orellana-Martín, M.A. Martínez-del-Amor, L. Valencia-Cabrera, A. Riscos-Núñez, M.J. Pérez-Jiménez, 11 years of P-Lingua: a backward glance, in *Proceedings of the 20th International Conference on Membrane Computing (CMC20)*, ed. by Gh. Păun (2019), pp. 451–462

40. I. Pérez-Hurtado, D. Orellana-Martín, G. Zhang, M.J. Pérez-Jiménez, P-Lingua in two steps: flexibility and efficiency. J. Membr. Comput. **1**(2), 93–102 (2019). https://doi.org/10.1007/s41965-019-00014-1

41. T. Song, L. Pan, Gh. Păun. Asynchronous spiking neural P systems with local synchronization. Inf. Sci. **219**, 197–207 (2013). https://doi.org/10.1016/j.ins.2012.07.023

42. A. Spicher, O. Michel, M. Cieslak, J.-L. Giavitto, P. Prusinkiewicz, Stochastic P systems and the simulation of biochemical processes with dynamic compartments. Biosystems, **91**(3), 458–472 (2008). https://doi.org/10.1016/j.biosystems.2006.12.009

43. The P-Lingua website. http://www.p-lingua.org

44. L. Valencia-Cabrera, *An Environment for Virtual Experimentation with Computational Models Based on P Systems*. Ph.D. Thesis (Universidad de Sevilla, Sevilla, 2015). http://hdl.handle.net/11441/45362

45. L. Valencia-Cabrera, B. Song, Tissue P systems with promoter simulation with MeCoSim and P-Lingua framework. J. Membr. Comput. **2**(2), 95–107 (2020). https://doi.org/10.1007/s41965-020-00037-z

46. L. Valencia-Cabrera, T. Wu, Z. Zhang, L. Pan, M.J. Pérez-Jiménez, A simulation software tool for cell-like spiking neural P systems. Rom. J. Inf. Sci. Technol. **20**(1), 71–84 (2017)

47. L. Valencia-Cabrera, D. Orellana-Martín, M.A. Martínez-del-Amor, A. Riscos-Núñez, M.J. Pérez-Jiménez, Computational efficiency of minimal cooperation and distribution in polarizationless P systems with active membranes. Fundam. Inform. **153**(1–2), 147–172 (2017). https://doi.org/10.3233/FI-2017-1535

48. L. Valencia-Cabrera, D. Orellana-Martín, M.A. Martínez-del-Amor, A. Riscos-Núñez, M.J. Pérez-Jiménez, Reaching efficiency through collaboration in membrane systems: dissolution, polarization and cooperation. Theor. Comput. Sci. **701**, 226–234 (2017). https://doi.org/10.1016/j.tcs.2017.04.015

49. L. Valencia-Cabrera, D. Orellana-Martín, M.A. Martínez-del-Amor, M.J. Pérez-Jiménez, An interactive timeline of simulators in Membrane Computing. J. Membr. Comput. **1**(3), 209–222 (2019). https://doi.org/10.1007/s41965-019-00016-z

50. T. Wu, Z. Zhang, Gh. Păun, L. Pan, Cell-like spiking neural P systems. Theor. Comput. Sci. **623**, 180–189 (2016). https://doi.org/10.1016/j.tcs.2015.12.038

Applications of Software Implementations of P Systems

3.1 Introduction

Since the introduction of membrane computing in 1998 [49], there has been a rapid theoretical development in this area with respect to computing models and their computing power and computational efficiency [50, 51]. Moreover, numerous real-world applications of membrane computing models [72, 76, 77] have been reported. P systems can perform specific tasks such as solving an NP-hard [48], NP-complete [37, 62], or PSPACE-complete problems [1], control language generation [63, 75], controlling robots [79], heuristic optimization problems [27, 71, 73], and arithmetic operation [78]. These tasks were accomplished manually, instead of by means of automatic design. The manual implementation of membrane computing models has some drawbacks. For example, it could be time-consuming, tedious, and impossible to implement large-scale systems. It limits the application scope of P system models. Therefore, the question on how to automatically design a P system by using programs, namely, the *programmability of a P system*, has become an urgent and attractive research direction in the area of membrane computing [74].

The automatic design of a P system is a very complicated and challenging task [70, 80]. There has been many works focused on the use of evolutionary algorithms to make a population of P systems evolve toward a successful one [34, 72]. These works start with the selection of an appropriate subset from a redundant set of evolution rules to design a cell-like P system, where a membrane structure and initial objects were predefined and fixed in the process of design [7, 23, 28, 66, 72]. In [23], a genetic algorithm was used to design a P system to calculate 4^2. In [28], a binary encoding technique was presented to denote an evolution rule set of a P system, and a quantum-inspired evolutionary algorithm (QIEA) was used to make a population of P systems evolve toward successful ones. This method successfully solved the design of P systems to compute 4^2 and n^2 (for natural numbers $n \geq 2$). In [66], an evaluation approach considering nondeterminism and halting penalty factors and a genetic algorithm with the binary encoding technique in [28] were introduced to

G. Zhang et al., *Membrane Computing Models: Implementations*, https://doi.org/10.1007/978-981-16-1566-5_3

design P systems for computing 4^2, n^2, and the generation of language $\{a^{2^n} b^{3^n} | n >$
1\}. In these studies mentioned above, a specific redundant evolution rule set was
designed for a specific computational task. This was developed in [7,72] by applying
one predefined redundant evolution rule set to design multiple different P systems,
each of which executes a computation task. In [7], an automatic design method
of a cell-like P system framework for performing five basic arithmetic operations
(addition, subtraction, multiplication, division, and power) was presented. In [72], a
common redundant set of evolution rules was applied to design successful P systems
for fulfilling eight computational tasks: $2(n-1)$, $2n-1$, n^2, $\frac{1}{2}[n(n-1)]$, $n(n-1)$,
$(n-1)^2 + 2^n + 2$, $a^{2^n} b^{3^n}$ and $\frac{1}{2}(3^n - 1)$, $(n > 1$ or 2$)$. In [21,31], the automatic
design of SN P systems is discussed.

This chapter is organized in the following manner: Sect. 3.2 discusses automatic
design of cell-like P systems with P-Lingua, Sect. 3.3 discusses automatic design
of spiking neural P systems with P-Lingua, Sect. 3.4 discusses modelling real
ecosystems with MeCoSim, and Sect. 3.5 discusses robot motion planning.

3.2 Automatic Design of Cell-Like P Systems with P-Lingua

In this section, some preliminaries are first provided. An automatic design approach
with a *genetic algorithm* (GA) for a cell-like P system through tuning membrane
structures, initial objects, and evolution rules is discussed. Next, an automatic design
method with a permutation penalty genetic algorithm (PPGA) for a deterministic
and non-halting membrane system by tuning membrane structures, initial objects,
and evolution rules is discussed.

3.2.1 Preliminaries

3.2.1.1 Alphabet and Multisets
An *alphabet* Γ is a non-empty set, and their elements are called *symbols*. A *string*
u over Γ is an ordered finite sequence of symbols, that is, a mapping from a natural
number $n \in \mathbb{N}$ onto Γ. The number n is called the *length* of the string u, and it is
denoted by $|u|$. The empty string (with length 0) is denoted by λ. A *multiset* over
an alphabet Γ is a mapping f from Γ onto the set of natural numbers $\mathbb{N}$. For each
symbol $a \in \Gamma$, the natural number $f(a)$ is called the *multiplicity* of symbol a in
multiset f. We denote by $M(\Gamma)$ the set of all multisets over Γ.

3.2.1.2 Rooted Tree
An *undirected graph* G is an ordered pair (V, E) where V is a set whose elements
are called *nodes* and $E = \{\{x, y\} \mid x, y \in V, x \neq y\}$ whose elements are called
edges. A *path* of length $k \geq 1$ from $x \in V$ to $y \in V$ is a sequence $(x_0, \ldots, x_k)$
such that $x_0 = x$ and $x_k = y$. If $x_0 = x_k$, then we say that the path is a *cycle*.
An undirected graph is *connected* if every pair of nodes is connected by a path. An

undirected graph with no cycle is said to be *acyclic*. A *rooted tree* is a connected, acyclic, undirected graph in which one of the vertices (called *the root of the tree*) is distinguished from the others.

3.2.1.3 Cell-Like P System/Transition P System

1. A cell-like P system with a hierarchical membrane structure can be formally represented as $\Pi = (V, O, \mu, W, \mathfrak{R}, i_o)$ [49], where
   (a) V is the (finite and non-empty) alphabet of objects.
   (b) $O \subseteq V$ is the output alphabet, namely, the set of output objects.
   (c) μ is a hierarchical membrane structure with $m \geq 1$ membranes labeled by the elements of a given set H, $H = \{0, 1, \ldots, m - 1\}$, and the skin membrane is labeled as 0. The hierarchical membrane structure can also be depicted through a rooted tree.
   (d) W is the vector of initial multisets $w_0, \ldots, w_{m-1}$ over V associated with the regions $0, 1, \ldots, m - 1$ delimited by the membranes of μ, namely, $W = [w_0, \ldots, w_{m-1}]$.
   (e) $\mathfrak{R}$ is the set of finite sets $R_0, \ldots, R_{m-1}$ of evolution rules associated with the regions $0, 1, \ldots, m - 1$ of the membrane structure μ, namely, $\mathfrak{R} = \{R_0, \ldots, R_{m-1}\}$. Three types of evolution rules, rewriting, dissolution, and rewriting-communication rules, are considered in this study. That is, R_i ($i = 0, 1, \ldots, m - 1$) has rules of one of the following forms:
      (i) *rewriting rule*: $[u \rightarrow v]_i$;
      (ii) *dissolution rule*: $[u]_i \rightarrow v$;
      (iii) *rewriting-communication rule*: $[u]_i \rightarrow [v]_i x$;
      where $i \in H$; $u \in V$; $v, x \in V^*$; where V^* denotes the set of all strings over V. The left-hand side of these rules is u, and the right-hand side of them is v or v, x. The length of u is called the radius of each rule. The rewriting rule $[u \rightarrow v]_i$ rewrites u by v. The dissolution rule $[u]_i \rightarrow v$ dissolves the compartment i, and its content is transferred to the surrounding membrane after all the other rules have been applied, and u is replaced by v. The rewriting-communication rule $[u]_i \rightarrow [v]_i x$ rewrites u by v inside the compartment i and, at the same time, sends x outside the compartment.
   (f) i_o is the output membrane of Π.
2. The system is called noncooperative if the length of the object in the left-hand side of an evolution rule is one.

The multisets associated to regions form a configuration of the P system. The computation begins by treating the initial multisets, w_i, $0 \leq i \leq m - 1$, and then the system will go from one configuration to a new one by applying the evolution rules associated to regions in a deterministic and maximally parallel way, that is, all the objects that may be transformed or communicated must be dealt with. The system will halt when no more rules are available to be applied. A computation is a sequence of configurations obtained as it is described above, starting with the initial configuration and ending with the configuration when the system halts. The result of a computation, a multiset of objects, is obtained in the output region, i_o.

Sometimes cell-like P systems are of the form $\Pi = (V, O, \mu, \mathcal{M}_0, \ldots, \mathcal{M}_{m-1}, (\mathcal{R}_0, \rho_0), \ldots, (\mathcal{R}_{m-1}, \rho_{m-1}), i_o)$, where $\mathcal{M}_0, \ldots, \mathcal{M}_{m-1}$ are multisets over O; $\mathcal{R}_0, \ldots, \mathcal{R}_{m-1}$ are rules associated with membrane $0, 1, \ldots, m-1$, respectively; and $\rho_0, \ldots, \rho_{m-1}$ are the partial order relations associated with the rules in $\mathcal{R}_0, \ldots, \mathcal{R}_{m-1}$. The ρ_i provides priorities between rules in $\mathcal{R}_i$, in such a manner that if $(r_1, r_2) \in \rho_i$ we say that rule r_1 has a higher priority than r_2, and we denote it by $r_1 > r_2$;

3.2.2 Automatic Design of P Systems with an Elitist Genetic Algorithm

In this subsection, *automatic design approach for a cell-like P system* through tuning membrane structures, initial objects, and evolution rules is discussed. In this method, a binary encoding technique is used to codify the P system with variable membrane structures, initial objects, and evolution rules; an elitist genetic algorithm is applied to evolve a population of P systems toward a successful P system for fulfilling a specific task, the calculation of the square of 4 [47]; an effective fitness function is employed to evaluate each candidate P system by a using *P-Lingua simulator* [58].

3.2.2.1 Problem Statement
Automatic design of cell-like P systems through tuning membrane structures, initial objects, and evolution rules [47] is performed by advancing the design of a cell-like P system step-by-step. While performing the task, a family of membrane systems $\prod$ of P systems, that is, $\prod = \{\Pi_i\}_{i \subseteq N}$, where N is the set of natural numbers and each P system Π_i has the structure $\Pi_i = (V, \mu, W, R, i_o)$, where V is a predefined alphabet of objects; μ is a hierarchical membrane structure with m membranes labeled by the elements of a given set H, $H = \{0, 1, \ldots, m-1\}$, and the skin membrane is labeled as 0; W is the set of initial multisets $w_0, \ldots, w_{m-1}$ over V associated with the regions $0, 1, \ldots, m-1$ of μ, that is, $W = \{w_0, \ldots, w_{m-1}\}$; R is the set of evolution rule sets $R_0, \ldots, R_{m-1}$ associated with the regions $0, 1, \ldots, m-1$ of μ, that is, $R = \{R_0, \ldots, R_{m-1}\}$. In order to perform the task of automatic design, μ, W, and R need to be designed. Moreover, only the rewriting and dissolution rules are considered in this design, and $i_0 = 0$ implies that the output result is inside the skin membrane.

Considering a family $\prod$ of P systems, $\prod = \{\Pi_i\}_{i \subseteq N}$, where each P system Π_i has a variable μ, W, and R, where μ, W, and R are attained by using an optimization approach. W and R coming from the alphabet V are generated in the process of design.

3.2.2.2 Design Method
The general steps of the design method can be summarized as follows:

Step 1 Design of membrane structure μ: A hierarchical membrane structure with m membranes is considered in the cell-like P systems.

Step 2 Definition of an alphabet V: As usual, a certain number of letters from English alphabet is chosen so that it satisfies the requirement of initial objects w_i and evolution rules R_i.

Step 3 Design of evolution rule set R: The evolution rule set R is obtained by using a genetic algorithm, where the maximal number of evolution rules in R_i, that is, the length of R_i, and the types of evolution rules are considered.

Step 4 Design of initial object set W: The initial objects inside each membrane w_i $(i = 0, 1, \ldots, m - 1)$ are obtained by using a genetic algorithm, where the maximal number of initial objects inside each membrane w_i $(i = 0, 1, \ldots, m - 1)$ need to be prescribed.

Step 5 Design of a genetic algorithm: This step has to consider four points: (1) an encoding technique for membrane structure μ, evolution rule set R or $\mathfrak{R}$, and initial object set W; (2) a fitness function for evaluating a candidate P system; (3) the choices of selection, crossover, and mutation operators; and (4) parameter setting.

The details are described as follows:

(1) The encoding techniques for initial object set W, evolution rule set $\mathfrak{R}$, and membrane structure μ are as follows.

(a) *Encoding* W: In a cell-like P system, encoding of an object in V is introduced and then turn to the representation of each initial object set w_i $(i = 0, 1, \ldots, m - 1)$ and the initial object set W. Suppose the alphabet $V = \{a_0, a_1, \ldots, a_{n_o-1}\}$, where n_o is the number of objects in V. In the genetic algorithm, a binary string with n $(n = ceil(\log_2 n_o))$ bits (0 or 1) is used to represent the object a_j $(j = 0, 1, \ldots, n_o - 1)$, where the *ceil* function returns the smallest integer value that is greater than or equal to the number $\log_2 n_o$. In this representation of each object, if the number of objects in V is less than 2^n, then $(2^n - n_o)$ copies of the empty set λ are inserted into V. For example, if $V = \{a, b, c, z_1, z_2, z_3, z_4\}$, then the binary string with 3 bits is used to represent each object in V. Thus, the codes corresponding to each object can be listed as follows:

$$000 \rightarrow a, 001 \rightarrow b, 010 \rightarrow c, 011 \rightarrow z_1$$
$$100 \rightarrow z_2, 101 \rightarrow z_3, 110 \rightarrow z_4, 111 \rightarrow \lambda.$$

Thus, the initial object set W can be encoded, $W = \{w_1, \ldots, w_m\}$, where w_i $(i = 0, 1, \ldots, m - 1)$ is the initial object set in the ith membrane and is composed of a certain number of copies of each object in V. So the maximal number is limited, denoted by n_{w_i} $(i = 0, 1, \ldots, m-1)$ of copies of objects for each w_i in the design of a P system. Therefore, the initial object set w_i in the ith membrane can be represented by using a binary string with nn_{w_i} bits, and consequently, W is denoted by using a binary string with L_W bits, where

$$L_W = \sum_{i=0}^{m-1} nn_{w_i}. \tag{3.1}$$

That is, W is obtained by concatenating w_i $(i = 0, 1, \ldots, m - 1)$ one by one. For example, if $V = \{a, b, c, z_1, z_2, z_3, z_4\}$, $W = \{w_0, w_1\}$, $n_{w_0} = 2$, and $n_{w_1} = 2$, W is represented by applying 12 bits. $W = 000000011111$ means that $w_0 = a^2$ and $w_1 = z_1$.

(b) *Encoding* $\mathfrak{R}$: Considers two types of evolution rules, that is,

$$[left ObSet \rightarrow right ObSet]_{label}$$
$$[left ObSet]_{label} \rightarrow right ObSet$$

where $left ObSet$ and $right ObSet$ are the multisets of objects selected from the alphabet V; $label$ represents the label of a membrane, that is, the location of the evolution rule. The value of $label$ needs to be preset. The first rule is a transition rule, and the second one is a dissolution rule. So a multi-tuple $(left ObSet, right ObSet, dissolution)$ is used to represent an evolution rule, where $dissolution$ is a binary bit, that is, '0' or '1', where '0' and '1' representing the rule will be dissolved or not. The encoding methods of $left ObSet$ and $right ObSet$ are the same as in w_i. So the binary string concatenating the three strings $left ObSet$, $right ObSet$, and $dissolution$ represents an evolution rule. For example, if $V = \{a, b, c, z_1, z_2, z_3, z_4\}$, $label = 1$, the length of $left ObSet$ equals 1, and the length of $rigth ObSet$ equals 2, an evolution rule can be denoted as a binary string with 13 bits. The string 0000010101111 means $r_1 \equiv [a]_1 \rightarrow b$.

Thus, the evolution rule set R, $R = \{r_1, r_2, \ldots, r_{n_R}\}$ is encoded, where n_R is the number of evolution rules in R. If an evolution rule is represented by using a binary string with L_r bits, the evolution rule set R can be represented as a binary string with $n_R L_r$. For example, if $R = \{r_1, r_2\}$, where $r_1 \equiv [a]_1 \rightarrow b$ and $r_2 \equiv [a \rightarrow bc]_1$, the evolution rule set R can be denoted as $0000010101111 0000010100010$, that is, $R = \{[a]_1 \rightarrow b, [a \rightarrow bc]_1\}$.

In this case, the membrane structure μ is fixed, and a candidate P system can be represented as the binary string concatenating W and R, that is, the string with $L_W + n_R L_r$ binary bits.

(c) *Encoding* μ: The hierarchical membrane structure of a cell-like P system can be represented as a tree structure, where each of the membranes except for the skin membrane has a parent membrane. For example, if $\mu = \left[[[]_2]_1\right]_0$, the parent membranes of the membranes with the label 2 and 1 are the membranes labeled as 1 and 0, respectively. The skin membrane in a cell-like P system is the outermost membrane. So only the codes of the rest $(m - 1)$ membranes are considered. In this section, a parent membrane encoding method to represent a membrane structure is introduced. Suppose that a cell-like P system has m membranes labeled as $0, 1, \ldots, m - 1$. The symbol n_m $(n_m = ceil(\log_2 m)$ binary bits (0 or 1) is used to encode each of the $m - 1$ membranes, where the $ceil$ function returns the smallest integer value that is greater than or equal to the number $\log_2 m$. The code of each membrane refers to the label of its parent membrane. Thus, the membrane structure μ can be represented by using a binary string with $(m - 1)n_m$ bits. In this representation of a membrane structure, if the number of membranes in μ is less than 2^{n_m}, the membrane structure with m membranes is extended to the new structure with 2^{n_m} membranes, where the last $(2^{n_m} - m)$membranes are represented by using the empty set λ. For example, if a cell-like P system has four membranes, μ is represented by applying six binary bits. Thus, the string 000010 means $\mu_1 = [[\ ]_1[[\ ]_3]_2]_0$, and the string 000000 corresponds to $\mu_2 = [[\ ]_1[\ ]_2[\ ]_3]_0$. It is worth noting that this representation of μ may result in unfeasible membrane structures. So the traversal of a tree is applied to check whether a candidate membrane structure is feasible or not. Each of the three traversal approaches, preorder, inorder, and postorder traversal, can effectively solve this problem.

In this case, a candidate P system can be represented as the binary string concatenating the codes of μ, W, and R, that is, the string with L_{W+n_R} $L_r+(m-1)n_m$ binary bits.

(2) The fitness function with penalty items is used to evaluate a candidate P system. The model of the fitness function is described as follows:

$$fitness = fitness + f(\mu) + f(W) + f(R) + f(Halt) \qquad (3.2)$$

where $f(W)$ is the penalty term of the undesired properties in the initial objects set, that is, when W contains redundant objects, an extra punishment is needed to the fitness function; $f(R)$ is the penalty term of the undesired properties in the evolution rules set. Four undesired properties are considered, and they are as follows: (1) The dissolution rule is a structural rule, and it is applied at most once per step. If R contains more than one dissolution rules in one membrane, the simulation will report errors. In order to avoid this kind of errors, a fitness function value with penalty term is directly returned to stop the simulation. (2) If R contains nondeterministic rules, the fitness function value with penalty term is directly returned. (3) A candidate P system contains useless rules: If a candidate P system contains a useless rule, then it will be added to a penalty term with η. (4) A candidate P system contains evolutionary rules which cannot forward the calculation process. $f(Halt)$ is the penalty term of the non-termination property, that is, if a candidate P system is not in a halting configuration, an extra punishment is added to the fitness function. If a candidate P system cannot satisfy the desired properties, a penalty term is added to the fitness function to reduce the probability of the selection in the candidate population. So the genetic algorithm can gradually remove the undesired candidate P systems. $f(\mu)$ is the penalty term of the undesired properties of the membrane structure. If a candidate P system has an invalid membrane structure, it cannot satisfy the basic syntax of the membrane systems. So in order to make error in the process of simulation, a penalty term is returned to stop its simulation in P-Lingua. The evaluation method is shown in Fig. 3.1.

In the evaluation method, the selection of these constants is based on the designers' experience, the experimental results, and some investigations such as in [66].

Evaluation method

$fitness \leftarrow 0$

Load the P system corresponding to the current chromosome

$NondePairs \leftarrow$ number of rule pairs with the same left hand side

$DisRuleNum \leftarrow$ number of dissolution rules in a membrane

$UselessNum \leftarrow$ number of useless initial objects in the process of the simulation

$UselessRule \leftarrow$ number of useless rules in the process of the simulation

$NotEvoRule \leftarrow$ number of not evolutionary rules in the simulation

$UselessMemSructure \leftarrow$ the value represents that the membrane structure is error

if $((NondePairs > 0)\|(UselessMemSructure > 0)\|(DisRuleNum > 1))$ **then**

    $fitness \leftarrow \delta * NondePairs + \delta * DisRuleNum + \delta * UselessMemSructure$

    return $fitness$

else

    {the P system is deterministic so we need to simulate only computation}

    $step \leftarrow 0$

    while $((P$ system is not a halting state$) \wedge (step < MaxSteps))$**do**

        evolve one step(move to the next configuration of the P system)

        $step \leftarrow step+1$

    end while

    if P system is in a halting configuration **then**

        $fitness \leftarrow fitness +| simulation\_result - desired\_result |$

    else

        $fitness \leftarrow fitness +| simulation\_result - desired\_result |+ \eta_1$

    end if

    if $fitness = 0$ **then**

        $fitness \leftarrow fitness + UselessNum * \eta_2 + NotUseRule * \eta_2 + NotEvoRule * \eta_2$

    end if

    return $fitness$

end if

Fig. 3.1 Evaluation methods. From [47]

(3) In this section, JGAP-Java Genetic Algorithms and Genetic Programming Package [43, 44] are used. The genetic algorithm applies an elitist selection operator, a single-point crossover operator, and a uniform mutation operator.

(4) There are four parameters in the genetic algorithm, and they are represented as a parameter set Pa_set where $Pa\_set = \{N_p, P_c, P_m, IterNum\}$, N_p, P_c, P_m, and $IterNum$ are the population size, the crossover rate, the mutation rate, and the maximal number of evolutionary generations in the genetic algorithm, respectively.

P system $\prod = \{V, \mu, W, R, i_o\}$ is considered, where the membrane structure consists of four membranes, and the skin membrane is labeled 0; the alphabet $V = \{a, b\}$; i_o=0; $W=\{w_0, w_1, w_2, w_3\}$, $R = \{R_0, R_1, R_2, R_3\}$, and μ are obtained by using JGAP. The parameters are assigned as follows: $n_{w_0} = n_{w_1} = n_{w_1} = n_{w_1} = 1$; $n_R = 4$, that is, the evolution rule set R consisting of four rules. In the experiment, each of R_0, R_1, R_2, and R_3 consists of only one rule. The maximal number of objects in the $leftObjSet$ and $leftObjSet$ of each rule are 1 and 4, respectively. According to the referring existing literature [66] and the design rules, the rest of the parameters in the experiments are set as follows: $m = 4, n = 2, L_W = 8, L_R = 44$, $\delta = 25, \eta_1 = 1, \eta_2 = 1$, and $MaxSteps = 25$.

In the following description, at first, the choices of the mutation rate P_m, the crossover rate P_c, the population size N_p, and the maximal number $IterNum$ of evolutionary generations in the genetic algorithm are discussed, and then the result of this design is provided.

In the experiments, the parameter sets for P_m, P_c, N_p, and $IterNum$ are set as follows:

$Pa\_set_{P_m} = \{30; 0.1; \{0.01, 0.05, 0.1, 0.125, 0.2, 0.25, 0.35, 0.5, 1.0\}; 300\}$

for P_m; $Pa\_set_{P_c} = \{30; \{0.01, 0.05, 0.09, 0.1, 0.2, 0.3, 0.4, 0.5, 0.6, 0.7, 0.8$ $, 0.9, 1.0\}; 0.1; 300\}$ for P_c; $Pa\_set_{N_p} = \{\{10, 20, 30, 40, 50, 60, 70\}; 0.1;$ $0.1; 300\}$ for N_p; $Pa\_set_{IterNum} = \{30; 0.1; 0.1; \{50, 100, 150, 200, 250,$ $300, 350, 400\}\}$ for $IterNum$.

Experimental results for the discussion of the four parameters are shown in Fig. 3.2, where the successful rate refers to the ratio of the number of successful computations to 100 independent runs; the average generation is the average of the evolutionary generations over 100 independent runs when the algorithm stops for each test, and the total number of function evaluations refers to the total number of the fitness function evaluations for candidate P systems in 100 independent runs.

Figure 3.2a shows that the highest successful rate and the lowest average generation are obtained when the value of P_m equals 0.100. Figure 3.2b shows that the best results of the successful rate and the average generation are obtained when $P_c = 1.0$. In Fig. 3.2c, when the value of N_p is greater than 30, the success rate arrives at 100%, while the best result of the total number of function evaluations is achieved when N_p=30. According to the results in Fig. 3.2d, as $IterNum$ increases from 50 to 400, the elapsed time per run gradually goes up; on the other hand, the success rate arrives at 100% if $IterNum$ is equal to or greater than 300. Therefore, it is better to assign P_m, P_c, N_p and $IterNum$ as 0.100, 1.0, 30, and 300, respectively.

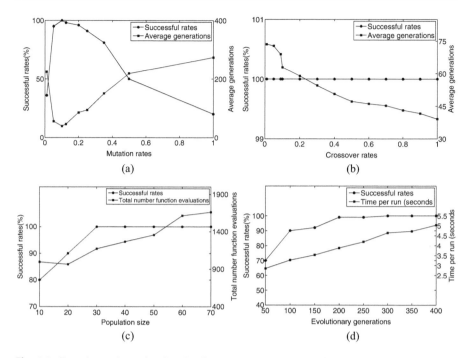

Fig. 3.2 Experimental results for the four parameters. From [47]. (**a**) Mutation rates. (**b**) Crossover rates. (**c**) Population sizes. (**d**) Evolutionary generations

In the design of a cell-like P system for calculating the square of 4, $Pa\_set = \{30; 0.1; 1.0; 300\}$. Next 1000 independent runs are performed, and it obtains 100% success rate. The introduced design approach obtains 65 different variants of cell-like P systems for successfully fulfilling the computation of 4^2. Their details can be referred to [47]. The design method obtains different solutions having different initial objects and evolution rules sets, due to the randomness of the selection of objects, the rules, and the membrane structure.

3.2.3   Automatic Design of P Systems with a Permutation Penalty Genetic Algorithm

In this section, an automatic design method, that is, *permutation penalty genetic algorithm* (PPGA), for a deterministic and non-halting membrane system generating the set $\{n^2 | n \geq 1\}$ of natural numbers, by tuning the syntactical ingredients consisting of membrane structures μ, initial objects W, and evolution rules $\Re$ [74] is discussed. The design approach is described in detail. And then a cell-like membrane system for computing the square of n (n is a natural number) is presented.

To design a P system with the prescribed requirements, it is necessary to consider the following three points: representation of a P system, evaluation of a candidate

P system, and evolution of a family of P systems toward the expected result. In this section, a P system permutation encoding representation, a penalty function evaluation of a candidate P system, and a genetic algorithm for the P system evolution toward the expected result are discussed. At first, three techniques are presented, and then the design method to provide an algorithmic elaboration is summarized.

1. Representation of P Systems

The permutation encoding technique [60] is used to codify a P system. The representation of a P system consists of the encoding approaches for the alphabet V, its membrane structure μ, the initial multiset vector W, evolution rules set $\Re$, and an individual chromosome corresponding to a candidate P system. Next, these approaches are discussed one by one.

(a) Encoding of V

Suppose that there are N_V objects (letters), and the N_V strictly positive integers are used to represent the objects and 0 to denote the empty set λ. Thus, V is encoded as an ordered string of numbers, namely, "01 ... N_V". For instance, if $V = \{a, b, c\}$, its codes are "0123".

(b) Encoding of μ

The hierarchical membrane structure of a cell-like P system can also be denoted as a rooted tree. Thus, the label of the parent (the neighboring outer membrane, like the parent of a node in a tree) of each membrane can be used to form an ordered string to represent a P system structure. It is worth noting that the skin membrane is not considered in the string because it is the outermost membrane in the structure. Thus, the hierarchical membrane structure of the P system with N_μ membranes is represented with a string with $(N_\mu - 1)$ numbers. For example, the structure in Fig. 3.3 can be represented as the codes "0001136".

(c) Encoding of W

Each element w_i, $i = 0, 1, \ldots, m - 1$, of the vector W are strings over V. The encoding approach of W is designed according to the encoding technique of V. Suppose that the largest number of objects in w_i is N_{w_i}, so w_i needs N_{w_i} codes, each of which may be 0, 1, ... or N_V. The codes of W can be obtained by concatenating

Fig. 3.3 An example for a cell-like P system membrane structure and its associated tree. From [60, 74]

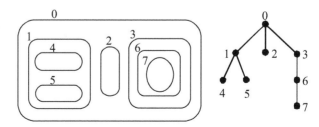

the string of w_i, $i = 0, 1, \ldots, m - 1$, and a separator symbol $N_V + 4$ is used to delimit the codes of w_i and w_{i+1}, $i = 0, 1, \ldots, m - 2$. Thus, the total number L_W of codes for W is

$$L_W = \sum_{i=0}^{m-1} N_{w_i} + m - 1 \tag{3.3}$$

For example, $W = [w_0, w_1, w_2]$ is the initial multiset vector of a P system. $N_{w_0}=\lambda$, $N_{w_1}=aa$, $N_{w_2}=bbcc$. Thus, $L_W=9$ and the string for encoding W is "071172233".

(d) Encoding of $\mathfrak{R}$

The left-hand side u and the right-hand side v of the rule (rewriting, dissolution, or rewriting-communication rule) are elements of V and V^*, respectively. On the basis of the representation of V, the set $\mathfrak{R}$ is encoded. Suppose that the number of rules in R_i is N_{R_i}, $i = 0, 1, \ldots, m - 1$, and the largest numbers of objects in the left-hand side u and in the right-hand side v of a rule are N_l and N_r, respectively. Thus, N_l codes are used, each of which may be $1, 2, \ldots$, or N_V, N_r codes, each of which may be $0, 1, \ldots$, or N_V, and additional one code to describe its rule type (here we use $N_V + 1$, $N_V + 2$, and $N_V + 3$ to denote a rewriting, dissolution, and rewriting-communication rules, respectively) to encode a rule. Thus, the code length L_{R_i} for the rule is $N_l + N_r + 1$, that is, $L_{R_i}=N_l + N_r + 1$. The codes of $\mathfrak{R}$ can be gained by concatenating the string of each rule and by using a separator symbol $N_V + 5$ between R_i and R_{i+1}, $i = 0, 1, \ldots, m - 2$. So the total code length $L_{\mathfrak{R}}$ of the set $\mathfrak{R}$ is

$$L_{\mathfrak{R}} = \sum_{i=0}^{m-1} (N_{R_i} * L_{R_i}) + m - 1 \tag{3.4}$$

It is worth noting that the dissolution rule is a structural rule, which is applied at most once at each step of a P system evolution, and rewriting and rewriting-communication rules can be normally applied in a maximally parallel mode. For instance, the set $\mathfrak{R}=\{R_0, R_1, R_2\}$ is encoded as the string 11124233481334221681235" where $R_0 = \{[a \rightarrow aab], [b \rightarrow cc]\}$, $R_1 = \{[a \rightarrow cc], [b] \rightarrow [b]a\}$, and $R_2 = \{[a] \rightarrow bc\}$.

(e) Encoding of a P System

Next, a P system through tuning membrane structure, initial objects, and evolution rules is designed where the codes for the P system can be attained by sequentially concatenating the codes of μ, W, and $\mathfrak{R}$, and a separator symbol $N_V +6$ to enable the separation of the codes of μ, W, and $\mathfrak{R}$. The encoding of a P system

Fig. 3.4 The initial configuration of Π_e (with rules included). From [74]

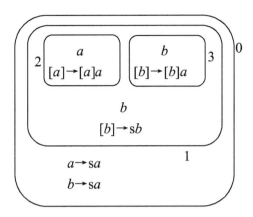

has been illustrated using the following example. Consider the following P system $\Pi_e = (V, O, \mu, W, \mathfrak{R}, i_o)$ where

1. $V = \{s, a, b\}$;
2. $O = \{s\}$;
3. $\mu = [[[\ ]_2[\ ]_3]_1]_0$;
4. $W = [w_0, w_1, w_2, w_3]$, $w_0 = \lambda$, $w_1 = b$, $w_2 = a$, $w_3 = b$;
5. $\mathfrak{R} = \{R_0, R_1, R_2, R_3\}$, $R_0 = \{a \rightarrow sa, b \rightarrow sa\}$, $R_1 = \{b \rightarrow sb\}$, $R_2 = \{[a] \rightarrow [a]a\}$, $R_3 = \{[b] \rightarrow [b]a\}$;
6. $i_o = 0$.

The initial configuration of the P system Π_e is illustrated in Fig. 3.4. If $N_{w_0} = N_{w_1} = N_{w_2} = N_{w_3} = 1$, $N_{R_0} = 2$, $N_{R_1} = N_{R_2} = N_{R_3} = 1$, $N_l = 1$, $N_r = 2$ and $L_{R_i} = 4$, ($i = 0, 1, 2, 3$), the P system Π_e is encoded as the string "011903239212431248313582 2683326".

2. Evaluation of P Systems
How to evaluate a candidate P system is a crucial step in the automatic design of membrane systems by using evolutionary algorithms. This step has a direct effect on the characteristics of the P systems obtained and the performance of the design algorithm. In the evaluation, the following seven aspects are considered:

1. The difference between the actual number(s) and the expected number(s) of output objects. The former refers to the simulated result that is returned from the specialized P system simulation software, P-Lingua [25, 26], through inputting a candidate P system into the software. The latter is designated by the designer according to the computational task or the problem to solve.
2. The feasibility of a P system due to its membrane structure μ. In the design, some infeasible membrane structures may be generated by the evolutionary operations such as crossover or mutation in a genetic algorithm. The infeasible membrane

structure refers to the one that does not satisfy the syntactical requirement of the P system.

3. The redundancy of objects in the initial multiset vector W. In this design, some objects exist in the initial multiset vector W, but they will not be used through the computation of the P system. They are called *redundant objects*. This redundancy results from the randomness of the generation of the population of initial P systems in an evolutionary algorithm.
4. The nondeterminism of a P system resulting from nondeterministic membrane systems due to evolution rules
5. The infeasibility of a P system due to more than one dissolution rules in one set R_i $(i = 0, 1, \ldots, m - 1)$
6. The redundancy of evolution rules in the set $\mathfrak{R}$. The redundant rules refer to the ones in the set $\mathfrak{R}$ that are not used through the computation of the P system.
7. A halting P system due to evolution rules

Based on the above analysis, the following evaluation functions are defined:

$$f = f_1 + f_2 + f_3 + f_4 + f_5 + f_6 + f_7 \tag{3.5}$$

where

$$f_1 = g_1(N_s) = \sum_{i=1}^{N_{obj}} |N_i^{ao} - N_i^{eo}| \tag{3.6}$$

$$f_2 = g_2(\mu) = \delta \cdot M_f \tag{3.7}$$

$$f_3 = g_3(W) = \eta \cdot N_{obs} \tag{3.8}$$

$$f_4 = g_4(\mathfrak{R}) = \alpha \cdot N_{non} \tag{3.9}$$

$$f_5 = g_5(\mathfrak{R}) = \beta \cdot R_{dis} \tag{3.10}$$

$$f_6 = g_6(\mathfrak{R}) = \gamma \cdot N_{red} \tag{3.11}$$

$$f_7 = g_7(\mathfrak{R}) = \xi \cdot H \tag{3.12}$$

where

- f_1 is the object error function; $g_1(N_s)$ is the function of the simulation step N_s of a candidate P system in the P-Lingua software and is designed according to the computational task; N_i^{ao} and N_i^{eo} are the actual number and the expected number of the ith $(i = 1, 2, \ldots, N_{obj})$ output objects, respectively; $N_{obj} = |O|$; and N_{obj} is the number of distinct letters involved in the output objects.

- f_2 is the penalty item of the infeasible membrane structure, $g_2(\mu)$ is the function of the membrane structure μ, δ is a penalty factor, and $M_f \in \{0, 1\}$, where "0" and "1" mean that the membrane structure of a candidate P system is feasible and infeasible, respectively.
- f_3 is the penalty item of the redundant objects in the initial multiset vector W, $g_3(W)$ is the function of the initial multiset vector W, η is a penalty factor, and N_{obs} is the number of the redundant objects in the initial multiset vector W.
- f_4 is the penalty item of a nondeterministic P system, $g_4(\Re)$ is a function of the set $\Re$, α is a penalty factor, and $N_{non} \in \{0, 1\}$, where "0" and "1" mean that there is not any nondeterministic evolution rule, and there is at least one pair of nondeterministic evolution rules in the set $\Re$, respectively.
- f_5 is the penalty item of the dissolution rules, $g_5(\Re)$ is a function of the set $\Re$, β is a penalty factor, and $R_{dis} \in \{0, 1\}$, where "0" and "1" mean that there is less than and at least two dissolution rules in one set R_i $(i = 0, 1, \ldots, m - 1)$, respectively.
- f_6 is the penalty item of the redundant rules, $g_6(\Re)$ is a function of the set $\Re$, γ is a penalty factor, and N_{red} is the number of the redundant rules in the set $\Re$.
- f_7 is the penalty item of the halting P system, $g_7(\Re)$ is a function of the set $\Re$, ξ is a penalty factor, and $H \in \{0, 1\}$, where "0" and "1" mean that the candidate P system is a non-halting and halting one, respectively.

In Eqs. (3.7)–(3.12), the purpose of introduction of the penalty factors δ, α, β, γ, and ξ is to reject the unexpected candidate P systems, and therefore, the five factors can be assigned as a larger value as possible, for example, $\delta=\alpha=\beta=\xi=999999$, while the purpose of the use of the two factors η and γ is to remove those candidate P systems having redundant objects or evolution rules as possible as we could, and accordingly, they can be prescribed as smaller values. They are empirically set to 1 and 1, respectively.

3. Evolution of P Systems
The genetic algorithm with the permutation encoding technique (GAPE) in JGAP [43] is used to evolve a family of P systems toward a successful one. GAPE uses the elitist selection strategy, where 20% of individuals with the best fitness values are selected to pass to the next generation, being free of the crossover and mutation operators. In GAPE, one-point crossover and uniform mutation are used.

It is worth noting that the evolutionary operators might produce the P systems violating the constraints in (3.7)–(3.12) including infeasible membrane structures μ, more than one dissolution rules in one set R_i $(i = 0, 1, \ldots, m - 1)$, the redundancy of objects in the initial multiset vector W, the redundancy of evolution rules in the set $\Re$, the nondeterministic evolution rule pairs, and the halting P system due to evolution rules.

Fig. 3.5 Pseudocode
algorithm of PPGA. From
[74]

> **Begin**
> $t \leftarrow 1$
> 1)   Initialization
>   **While** (not termination condition) **do**
> 2)   Evaluation
> 3)   Storage of the best solution
> 4)   Selection
> 5)   Crossover
> 6)   Mutation
> $t \leftarrow t + 1$
>   **End**
> **End**

4. Algorithmic Elaboration

This subsection summarizes the design method PPGA as shown in Fig. 3.5, where each step is described as follows:

1. This step consists of two processes: the setting of initial parameter values and the generation of initial population. The former process is used to set initial values for N_V N_{w_i}, N_{R_i}, L_{R_i}, $i = 0, 1, \ldots, m - 1$, N_l, N_r, population size N_P, P_c and P_m, δ, η, α, β, γ, ξ, the maximal number $MaxGen$ of evolutionary generations as the termination condition of GAPE, and the maximal number $MaxStep$ of simulation steps for a P system in the P-Lingua software. The latter process produces a population with N_P individuals, each of which corresponds to a candidate P system.

2. Each individual is evaluated by using Algorithm 1 and, thus, obtains its fitness. In Algorithm 1, the values of the variables, M_f, N_{obs}, N_{non}, R_{dis}, N_{red}, and H, depend on the following constraint recognition techniques:

    (a) Infeasible P systems due to infeasible membrane structures: A P system is an infeasible one if it satisfies one of the three conditions: (i) The parent membrane of any one membrane is itself, (ii) the system has not the skin membrane, and (iii) two or more membranes form a parent membrane loop. For example, membrane 1 is the parent of membrane 2, membrane 2 is the parent of membrane 3, and membrane 3 is the parent of membrane 1.

    (b) Redundant objects: The objects in W do not appear in the left-hand side u of all evolution rules in $\Re$.

    (c) Nondeterministic P systems have two cases: (i) Two or more evolution rules in R_i ($i = 0, 1, \ldots, m - 1$) have the identical left-hand side u. (ii) Two or more evolution rules in R_i ($i = 0, 1, \ldots, m - 1$) can be applied within one transition. That is, the left-hand side objects of two or more evolution rules in R_i ($i = 0, 1, \ldots, m - 1$) can be provided in the current configuration.

(d) Infeasible P systems due to dissolution rules: A P system is an infeasible one if there are two or more dissolution rules in R_i $(i = 0, 1, \ldots, m - 1)$ according to the codes describing the rule types.

(e) Redundant evolution rules: An evolution rule is redundant in two cases: (i) if the evolution rule in which all the objects in the left-hand side do not appear both in the initial multiset and in the right-hand side of any one rule in the membrane and (ii) if the evolution rule in which the objects in the left-hand side are identical with those in the right-hand side, and they are neither the expected ones nor appear in the left-hand side of any rule in the membrane.

(f) Halting P systems: If there is not any *iterative loop* consisting of one or more evolution rules, the system is a halting one. An *iterative loop* may be one of the following cases: (i) One evolution rule forms an *iterative loop*. That is, if one evolution rule $left Obj \rightarrow right Obj$ has the feature $left Obj \subset right Obj$, the rule forms an *iterative loop*. (ii) Several evolution rules form an *iterative loop*. If N_{il} evolution rules, $left Obj_1 \rightarrow right Obj_1$, $left Obj_2 \rightarrow right Obj_2$, $left Obj_3 \rightarrow right Obj_3$, $\ldots$, $left Obj_{N_{il}-1} \rightarrow right Obj_{N_{il}-1}$, $left Obj_{N_{il}} \rightarrow right Obj_{N_{il}}$, have the features, $left Obj_2 \subseteq right Obj_1$, $left Obj_3 \subseteq right Obj_2$, $\ldots$, $left Obj_{N_{il}} \subseteq right Obj_{N_{il}-1}$, $left Obj_1 \subseteq right Obj_{N_{il}}$, the rules form an *iterative loop*.

3. The best solution and its corresponding P system are stored.
4. The elitist selection strategy described is considered.
5. The one-point crossover operator is used and depicted.
6. The uniform mutation operator is employed and illustrated.

Algorithm 1: Evaluation method

Require: A candidate P system
1: $f \leftarrow 0$
2: Compute M_f, N_{obs}, N_{non}, R_{dis}, N_{red}, H
3: **if** $((M_f > 0)\|(N_{non} > 0)\|(R_{dis} > 0))$ **then**
4:      $f \leftarrow f_2 + f_4 + f_5$
5: **else**
6:      $N_s \leftarrow 0$
7:      **while** $(H < 1) \wedge (N_s \leq Max Step)$ **do**
8:          Evolve the P system for one step
9:          $N_s \leftarrow N_s + 1$
10:         $f \leftarrow f + f_1$
11:     **end while**
12:     **if** $(H > 0)$ **then**
13:         $f \leftarrow f_7$
14:     **end if**
15:     **if** $(f = 0)$ **then**
16:         $f \leftarrow f + f_3 + f_6$
17:     **end if**
18: **end if**
Ensure: Fitness f

Table 3.1 Successful P systems

No	μ	W	$\mathfrak{R}$
1	$[[\ ]_1[\ ]_2[\ ]_3]_0$	$w_0 = \lambda$ $w_1 = b$ $w_2 = a$ $w_3 = a$	$[b \to bs]_0$ $[a \to ba]_0$ $[b]_1 \to ab$ $[a]_2 \to ab$ $[a]_3 \to sb$
2	$[[[\ ]_1]_2[\ ]_3]_0$	$w_0 = \lambda$ $w_1 = a$ $w_2 = a$ $w_3 = a$	$[b \to bs]_0$ $[a \to b^2]_0$ $[a]_1 \to [a]_1 a$ $[a]_2 \to sb$ $[a]_3 \to b^2$
3	$[[\ ]_1[\ ]_2[\ ]_3]_0$	$w_0 = \lambda$ $w_1 = a$ $w_2 = a$ $w_3 = b$	$[b \to bs]_0$ $[a \to ab]_0$ $[a]_1 \to ab$ $[a]_2 \to sb$ $[a]_3 \to ab$
4	$[[[\ ]_1[\ ]_3]_2]_0$	$w_0 = \lambda$ $w_1 = a$ $w_2 = b$ $w_3 = a$	$[b \to as]_0$ $[a \to sa]_0$ $[a]_1 \to [a]_1 a$ $[b]_2 \to sb$ $[a]_3 \to [a]_3 a$
5	$[[\ ]_1[\ ]_2[\ ]_3]_0$	$w_0 = \lambda$ $w_1 = b$ $w_2 = b$ $w_3 = a$	$[b \to sa]_0$ $[a \to sa]_0$ $[b]_1 \to [b]_1 a$ $[b]_2 \to [b]_2 a$ $[a]_3 \to sb$

The design of the cell-like P system Π_{ex} for fulfilling the computation n^2 is discussed to show the results. The parameters, P_m, P_c, N_P, $MaxGen$, η, and γ, are set to 0.1, 0.8, 20, 200, 1, and 1, respectively. Next, 5000 independent runs of the design experiment are performed, and it obtains the success rate 100%. The introduced design approach obtains 2930 different variants of cell-like P systems Π_{ex} for successfully fulfilling the computation of n^2. Table 3.1 lists only five successful P systems. The complete list of the 1936 successful P systems can refer to [74]. Due to the randomness of the selection of membrane structure, objects, and rules, multiple solutions for the same computational task can be obtained on the identical condition to provide multiple possibilities to construct different complex membrane systems.

3.3 Automatic Design of Spiking Neural P Systems with P-Lingua

In this section, an automatic design method based on genetic algorithms for evolving SN P systems for generating natural numbers within P-Lingua [20, 21, 54, 67] is discussed.

An SN P system consists of five main elements: the amount of neurons in the system, the synapse connections between neurons, the amount of rules within each neuron, the regular expressions which define each rule, and the initial number of spikes within each neuron.

A, SN P system [30] of degree $m \geq 1$ is a tuple $\Pi = (O, \sigma_1, \cdots, \sigma_m, syn, i_o)$, where:

(1) $O = \{a\}$ is the singleton alphabet (a is called spike);
(2) $\sigma_1, \cdots, \sigma_m$ are neurons, identified by pairs

$$\sigma_i = (n_i, R_i), 1 \leq i \leq m \tag{3.13}$$

where:
(a) $n_i \geq 0$ is the initial number of spikes contained in σ_i.
(b) R_i is a finite set of rules of the following two forms:
   (i) $E/a^c \rightarrow a; d$ where E is a regular expression over O, and $c \geq 1, d \geq 0$;
   (ii) $a^s \rightarrow \lambda$, for some $s \geq 1$, with the restriction that for each rule $E/a^c \rightarrow a; d$ of type (i) from R_i, we have $a^s \notin L(E)$;
(3) $syn \subseteq \{1, \ldots m\} \times \{1, \ldots m\}$ with $(i, i) \notin syn$ for $i \in \{1, \ldots m\}$ (synapses between neurons);
(4) $i \in \{1, \ldots m\}$ indicates the output neuron (i.e., σ_{i_o} is the output neuron).

The firing and forgetting rules of an SN P system are described and discussed in detail in [30, 73]. The distinguishing feature of SN P system is that the sequence of configurations can produce an associated spike train. If the output neuron spikes, then we have 1, and otherwise, we have 0. Hence, the spike train can be represented by the sequence of ones and zeros.

In order to automatically generate an SN P system, we should consider each aspect in an SN P system. The number of neurons in system, the synapse connections between neurons, the number of rules within each neurons, and the number of spikes within each neuron, according to specific task, are previously determined, but the regular expressions which define each rule and the delays on each rule are randomly generated in an SN P system. Then we can generate a population of SN P systems by same method. The aim is to use genetic algorithms to get an optimal SN P system by appropriately evolving an SN P system. The steps are listed as follows:

Step 1: First of all, we define a population of SN P systems $\Pi = \{\Pi_i\}_{i \in H}$, where H is a subset of natural numbers, and each SN P system Π_i of degree $m \geq 1$ is described as follows:

$$\Pi_i = (O, \sigma_1, \cdots, \sigma_m, syn, i_o) \tag{3.14}$$

where

(1) $O = \{a\}$ is a predefined singleton alphabet;
(2) $\sigma_1, \cdots, \sigma_m$ is the neurons from 1 to m.

$$\sigma_i = (n_i, R_i), 1 \leq i \leq m \tag{3.15}$$

where:
(a) $n_i \geq 0$ is the initial number of spikes contained in σ_i.
(b) R_i is a finite set of rules of the following two forms:
   (i) **Spike transfer rules:** $E/a^c \rightarrow a; d$. When fulfilling spike transfer rules and $d = 0$, a spike in the neuron should leave along the synapses and travel to the neurons connected to the neuron where the rule is applied.
   (ii) **Spike forgetting rules:** $a^s \rightarrow \lambda$. When performing spike forgetting rules, s spikes are consumed.

Step 2: Determine fitness of each individual in the population.
Step 3: Reserve the individual with higher fitness from the population.
Step 4: Select parents from the population and produce offsprings.
Step 5: Randomly perform mutation.
Step 6: Check whether any individual meets the requirements. If so, terminate the algorithm; otherwise, continue the algorithm.

The pseudocode algorithm of automatic design method is shown in Fig. 3.6. More explanations for each step are provided as follows:

Step 1: Input required parameters, which include m, n_i, syn, i_o, H, $MaxSteps$, $StepRepetition$, $MutationRate$, $MinFitness$, $MaxGeneration$, $BestFitness$, and $ExpectedSet$,
where:

(a) m, n_i, syn, and i_o represent the number of neurons in each P system, the number of spikes in each neuron, the synapse connections between each neuron, and the output neurons, respectively.
(b) H is population size.
(c) $MaxSteps$ represents the maximum steps that each network will take.
(d) $StepRepetition$ is the amount of repetitions each network will undergo to generate an output list.
(e) $MutationRate$ is the percentage chance for mutation.
(f) $MinFitness$ represents minimal fitness.
(g) $MaxGeneration$ is the max amount of generations.

```
Require: Initial membrane construction and objects and genetic algorithm
 1:  i=1
 2:  while (i ≤ H) do
 3:    Generating random SN PS_i
 4:    Caculating fitness value F(SN PS_i)
 5:    if (F(SN PS_i) ≤ MinFitness||F(SN PS_i) == null) then
 6:      Generating new SN PS_i and replacing old SN PS_i
 7:    end if
 8:    i = i + 1
 9:  end while
10:  while (generation ≤ MaxGeneration) do
11:    Caculating fitness value each SNPS
12:    Sorting population accordding to set F(SN PS)
13:    i=1
14:    while (i ≤ H) do
15:      if (i ≤ Elitism && i ≤ H) then
16:        New population[i] = Population[i]
17:        if (F(SN PS_i > BestFitness)) then
18:          BestFitness = SN PS_i
19:        end if
20:      else
21:        Parent1=ChooseParent( )
22:        Parent2=ChooseParent( )
23:        Child=Crossover(Parent1,Parent2)
24:        Child=Mutate(Child)
25:        New population[i] = Child
26:      end if
27:      if (F(SN PS_i) == 0||F(SN PS_i) == null) then
28:        F(SN PS_i) = 0
29:      else
30:        F(SN PS_i) = F(SN PS_i)
31:      end if
32:    end while
33:    genration = gneration + 1
34:  end while
Ensure: Spiking neural P system
```

Fig. 3.6 Automatic design algorithm of SN P systems

(h) *BestFitness* represents the best fitness through generations.
(i) *ExpectedSet* is the expected set.

Step 2: A population of SN P systems and their fitness values are calculated. $F(SNPS_i)$ and $F(SNPS)$ represent the fitness value of the ith SN P system and the fitness set of all SN P systems in the population, respectively. Check whether SN P systems are correct according to the fitness function value of each SN P system in the population.

Step 3: The genetic algorithm is used to automatically design each SN P system in the population. *Elitism* represents the number of reserving a certain number of better SN P systems in the population. *Parent1* and *Parent2* are two randomly selected SN P system with larger fitness values. *Crossover()* and *Mutate()* represent the crossover and mutate functions, respectively.

Step 4: Output a new SN P system with high sensitivity and precision after completion of automatic design.

The most important three steps in Fig. 3.6 including building a population of SN P systems, designing a fitness function, and setting elitism, crossover, and mutation are detailed in the following description.

1. Building a Population of SN P Systems

An SN P system includes the number of neurons, the synapse connections between neurons, the number of rules within each neuron, the regular expressions which define each rule, and the number of spikes in each neuron. An SN P system represents an individual (DNA, $SNPS_i$) in the population. Here, an individual is also thought of as a set, which contains above five aspects. As a result, the building of a population of SN P systems can be divided into the following steps.

Step 1:   Generate a random individual, where rules are randomly generated and other elements are predefined.

Step 2:   Repeat the first step until all the individuals($SNPS_i$) in the population are produced.

Step 3:   Check whether each individual is correct.

Step 4:   Delete and replace individuals with incorrect and low fitness values.

Step 5:   Save the initial population.

With the initial population, it is necessary to have an appropriate evaluation function to guide the population to evolve to the optimal solution. Therefore, it is worth noting that the fitness function plays an important role throughout the automatic design process. We describe the details of the fitness function as follows.

2. Design of Fitness Function

Here, we discuss how to design the fitness function, which is used to calculate the sensitivity and the precision of SN P systems. There are two data sets after the establishment of the SN P systems. One is a real output set $Output Set$. Another is given expected set $Expected Set$. $Output Set$ represents generating number set of repeating execution of SN P systems for a specifical task. $Expected Set$ is expected number set for a special task. So a fitness function is established by comparing elements in the real output set and the expected set. The pseudocode of the fitness function is shown in Fig. 3.7.

The category of an element in the above two sets is as follows:

(1) The output set is compared with the expected set, and for every number that is in both of the sets, the true positive count tp increases.

(2) The output set is compared with the expected set, and for every number that is in the output set but not in the target set, the false positive count fp increases.

(3) The output set is compared with the expected set, and for every number that is not in the output set but is in the target set, the false negative count fn increases.

(4) The true negative values, those that are not in the output set and not in the target set, are not counted as they are not needed for this design.

3. Elitism, Crossover, and Mutations

An individual consists of genes, which in the case of this section are represented by an SN P system. The crossover function allows the exchange of genes between two

Require: $OutputSet, ExpectedSet, tp = 0, fp = 0, fn = 0$
1: Initialization settings
2:    Merging elements from $OutputSet$ and $ExpectedSet$ into $OutExSet$. The length of $OutExSet$ is n
3: $i = 1$
4: **while** $(i \leq H)$ **do**
5:     $i = i + 1$
6:    **if** $OutExSet(i) \in OutputSet$ **then**
7:     **if** $OutExSet(i) \in ExpectedSet$ **then**
8:        $tp = tp + 1$
9:         Turn to **Step 21**
10:    **else**
11:        $fp = fp + 1$
12:        Turn to **Step 21**
13:    **end if**
14:    **else**
15:      **if** $OutExSet(i) \in ExpectedSet$ **then**
16:        $fn = fn + 1$
17:        Turn to **Step 21**
18:     **else**
19:        Turn to **Step 21**
20:    **end if**
21:    **end if**
22:    **if** $i \geqslant n$ **then**
23:       Turn to **Step 26**
24:    **else**
25:       Turn to **Step 4**
26:    **end if**
27: $Fitness = (\frac{2 \times tp}{2 \times tp + fp + fn}) \times sf$
28: **end while**
Ensure: Return $Fitness$

Fig. 3.7 The design of the fitness function

parents, creating a new child individual with the characteristics of the parents that were used. After the crossover, there is also a chance for the new child individual to mutate, changing one of the rules in the generated network at random. To ensure diversity in the population, a certain number of individuals are added to the population pool at each generation.

Except for crossover and mutation, this algorithm also allows the use of elitism selection. This feature allows a selected number of best SN P systems to be introduced with a new generation.

The detailed procedure of elitism, crossover, and mutation are described as follows:

Elitism: Elitism, the best optimal individuals in the current population, is set to 1 in the method of the automatic design, *that is*, an SN P system with the high sensitivity and precision can be saved to new population of each generation.

Crossover: The crossover is mainly composed of two steps, one is to choose the parent individuals (parents with a higher fitness will have a higher chance of reproducing), and the other is to exchange the corresponding rules in the two parent individuals.

```
Require: GlobleBestFitness  =  0,  CurrentBestFitness,  RateChange  =  0,
         MutationRate = 0
 1:  i = 1
 2:  while (i ≤ H) do
 3:     i = i + 1
 4:     if GlobleBestFitness ≤ CurrentBestFitness then
 5:        GlobleBestFitness = CurrentBestFitness
 6:        RateChange + +
 7:     else
 8:        RateChange = 0
 9:     end if
10:     if RateChange ≥ 10 then
11:        MutationRate = random(0, 10)
12:     else
13:        MutationRate = random(10, 20)
14:     end if
15:  end while
Ensure:  Return MutationRate
```

Fig. 3.8 Dynamic adjustment procedure of mutation probability

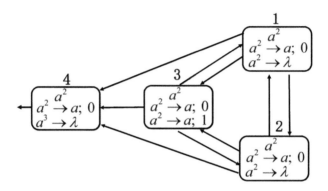

Fig. 3.9 A SN P system generating all natural numbers

Mutations: After getting new sub-individuals from the crossover of two parent individuals, new sub-individuals are mutated and added to new population, where *MutationRate* is dynamically adjusted according to the detailed problem. The pseudocode algorithm of dynamic adjustment is described in Fig. 3.8.

The automatic design method is further expounded by considering an SN P system generating all even natural numbers.

An SN P system generating all natural numbers mainly contains four elements: four neurons, ten synapse connections between neurons, eight rules, and two starting spikes each neuron. Out of four neurons, three neurons are general neurons, and remaining one is an output neuron. The specific sketch of an SN P system generating all natural numbers is shown in Fig. 3.9.

To illustrate the performance of the design method when simulating an SN P system generating all natural numbers, we make a dynamic behavior analysis from the fitness function value of the experimental testing process.

The average fitness value across ten runs is denoted by F_{av}. A larger value of F_{av} represents a smaller difference between the expected set and the output set.

$$F_{av} = \sum_{j=1}^{10} \sum_{i=1}^{n} F(SNPS_i) \qquad (3.16)$$

where $F(SNPS_i)$ represents the fitness value of the ith SN P systems, n is the number of SN P systems in the population, and j represents the jth run.

In the process of simulated evolution, the design parameters are set as follows: expected output set for the natural numbers system, 1, 2, 3, 4, 5, 6, 7, 8, 9; the population size, 4; maximum number of steps per system, 50; maximum number of repeats per system, 50; and maximum number of generations, 200.

We obtain the change curves of the average fitness value of static and dynamic mutation probabilities in Fig. 3.10, respectively. As can be seen from Fig. 3.11, the results of the correct natural data output are produced by a real natural SNP system and is the same as the expected set.

3.4 Modelling Real Ecosystems with MeCoSim

Membrane computing was not conceived in 1998 as a computational modelling framework for complex systems. It was far from the initial studies proposing a novel bioinspired computing model, with roots in formal languages theory and computation theory. The computational power and efficiency of these devices were studied in order to provide alternative paths to traditional computers based on Turing machines, proving the universality of different types of P systems. Besides, these new machines presented desirable properties in terms of the inherent parallelism and the promising effects derived from mechanisms as the cellular division, doubling the computation resources at any given step, trading space for time in order for these systems to present a great ability to solve NP-complete problems in reasonable time. Therefore, nothing in this new paradigm made its founder imagine that the research lines opened could diverge so significantly as it started to happen a few years after the first technical report published in 1998.

3.4.1 Problem Description

As a general idea, the primary intent we pursue is problem-solving through membrane systems. Thus, given a certain abstract problem (as 3-COL problem, deciding if a coloring with three colors is possible for a given graph), a membrane system is designed to solve the problem, according to the rules satisfying the constraint of the specific computing model chosen among all the possible types and variants of P systems. Then, the design is translated into a P-Lingua format specification and saved in a file with *.pli* extension. For instance, if the solution is

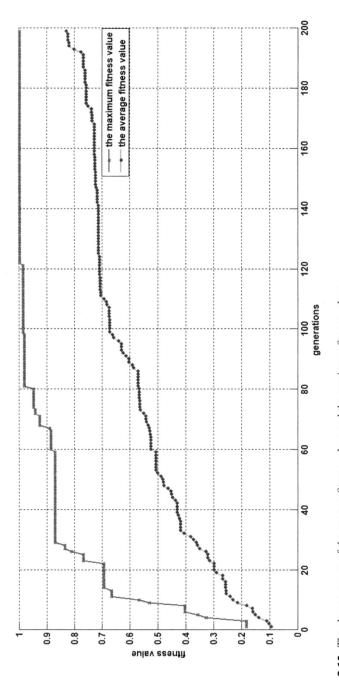

Fig. 3.10 The change curves of the average fitness values and the maximum fitness values

```
Final output set:
1       1       2       2       2       2       2       2       2       2
2       2       2       2       2       2       2       2       2       2
2       2       2       2       2       2       2       2       2       2
2       2       2       2       2       2       2       2       2       2
2       2       2       2       2       2       2       2       2       2
2       2       2       2       2       2       2       2       2       2
2       2       2       2       2       2       2       2       2       2
3       3       3       3       3       3       3       3       3       3
3       3       3       3       3       3       3       3       3       3
3       3       3       3       3       3       3       3       3       3
3       3       3       3       3       3       3       3       3       3
3       3       3       3       3       4       4       4       4       4
4       4       4       4       4       4       4       4       4       4
4       4       4       4       4       4       4       4       4       5
5       5       5       5       5       5       5       5       5       5
5       5       5       5       5       5       5       5       5       5
5       6       6       6       6       6       7       7       7       7
7       7       7       7       7       8       8       10
Press any key to exit, time elapsed: 00:00:01.5532086s
```

Fig. 3.11 The output set of SN P systems generating all natural numbers

using a cell-like P system with active membranes, the following elements should be given: the membrane structure, μ, the initial multisets for each region, and their corresponding sets of rules.

A file as the one described above could specify a concrete P system, but in our approach, we generally provide solutions for an abstract problem, through a family of P systems (let us denote it by $\Pi(< pars >)$), subject to certain parameters. Thus, for instance, if a solution $\Pi(< n >)$ for 3-COL problem is provided (with the parameter n representing the number of nodes in the graph, getting possibly involved in the sets of rules, alphabet, initial multisets, and membrane structure), the P-Lingua file will generically define the structure applicable to every P system member of the family. Thus, for each particular value of the parameters involved (n in the example), a different P system will be instantiated. Then, for a given member of the family (e.g., the P system $\Pi(5)$, solving 3-COL with $n = 5$, i.e., graphs with five nodes), many different possible inputs could be provided (in the example, one for each possible graph with five nodes, determined by its specific nodes and edges). In our approach, P-Lingua files should specify the solution for the abstract problem, while the introduction of the specific parameter values to instantiate the member of the family and the input to accompany the problem with the particular input is performed through MeCoSim layer. This imposes a clear separation between the abstract problem solved (P-Lingua specification) and the virtual experimentation with each specific instance and input, constituting what is called a scenario (MeCoSim [42, 55]).

For sure, P-Lingua files accept solutions providing non-parameterized models, or models whose parameters are also hard-coded in the same files, but this would break the proper separation of the responsibilities of each tool and consequently the adequate separation of the roles involved (P system designer, solving the general problem, and end users, running their virtual experiments through the provision of the particular data of each scenario of interest). The approach proposed is even more interesting when we are dealing with models representing real-life problems, for instance, ecology, where the profiles of people in charge of P system design and those managing the actual ecosystem are more clearly identified, in such a way that their background, knowledge, and main focus are generally different, being the former ones interested in designing solutions based on their computing models, taking advantage of their novel theories, and the latter ones interested in managing their ecosystems, getting abstracted from internal details of the models once they have experimentally validated with the experts in the models that they seem to behave properly according to their well-known scenarios, and therefore, the tools provided are useful for their virtual experiments aiding them in their decision-making process to manage their populations.

All in all, MeCoSim raised with this twofold intention now clearer with the roles described above: (1) providing a high-level visual environment to design, debug, simulate, analyze, and visualize models based on P systems and (2) putting at disposal a simulation environment for end users to introduce different instances of the problems and run their experiments according to their final needs.

The needs leading the such development were first detected in the context of ecological modelling and simulation of certain real ecosystems, as the ones described in Sect. 3.4. The managers of the ecosystems under study needed some tools to predict the evolution of the population of certain species in the corresponding systems (for different purposes, such as endangered species conservation or invasive species control). Initially, certain software applications were developed (Ecosim 1.0 family (see Refs. [20, 54]) to allow the introduction of different initial scenarios and visualize specific outputs, showing certain elements of the ecosystems. The effort was significant to develop each of these specific-purpose applications handling models of different ecosystems (in tasks from the analysis and design to the pure development).

Then, after those experiences, a number of common needs were identified. Investing that amount of effort for each possible future model designed was unfeasible, so a new approach emerged requiring the development of a software environment providing the generic mechanisms not only to handle P system-based models but also to allow the guided delivery of custom applications for each model designed, hence adapted for each end user problem addressed. With this view, MeCoSim environment would act as a meta-simulation app, allowing the definition of a customized simulation app for each problem, with the specific inputs and outputs required by that problem. Just to summarize, the definition of such custom user interfaces would imply the following mechanisms:

1. Definition of *input tables* where the user could introduce the external data of each particular scenario (possibly including both data involved in parameter values generation and input data for the specific instance for the experiment to conduct)

2. Calculation of *parameters* and inputs of the P system, from the data of the instance just introduced
3. Definition of the *output tables and charts*, to show the end users requested information for their target application (depending on their user view, but designed by the experts in the underlying P systems, configuring which specific elements of the computation should be extracted and how)
4. Specification of the arrangement of all these inputs and outputs in the custom app.

Further details of this approach are provided in Refs. [42, 55, 67]

Among all the possible practical applications emerged along the years in membrane computing, probably one of the most successful ones is the provision of a very useful methodology [13] for ecologists interested in certain problems related with real ecosystems, involving a number of species, in competition or cooperation, with a number of processes taking place simultaneously in the ecosystem and many biotic and abiotic factors and parameters playing different roles in the interactions.

In what follows, we list in Tables 3.2, 3.3, and 3.4 the main models created following the approach proposed of P systems as modelling framework and P-Lingua and MeCoSim as the tools for virtual experimentation.

3.5   Robot Motion Planning

The problem of motion planning is a crucially important problem in mobile robotics. The problem consists of finding a sequence of motion commands to move a robot in a complex environment from a starting point to a goal area while avoiding static and dynamic obstacles. The problem is even more complex if kinematic and nonholonomic constraints are considered. This problem has been studied from several years ago [35, 59], proving it is PSPACE-hard when the positions of obstacles are known. Several approximate algorithms have been proposed in the literature [19, 64]. A special mention should be given to a category of algorithms to build rapidly exploring random trees (RRTs) [36]. They are based on the randomized exploration of the configuration space by building a tree where nodes represent reachable points in the configuration space, and edges represent the corresponding transitions. In particular, the RRT* algorithm [33] is able to build an RRT whose paths asymptotically converge in time of computation to optimal solutions with respect to a predefined cost function. One of the main challenges by applying motion planning algorithms in robotics is the parallelization in software or hardware of such algorithms in order to accelerate them. For example, in [2], a GPU-based version of the RRT algorithm is presented. One alternative is to model the algorithms over an inherently parallel model of computation and then apply software/hardware simulators. With this idea, membrane computing has been used to design bioinspired parallel RRT models that can be efficiently simulated by means of parallel software/hardware architectures such as OpenMP [46] and CUDA [45]. The first approximation was introduced in [56] by using an extension

Table 3.2 Ecosystems models based on P systems, simulated with EcoSim/MeCoSim (I)

Reference	Case study	Comments
M. Cardona et al. 2008 [4]	**Bearded Vulture** The cliff-nesting and territorial mountains in Catalan Pyrenees (Northeastern Spain)	Five wild and domestic ungulates are included as carrion (prey) species.
M. Cardona et al. 2008 [3]	**Bearded Vulture** Catalan Pyrenees(NE)	Similar structure to [4]
M. Cardona et al. 2010 [5]	**Scavenger Birds** Catalan Pyrenees(NE)	Nomadic and non-nomadic species, and density regulation. Thirteen species, including two scavenger birds in competition with bearded vulture
M.A. Colomer et al. 2010 [10]	**Pyrenean Chamois** Catalan Pyrenees(NE)	Four influencing factors: introduced disease such as pestivirus infection, climate change, hunting, and migrations among areas
M.A. Colomer et al. 2010 [8]	**Bearded Vulture** The cliff-nesting and territorial mountains in Catalan Pyrenees (NE Spain)	Same model presented in [10]
M. Cardona et al. 2011 [6]	**Scavengers/Zebra mussel** Catalan Pyrenees (NE Spain) and a fluvial reservoir (Riba-roja-Ebro river, NE Spain)	For the scavengers, a simplified version of [4]. For mussels, focus on temperature and its effect on reproduction, fixation of the mussel to the substrate, movement of larvae, and density regulations.
M.A. Colomer et al. 2011 [11]	**Scavenger Birds** Catalan Pyrenees /Pyrenean and Pre-pyrenean mountains.	Species move among areas if lack of feeding resources in origin region. The model studied: (a) 13 species, including three avian scavengers (predators), six wild ungulates, and four domestic ungulates (preys); (b) interactions among species; (c) communication among areas; (d) load capacity regulation
M.A. Colomer et al. 2011 [9]	**Plant Communities** (sub)Alpine(NE Spain)	Model with climatic variability and orographic factors. Impact of the plant community module on population dynamics
A. Margalida et al. 2011 [39]	**Scavenger Birds** Catalan Pyrenees(NE)	Wild ungulates considered due to limitation of domestic carcasses. It causes an impact on the biomass. When only considering wild ungulates, the ecosystem cannot offer enough food for predators.
M.A. Colomer et al. 2012 [12]	**A carnivore that predates on ungulates and five ungulates** Catalan Pyrenees(NE)	Impacts of environment factors such as weather, orography, and soil conditions on carnivore size
A. Margalida et al. 2012 [38]	**European vultures** as the **Bearded vulture, Egyptian vulture, and Cinereous vulture** 10 municipalities in Catalonia, Northern Spain.	Food source: four scenarios of food availability. Taking 10 areas and 4 avian scavengers as research object. Impact of climate variations, such as seasons (summer and winter), food shortage, density regulation, and changes in species habitats (insufficient resources)

Table 3.3   Ecosystems models based on P systems, simulated with EcoSim/MeCoSim (II)

Reference	Case study	Comments
M.A. Colomer et al. 2013 [13]	**Birds, cats, and rats** General model	Prey-predator. Natural mortality, intraguild predation, and mesopredator release effect on long-lived prey
M.A. Colomer et al. 2014 [14]	**Zebra mussel** Reservoir of Ribarroja	Twenty membranes used for 20 weeks first reproductive cycle, 16 for the weeks of second reproductive cycle, and 2 membranes to handle regulation and mortality
M.A. Colomer et al. 2014 [15]	**Calotriton asper (newt)** Pi Valley (Noth Spain) water streams	Reproduction, mortality, and displacements in the terrestrial environment, possibly colonizing new streams
A. Margalida et al. 2015 [40]	**Avian scavengers** Pi Valley (Noth Spain) water streams	Impact of removal scenarios on population viability
A. Cortés-Avizanda et al. 2015 [18]	**Wild rabbits and avian scavengers** Mediterranean landscapes	Reproduction, mortality, foraging behavior of Egyptian vultures, wild rabbit carcass biomass availability, maximum carrying capacity, and carcass-sharing with competitors
A. Kane et al. 2015 [32]	**Gyps africanus** Hlane-Mlawula-Mbuluzi reserve network in Swaziland	Carrion feeding, feeding needs analysis, natural mortality, and many interacting species
C. Fondevilla et al. 2016 [24]	**Land use and land cover (plant communities)** Stubai Valley (Central Alps)	Grazing, foraging, natural mortality of animal species, movement, and land use
Z. Huang, G. Zhang, et al. 2017 [29]	**Domestic Giant Panda** Chengdu Research Base of Giant Panda Breeding (GPBB), Wolong China Conservation and Research Center for Giant Panda (CCRCGP)	The evolution process of the species: RMF+Rescue module, where RMF is also modified as RFM, FMR, or other forms, showing the robustness of the system independently on the order of the modules
H. Tian, G. Zhang, et al. 2018 [65]	**Domestic Giant Panda** Two regions: GPBB/CCRCGP	The membrane structure is the same as in [29], and the only difference is that release module is added to the previous module, that is, RMF+Rescue module+Release module.
A. Margalida, et al. 2018 [41]	**European avian scavengers** North Spain	Two periods (summer, breeding), reproduction, mortality, feeding, and carrying capacity. Forage in peripheral areas depending on availability in origin
M.A. Colomer, et al. 2019 [17]	**Porcine Reproductive and Respiratory Syndrome** Spain	Births, lactation, transmission, and fattening
M.A. Colomer, et al. 2020 [16]	**Porcine production** Vaccination against Aujeszky's disease Spain	Based on [17]
Y. Duan, et al. 2020 [22]	**Giant Panda in captivity** GPBB and related centers	Reproduction, mortality, feeding, and rescue models

Table 3.4 Ecosystems models based on P systems, simulated with EcoSim/MeCoSim (III)

Reference	Case study	Comments
L. Valencia-Cabrera, et al. 2013[68]	**Gene regulatory networks** General model	The first membrane computing model applied to reconstruct the behavior of logic networks of species with PDP systems
L. Valencia-Cabrera, et al. 2013[69]	**Gene regulatory networks** Arabidopsis thaliana	Based on [68], P systems are used to reproduce a logic gene network of (real) Arabidopsis thaliana in order to regulate the flowering processes.
M.A. Colomer et al. 2014 [14]	**Pandemics** General model	Different areas, neighborhoods, families, and infections at home, in school, workplace, among communities, etc.
E. Sánchez-Karhunen, et al. 2019[61]	**Market interactions**	Economic ecosystem modelled with PDP systems

of the enzymatic numerical P systems (ENPS) [53] framework to simulate basic RRT algorithms. In [57], the framework of ENPS was used for modelling the RRT and RRT* algorithms. It is worth pointing out that in [57], no additional ingredients to the ENPS framework were included. In consequence, the resulting models are compatible with existent ENPS robot controllers [52,53,77]. In [57], two simulators were also presented: The first one is based on OpenMP, and the second one is based on CUDA. The current challenges in this research line are related to simulate on hardware (FPGA) the models, to adapt the software/hardware simulators to actual robots, and, finally, to study the inclusion of dynamic obstacles such as people surrounding the robot.

3.5.1 Problem Definition

Let $X \subseteq \mathbb{R}^d$ be the *configuration space* of the robot, where $d \in \mathbb{N}, d \geq 2$. Let X_{obs} be the *obstacle space* and X_{free} be the *obstacle-free space* such that $X = X_{obs} \cup X_{free}$ and $X_{obs} \cap X_{free} = \emptyset$. Let the *initial configuration* $x_{init} \in X_{free}$ and the *goal region* $X_{goal} \subsetneq X_{free}$. A motion planning problem is defined by $(X_{free}, x_{init}, X_{goal})$.

A function $\sigma : [0, 1] \to \mathbb{R}^d$ is called:

- Path, if it is continuous;
- Collision-free path, if it is a path and $\sigma(\tau) \in X_{free}$, for all $\tau \in [0, 1]$;
- Feasible path, if it is a collision-free path, $\sigma(0) = x_{init}$ and $\sigma(1) \in X_{goal}$.

The motion planning problem can be solved in two ways:

1. Given a motion planning problem $(X_{free}, x_{init}, X_{goal})$, find a feasible path σ. If no such path exists, return failure. This is called *the feasible motion planning*.

2. Given a motion planning problem $(\mathcal{X}_{free}, x_{init}, \mathcal{X}_{goal})$ and a cost function c : $\sigma \rightarrow \mathbb{R}$, find a feasible path σ^* such that $c(\sigma^*) = min\{c(\sigma) : \sigma\ is\ feasible\}$. If no such path exists, return failure. This is called *the optimal motion planning*.

3.5.2 Path Planning for Mobile Robots

The path planning problem for mobile robots is a type of motion planning problem in which a wheeled or legged robot is considered, and it should navigate from an initial position to a goal region while avoiding obstacles. We can consider two types of mobile robots: On the one hand, *holonomic robots* are those that can move in any direction from its current state. On the other hand, *nonholonomic robots* have constrained motions with respect to its current state. For example, a two-wheeled robot is a nonholonomic robot that cannot follow a direction along its axes without applying previously a rotation in-place motion.

For the sake of simplicity, we will consider holonomic robots in the rest of this section. For this type of robots, the configuration space can be defined as $\mathcal{X} = \{(x, y)\} \subseteq \mathbb{R}^2$ where (x, y) are the Cartesian coordinates of the center of the robot. The radius of the robot is given by a constant R, and the sets $\mathcal{X}_{obs}$ and $\mathcal{X}_{free}$ are given by an occupancy matrix.

3.5.3 Rapidly-Exploring Random Tree (RRT) Algorithm

The RRT algorithm [36] is a classical solution to the feasibility motion planning problem. On the other hand, the RRT* algorithm [33] provides an approximate solution to the optimal motion planning problem. The original algorithms are sequential, but there are parallel versions as [2].

In [56] and [57], membrane computing has been used as computational framework to model parallel versions of such algorithms, providing also simulators in parallel architectures such as OpenMP and CUDA.

In general terms, the RRT algorithm gives a solution to the feasible motion planning problem by making a random tree exploring the free-obstacle configuration space. The nodes in the tree represent states in the obstacle-free space, and the edges represent transitions or movements between such states. The root is located in the initial robot position. The algorithm explores the space until a node in the goal region is reached or until a number of iterations. For a holonomic robot, nodes contain Cartesian coordinates in a 2D space, and edges represent straight-line movements.

In Fig. 3.12, an example of the RRT is represented. It can be seen as the free space is explored by the edges of the tree.

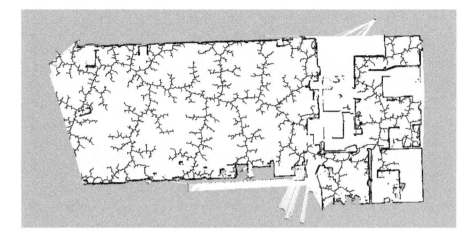

Fig. 3.12 A rapidly exploring random tree example

3.6   Conclusion

Following software implementation of P systems in Chap. 2, this chapter discussed
the use of P-Lingua and MeCoSim to fulfill some applications such as automatic
design of cell-like P systems and spiking neural P systems for performing specific
tasks, and modelling ecosystems and robot path planning. P-Lingua is a widely used
simulator for many variants of P systems such as cell- and tissue-like P systems,
spiking neural P systems, fuzzy reasoning spiking neural P systems, and kernel P
systems. MeCoSim is a visualization simulator based on P-Lingua. Both of them
are very useful to support the exploration of more and more applications with
automation, such as power system fault diagnosis, modelling giant panda ecosystem,
and mobile robot controller design.

References

1. A. Alhazov, C. Martín-Vide, L. Pan, Solving a PSPACE-complete problem by recognizing P
   systems with restricted active membranes. Fundam. Inform. **58**(2), 66–77 (2003)
2. J. Bialkowski, S. Karaman, E. Frazzoli, Massively parallelizing the RRT and the
   RRT*Massively parallelizing the RRT and the RRT*, in *Proceedings of the 2011 IEEE/RSJ
   International Conference on Intelligent Robots and Systems, San Francisco, CA, 2011* (2011),
   pp. 3513–3518. https://doi.org/10.1109/IROS.2011.6095053
3. M. Cardona, M.A. Colomer, M.J. Pérez-Jiménez, D. Sanuy, A. Margalida, A P System modeling an ecosystem related to the bearded vulture, in *Proceedings of the Sixth Brainstorming
   Week on Membrane Computing*, Fénix Editora, ed. by D. Díaz-Pernil, C. Graciani, M.A.
   Gutiérrez-Naranjo, Gh. Păun, I. Pérez-Hurtado, A. Riscos-Núñez (2008), pp. 51–66
4. M. Cardona, M.A. Colomer, M.J. Pérez-Jiménez, Modeling ecosystems using P systems: the
   bearded vulture, a case study, in *Membrane Computing (WMC 2008)*, ed. by D.W. Corne, P.
   Frisco, Gh. Păun, G. Rozenberg, A. Salomaa. Lecture Notes in Computer Science, vol. 5391

(2009), pp. 137–156. https://doi.org/10.1007/978-3-540-95885-7_11

5. M. Cardona, M.A. Colomer, A. Margalida, I. Pérez-Hurtado, M.J. Pérez-Jiménez, D. Sanuy, A P system based model of an ecosystem of some scavenger birds, in *Membrane Computing (WMC 2009)*, ed. by Gh. Păun, M.J. Pérez-Jiménez, A. Riscos, G. Rozenberg, A. Salomaa. Lecture Notes in Computer Science, vol. 5957 (2010), pp. 182–195. https://doi.org/978-3-642-11467-0_14

6. M. Cardona, M.A. Colomer, A. Margalida, A. Palau, I. Pérez-Hurtado, M.J. Pérez-Jiménez, D. Sanuy, A computational modeling for real ecosystems based on P systems. Nat. Comput. **10**(1), 39–53 (2011). https://doi.org/10.1007/s11047-010-9191-3

7. Y. Chen, G. Zhang, T. Wang, X. Huang, Automatic design of a P system for basic arithmetic operations. Chin. J. Electron. **23**(2), 302–304 (2014)

8. M.A. Colomer, M.A. Martínez-del-Amor, I. Pérez-Hurtado, M.J. Pérez Jiménez, A uniform framework for modeling based on P systems, in *Proceedings of the 2010 IEEE Fifth International Conference on Bio-Inspired Computing: Theories and Applications (BIC-TA 2010), Changsha, China*, vol. 1 (IEEE Press, New York, 2010), pp. 616–621. https://doi.org/10.1109/BICTA.2010.5645196

9. M.A. Colomer, C. Fondevilla, L. Valencia-Cabrera, A new P system to model the subalpine and alpine plant communities, in *Proceedings of the Ninth Brainstorming Week on Membrane Computing*, Fénix Editora, ed. by M.A. Martínez-del-Amor, Gh. Păun, I. Pérez-Hurtado, F.J. Romero-Campero, L. Valencia-Cabrera (2011), pp. 91–112

10. M.A. Colomer, S. Lavín, I. Marco, I. Pérez-Hurtado, M.J. Pérez-Jiménez, D. Sanuy, E. Serrano, L. Valencia-Cabrera, Modeling population growth of Pyrenean chamois (Rupicapra p. pyrenaica) by using P-systems, in *Membrane Computing (CMC 2010)*, ed. by M. Gheorghe, T. Hinze, Gh. Păun, G. Rozenberg, A. Salomaa. Lecture Notes in Computer Science, vol. 6501 (2011), pp. 144–159. https://doi.org/10.1007/978-3-642-18123-8_13

11. M.A. Colomer, A. Margalida, D. Sanuy, M.J. Pérez-Jiménez, A bio-inspired computing model as a new tool for modeling ecosystems: the avian scavengers as a case study. Ecol. Modell. **222**(1), 33–47 (2011). https://doi.org/10.1016/j.ecolmodel.2010.09.012

12. M.A. Colomer, I. Pérez-Hurtado, M.J. Pérez-Jiménez, A. Riscos-Núñez, Comparing simulation algorithms for multienvironment probabilistic P systems over a standard virtual ecosystem. Nat. Comput. **11**(3), 369–379 (2012). https://doi.org/10.1007/s11047-011-9289-2

13. M.A. Colomer, A. Margalida, M.J. Pérez-Jiménez, Population Dynamics P System (PDP) models: a standardized protocol for describing and applying novel bio-inspired computing tools. PloS One **8**(4) (2013). https://doi.org/10.1371/journal.pone.0060698

14. M.A. Colomer, A. Margalida, L. Valencia-Cabrera, A. Palau, Application of a computational model for complex fluvial ecosystems: the population dynamics of zebra mussel dreissena polymorpha as a case study. Ecol. Complexity **20**, 116–126 (2014). https://doi.org/10.1016/j.ecocom.2014.09.006

15. M.A. Colomer, A. Montori, E. García, C. Fondevilla, Using a bioinspired model to determine the extinction risk of Calotriton asper populations as a result of an increase in extreme rainfall in a scenario of climatic change. Ecol. Modell. **281**, 1–14 (2014). https://doi.org/10.1016/j.ecolmodel.2014.02.018

16. M.A. Colomer, A. Margalida, L. Fraile, Improving the management procedures in farms infected with the porcine reproductive and respiratory syndrome virus using PDP models. Sci. Rep. **9**, 9959 (2019). https://doi.org/10.1038/s41598-019-46339-w

17. M.A. Colomer, A. Margalida, L. Fraile, Vaccination is a suitable tool in the control of Aujeszky's disease outbreaks in pigs using a Population Dynamics P Systems model. Animals **10**, 909 (2020). https://doi.org/10.3390/ani10050909

18. A. Cortés-Avizanda, M.A. Colomer, A. Margalida, O. Ceballos, J.A. Donázar, Modeling the consequences of the demise and potential recovery of a keystone-species: wild rabbits and avian scavengers in Mediterranean landscapes. Sci. Rep. **5**, 17033 (2015). https://doi.org/10.1038/srep17033

19. K. Daniel, A. Nash, S. Koenig, A. Felner, Theta*: Any-Angle Path Planning on Grids. J. Artif. Intell. Res. **39**, 533–579 (2010). https://doi.org/10.1613/jair.2994

20. D. Díaz-Pernil, I. Pérez-Hurtado, M.J. Pérez-Jiménez, A. Riscos-Núñez, A P-Lingua programming environment for Membrane Computing, in *Membrane Computing (WMC 2008)*, ed. by D.W. Corne, P. Frisco, Gh. Păun, G. Rozenberg, A. Salomaa. Lecture Notes in Computer Science, vol. 5391 (2009), pp. 187–203. https://doi.org/10.1007/978-3-540-95885-7_14

21. J. Dong, M. Stachowicz, G. Zhang, M. Cavaliere, H. Rong, P. Paul, Automatic design of spiking neural P systems based on genetic algorithms. Int. J. Unconv. Comput. **16**(2–3), 201–216 (2021)

22. Y. Duang, H. Rong, D. Qi, L. Valencia-Cabrera, G. Zhang, M.J. Pérez-Jiménez, A review of membrane computing models for complex ecosystems and a case study on a complex Giant Panda system. Complexity 2020, Article ID 1312824, 26, (2020). https://doi.org/10.1155/2020/1312824

23. G. Escuela, M.A. Gutiérrez-Naranjo, An application of genetic algorithms to Membrane Computing, in *Proceedings of the Eighth Brainstorming Week on Membrane Computing*, Fénix Editora, ed. by M.A. Martínez-del-Amor, Gh. Păun, I. Pérez-Hurtado, A. Riscos-Núñez (2010), pp. 101–118

24. C. Fondevilla, M.A. Colomer, F. Fillat, U. Tappeiner, Using a new PDP modelling approach for land-use and land-cover change predictions: a case study in the Stubai Valley (Central Alps). Ecol. Modell. **322**, 101–114 (2016). https://doi.org/10.1016/j.ecolmodel.2015.11.016

25. M. García-Quismondo, R. Gutiérrez-Escudero, M.A. Martínez-del-Amor, E. Orejuela-Pinedo, I. Pérez-Hurtado, P-Lingua 2.0: a software framework for cell-like P systems. Int. J. Comput. Commun. Control **4**(3), 234–243 (2009). https://doi.org/10.15837/ijccc.2009.3.2431

26. M. García-Quismondo, R. Gutiérrez-Escudero, I. Pérez-Hurtado, M.J. Pérez-Jiménez, A. Riscos-Núñez. An Overview of P-Lingua 2.0, in *Membrane Computing (WMC 2009)*, ed. by Gh. Păun, M.J. Pérez-Jiménez, A. Riscos, G. Rozenberg, A. Salomaa. Lecture Notes in Computer Science, vol. 5957 (2010), pp. 264–288. https://doi.org/10.1007/978-3-642-11467-0_20

27. J. He, J. Xiao, X. Liu, T. Wu, T. Song, A novel membrane-inspired algorithm for optimizing solid waste transportation. Optik—Int. J. Light Electron Opt. **126**(23), 3883–3888 (2015). https://doi.org/10.1016/j.ijleo.2015.07.152

28. X. Huang, G. Zhang, H. Rong, F. Ipate, Evolutionary Design of a Simple Membrane System, in *Membrane Computing (CMC 2011)*, ed. by M. Gheorghe, Gh. Păun, G. Rozenberg, A. Salomaa, S. Verlan. Lecture Notes in Computer Science, vol. 7184 (2012), pp. 203–214. https://doi.org/10.1007/978-3-642-28024-5_14

29. Z. Huang, G. Zhang, D. Qi, H. Rong, M.J. Pérez-Jiménez, L. Valencia-Cabrera, Application of probabilistic membrane systems to model giant panda population data. Comput. Syst. Appl. **26**(8), 252–256 (2017). https://doi.org/10.15888/j.cnki.csa.005878 (in Chinese)

30. M. Ionescu, Gh. Păun, T. Yokomori, Spiking Neural P Systems. Fundam. Inform. **71**(2–3), 279–308 (2006)

31. J. Juico, J. Silapan, F.G.C. Cabarle, I. Macababayao, R.T.A. De la Cruz. Evolving spiking neural P systems with polarization. Philipp. Comput. J. (Special Issue on P systems) **14**(2), 11–20 (2020)

32. A. Kane, A.L. Jackson, A. Monadjem, M.A. Colomer, A. Margalida, Carrion ecology modelling for vulture conservation: are vulture restaurants needed to sustain the densest breeding population of the African white-backed vulture? Anim. Conserv. **18**(3), 279–286 (2015). https://doi.org/10.1111/acv.12169

33. S. Karaman, E. Frazzoli, Sampling-based algorithms for optimal motion planning. Int. J. Rob. Res. **30**(7), 846–894 (2011). https://doi.org/10.1177/0278364911406761

34. S. Kazarlis, A. Bakirtzis, V. Petridis, A genetic algorithm solution to the unit commitment problem. IEEE Trans. Power Syst. **11**(1), 83–92 (1996). https://doi.org/10.1109/59.485989

35. J. Latombe, Motion planning: a journey of robots, molecules, digital actors, and other artifacts. Int. J. Rob. Res. **18**(11), 1119–1128 (1999). https://doi.org/10.1177/02783649922067753

36. S. LaValle, *Rapidly-exploring Random Trees: A New Tool for Path Planning, TR 98-11* (Computer Science Department, Iowa State University, Iowa, 1998). http://lavalle.pl/papers/Lav98c.pdf

37. X. Liu, J. Suo, S. Leung, J. Liu, X. Zeng, The power of time-free tissue P systems: Attacking NP-complete problems. Neurocomputing **159**, 151–156 (2015). https://doi.org/10. 1016/j.neucom.2015.01.072

38. A. Margalida, M.A. Colomer, Modelling the effects of sanitary policies on European vulture conservation. Sci. Rep. **2**, 753 (2012). https://doi.org/10.1038/srep00753

39. A. Margalida, M.A. Colomer, D. Sanuy, Can wild ungulate carcasses provide enough biomass to maintain avian scavenger populations? An empirical assessment using a bio-inspired computational model. PloS One **6**(5), e20248 (2011). https://doi.org/10.1371/journal.pone. 0020248

40. A. Margalida, M.A. Colomer, D. Oro, R. Arlettaz, J.A. Donázar, Assessing the impact of removal scenarios on population viability of a threatened, long-lived avian scavenger. Sci. Rep. **5**, 16962 (2015). https://doi.org/10.1038/srep16962

41. A. Margalida, P. Oliva-Vidal, A. Llamas, M.A. Colomer, Bioinspired models for assessing the importance of transhumance and transboundary management in the conservation of European avian scavengers. Biol. Conserv. **228**, 321–330 (2018). https://doi.org/10.1016/j.biocon.2018. 11.004

42. MeCoSim website. http://www.p-lingua.org/mecosim

43. K. Meffert, J. Meseguer, E.D. Mart, A. Meskauskas, J. Vos, N. Rotstan (last visited-July 2011), *JGAP—Java Genetic Algorithms and Genetic Programming Package* (2011). http://jgap.sf.net

44. M. Mitchell, *An Introduction to Genetic Algorithms* (MIT Press, Cambridge, 1998)

45. NVIDIA CUDA Toolkit. https://developer.nvidia.com/cuda-toolkit. NVIDIA Corporation. Online (accesed August 2019)

46. OpenMP specification, version 4.5. https://www.openmp.org/specifications. The OpenMP ARB (Architecture Review Boards). Online (accessed August 2019)

47. Z. Ou, G. Zhang, T. Wang, X. Huang, Automatic design of cell-like P systems through tuning membrane structures, initial objects and evolution rules. Int. J. Unconv. Comput. **9**(5–6), 425–443 (2013)

48. L. Pan, Gh. Păun, M.J. Pérez-Jiménez, Spiking neural P systems with neuron division and budding. Sci. China Inf. Sci. **54**(8), 1596–1607 (2011). https://doi.org/10.1007/s11432-011-4303-y

49. Gh. Păun, Computing with membranes. J. Comput. Syst. Sci. **61**(1), 108–143 (2000). https:// doi.org/10.1006/jcss.1999.1693 (first circulated at TUCS Research Report No. 208, November 1998. http://www.tucs.fi)

50. Gh. Păun, G. Rozenberg, A guide to membrane computing. Theor. Comput. Sci. **287**, 73–100 (2002). https://doi.org/10.1016/S0304-3975(02)00136-6

51. Gh. Păun, G. Rozenberg, A. Salomaa, *The Oxford Handbook of Membrane Computing* (Oxford University, Oxford, 2010)

52. A.B. Pavel, C. Buiu, Using enzymatic numerical P systems for modeling mobile robot controllers. Nat. Comput. **11**(3), 387–393 (2012). https://doi.org/10.1007/s11047-011-9286-5

53. A.B. Pavel, O. Arsene, C. Buiu, Enzymatic numerical P systems: a new class of Membrane Computing systems, in *Proceedings of the 2010 IEEE Fifth International Conference on Bio-Inspired Computing: Theories and Applications (BIC-TA), Changsha, 2010* (2010), pp. 1331–1336. https://doi.org/10.1109/BICTA.2010.5645071

54. I. Pérez-Hurtado, *Desarrollo y Aplicaciones de un Entorno de Programación para Computación Celular: P-Lingua*. Ph.D. Thesis (Universidad de Sevilla, Sevilla, 2010, in Spanish). http://hdl.handle.net/11441/66241

55. I. Pérez-Hurtado, L. Valencia-Cabrera, M.J. Pérez-Jiménez, M.A. Colomer, A. Riscos-Núñez, MeCoSim: a general purpose software tool for simulating biological phenomena by means of P systems, in *Proceedings of the IEEE Fifth International Conference on Bio-inspired Computing: Theories and Applications (BIC-TA 2010)*, vol. I, ed. by K. Li, Z. Tang, R. Li, A.K. Nagar, R. Thamburaj (2010), pp. 637–643. https://doi.org/10.1109/BICTA.2010.5645199

56. I. Pérez-Hurtado, M.J. Pérez-Jiménez, G. Zhang, D. Orellana-Martín. Simulation of rapidly-exploring random trees in Membrane Computing with P-lingua and automatic programming. Int. J. Comput. Commun. Control **13**(6), 1007–1031 (2019). https://doi.org/10.15837/ijccc.2018.6.3370
57. I. Pérez-Hurtado, M.A. Martínez-del-Amor, G. Zhang, F. Neri, M.J. Pérez-Jiménez, A membrane parallel rapidly-exploring random tree algorithm for robotic motion planning. Integr. Comput.-Aided Eng. **27**, 1–18 (2020). https://doi.org/10.3233/ICA-190616
58. P-Lingua website (last visited, July 2011). http://www.p-lingua.org
59. J.H. Reif, Complexity of the mover's problem and generalizations, in *Proceedings of the 20th Annual Symposium on Foundations of Computer Science (SFCS 1979), San Juan, Puerto Rico, USA* (1979), pp. 421–427. https://doi.org/10.1109/SFCS.1979.10
60. S. Ronald, Robust encodings in genetic algorithms: a survey of encoding issues, in *Proceedings of 1997 IEEE International Conference on Evolutionary Computation (ICEC '97), Indianapolis, IN, USA, 1997* (1997), pp. 43–48. https://doi.org/10.1109/ICEC.1997.592265
61. E. Sánchez-Karhunen, L. Valencia-Cabrera, Modelling complex market interactions using PDP systems. J. Membr. Comput. **1**(1), 40–51 (2019). https://doi.org/10.1007/s41965-019-00008-z
62. T. Song, L.F. Macías-Ramos, L. Pan, M.J. Pérez-Jiménez, Time-free solution to SAT problem using P systems with active membranes. Theor. Comput. Sci. **529**, 61–68 (2014). https://doi.org/10.1016/j.tcs.2013.11.014
63. T. Song, Q. Zou, X. Liu, X. Zeng, Asynchronous spiking neural P systems with rules on synapses. Neurocomputing **151**, 1439–1445 (2015). https://doi.org/10.1016/j.neucom.2014.10.044
64. A. Stentz, The focussed D* algorithm for real-time replanning, in *IJCAI95: Proceedings of the 14th International Joint Conference on Artificial Intelligence*, vol. 2 (1995), pp. 1652–1659
65. H. Tian, G. Zhang, H. Rong, et al. Population model of giant panda ecosystem based on population dynamics P system. J. Comput. Appl. **38**(5), 1488–1493 (2018). https://doi.org/10.11772/j.issn.1001-9081.2017102551 (in Chinese)
66. C. Tudose, R. Lefticaru, F. Ipate, Using genetic algorithms and model checking for P systems automatic design, in *Nature Inspired Cooperative Strategies for Optimization (NICSO 2011). Studies in Computational Intelligence*, vol 387, ed. by D.A. Pelta, N. Krasnogor, D. Dumitrescu, C. Chira, R. Lung (2012), pp. 285–302. https://doi.org/10.1007/978-3-642-24094-2_20
67. L. Valencia-Cabrera, *An Environment for Virtual Experimentation with Computational Models Based on P Systems*. Ph.D. Thesis (Universidad de Sevilla, Sevilla, 2015). http://hdl.handle.net/11441/45362
68. L. Valencia-Cabrera, M. García-Quismondo, M.J. Pérez-Jiménez, Y. Su, H. Yu, L. Pan, Modeling logic gene networks by means of probabilistic dynamic P systems. Int. J. Unconv. Comput. **9**(5–6), 445–464 (2013)
69. L. Valencia-Cabrera, M. García Quismondo, M.J. Pérez-Jiménez, Analysing gene networks with PDP systems. Arabidopsis thailiana, a case study, in *Proceedings of the Eleventh Brainstorming Week on Membrane Computing*, Fénix Editora, ed. by L. Valencia-Cabrera, M. García-Quismondo, L.F. Macías-Ramos, M.A. Martínez-del-Amor, Gh. Păun, A. Riscos-Núñez (2013), pp. 257–272
70. M. Yuan, G. Zhang, M.J. Pérez-Jiménez, T. Wang, Z. Huang, P systems based computing polynomials: design and formal verification. Nat. Comput. **15**, 591–596 (2016). https://doi.org/10.1007/s11047-016-9577-y
71. G. Zhang, J. Cheng, M. Gheorghe, Q. Meng, A hybrid approach based on differential evolution and tissue membrane systems for solving constrained manufacturing parameter optimization problems. Appl. Soft Comput. **13**(3), 1528–1542 (2013). https://doi.org/10.1016/j.asoc.2012.05.032
72. G. Zhang, M. Gheorghe, L. Pan, M.J. Pérez-Jiménez, Evolutionary membrane computing: a comprehensive survey and new results. Inf. Sci. **279**, 528–551 (2014). https://doi.org/10.1016/j.ins.2014.04.007

73. G. Zhang, H. Rong, F. Neri, M.J. Pérez-Jiménez, An optimization spiking neural P system for approximately solving combinatorial optimization problems. Int. J. Neural Syst. **24**(5), 01–16 (2014). https://doi.org/10.1142/S0129065714400061

74. G. Zhang, H. Rong, Z. Ou, M.J. Pérez-Jiménez, M. Gheorghe, Automatic design of deterministic and non-halting membrane systems by tuning syntactical ingredients. IEEE Trans. Nanobiosci. **13**(3), 363–371 (2014). https://doi.org/10.1109/TNB.2014.2341618

75. X. Zhang, Y. Liu, B. Luo, L. Pan, Computational power of tissue P systems for generating control languages. Inf. Sci. **278**, 285–297 (2014). https://doi.org/10.1016/j.ins.2014.03.053

76. G. Zhang, J. Cheng, T. Wang, X. Wang, J. Zhu, *Membrane Computing: Theory and Applications* (Science China Press, Beijing, 2015) (in Chinese)

77. G. Zhang, M.J. Pérez-Jiménez, M. Gheorghe, *Real-life Applications with Membrane Computing*. Series Emergence, Complexity and Computation (Springer, Berlin, 2017)

78. G. Zhang, H. Rong, P. Paul, Y. He, F. Neri, M.J. Pérez-Jiménez, A complete arithmetic calculator constructed from spiking neural P systems and its application to information fusion. Int. J. Neural Syst., 2050055 (2020). Available online, published 16 September 2020. https://doi.org/10.1142/S0129065720500550

79. J. Zhao, X. Wang, G. Zhang, F. Neri, T. Jiang, M. Gheorghe, F. Ipate, R. Lefticaru, Design and implementation of membrane controllers for trajectory tracking of nonholonomic wheeled mobile robots. Integr. Comput.-Aided Eng. **23**, 15–30 (2016). https://doi.org/10.3233/ICA-150503

80. M. Zhu, G. Zhang, Q. Yang, H. Rong, W. Yuan, M.J. Pérez-Jiménez. P systems based computing polynomials with integer coefficients: design and formal verification. IEEE Trans. NanoBiosci. **17**(3), 272–280 (2018). https://doi.org/10.1109/TNB.2018.2836147

Infobiotics Workbench: An In Silico Software Suite for Computational Systems Biology

4

4.1 Introduction

The modelling and analysis of biological systems using computational approaches alternative to mathematical methods have been the focus of many recent studies since these approaches can reveal more information about system behavior. Various computational formalisms have been introduced and studied in this context, including *state transition systems* [32], *rule-based systems* [33], *Petri nets* [68], and *process algebra* [59].

Membrane computing is a popular subfield of rule-based systems. Due to its affinity with the functioning and structure of living cells, it has been utilized in modelling and analysis of a number of biological systems [12, 44, 49, 50, 65].

In membrane computing, where models are called *P systems*, computations represent biological processes that take place within compartments of a living cell. Membrane structures mimic cell structures of living organisms, where compartments contain multisets of objects that evolve by the execution of a set of rules.

Stochastic P systems [64] are a probabilistic variant of P systems, where reaction rates are obtained from elementary rate constants according to the law of mass action kinetics. Stochastic P systems offer a suitable, intuitive, and amenable modeling framework for biological and chemical systems, where the inherent noise that exists in stochastic dynamics of small copy number of systems cannot be properly captured by more traditional mathematical methods. The reaction rules with associated rate constants translate directly and without additional input into probabilistic transitions of the continuous time Markov process that defines the stochastic model.

© The Author(s), under exclusive license to Springer Nature Singapore Pte Ltd. 2021
G. Zhang et al., *Membrane Computing Models: Implementations*,
https://doi.org/10.1007/978-981-16-1566-5_4

The Infobiotics Workbench (IBW) is an integrated software suite built upon stochastic P systems models. The platform utilizes computer-aided modelling and analysis of biological systems through a number of important features:

Modelling Language IBW features a domain-specific language, where individual cells are represented by stochastic P systems. The language also allows specifications of multicellular populations distributed over various geometric surfaces, such as lattices.

Simulation IBW implements a native stochastic simulator that enables molecular populations to be visualized over cellular populations in space and time. The results can be viewed in different formats, including time series, histograms, and 3D surface plots.

Verification IBW has a verification component used for validating biological properties. Using powerful probabilistic model checking tools, the platform enables inferring novel system information through formal probabilistic queries and exhaustive analysis of all possible system behaviors.

Optimization The optimization engine permits optimization parameters by estimating the rate constants in order to converge model dynamics toward laboratory observations. It also optimizes model structures by changing the composition of rule sets managing potential state transitions in compartments to generate alternative reaction networks recreating target dynamics more accurately.

IBW allows modelling and analysis of not only cell-level behavior but also multicompartmental population dynamics. This enables comparing between macroscopic and mesoscopic interpretations of molecular interaction networks and investigating temporospatial phenomena in multicellular systems.

This chapter is divided into the following sections: a presentation of the stochastic P systems, a description of IBW's key features, two case studies where we illustrate using the IBW features, a short description of a related tool used for qualitative analysis, and finally, a presentation of the next-generation infobiotics for synthetic biology.

4.2   Stochastic P Systems

In IBW, each cell is represented by a *stochastic P system* (Definition 4.1). The definitions given in this section are borrowed from [12].

Definition 4.1. A **stochastic P system (SP system)** is a probabilistic variant of P systems, whose semantics is given by a tuple:

$$SP = (O, L, \mu, M_1, \ldots, M_n, R_1, \ldots, R_n) \qquad (4.1)$$

where:

- O is a finite set of objects that specify the entities that are part of the system (such as genes, RNAs, proteins, etc.);
- $L = \{l_1, \ldots, l_n\}$ is a finite set of labels that name compartments (such as cells, nucleus, cytoplasm, etc.);
- μ is a membrane structure containing $n \geq 1$ membranes that define the regions or compartments;
- $M_i = (l_i, w_i, s_i)$, for each $1 \leq i \leq n$, is the initial configuration of the membrane i (defining a compartment or a region), where $l_i \in L$ is the membrane label, $w_i \in O^*$ is a finite multiset of objects, and s_i is a finite set of strings over O;
- $R_{l_k} = \{r_1^{l_k}, \ldots, r_{m_{l_k}}^{l_k}\}$, for each $1 \leq k \leq n$, are a set of multiset rewriting rules that describe molecular interactions, for example, complex formation and gene regulation. Here, each set of rewriting rules R_{l_k} are linked to the corresponding compartment identified by the label l_k. The multiset rewriting rules are defined as:

$$r_i^{l_k} : o_1 [o_2]_l \xrightarrow{c_i^{l_k}} o_1' [o_2']_l \qquad (4.2)$$

where o_1, o_2 and o_1', o_2' are multisets of objects (that might be empty), over O, representing molecular species that are consumed/produced in corresponding molecular reactions. The label l (linked to the square brackets) specifies the compartment where the interaction takes place. When such a rule is applied, the contents of the membrane with label l change by replacing the objects o_2 with o_2'. The contents of the outside membrane also change by replacing the objects o_1 with o_1'. The stochastic constant $c_i^{l_k}$ is used to compute the rule propensity (i.e., probability and time required to apply the rule [23]).

Definition 4.1 provides the formal specification for an individual cell. Many biological systems are multicompartmental in nature, that is, they have spatial characteristics in that molecule exchanges between *adjacent* cells determine overall phenotypes. However, this type of structures cannot be defined by stochastic P systems as these systems have only hierarchical (nested) membrane structures that do not capture multicompartments. Therefore, stochastic P systems should be complemented with a spatial framework. Here, we define such a framework as a two-dimensional geometric lattice, which consists of a population of cells represented by SP systems. Rules moving objects from one cell to another on the lattice are associated with a vector describing where to place these molecules. This geometric extension of stochastic P systems is called *lattice population P systems* (*LPP systems* for short) [64].

To capture the spatial distribution of cells forming colonies and tissues, we define a *finite point lattice* or *grid* with regularly distributed points [56] that can describe possible spatial geometries in Fig. 4.1. The spatial distribution of cells is defined by a *finite point lattice*, Definition 4.2.

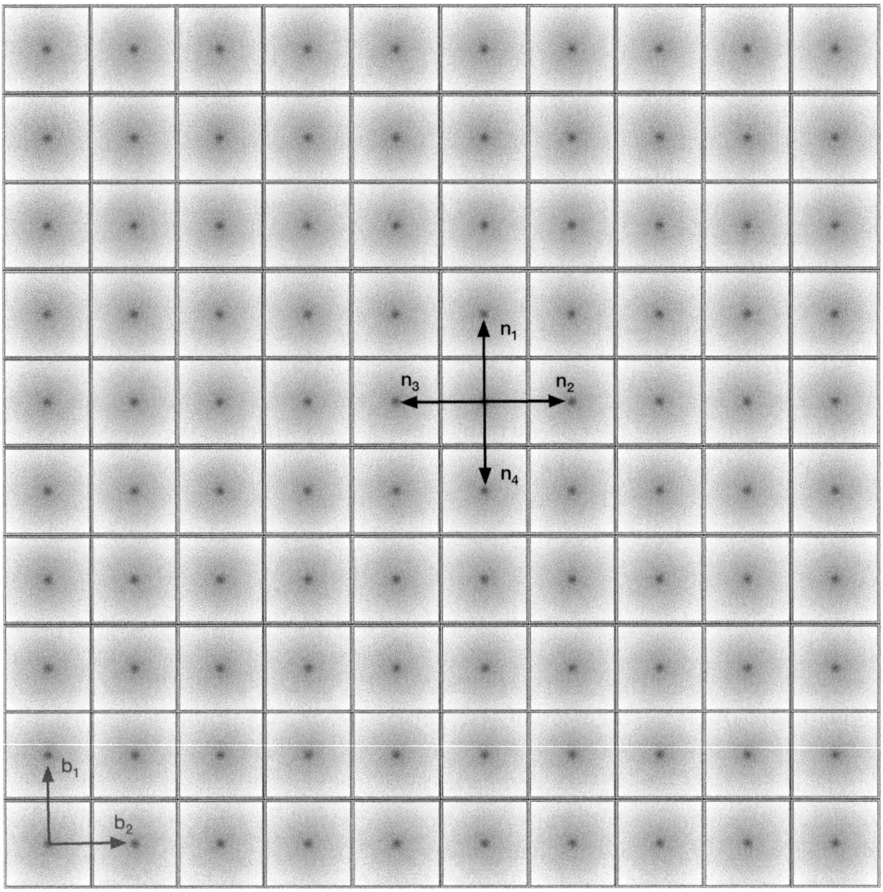

Fig. 4.1 A square lattice

Definition 4.2. Given $B = \{v_1, \ldots, v_n\}$ a list of linearly independent basis vectors, $o \in \mathbb{R}^n$ a point referred to as origin, and a list of integer bounds $(\alpha_1^{min}, \alpha_1^{max}, \ldots, \alpha_n^{min}, \alpha_n^{max})$, a **finite point lattice** generated by:

$$Lat = (B, o, (\alpha_1^{min}, \alpha_1^{max}, \ldots, \alpha_n^{min}, \alpha_n^{max})) \qquad (4.3)$$

is a collection of regularly distributed points, $P(Lat)$, defined as:

$$P(Lat) = \{o + \sum_{i=1}^{n} \alpha_i v_i \; : \; \forall i = 1, \ldots, n \; (\alpha_i \in \mathbb{Z} \wedge \alpha_i^{min} \leq \alpha_i \leq \alpha_i^{max})\} \qquad (4.4)$$

Given a *finite point lattice*, generated by *Lat*, where the coefficients $\{\alpha_i : i = 1, \ldots, n\}$ uniquely identify each point $x = o + \sum_{i=1}^{n} \alpha_i v_i \in P(Lat)$, hence denoted as $x = (\alpha_1, \ldots, \alpha_n)$.

LPP systems allow the distribution of instances of stochastic P systems representing cells on a lattice according to Definition 4.3.

Definition 4.3. A **lattice population P (LPP) system** is a formal specification of a set of geometrically organized cells, denoted by the following tuple:

$$LPP = (Lat, \{SP_1, \ldots, SP_p\}, Pos, \{T_1, \ldots, T_p\}) \tag{4.5}$$

where

- *Lat* defines a finite point lattice in $\mathbb{R}^n$ (typically $n = 2$) as in Definition 4.2 describing the geometry of cellular population.
- $SP_1, \ldots, SP_p$ are SP systems as in Definition 4.1 representing different cell types in the population.
- $Pos : P(Lat) \rightarrow \{SP_1, \ldots, SP_p\}$ is a function that distributes different instances of SP systems $SP_1, \ldots, SP_p$ over the lattice points.
- $T_k = \{r_1^k, \ldots, r_{n_k}^k\}$ for each $1 \leq k \leq p$ is a finite set of *translocation rules* included in the skin membrane of the corresponding SP system SP_k, allowing the interchange of objects between different SP systems located in different geometrical locations. The translocation rules are specified as follows:

$$r_i^k : [\, obj \,]_k \overset{\mathbf{v}}{\bowtie} [\ ]_{k'} \xrightarrow{c_i^k} [\ ]_k \overset{\mathbf{v}}{\bowtie} [\, obj \,]_{k'} \tag{4.6}$$

where *obj* is a multiset of objects, $\mathbf{v}$ is a vector in $\mathbb{R}^n$, and c_i^k is the stochastic constant. When a translocation rule is applied in the skin membrane of an SP system SP_k located at the point $\mathbf{p}$ ($Pos(\mathbf{p}) = SP_k$), the objects *obj* are removed from this membrane and placed in the skin membrane of $SP_{k'}$ located at the point $\mathbf{p} + \mathbf{v}$, $Pos(\mathbf{p} + \mathbf{v}) = SP_{k'}$.

In system biology, there are cases where molecular reaction networks can be divided into modules, each of which performs a specific task [27]. It has been shown some modules, called *motifs*, appear recurrently in transcriptional networks. Motifs carry out particular functions like response acceleration and noise filtering [2].

In order to capture the *modularity* in LPP systems, hence to be able to model motifs, we have introduced *P system modules* [12], defined as follows:

Definition 4.4. A **P system module**, *Mod*, is defined using three finite ordered sets of variables $O = \{O_1, \ldots, O_x\}$, $C = \{C_1, \ldots, C_y\}$, and $Lab = \{L_1, \ldots, L_z\}$ (where O, C and *Lab* represent objects, stochastic kinetic constants, and compartment labels, respectively). Modules contain a finite set of rewriting rules that have the same form in Eq. (4.2):

$$Mod(O, C, Lab) = \{r_1, \ldots, r_m\} \tag{4.7}$$

O, C, and Lab can be *instantiated* with specific values $o = \{o_1, \ldots, o_x\}$, $c = \{c_1, \ldots, c_y\}$, and $lab = \{l_1, \ldots, l_z\}$ for O, C, and Lab, respectively, as in:

$$Mod(\{o_1, \ldots, o_x\}, \{c_1, \ldots, c_y\}, \{l_1, \ldots, l_z\}) \tag{4.8}$$

The rules are generated according to the corresponding substitutions $O_1 = o_1, \ldots,$ $O_x = o_x, C_1 = c_1, \ldots, C_y = c_y$ and $L_1 = l_1, \ldots, L_z = l_z$.

The use of modularity allows us to define libraries or collections of modules:

$$Lib = \{Mod_1(O_1, C_1, Lab_1), \ldots, Mod_p(O_p, C_p, Lab_p)\} \tag{4.9}$$

In order to specify and manipulate LPP system models, we have introduced LPP XML [12], a set of machine-readable data formats closely mirroring our formal definitions. LPP XML allows us to define LPP system models which consist of stochastic P system modules with initial multisets and instantiations of rules and a geometric lattice and distribution of stochastic P systems over the lattice.

The LPP XML formats are very convenient for software implementation, but writing, reading, and manipulating models in XML by hand is a very cumbersome task with syntax obscuring information. Hence, to utilize this process, we have defined a user-friendly DSL (domain-specific language), called *LPP DSL*. IBW implements a parser that directly reads LPP DSL files and automatically converts them into XML.

The LPP formalism permits the reuse of some components:

- *Inter-model reuse*: Modules (in libraries), stochastic P systems, and lattices are put into different files that can be used and referred from multiple LPP system models.
- *Intra-model reuse*: Multiple SP systems can reside within each LPP system, utilizing the model construction of homogeneous or heterogeneous bacterial colonies or tissues.
- *Intra-submodel reuse*: Modules of rules can be parameterized and instantiated multiple times within an SP system using different instantiations.

P systems modules can be made more or less abstract by parameterizing different elements, such as species and stochastic rate constants. Motifs, corresponding to the topology of the underlying biological network, can be specified by modules that are made fully abstract by representing all components as parameters. In this scenario, parameter names should point out what role their values will play in the module.

4.3 Software Description

The Infobiotics Workbench (IBW) [30] is an integrated in silico platform built upon lattice population P (LPP) systems models [11, 12]. IBW has several functionalities. It allows simulating LPP models using a custom-built stochastic simulator, MCSS, and provides a user-friendly dashboard to visualize the simulation experiments in various formats. The dashboard uses adjustable editor views, allowing to edit and run model files easily.

The platform features a model checking component, PMODELCHECKER, that permits users verify temporospatial dynamic system properties using probabilistic or statistical model checking. IBW also offers parameter and model structure optimization using evolutionary algorithms via POPTIMIZER.

The users can perform *experiments* using the integrated dashboard or individual components separately outside the workbench. IBW makes the flow of information between different components seamless and easy by passing parameter files and model files through different components (see Fig. 4.2 [12]).

4.3.1 Simulation

The Infobiotics Workbench features a custom-built simulation platform, MCSS (multicompartmental stochastic simulation), comprising two types of quantitative simulations: *deterministic numerical approximation* with standard solvers and *stochastic simulation* using Gillespie algorithms [23]. MCSS extends the baseline Gillespie method with multicompartmental stochastic algorithms [63] that relies on compartmentalized nature of lattice population P systems models. The algorithm uses queues that store the next rule to execute in each compartment in the heap and only recalculates the reaction propensities in a compartment where a rule is fired. This approach significantly improves performance by reducing the simulation time for models that consist of a large number of compartments.

IBW features a very user-friendly simulation dashboard (see Fig. 4.3) [12]. The simulation environment allows tweaking various simulation parameters, for example, number of runs, time points, and intervals, concentration units, and species to be displayed. The results can be displayed as time series and histograms. System population dynamics can also be observed as surface plotting functions in 3D by selecting a subset of compartments. The results can be exported in common data formats (e.g., csv) for manipulating by third-party software.

The simulation dashboard has a number of features to make the simulation experiments simple, customizable, and reproducible. Users can: (i) select a subset of (or all) entries, multiple, species, and compartments; (ii) filter species or sort them in alphabetical order; (iii) filter compartments or sort them by their geometric positions on the lattice; (iv) adjust simulation time points and intervals; (v) set data and display units (species concentrations as *molecules*, *moles*, or *concentrations*; compartment volumes as *liters*, *milliliter*, *microliters*, and *nanoliters*; and time

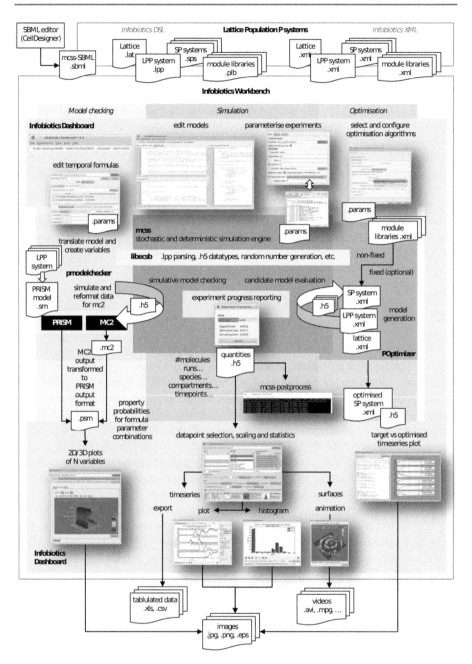

Fig. 4.2 Summary of the data flow between different components of IBW. Information is passed as files: parameters (`.params`) and models (`.sbml`, `.lpp` or `.xml`). Various intermediary files are generated: simulation data (`.h5`) and verification data (`.psm`). The results can be exported in various formants: tabulated data (`.csv`), image (`.jpg`, `.png`, `.eps`), and videos (`.avi`, `.mpg`)

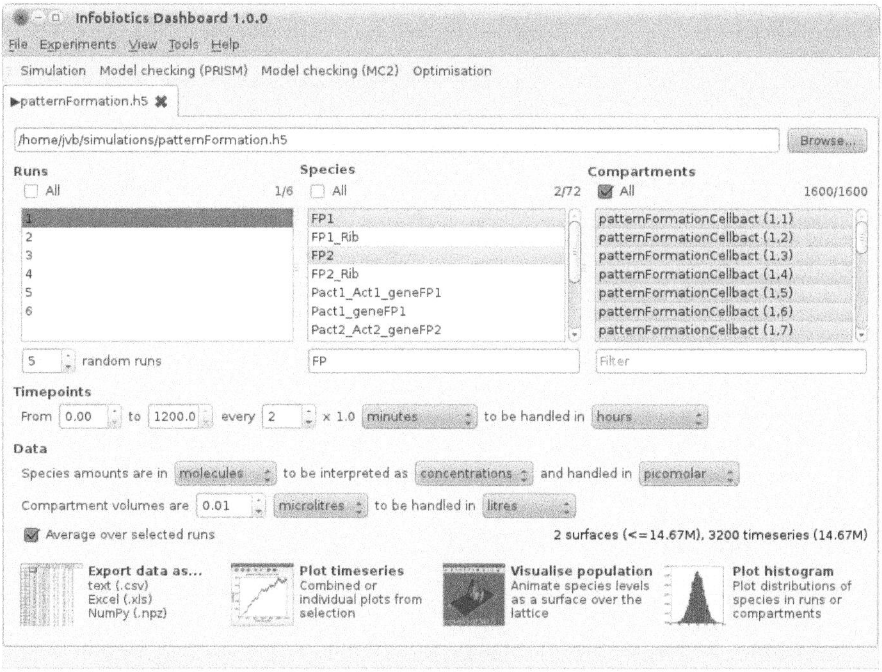

Fig. 4.3 The simulation dashboard

points as *seconds*, *minutes*, or *hours*); (vi) select whether species' amounts in each compartment over the selected runs should be averaged for obtaining approximate results; (vii) get an estimated memory requirement for each simulation experiment to predict how fast the experiment can be carried out; (viii) export the selected and rescaled datapoints in various data formats (.csv, .xls, .npz); and (ix) plot results for selected runs and compartments as time series or histograms, which allows making exact (`combined`) or relative (`stacked`/`tiled`) comparisons of the temporal behavior of different molecular species of same/different compartments based on specific, several, or averaged over many simulation runs. (x) export plots as images for further comparison with experimental observations (see Fig. 4.4) [12]. The figure toolbar enables zooming, panning, and subplot configuration and (xi) visualize the system dynamics at real-time in 2D space using 3D heat-mapped meshes or *surface* plots to capture the dynamic distribution of selected species over time (see Fig. 4.5) [12]. Surfaces plots provide an intuitive means of qualitative evaluation of population level dynamics that may (cautiously) be compared to laboratory observations.

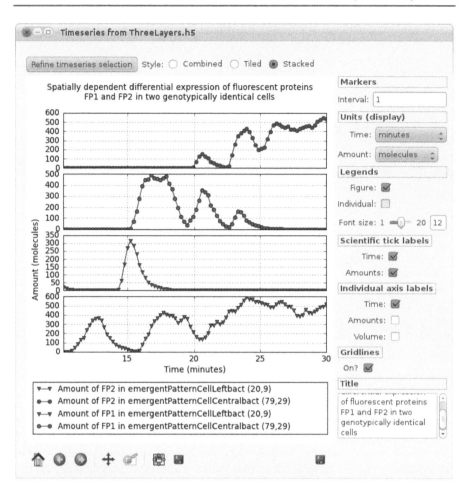

Fig. 4.4 Time series plot styles (stacked view)

4.3.2 Verification

Formal methods have been used in systems biology in order to better understand system behavior. As a complementary approach to simulation, *formal verification* is a method which *exhaustively* analyzes *all* possible system behaviors, which cannot be done via simulation, to evaluate the correctness of systems. It allows inferring "more novel information about system properties" [44].

Model checking [14], an *algorithmic* verification approach, is used to verify whether a model with a finite structure satisfies certain system properties. Model checking requires a formal system model and a formal specification, expressed in a logical notation [34–39]. It then evaluates the formal specification against all possible behaviors of the system model, which are computed by enumerating all possible sequence of traces.

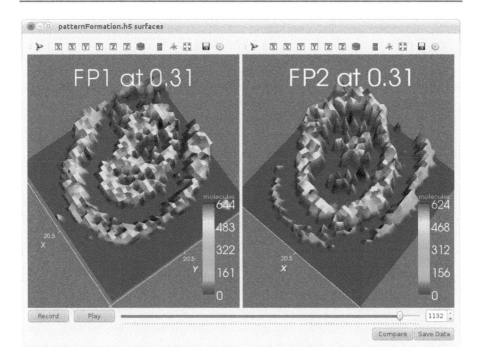

Fig. 4.5 Surface plots illustrating dynamic expression patterns for two proteins. Users can progress time either by moving the time point index slider forward or backward or by pressing the Play/Pause button

Model checking has been widely utilized in computing and engineering applications for the last two decades in verifying various systems, for example, safety-critical systems [40], concurrent systems [3], distributed systems [69], network protocols [42], stochastic systems [41], multi-agent systems [1, 47], pervasive systems [4, 43, 48], and swarm robotics [45, 46] as well as some engineering applications [57, 58]. Due to its novel features to infer information about system behavior, there is a growing interest to apply this technique in systems biology [8, 9]. Recently, it has been applied to analysis of various biological systems [21, 49, 49, 50, 52, 65].

Probabilistic model checking is a stochastic extension of classical model checking complemented with quantitative techniques to verify properties about the *likelihood* of the observation of certain behavior. However, they require a *probabilistic state machine* (such as *Discrete-Time Markov Chains (DTMCs)*, *Continuous-Time Markov Chains (CTMCs)*) or *Markov Decision Processes (MDPs)* in a dedicated syntax. System properties are written as probabilistic logical statements, often *probabilistic logics*: CSL *(Continuous Stochastic Logic)* [5] for CTMCs and PCTL *(Probabilistic Computation Tree Logic)* [26] for DTMCs and MDPs. A probabilistic model checker then automatically verifies if the system model satisfies the property using some analytical methods.

The Infobiotics Workbench features a verification module, called PMOD-ELCHECKER, which integrates two third-party probabilistic models checkers PRISM [28] and MC2 [15]. Properties of stochastic P system models are written as probabilistic logic formulas and automatically verified using either PRISM or MC2. PMODELCHECKER extends the verification capability to multicompartments so as to verify LPP system models.

PMODELCHECKER supports both *exact* (i.e., *numerical*) and *approximate* (i.e., *statistical*) model checking methods. To perform *exact* probabilistic model checking, LPP systems are automatically converted into the *reactive modules* specification, from which PRISM is executed. In this approach, the full state space is generated and each property is verified against all states of the model, which is usually computationally very demanding. The *approximate* probabilistic model checking does not require generating all system states. Instead, simulations are run up to a specified maximum number of runs or a confidence threshold (defined by users), and properties are verified against the simulation traces instead of the system model. To perform *approximate* probabilistic model checking, users can either (i) call PRISM's discrete event simulator or (ii) run MC2 using previous simulation results or running new simulations.

The PMODELCHECKER dashboard provides an interface for both PRISM and MC2 (see Fig. 4.6) [12]. Users can adjust verification parameters for each model checker, accordingly. The dashboard allows loading multiple formulas from a file and selecting a specific formula that can be edited or removed. Users can also add a new formula using the respective buttons.

The PMODELCHECKER dashboard features a result view which displays the outcome of a model checking experiment (see Fig. 4.7) [12]. The results can be displayed in 2D if the probability of a property in question is compared against one selected variable, or the results can be displayed in 3D if the probability is checked against two variables. The dashboard allows performing queries that depend on several variables by enabling the choice of variables so that the results of n-dimensional queries to be viewed in a consistent manner.

4.3.3   Optimization

The correct reproduction of cellular behavior depends on the accuracy of kinetic rate constants used in both deterministic and stochastic models. Unfortunately, well-characterized rate constants are not often available in many systems, and those that are known for some models use artificial values that are obtained from similar systems. One possible solution to this problem is using parameter optimization to estimate the rate constants in order to fit model dynamics to laboratory observations.

For this purpose, IBW features the POPTIMIZER component, which optimizes models in two ways:

1. Numerical model parameters: The stochastic kinetic constants linked to each rule can be tweaked to fit the given target.

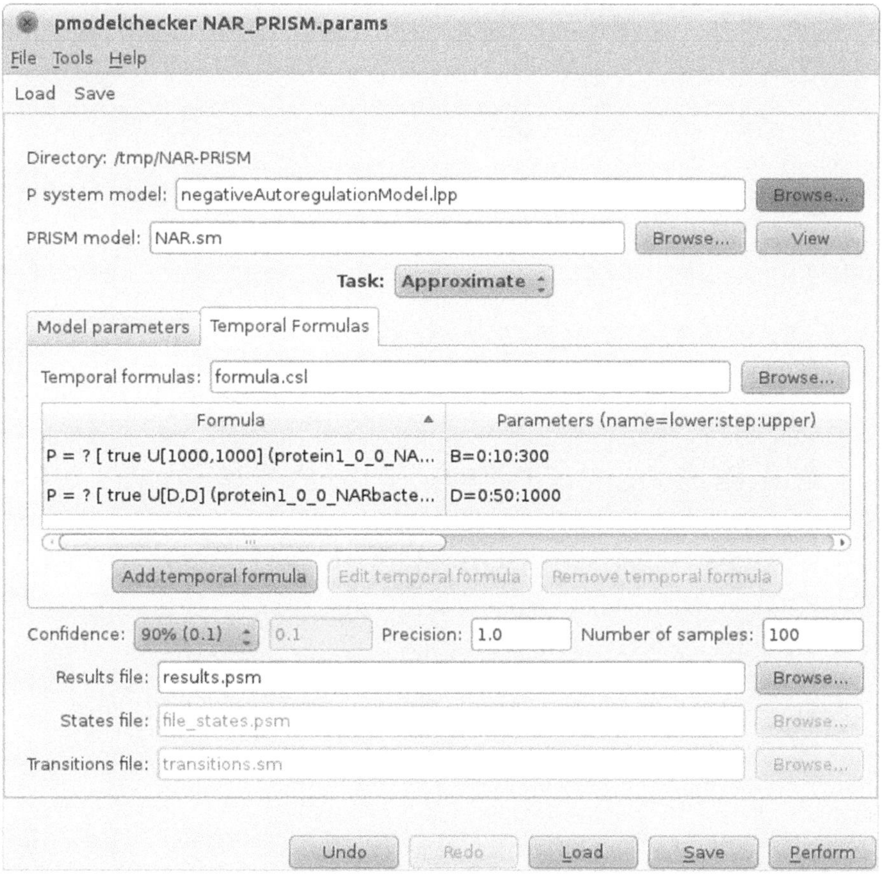

Fig. 4.6 PMODELCHECKER parameterization interfaces

2. Model structure: The composition and structure of the rule sets managing possible state transitions occurring in compartments can be changed to generate alternative reaction networks recreating the target dynamics more accurately.

Both of these optimization steps aim to *minimize* the distance between the stochastically simulated and user-provided quantities of molecular species at every target time point, quantitatively evaluating the fitness of candidate models and automatically discriminating between them.

POPTIMIZER searches both parameter and structure spaces using well-known population-based optimization algorithms: Covariance Matrix Adaptation Evolution Strategies (CMA-ES) [25], Estimation of Distribution Algorithms (EDA), Differential Evolution (DE) [67], and genetic algorithms (GA) [24]. The current version of the optimization process is limited to single compartment models because multicompartmental structures significantly increase the algorithmic complexity.

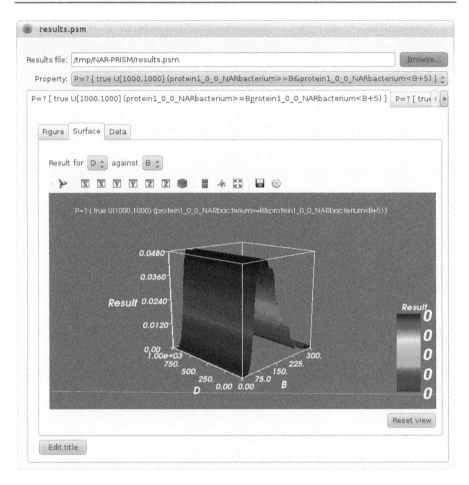

Fig. 4.7 Model checking results interface

This is mainly due to the fact that simulating many copies of the cells at those compartments would increase the computational cost and makes it difficult to provide accurate target data. Hence, model optimization is generally feasible for smaller models, which can then be reintegrated, provided they can be decoupled.

POPTIMIZER implements a *genetic algorithm* [13, 62] to produce candidate models. This is initially done by random choice and then by mutating the fittest models of the previous round, performing several runs of parameter optimization steps on each model to ensure that the candidate models have fair chance of fitting the target behavior before using the final fitness function to choose the next generation.

The result of an optimization process is the fittest model generated, and the outcome is displayed at the dashboard. POPTIMIZER also allows a visual comparison of the quantities of each species for target and the optimized models (see Fig. 4.8) [12].

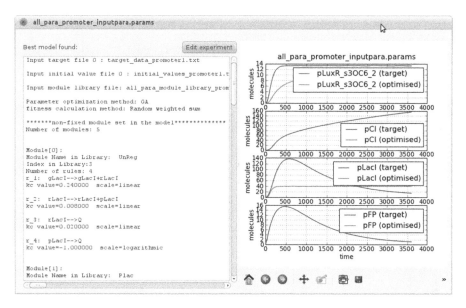

Fig. 4.8 POPTIMIZER results interface

4.4   Case Studies

In this section, we will illustrate using the IBW features in two case studies. In the first case study, we will use the *pulse generator* system [10], consisting of a bacterial colony that displays a propagation behavior of a wave of gene expression. The second case study is a genetic circuit, repressilator.

4.4.1   Pulse generator

The pulse generator system [10] synthesizes a signalling molecule AHL, triggering the production of the green fluorescent protein (GFP). The system exhibits a propagation behavior, that is, the propagation of the GFP expression along the bacterial colony (see Fig. 4.11 and 4.12) [12]. The system consists of two different bacterial strains, *sender cells* and *pulsing cells* (see Fig. 4.9) [50], which work as follows:

"Sender cells contain the gene luxI from *Vibrio fischeri*. This gene codifies the enzyme LuxI responsible for the synthesis of the molecular signal 3OC12HSL (AHL). The luxI gene is expressed constitutively under the regulation of the promoter PLtetO1 from the tetracycline resistance transposon."

"Pulsing cells contain the luxR gene from *Vibrio fischeri* that codifies the 3OC12HSL receptor protein LuxR. This gene is under the constitutive expression of the promoter PluxL. It also contains the gene cI from lambda phage codifying the repressor CI under the

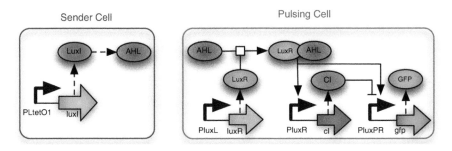

Fig. 4.9 The sender and pulsing cells of the pulse generator.

regulation of the promoter PluxR that is activated upon binding of the transcription factor LuxR_3OC12. Finally, this bacterial strain carries the gene gfp that codifies the green fluorescent protein under the regulation of the synthetic promoter PluxPR combining the Plux promoter (activated by the transcription factor LuxR_3OC12) and the PR promoter from lambda phage (repressed by the transcription factor CI)."

The sender and pulsing bacterial strains are distributed along a lattice, where the sender cells are located at one end of the lattice, and the pulsing cells are placed at the rest of the lattice (see Fig. 4.10).

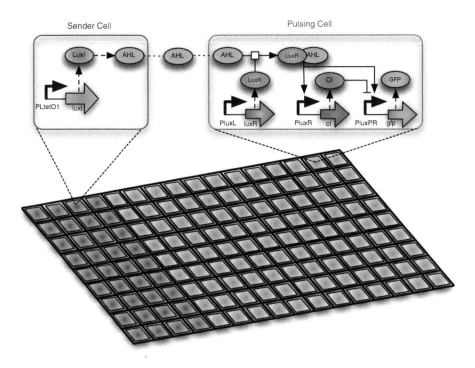

Fig. 4.10 Spatial distribution of two bacterial strains

Modelling

As discussed in Sect. 4.2, IBW accepts lattice population systems as input. The pulse generator system is captured by an LPP model, representing a bacterial colony over a rectangular lattice, which distributes the sender cells at one end of the lattice and the pulsing cells over the rest of the lattice. The LPP model contains two stochastic P systems models, one for each different cell type. The first SP model represents the stochastic behavior of the sender cell, capturing the production of the signal 3OC6-HSL (AHL). The second model represents the pulsing cell, capturing the production of GFP protein as a response to the signal 3OC6-HSL (AHL). In both SP models, the reaction rules govern the regulation of the corresponding promoters used in the sender and pulsing cells. The complete stochastic model of the pulse generator example (written in LPP) is available in the IBW website [60].

Simulation

The IBW simulation dashboard visualizes the system behavior via time series, histogram, or surface plotting functions. Users are able to choose species they want to simulate over a subset of datapoints. Below, we present a set of simulation experiments [12, 44, 50].

Figure 4.11 shows the propagation of a pulse of GFP over a single pulsing cell using time series. Figure 4.12 illustrates the spatial propagation over a bacterial colony using 3D animation. The propagation of the GFP protein continues through pulsing cells until the concentration level drops to 0.

Figure 4.13 shows the signalling molecule signal3OC6 amount, the number of molecules, over time, suggesting that the pulsing cells located further away from the sender cells produce lower concentrations of GFP.

These experiments suggest IBW's stochastic simulation algorithms allow users to generate realistic trajectories of molecular dynamics that can be compared to laboratory data.

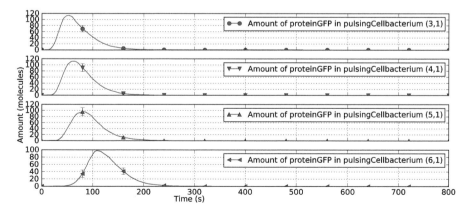

Fig. 4.11 Propagation of GFP over a pulsing cell

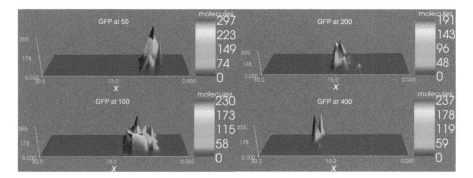

Fig. 4.12 Propagation of GFP along the bacterial colony

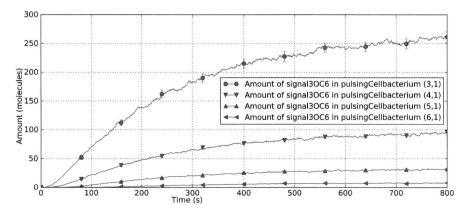

Fig. 4.13 Signalling molecule level over time

Verification

IBW's PMODELCHECKER component allows users to perform verification using two third-party probabilistic model checkers PRISM and MC2 to infer more information about system behavior.

Below, we present a set of verification experiments [50] based on probabilistic model checking. Here, we consider a lattice of size 2×6. The sender cells are positioned to the initial 2×2 segment of the lattice, followed by the pulsing cells that are distributed to the rest (2×4) of the lattice (see Fig. 4.10).

In the following, we show the informal representation of *queries* (i.e., system requirements to be verified) and their corresponding translations to the language that PMODELCHECKER accepts as input.

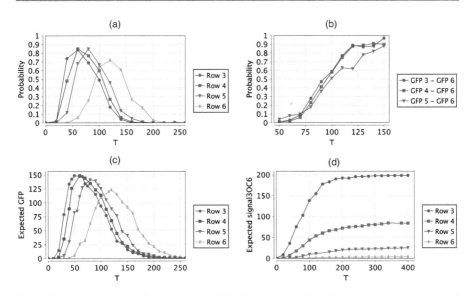

Fig. 4.14   Quantitative analysis using probabilistic model checking. Row *n* denotes the *n*th row of the pulsing cells in the lattice and *T* denotes time. (**a**) Prob. of GFP exceeds threshold (Prop. 1). (**b**) Prob. of relative GFP (Prop. 2). (**c**) Expected GFP protein (Prop. 3). (**d**) Expected signal3OC6 (Prop. 4)

Query 1.   *"What is the probability that GFP concentration at row $n \in \{3, 4, 5, 6\}$ exceeds 100 at the time instant T ?"*

This query is expressed formally as follows:

$$P_{=?}[\text{true } U^{[T,T]} \text{ GFP\_pulsing\_n} \geq 100].$$

The verification results are illustrated in Fig. 4.14a.

Query 2.   *"What is the probability that GFP concentration at row $n \in \{3, 4, 5\}$ stays greater than GFP concentration at row 6 until the time instant T where GFP concentration at row 6 exceeds GFP concentration at row n?"*

The formal translation of this query is:

$$P_{=?}[\text{GFP\_pulsing\_n} \geq \text{GFP\_pulsing\_6 } U^{[T,T]} \text{ GFP\_pulsing\_6} >$$

$$\text{GFP\_pulsing\_n}].$$

The verification results are presented in Fig. 4.14b.

Query 3. *"What is the expected GFP concentration at row $n \in \{3, 4, 5, 6\}$ at the time instant T?"*

This query is formally expressed as:

$$R\{\text{"GFP\_pulsing\_n"}\}_{=?}[I = T].$$

The results are shown in Fig. 4.14c.

Query 4. *"What is the expected signal3OC6 concentration at row $n \in \{3, 4, 5, 6\}$ at the time instant T?"*

The query is formally translated as:

$$R\{\text{"signal3OC6\_pulsing\_n"}\}_{=?}[I = T].$$

The corresponding verification results are shown in Fig. 4.14d.

Figure 4.14a,c confirm the propagation of a pulse of GFP, whose concentration first increases in the rows near to the sender cells and then gradually drops to zero. The rows distant from the sender cells exhibit a similar behavior with some delay, which is proportional to the distance between the row and the sender cells. Figure 4.14d shows that pulsing cells located further away from the sender cells produce lower concentrations of GFP.

These results show verification, by means of formal queries, can provide more novel information about the system behavior and dynamics, complementary to simulation.

4.4.2 Repressilator

The repressilator is a genetic circuit [17] used as a canonical example in some P system models [19].

The system contains three genes codifying the corresponding repressors: the operon lactose repressor, lacI; the repressor from the tetracycline transposon, tetR; and a repressor from the λ phage virus, cI. These three genes are linked in a gene regulatory network in such a way that lacI represses the expression of tetR; the tetR gene then represses cI. Finally, cI represses the expression of lacI to close the cycle.

Modelling

The repressilator system is captured as a stochastic P system. The molecular interactions within the stochastic P system are defined in a modular manner. The bacterial colony is modelled by a lattice population system over a rectangular lattice. This is done by distributing the copies of this cell type over the points of a rectangular lattice. The complete stochastic model of the repressilator system is available in the IBW website [61].

Simulation
Figure 4.15 shows the system evolution over time for the LacI, CI, and TetR proteins, confirming that the circuit generates oscillations of these repressor molecules based on the order they are connected within the regulatory network.

The oscillations significantly differ in amplitude and frequency due to stochastic effects. Therefore, different cells in the lattice might exhibit different oscillatory behavior, not necessarily synchronous (as illustrated in Fig. 4.15).

The asynchronous oscillatory behavior in different cells can be better observed using the population dynamics. Figure 4.16 shows the spatiotemporal evolution of LacI, CI, and TetR in the entire colony carrying the repressilator.

Verification
Below, we show two queries used to calculate the probability of having more or fewer than 300 proteins of LacI, CI, and TetR simultaneously over different time points of the evolution.

Query 1. *"What is the probability that LacI, CI, and TetR can simultaneously be below 300 molecules?"*

This query is expressed formally as follows:

$$P_{=?}[\text{time} = t \text{ U LacI} < 300 \wedge \text{CI} < 300 \wedge \text{TetR} < 300].$$

The verification results for $t = 20,000 \ldots 40,000$ (with increments of 5000) are zero.

Query 2. *"What is the probability that LacI, CI, and TetR can simultaneously be above 300 molecules?"*

The query is translated as:

$$P_{=?}[\text{time} = t \text{ U LacI} > 300 \wedge \text{CI} > 300 \wedge \text{TetR} > 300].$$

Similarly, the verification results for $t = 20,000 \ldots 40,000$ (with increments of 5000) are zero.

The results obtained in both scenarios suggest that these three proteins cannot be above or below 300 molecules simultaneously, confirming oscillating behavior.

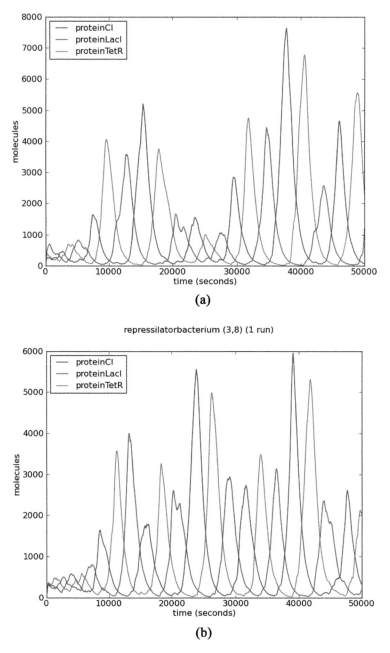

Fig. 4.15   Oscillation behavior in two different cells [19]

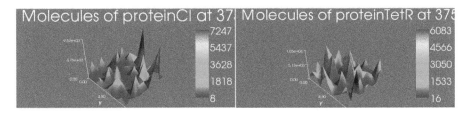

Fig. 4.16   Spatiotemporal evolution of the CI and TetR proteins in the colony

4.5   KPWorkbench: A Qualitative Analysis Tool

We have illustrated how IBW facilitates the *quantitative* analysis of biological systems using stochastic P systems. However, in some cases, quantitative analysis might not be needed if, for example, we only want to observe the detection of molecular species rather than measuring their concentration. In such cases, we can only rely on *qualitative* analysis where we can apply some abstraction methods to reduce the model complexity. One typical abstraction method is removing kinetic constants from a stochastic model. In this way, we can obtain much simpler nondeterministic models that can be used for detecting the existence of molecular species.

A nondeterministic model captures all interactions included in its stochastic counterpart but in a rather symbolic and qualitative way in that it removes more precise quantitative aspects of the system. All possible system pathways are still contained in the nondeterministic model but as exact molecular concentrations are not necessary for these models. In certain circumstances, the multisets are bounded, even restricted to one or two elements, describing their presence rather than their molecular concentrations.

In order to facilitate the qualitative modelling, we have introduced *kernel P systems* [22], a non-probabilistic variant of stochastic P systems, which mimic biological membranes without any quantitative information. Kernel P systems allow building nondeterministic models, which are used for qualitative analyses where molecular concentrations are not necessary or a chain of reactions already analyzed can be replaced by some abstractions mimicking their behavior through simpler rewriting mechanisms.

The expressive power and efficiency of kP systems have been illustrated by a number of representative case studies [49, 50, 58]. In this respect, we have also introduced a modelling language, called *kP–Lingua*, allowing one to write kP system models. The theoretical aspects of the methods and techniques developed for kP systems have been discussed in [6, 7, 16, 20].

We have also developed the kPWORKBENCH platform [53] (available and down-loadable from its website [54]), which allows modelling and analysis of membrane systems through various computational approaches, including modelling, simulation, agent-based high-performance simulation [51], and verification. To simplify verification queries, we have introduced a user-friendly property language based on *natural language* statements. These unique features allow kPWORKBENCH to support the non-probabilistic modelling and analysis of membrane systems using various computational approaches. The usability and novelty of our approach have been illustrated by some case studies from systems and synthetic biology [49, 50] to some engineering problems [57, 58].

4.6   Next-Generation Infobiotics for Synthetic Biology

Systems biology mainly focuses on studying existing organisms. In computational biology, there is a growing trend to study biological phenomena that do not exist in nature. To this end, synthetic biology, aiming to design new biological entities, is emerging rapidly. As DNA sequencing and synthesis technology get cheaper and become easy to reach [55], the scale and complexity of engineered biology systems will grow. Moreover, rapidly emerging biotechnology is accelerating the adoption of synthetic biology across various disciplines including computing science as well as industrial applications.

In line with these advances, synthetic biology introduces new challenges difficult for existing tools and approaches to address. It is well known that most of synthetic biology models are complex, with a rich combinatorics of biochemical interactions and certain motifs occurring.

Although IBW provides a good tool support for systems biology, and it can be utilized for some small-scale synthetic biology systems, it cannot address the challenges imposed by synthetic biology. The IBW language allows modelling systems at a relatively high abstraction level but does not provide any support for further refinements at the DNA level, which is a requirement of synthetic biology, where different operations at that level have to be specified. Also, the simulation and verification processes that are normally efficient for systems biology can be very cumbersome depending on the complexity of synthetic systems.

In an attempt to provide a robust tool support for synthetic biology, we have developed a new version of Infobiotics Workbench [31] that can assist synthetic biologists in an informed, iterative workflow of system specification, verification, simulation, and biocompilation. This new version of IBW features a unique domain-specific language, called *IBL* (Infobiotics Language), offering a combined grammar for modelling, verification, and biocompilation statements rather than relying upon individual complex formalisms for each computational aspect. This novel approach offers seamless interoperability across different tools as well as compatibility with common data exchange formats, for example, SBOL (Synthetic Biology Open Language) [18] and SBML (Systems Biology Markup Language) [29], and eliminates the need of manual translations for stand-alone applications.

The new IBW also significantly improves the efficiency of computational processes so as to cope with scaling-up demand of synthetic biology. The platform implements a new simulation module, incorporating all the variants of Gillespie's stochastic simulation algorithms (SSAs) complemented with prediction tool that selects the best performing SSA using machine learning algorithms. The simulation algorithms are also speeded up via parallel implementation and executed on cloud-based GPU clusters.

The verification queries use natural language statements, which are embedded within the IBL language. This makes IBL easy to use and intuitive for nonexperts. The verification process relies on statistical model checking approach [66], which significantly improves model checking times. This allows verifying queries for large systems in seconds rather than hours.

IBW also features a biocompilation module that allows automated compilation of a specified synthetic circuit into eventual genetic sequence information and import from/export to standard data exchange formats.

These unique features make IBW a very useful in silico tool for synthetic biology.

4.7 Conclusion

In this chapter, we have presented the Infobiotics Workbench, a computer-aided in silico design suite for systems biology. We have provided an overview of the platform's important features: (a) a domain-specific language, where individual cells are represented by stochastic P systems and multicellular populations are represented by lattice population P systems; (b) a multicellular stochastic simulator that enables molecular populations to be visualized over cellular populations in space and time using a variety of visualization formats; (c) a verification component that validates biological properties using probabilistic model checking; and (d) an optimization engine that optimizes model parameters and model structures.

We have shown the usability and applicability of the platform with two case studies: pulse generator and repressilator. For each case study, we have discussed the respective modelling, along with its simulation and verification results.

We have also provided a brief overview of the new version of Infobiotics Workbench [31] developed to address the challenges and requirements of synthetic biology by providing an informed, iterative workflow of system specification, verification, simulation, and biocompilation.

References

1. H. Abbink, R. van Dijk, T. Dobos, M. Hoogendoorn, C. Jonker, S. Konur, P.P. van Maanen, V. Popova, A. Sharpanskykh, P. van Tooren, J. Treur, J. Valk, L. Xu, P. Yolum, Automated support for adaptive incident management, in *Proceedings of the 1st International Workshop on Information Systems for Crisis Response and Management (ISCRAM'04)* (Brussels, Belgium, 2004), pp. 153–170
2. U. Alon, Network motifs: theory and experimental approaches. Nat. Rev. Genet. **8**(6), 450–61 (2007). https://doi.org/10.1038/nrg2102
3. R. Alur, K. McMillan, D. Peled, Model-checking of correctness conditions for concurrent objects. Inf. Comput. **160**(1–2), 167–188 (2000). https://doi.org/10.1006/inco.1999.2847
4. M. Arapinis, M. Calder, L. Denis, M. Fisher, P. Gray, S. Konur, A. Miller, E. Ritter, M. Ryan, S. Schewe, C. Unsworth, R. Yasmin, Towards the verification of pervasive systems. Electron. Commun. EASST **22**, 1–15 (2009). https://doi.org/10.14279/tuj.eceasst.22.315

5. C. Baier, B Haverkort, H. Hermanns, J.P. Katoen, Model-checking algorithms for continuous-time markov chains. IEEE Trans. Software Eng. **29**, 524–541 (2003). https://doi.org/10.1109/TSE.2003.1205180

6. M.E. Bakir, F. Ipate, S. Konur, L. Mierlă, I. Niculescu, Extended simulation and verification platform for kernel P systems, in *Membrane Computing (CMC 2014)*, ed. by M. Gheorghe, G. Rozenberg, A. Salomaa, P. Sosík, C. Zandron. Lecture Notes in Computer Science, vol. 8961 (2014), pp. 158–178. https://doi.org/10.1007/978-3-319-14370-5_10

7. M.E. Bakir, S. Konur, M. Gheorghe, I. Niculescu, F. Ipate, High performance simulations of kernel P systems, in *Proceedings of the 2014 IEEE International Conference on High Performance Computing and Communications, 2014 IEEE 6th International Symposium on Cyberspace Safety and Security, 2014 IEEE 11th International Conference on Embedded Software and System (HPCC,CSS,ICESS)* (2014), pp. 409–412. https://doi.org/10.1109/HPCC.2014.69

8. M.E. Bakir, M. Gheorghe, S. Konur, M. Stannett, Comparative analysis of statistical model checking tools, in *Membrane Computing (CMC 2016)*, ed. by A. Leporati, G. Rozenberg, A. Salomaa, C. Zandron. Lecture Notes in Computer Science, vol. 10105 (2017), pp. 119–135. https://doi.org/10.1007/978-3-319-54072-6_8

9. M.E. Bakir, S. Konur, M. Gheorghe, N. Krasnogor, M. Stannett, Automatic selection of verification tools for efficient analysis of biochemical models. Bioinformatics **34**(18), 3187–3195 (2018). https://doi.org/10.1093/bioinformatics/bty282

10. S. Basu, Y. Gerchman, C.H. Collins, F.H. Arnold, R. Weiss, A synthetic multicellular system for programmed pattern formation. Nature **434** (2005), 1130–1134. https://doi.org/10.1038/nature03461

11. J. Blakes, J. Twycross, F.J. Romero-Campero, N. Krasnogor, The Infobiotics Workbench: an integrated in silico modelling platform for systems and synthetic biology. Bioinformatics **27**(23), 3323–3324 (2011). https://doi.org/10.1093/bioinformatics/btr571

12. J. Blakes, J. Twycross, S. Konur, F.J. Romero-Campero, N. Krasnogor, M. Gheorghe, Infobiotics workbench: a P systems based tool for systems and synthetic biology, in *Applications of Membrane Computing in Systems and Synthetic Biology*. Series Emergence, Complexity and Computation, Chapter **7** (2014), pp. 1–41. https://doi.org/10.1007/978-3-319-03191-0_1

13. H. Cao, F.J. Romero-Campero, S. Heeb, M. Cámara, N. Krasnogor, Evolving cell models for systems and synthetic biology. Syst. Synth. Biol. **4**(1), 55–84 (2010). https://doi.org/10.1007/s11693-009-9050-7

14. E.M. Clarke, O. Grumberg, D.A. Peled, *Model checking* (MIT Press, New York, 1999)

15. R. Donaldson, D. Gilbert, A Monte Carlo model checker for probabilistic LTL with numerical constraints. Res. Rep. (2008), TR-2008-282. Department of Computing Science, University of Glasgow

16. C. Dragomir, F. Ipate, S. Konur, R. Lefticaru, L. Mierlă, Model checking kernel P systems, in *Membrane Computing (CMC 2013)*, ed. by A. Alhazov, S. Cojocaru, M. Gheorghe, Y. Rogozhin, G. Rozenberg, A. Salomaa. Lecture Notes in Computer Science, vol. 8340 (2013), pp. 151–172. https://doi.org/10.1007/978-3-642-54239-8_12

17. M.B. Elowitz, S. Leibler, A synthetic oscillatory network of transcriptional regulators. Nature **403**(6767), 335–338 (2000). https://doi.org/10.1038/35002125

18. M. Galdzicki, K.P. Clancy, E. Oberortner, M. Pocock, J.Y. Quinn, C.A. Rodriguez, R. Nicholas, M.L. Wilson, L. Adam, J.C. Anderson, The synthetic biology open language (SBOL) provides a community standard for communicating designs in synthetic biology. Nat. Biotechnol. **32**(6), 545–550 (2014). https://doi.org/10.1038/nbt.2891

19. M. Gheorghe, V. Manca, F.J. Romero-Campero, Deterministic and stochastic P systems for modelling cellular processes. Nat. Comput. **9**(2), 457–473 (2009). https://doi.org/10.1007/s11047-009-9158-4

20. M. Gheorghe, S. Konur, F. Ipate, L. Mierlă, M.E. Bakir, M. Stannett, An integrated model checking toolset for kernel P systems, in *Membrane Computing (CMC 2015)*, ed. by G. Rozenberg, A. Salomaa, J.M. Sempere, C. Zandron. Lecture Notes in Computer Science, vol. 9504 (2015), pp. 153–170. https://doi.org/10.1007/978-3-319-28475-0_11

21. M. Gheorghe, S. Konur, F. Ipate, Kernel P systems and stochastic P Systems for modelling and formal verification of genetic logic gates, in *Advances in Unconventional Computing*, ed. by A. Adamatzky. Series Emergence, Complexity and Computation, vol. 22 (2017), pp. 661–675. https://doi.org/10.1007/978-3-319-33924-5_25

22. M. Gheorghe, R. Ceterchi, F. Ipate, S. Konur, R. Lefticaru, Kernel P systems: from modelling to verification and testing. Theor. Comput. Sci. **724**, 45–60 (2018). https://doi.org/10.1016/j.tcs.2017.12.010

23. D. Gillespie, A general method for numerically simulating the stochastic time evolution of coupled chemical reactions. J. Comput. Phys. **22**(4), 403–434 (1976). https://doi.org/10.1016/0021-9991(76)90041-3

24. D.R. Goldberg, *Genetic Algorithms in Search, Optimization and Machine Learning* (Addison Welsey, Reading, 1989)

25. N. Hansen, A. Ostermeier, Completely derandomized self-adaptation in evolution strategies. Evol. Comput. **9**(2), 159–195 (2001). https://doi.org/10.1162/106365601750190398

26. H. Hansson, B. Jonsson, A logic for reasoning about time and reliability. Formal Aspects Comput. **6**, 102–111 (1994). https://doi.org/10.1007/BF01211866

27. L.H. Hartwell, J.J. Hopfield, S. Leibler, A.W. Murray, From molecular to modular cell biology. Nature **402**, C47–C52 (1999). https://doi.org/10.1038/35011540

28. A. Hinton, M. Kwiatkowska, G. Norman, D. Parker, Prism: a tool for automatic verification of probabilistic systems, in *Tools and Algorithms for the Construction and Analysis of Systems, 12th International Conference, TACAS 2006 Held as Part of the Joint European Conferences on Theory and Practice of Software, ETAPS 2006, Vienna, Austria, March 25—April 2, 2006*. Lecture Notes in Computer Science, vol. 3920 (2006), pp. 441–444. https://doi.org/10.1007/11691372_29

29. M. Hucka, A. Finney, H.M. Sauro, et al. The systems biology markup language (SBML): a medium for representation and exchange of biochemical network models. Bioinformatics **19**(4), 524–531 (2002). https://doi.org/10.1093/bioinformatics/btg015

30. *Infobiotics Workbench*. http://sysbio.infobiotics.org

31. *Infobiotics Workbench for Synthetic Biology*. http://infobiotics.org

32. S.A. Kauffman, Metabolic stability and epigenesis in randomly constructed genetic nets. J. Theor. Biol. **22**(3), 437–467 (1969). https://doi.org/10.1016/0022-5193(69)90015-0

33. J.W. Klop, Term rewriting systems, in *Handbook of Logic in Computer Science*, vol. 2 (Oxford University, Oxford, 1993), pp. 1–116

34. S. Konur, A decidable temporal logic for events and states, in *Proceedings of the Thirteenth International Symposium on Temporal Representation and Reasoning (TIME'06), Budapest, 2006* (2006), pp. 36–41. https://doi.org/10.1109/TIME.2006.1

35. S. Konur, An interval logic for natural language semantics, in *Proceedings of the Seventh Conference on Advances in Modal Logic, Nancy, France, 9–12 September 2008*, ed. by C. Areces, R. Goldblatt (2008), pp. 177–191

36. S. Konur, *Real-time and Probabilistic Temporal Logics: An Overview*. CoRR **abs/1005.3200** (2010)

37. S. Konur, *A Survey on Temporal Logics*. CoRR **abs/1005.3199** (2010)

38. S. Konur, An event-based fragment of first-order logic over intervals. J. Logic Lang. Inf. **20**, 49–68 (2011). https://doi.org/10.1007/s10849-010-9126-5

39. S. Konur, A survey on temporal logics for specifying and verifying real-time systems. Front. Comput. Sci. **7**(3), 370–403 (2013). https://doi.org/10.1007/s11704-013-2195-2

40. S. Konur, Specifying safety-critical systems with a decidable duration logic. Sci. Comput. Program. **80**(Part B), 264–287 (2014). https://doi.org/10.1016/j.scico.2013.07.012

41. S. Konur, Towards light-weight probabilistic model checking. J. Appl. Math. **2014**, Article ID 814159, 1–15 (2014). https://doi.org/10.1155/2014/814159

42. S. Konur, M. Fisher, Formal analysis of a VANET congestion control protocol through probabilistic verification, in *Proceedings of the 2011 IEEE 73rd Vehicular Technology Conference (VTC Spring), Yokohama, 2011* (2011), pp. 1–5. https://doi.org/10.1109/VETECS.2011.5956327

43. S. Konur, M. Fisher, A roadmap to pervasive systems verification. Knowl. Eng. Rev. **30**(3), 324–341 (2015). https://doi.org/10.1017/S0269888914000228
44. S. Konur, M. Gheorghe, A property-driven methodology for formal analysis of synthetic biology systems, in *IEEE/ACM Transactions on Computational Biology and Bioinformatics*, vol. 12(2), 360–371 (2015). https://doi.org/10.1109/TCBB.2014.2362531
45. S. Konur, C. Dixon, M, Fisher, Formal verification of probabilistic swarm behaviours, in *Swarm Intelligence (ANTS 2010)*, ed. by M. Dorigo et al. Lecture Notes in Computer Science, vol. 6234 (2010), pp. 440–447. https://doi.org/10.1007/978-3-642-15461-4_42
46. S. Konur, C. Dixon, M. Fisher, Analysing robot swarm behaviour via probabilistic model checking. Rob. Auton. Syst. **60**(2), 199–213 (2012). https://doi.org/10.1016/j.robot.2011.10.005
47. S. Konur, M. Fisher, S. Schewe, Combined model checking for temporal, probabilistic, and real-time logics. Theor. Comput. Sci. **503**, 61–88 (2013). https://doi.org/10.1016/j.tcs.2013.07.012
48. S. Konur, M. Fisher, S. Dobson, S. Knox, Formal verification of a pervasive messaging system. Formal Aspects Comput. **26**(4), 677–694 (2014). https://doi.org/10.1007/s00165-013-0277-4
49. S. Konur, M. Gheorghe, C. Dragomir, F. Ipate, N. Krasnogor, Conventional verification for unconventional computing: a genetic XOR gate example. Fundam. Inform. **134**, 97–110 (2014). https://doi.org/10.3233/FI-2014-1093
50. S. Konur, M. Gheorghe, C. Dragomir, L. Mierlă, F. Ipate, N. Krasnogor, Qualitative and quantitative analysis of systems and synthetic biology constructs using P systems. ACS Synth. Biol. **4**(1), 83–92 (2015). https://doi.org/10.1021/sb500134w
51. S. Konur, M. Kiran, M. Gheorghe, M. Burkitt, F. Ipate, Agent-based high-performance simulation of biological systems on the GPU, in *Proceedings of the 2015 IEEE 17th International Conference on High Performance Computing and Communications, 2015 IEEE 7th International Symposium on Cyberspace Safety and Security, and 2015 IEEE 12th International Conference on Embedded Software and Systems, New York, NY* (2015), pp. 84–89. https://doi.org/10.1109/HPCC-CSS-ICESS.2015.253
52. S. Konur, H. Fellermann, L.M. Mierlă, D. Sanassy, C. Ladroue, S. Kalvala, M. Gheorghe, N. Krasnogor, An integrated *in silico* simulation and biomatter compilation approach to cellular computation, in *Advances in Unconventional Computing*, ed. by A. Adamatzky. Series Emergence, Complexity and Computation, vol. 23 (2017), pp. 655–676. https://doi.org/10.1007/978-3-319-33921-4_25
53. S. Konur, L. Mierlă, F. Ipate, M. Gheorghe, kPWorkbench: a software suit for membrane systems. SoftwareX **11**, 100407 (2020). https://doi.org/10.1016/j.softx.2020.100407
54. *kPWorkbench*. https://github.com/kernel-p-systems/kpworkbench
55. P. Kuhn, K. Wagner, K. Heil, M. Liss, N. Netuschil, Next generation gene synthesis: from microarrays to genomes. Eng. Life Sci. **17**(1), 6–13 (2017). https://doi.org/10.1002/elsc.201600121
56. J.C. Lagarias, Point lattices, in *Handbook of Combinatorics*, vol. 1 (1996), pp. 919–966
57. R. Lefticaru, S. Konur, Ü. Yildirim, A. Uddin, F. Campean, M. Gheorghe, Towards an integrated approach to verification and model-based testing in system engineering, in *Proceedings of the 2017 IEEE International Conference on Internet of Things (iThings) and IEEE Green Computing and Communications (GreenCom) and IEEE Cyber, Physical and Social Computing (CPSCom) and IEEE Smart Data (SmartData), Exeter, 2017* (2017), pp. 131–138. https://doi.org/10.1109/iThings-GreenCom-CPSCom-SmartData.2017.25
58. R. Lefticaru, M.E. Bakir, S. Konur, M. Stannett, F. Ipate, Modelling and validating an engineering application in kernel P systems, in *Membrane Computing (CMC 2017)*, ed. by M. Gheorghe, G. Rozenberg, A. Salomaa, C. Zandron. Lecture Notes in Computer Science, vol. 10725 (2018), pp. 183–195. https://doi.org/10.1007/978-3-319-73359-3_12
59. C. Priami, Stochastic π-calculus. Comput. J. **38**(7), 578–589 (1995). https://doi.org/10.1093/comjnl/38.7.578
60. *Pulse Generator Case Study*. https://sysbio.infobiotics.org/models/pulseGenerator/pulseGenerator.html

61. *Repressilator Case Study*. http://sysbio.infobiotics.org/models/repressilator/repressilator.html
62. F.J. Romero-Campero, H. Cao, M. Camara, N. Krasnogor, Structure and parameter estimation for cell systems biology models, in *Proceedings of the 10th Annual Conference on Genetic and Evolutionary Computation (GECCO '08), Atlanta, GA, USA, July 12–16, 2008* (2008), pp. 331–339. https://doi.org/10.1145/1389095.1389153
63. F.J. Romero-Campero, J. Twycross, M. Cámara, M. Bennett, M. Gheorghe, N. Krasnogor, Modular assembly of cell systems biology models using P systems. Int. J. Found. Comput. Sci. **20**(3), 427–442 (2009). https://doi.org/10.1142/S0129054109006668
64. F.J. Romero-Campero, J. Twycross, H. Cao, J. Blakes, N. Krasnogor, A multiscale modeling framework based on P systems, in *Membrane Computing (WMC 2008)*, ed. by D.W. Corne, P. Frisco, Gh. Păun, G. Rozenberg, A. Salomaa. Lecture Notes in Computer Science, vol. 5391 (2009), pp. 63–77. https://doi.org/10.1007/978-3-540-95885-7_5
65. D. Sanassy, H. Fellermann, N. Krasnogor, S. Konur, L. Mierlă, M. Gheorghe, C. Ladroue, S. Kalvala, Modelling and stochastic simulation of synthetic biological Boolean gates, in *Modelling and Stochastic Simulation of Synthetic Biological Boolean Gates, 2014 IEEE International Conference on High Performance Computing and Communications, 2014 IEEE 6th International Symposium on Cyberspace Safety and Security, 2014 IEEE 11th International Conference on Embedded Software and Syst (HPCC,CSS,ICESS), Paris, 2014* (2014), pp. 404–408. https://doi.org/10.1109/HPCC.2014.68
66. K. Sen, M. Viswanathan, G. Agha, Statistical model checking of black-box probabilistic systems, in *Computer Aided Verification (CAV 2004)*, ed. by R. Alur, D.A. Peled. Lecture Notes in Computer Science, vol. 3114 (2004), pp. 202–215. https://doi.org/10.1007/978-3-540-27813-9_16
67. R. Storn, K. Price, Differential evolution: a simple and efficient heuristic for global optimization over continuous spaces. J. Global Optim. **11**, 341–359 (1997). https://doi.org/10.1023/A:1008202821328
68. F.J.W. Symons, Introduction to numerical Petri nets, a general graphical model of concurrent processing systems. Aust. Telecommun. Res. **14**(1), 28–32 (1980)
69. M. Yabandeh, Model checking of distributed algorithm implementations, Ph.D. thesis, IC (2011). École Polytechnique Fédérale de Lausanne. https://doi.org/10.5075/epfl-thesis-4858

Molecular Physics and Chemistry in Membranes: The Java Environment for Nature-Inspired Approaches (JENA)

5

5.1 Introduction

Molecules turn out to form a perfect medium for data storage and information processing carried out by dedicated chemical reactions or physical effects. By means of these interactions, molecules might be modified, selected, or spatially separated by specific attributes. Moreover, molecules stand out due to their miniaturized size within a nanometer scale [36]. Since molecules are composed of atoms or ions, they come with an inner spatial structure sustained by specific chemical bonds and resulting forces [29]. A molecule "stores" its inner structure which is responsible for molecular attributes like overall mass, binding energy, electric charge, and chemical reactivity reflecting unsaturated binding sites and valences. From a descriptive point of view, molecules represent an excellent workpiece: On the one hand, they are small enough in a way that gravity has merely an insignificant and mostly negligible effect on their behavior, but on the other hand, they are large enough to commonly overcome influences of stochastic quantum physics and partially unknown consequences of strong nuclear power [12]. The behavior of molecules follows the laws of thermodynamics [1, 34] and mechanics mainly driven by mechanical and electrical forces, especially electrostatics [3]. The underlying rules, formulated either in an explicit manner or by statistical statements, provide a well-balanced basis for modelling and simulation in membrane computing.

Having these facts in mind, the idea arises to create a software system for membrane computing operating at the level of single spatially distributed molecules in a vessel and emulating their interactions. Its aim is bridging the gap between highly abstract and strongly idealized formal term-rewriting modelling tools like *P-Lingua* [8, 27] and expensive systems for detailed molecular dynamics like *Amber* [2, 31] including almost all known physical effects able to slightly influence molecular structures in time and space which implies advanced demands in high-performance computing. For our approach, we envisage a software tool acting at

G. Zhang et al., *Membrane Computing Models: Implementations*, https://doi.org/10.1007/978-981-16-1566-5_5

a medium level of abstraction and able to exhibit the most relevant aspects of the dynamical behavior of a molecular system under study. In this way, we are going to capture principles of biological information processing along with an illustrative visualization.

Interestingly, biochemistry and biophysics typically take place within *liquids*, particularly within water in its liquid form [14, 17]. A biological cell in a living organism is formed by an outer delimiting but flexible and permeable phospholipid *membrane* mainly filled with water. Inner membranes define subcellular compartments in which the presence of special molecules along with specific environmental conditions like pH value enables different specialized tasks [21]. An average biological cell consists of approximately 10^9 molecules, between 60% and 80% of them water [20]. Beyond molecular interactions within living cells in vivo, molecular biological processes can also be carried out in vessels or test tubes in vitro [5]. Corresponding laboratory techniques have in common that the molecules are treated in liquid water as well. Aiming at a virtual cell and a virtual laboratory, our membrane computing software is conceived by the imagination to have at least one reaction space surrounded by a membrane or a barrier and filled with a liquid.

The software as a whole should cover four tasks: (1) definition of a *molecular system* with its initial spatial placement of molecules in terms of a liquid and specification of a delimiting vessel or outer membrane, (2) configuration of *processing specifications* like chemical reactions, electrical or mechanical forces the vessel or membrane is exposed to, (3) *simulation of system's behavior* by running the process in time and space with motion of molecules, tracing the interactions among molecules and between molecules and membrane, and visualization of system's dynamics, and (4) *analysis* of the emulated process by histograms and statistical evaluations (see Fig. 5.1).

From a technical point of view, the software is planned to be *modular*. So it can be successively extended in order to manage more and more types of processes beyond chemical reactions like diffusion or osmosis, but also blotting, separation, and filtering techniques based on dedicated physical effects. In addition, the pool of visualization, analysis, and evaluation methods is intended to grow in the long term as well. All modules communicate to each other and exchange data via interfaces. Another crucial feature lies in a strict *object-oriented* implementation which supports the handling of molecules at different stages of detailedness such as with or without inner structure and with varying settings of attributes. The response of molecules to consequences of the process under study can be adapted in accordance with the available amount of molecular data. Moreover, the user interface should be appropriate and easy to obtain. We decided to utilize *Java* as programming language due to its advantageous properties [7]. Since teams of students are involved in software development, the popularity of Java in teaching and in practice gives a further argument. Summarizing all together, we created the name *"Java Environment for Nature-inspired Approaches"*, JENA for short [15], for our membrane computing software which expresses a homage to our university located in the city with the same name.

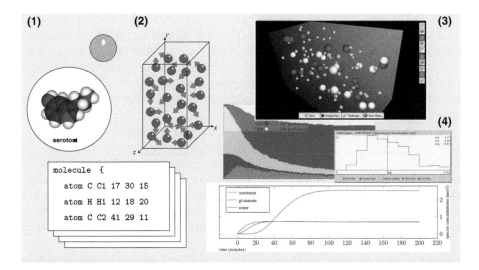

Fig. 5.1 Schematic illustration of the main steps when employing the Java Environment for Nature-inspired Approaches (JENA): (1) definition of a molecular system, (2) configuration of processing specifications, (3) simulation of system's behavior, and (4) analysis and evaluation

Our main motivation for the JENA project is the idea to bring models of membrane computing closer to real-life processes. Particularly, the role of *time* for adjustment of processing schemes toward orchestrated functional units might be a major clue for understanding of biological control loops [18] and clock systems [16] acting as triggers for numerous facets of life.

When examining state-of-the-art models of systems biology or bioinformatics in which the course of molecule concentrations over time is obtained, we notice that the mathematical formulation of the model often contains *abstract process parameters* whose values are hard to determine or need to be fitted. In case of chemical reactions described by ordinary differential equations according to the rules of mass action or other kinetics. For instance, there are rate constants so-called Arrhenius terms [4]. It belongs to a common practice to assign a rate constant value that reaches the best possible fit of the model to the observations. More or less, abstract macroscopic parameters like rate constants reflect the most likely superposition of a large number of microscopic effects at the molecular level. The microscopic effects in turn result from the natural laws of thermodynamics and molecular mechanics. Here, molecules move within space able to collide and to interact like billiard balls. This coincides with the basic idea we adopt for our modelling approach. Since the *Brownian motion* of molecules characterizes liquids [25], we combine it with force fields able to deflect, to accelerate, and to slow down molecules. Forces arise from molecular motion, from unsaturated binding sites of molecules, or from environmental influences like an applied voltage. Simulation studies of a molecular system's behavior conducted in this way can help to reveal abstract process parameter values and explain their assignment.

Biological information processing can be seen as an *interplay* of manifold chemical reactions and physical processes operating in concert [28]. They might run simultaneously inside the same membrane, but they can also be organized within a cascade of adjacent membranes, or they utilize *dynamical membrane structures* capable of dividing a membrane into two parts or unification of either membranes into one. Due to the permeable nature of a membrane, molecules can selectively pass via channels or get blocked.

A fascinating biological example for an interplay of distinct processes and membranes is given by *neural signal transduction* across a synaptic cleft between connected neurons in higher-order multicellular organisms [22]. A neuron produces a *sequence of spikes* based on its input stimulations and their weighted summation. The spikes represent *electrical signals* mediated by subsequent thrusts of positively charged natrium (sodium) and other ions. They spread through the axon of the neuron towards its synapse. The distance of an axon varies from less than 1 mm up to more than 1 m [6]. An axon is equipped with a cascade of membranes connected via ion channels. A spike of ions generates a so-called action potential which in turn temporarily opens one ion channel after the other in a way that the spike runs through the entire axon. Its speed reaches up to $140 \frac{m}{s}$ [10]. Typically, a spike is followed by other ones forming a sequence over time whose duration and frequency (temporal distance between consecutive spikes) determine the information to transmit. The opposite tail of an axon is called synapse in which vesicles filled with neurotransmitters reside. There are around 60 variants of neurotransmitters available, each of them symbolizing a molecular messenger [23]. Subject to duration and frequency of the spike sequence entering the synapse, a specific combination of neurotransmitters gets released. To this end, corresponding vesicles move to the surface of the synapse and undergo an *exocytosis* [32]. This process opens vesicle's membrane, and its containing neurotransmitters leave the hosting neuron. By *diffusion* [33], they traverse the synaptic cleft to the adjacent neuron and finally *bind* to receptors placed on its outer dendritic face. This implies an activation of ion channels and leads to transformation of the chemical signal into an electrical signal to be evaluated as an input stream. A neuron is able to receive several thousands of input streams from its dendrites connected with upstream neurons. These input signals are weighted and summarized. When exceeding a threshold, they stimulate the neuron to fire by producing a new sequence of spikes. What stands out is that underlying processing schemes incorporate several compartments and a variety of cells to achieve the final outcome. So biological information processing becomes manifest in time and *space* [26]. We accommodate this property by taking into account the *outer environment* of a membrane for input and output of molecules. Additionally, we allow the JENA system to manage a *multiplicity* of membranes and vessels.

The JENA chapter is structured as follows: In Sect. 5.2, we familiarize the reader with the configurability and the features of JENA at its current state of implementation in 2020 from a user's perspective along with the underlying natural laws and basic knowledge from chemistry and physics relevant for employment of JENA. We shed light on JENA's descriptive capacity from a modelling point of view. We show how to specify molecules, membranes, vessels, physical processes, chemical reactions, and handling of multiple membranes. Furthermore, we introduce the simulation engine and tools for visualization and analysis. After all, Sect. 5.3 is dedicated to the JENA source code design from a technical standpoint. We give an overview of modules, packages, and their structure and interplay. Especially for visualization, some predefined classes from the SRSim Library [11] have been used. Finally, four case studies presented in Sect. 5.4 demonstrate the practicability of JENA for modelling and simulation in membrane computing. We exemplify a chemical Lotka-Volterra oscillator [24], show the effects of electrophoresis [19] and centrifugation as laboratory techniques driven by external forces, and present a model of neural signal transduction across a synaptic cleft.

5.2 JENA at a Glance and Its Descriptive Capacity

In this section, we introduce the features and expressiveness of JENA for modelling and simulation of molecular systems over time and in space. In this context, we reflect and recall the underlying natural laws and their formalisms from physics and chemistry the JENA software is based on. So the adopted medium level of abstraction becomes apparent, and the descriptive capacity together with its capabilities and limitations emerges from the range of knowledge in natural sciences incorporated into JENA's engines.

We start with the smallest elementary entities managed in the system: *atoms* and *ions*. Their attributes like mass, electric charge, and degree of saturation of the outer orbital of electrons are responsible for their properties and for their behavior since a variety of forces (strength and direction) affecting motion, acceleration, speed, and reactivity result from the entire force field. Atoms can bind to each other forming *molecules* with a three-dimensional structure of atoms. Each chemical bond comes with additional parameters like binding energy and binding length which defines molecule's stability and the activation energy necessary to modify its structure by breaking or setting chemical bonds. Molecules can also arise from ions attached to each other with alternating positive and negative electric charge composing an ion lattice which in turn acts and reacts with respect to the force field. We assume atoms, ions, and molecules to follow a Brownian motion typical for a solution of liquid water. The existence of *membranes* and barriers from solid material delimiting a processing space requires consideration of elements and building blocks able to resist a permanent motion. Instead, they keep their position within a nearly fixed, large, and dense spatial structure sticked together by stronger forces. To this end, we allow for formation of *particles* either composed of atoms, ions, and molecules or freely configured as sized building blocks. Membranes may contain channels, receptors, and openings making them permeable and able to control passage from outside to inside and vice versa. Beyond creation of solid membranes or delimiters, particles are helpful entities in order to capture abstract substrates without definition of an inner structure but moveable within the surrounding liquid volume.

Having the specification of initial atoms, ions, molecules, and particles at hand, one or more *vessels* can be created and filled together with additional water molecules. A vessel is a coherent finite three-dimensional space placed within a Cartesian coordinate system and completely enclosed by *membranes* and/or *delimiters*. A vessel consists of a finite number of inner adjacent volume elements. Membranes or delimiters are built by connected particles whose spatial placement decides about the shape of a vessel. Membranes and delimiters can be defined in a way that several vessels occur. Each of them constitutes an individual volume given by the number of inner volume elements. Eventually, each vessel becomes initially filled with the corresponding atoms, ions, molecules, and moveable particles according to given substance concentrations. Additional water molecules complement each vessel. When filling a vessel, the spatial distribution of all containing elements matters which can either represent a homogeneous placement or emulate a punctiform injection. All elements of a vessel have been assigned an initial speed, orientation, and direction of movement in accordance with the Maxwell-Boltzmann distribution which relies on the configurable temperature among others. Now, the *Brownian motion* of all moveable elements of all vessels might start after the initial configuration of the whole molecular system under study is set (see Fig. 5.2).

Assuming a liquid to be existing within each vessel of the system, the average spatial distance between neighbored moveable elements lies within the magnitude of the medium size of a molecule. This implies a quite dense package of the atoms, ions, molecules, and particles which enables numerous interactions. Each moveable element comes with an individual amount of kinetic energy which mainly marks out its movement. Additional accelerations or slowdowns might be caused by electrostatic charges located in atoms or ions whose outer orbital of electrons is unsaturated. Resulting Coulomb forces can deviate other moveable elements

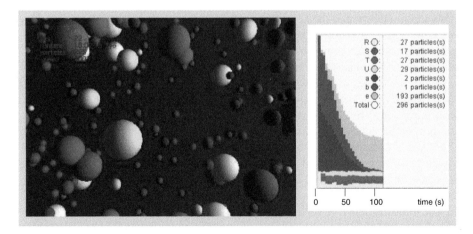

Fig. 5.2 Artificial molecular system composed of different types of particles during Brownian motion. Collisions among particles might cause chemical reactions

with similar or with complement properties from their trajectory. We organize the simulation of Brownian motion in a time-discrete manner. Each atom, ion, molecule, or particle is located within a volume element of the residing vessel. By conducting a time step, it might leave this volume element and enter a different one. Interactions of atoms, ions, molecules, and particles result in *collisions* among each other and with the solid particle structures forming membranes and delimiters. A collision can initiate a chemical reaction in case the kinetic energy of all involved atoms, ions, molecules, and particles in total reaches or exceeds the required activation energy. A configurable list of possible reactions together with activation energies has been defined for each vessel. When reacting, the collision is said to be nonelastic and effective. Chemical bonds of the substrates get rearranged, and reaction products emerge which in turn move through the vessel along a new route. Particles incorporated in the solid structures of membranes or delimiters might be involved in reactions as well. Collisions with too less kinetic energy run in an elastic manner similar to a reflection. Here, all atoms, ions, molecules, and particles stay intact without any modification of chemical bonds, and they continue their movement with a different direction. A special case of a chemical reaction is called decay. Here, a molecule or particle can spontaneously decompose without any collision. If a decay reaction has been defined in a vessel, its substrate molecules or particles have been marked with individual points in time in which the decay will occur. The point in time is estimated from the speed and from the decay reaction's activation energy in accordance with laws of thermodynamics.

Furthermore, *external forces* applied to a vessel might affect the movement of containing atoms, ions, molecules, and particles constituting the liquid. We distinguish mechanical and electrical external forces. A typical example for application of mechanical forces is centrifugation. Here, all moveable elements of a vessel receive an additional acceleration in the direction of the applied force. The intensity of acceleration depends on their individual mass. Since all moveable constituents of the vessel undergo applied mechanical forces, the Brownian motion gets perturbed for a while commonly resulting in more elastic collisions reflecting the effect of friction. In contrast, application of electrical external forces can be done by a voltage causing an electric field spatially distributed throughout the hosting vessel. It influences the movement of all electrically charged ions, molecules, and particles while atoms remain unaffected. A typical example is electrophoresis but also the functioning of ion channels.

Membranes and *delimiters* composed of particles are helpful in order to separate a processing space into different vessels or compartments which in turn can be equipped with various initial settings of substrate atoms, ions, molecules, and particles. Membranes and delimiters have been treated as solid structures without Brownian motion and surrounded by liquids. Delimiters intend to act as a barrier impassable for moveable atoms, ions, molecules, and particles forming a liquid. In contrast, a membrane enables passage of constituents of a liquid by presence of ion channels or by small openings, and it might interact with their environment by receptors. An ion channel residing in a membrane is shaped by some particles representing the outer cover, a particle having the function of a gate and electrical external forces able to temporarily open and to close the gate. Particles utilized for delimiters and membranes are allowed to act as substrates or catalysts for chemical reactions. In this way, delimiters and membranes can be dissolved. Remaining single particles with no bond to the solid structure become moveable and can be degraded by further reactions. Moreover, we allow placement of particles into the molecular system by configuration at any discrete point in time. This feature can be employed to create delimiters and membranes on the fly. The dynamics of active membranes and variable delimiters makes the JENA software more flexible for modelling and simulation.

The entire molecular system under study captured by JENA is embedded into a *cuboid* placed in a three-dimensional Cartesian coordinate system and composed of many small cubical-shaped *volume elements*. These volume elements represent the smallest unit (lattice) for particles as parts of solid structures and for atoms, ions, molecules, and particles forming the liquids. A configuration of the entire molecular system is given by a list of all volume elements indicating for each volume element the contained atoms, ions, molecules, and particles. A simulation of system's behavior over time sums up all configurations over the discrete points in time resulting in a *logging data set*. This data set becomes employed for all subsequent *visualizations* and *analyses*. Visualizations depict configuration series of the system under study from a freely configurable observer's perspective or at an arbitrary plane (layer) parallel to two of the coordinate system's axes. Analyses result in histograms and diagrams obtained from evaluation of the data set. Abundance of atoms, ions, molecules, and particles can be showed over time. The spatial trace of a single molecule or particle is available as well. In addition, statistical parameters like temperature and speed distribution, collision frequency, and percentage of different energy forms complete the analytic features of JENA.

5.2.1   Atoms, Ions, Molecules, and Particles

Atoms

Atoms embody the spheric components from which matter as physical substance in its solid, liquid, or gaseous state is made up. Material properties of substances as well as their behavior in chemical reactions have been defined by the atoms and their spatial arrangement. Each atom belongs to a *chemical element* listed in the *periodic table*. There are 92 naturally produced elements found on earth. They differ by their inner structure, by their mass, by their spheric size, and by their reactivity.

An atom consists of a small nucleus surrounded by an atomic shell. The nucleus is composed of a dense packing of protons and neutrons. Protons are positively electrically charged, sticked together by strong nuclear power active within the small radius of the nucleus. Each chemical element is characterized by an individual number of protons residing in the atomic nucleus ranging from 1 (hydrogen) to 92 (uranium). There exist further unstable chemical elements with more than 92 protons which have been artificially produced and tend to spontaneously decay in the short term. Most of the chemical elements host a specific number of neutrons inside the nucleus in addition to the protons. For one element, the number of neutrons might slightly vary. So a chemical element might be available in several isotopes according to the number of neutrons. The nucleus of an atom as a whole is positively electrically charged due to the contained protons. Although a nucleus is extremely small within a magnitude of few femtometers (10^{-15} m), it summarizes more than 99% of the mass of an atom.

The surrounding atomic shell comprises around 100,000-fold of the nucleus' diameter. It is structured by nearly spherically layers of orbitals in which electrons are located. An electron is negatively electrically charged. In an atom, the number of protons in the nucleus is in parity with the total number of electrons in the shell. This implies an electrically neutral state of the entire atom taken as an entity. The orbitals forming the atomic shell conically enclose the nucleus. Each orbital comes with a maximum number of electrons able to include. While the innermost orbital can merely host up to two electrons, each of the next both orbitals might manage 8 of them followed by two orbitals, each of them able to carry up to 18 electrons and finally having two orbitals with each of them giving room for up to 32 electrons. Electrons start to fill the innermost orbital. After its capacity has been exhausted, the next orbital gets occupied.

The degree of saturation of the outermost orbital with electrons (valence) is mainly responsible for the reactivity and for the kind of chemical reactions the atom can be involved in. Electrons in the outermost orbital might interact with corresponding electrons from another atom nearby. To do so, both atoms can completely fill their outermost orbitals by sharing common electrons. To this end, both outermost orbitals interfere with each other. A residing electron of the one atom can pair with its counterpart from the other atom to form a covalent chemical bond sticking both atoms to each other. In case of atoms whose outermost orbital is completely filled from the beginning with a number of electrons at its capacity limit (inert gases), there is no reactivity.

The mass of an atom results from the number of protons, neutrons, and electrons it is composed of. A proton contributes a mass of $1.672621923 \cdot 10^{-27}$ kg, a neutron $1.674927498 \cdot 10^{-27}$ kg, and an electron merely $9.109383702 \cdot 10^{-31}$ kg. Since the majority of chemical elements found on earth is available in a mixture of isotopes whose number of neutrons slightly varies, it is a common practice to choose an average number of neutrons according to the relative abundance of all known stable isotopes. The periodic table assigns a corresponding molar mass to each chemical element which stands for the mass in g of $6.02214076 \cdot 10^{23}$ atoms (amount of 1mol).

In case of the chemical element *carbon* (symbolized by C; see Fig. 5.3) over all stable isotopes, the periodic table exhibits an average molar mass of $12.0116 \frac{g}{mol}$. This corresponds to a mass of approximately $2.008 \cdot 10^{-26}$ kg. Moreover, the periodic table reveals a radius of 76 pm (picometers whereas 1 pm $= 10^{-12}$ m) for carbon atoms. Their nucleus accommodates six protons, and their outermost orbital hosts four electrons having a capacity of eight.

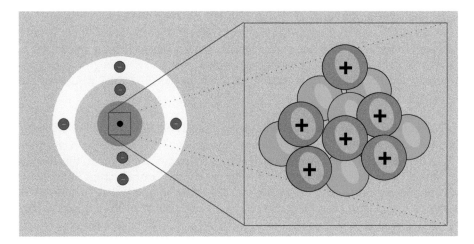

Fig. 5.3 Schematic representation of an atom of the chemical element carbon (isotope ^{12}C). Its nucleus contains six protons (+) and six neutrons. Six electrons (−) have been distributed within two orbitals. The inner one is completely filled with two electrons while the outer one possesses four having a capacity of eight. Seldomly (<1%), naturally produced carbon atoms exist as ^{13}C isotopes accommodating seven instead of six neutrons in its nucleus

For all 92 naturally occurring and stable chemical elements from hydrogen (H, 1 proton) to uranium (U, 92 protons), we keep at hand the name, the symbol, the mass, the radius of the atoms, the number of protons, and the number of electrons in the outermost orbital in relation to its capacity. This set of parameters marks each atom. For schematic representation, we depict an atom by a sphere without inner structure.

Ions

While atoms have in common that the number of protons residing within the nucleus is in parity with the number of electrons distributed within the orbitals of the atomic shell, *ions* deviate from this property. They can either accumulate additional electrons which leads to a negative electric charge or they might emit electrons from their outermost orbital which in turn results in a positive electric charge. Ions tend to have completely filled orbitals of electrons avoiding orbitals whose capacity is not exhausted. In case the outermost orbital carries only one or few electrons, they typically get emitted to obtain a positively charged ion. In contrast, a nearly filled outermost orbital attracts further electrons generating negatively charged ions. A configuration of electrons in which all used orbitals have been completely filled turns out to be more energy efficient for the ion than others making the entire subatomic structure more stable. Typically, the number of accumulated or emitted electrons ranges from one up to three, whereas chemical elements being metals produce mainly onefold, twofold, or threefold positively charged ions (cations) like sodium ions (Na^+), magnesium ions (Mg^{2+}), or iron ions (Fe^{3+}). Nonmetals mostly generate negatively charged ions (anions). Examples are chlorine ions (Cl^-), oxygen ions (O^{2-}), or phosphide ions (P^{3-}). Ions with an *electric charge balance* greater than $+3$ or smaller than -3 are extremely rare. It might happen that several atoms chemically bind to each other before becoming a polyatomic ion.

We illustrate an ion by a sphere whose radius corresponds to the radius of the underlying atom. Since the electrons contribute to an ion's mass merely in a negligible manner, the mass of an ion is set to the same value of its underlying atom. Having in mind the ion model consisting of nucleus and surrounding spherical electron orbitals, we assign ion's radius by copying the radius of its underlying atom which holds in acceptable approximation. For the parameter set characterizing an ion, we add to the parameters of the underlying atom its electric charge balance by the corresponding integer number.

Since ions are electrically charged with respect to their environment, they induce an electrical force (*Coulomb force*) attracting other ions with opposite charge and pushing away other ions with correspondent charge. These forces can be strong enough to affect the motion route of ions present close to each other in a vessel. So we need to capture all electrical forces by modelling their influence to the motion of ions.

The *elementary electric charge* of $e = 1.602176634 \cdot 10^{-19}$As (Ampere seconds) is the smallest portion of electric charge to be distinguished. An electron is said to exhibit the charge $-e$, while a proton possesses $+e$. In consequence, an ion marked with a charge balance $-n$ has a total charge of $-n \cdot e$, while an ion with $+n$ reaches $n \cdot e$, respectively.

Two (spherical) ions with charges q_1 and q_2 whose spatial distance is r affect to each other by a *Coulomb force* $|\mathbf{F}_Q|$ of

$$|\mathbf{F}_Q| = \frac{1}{4 \cdot \pi \cdot \epsilon_0} \cdot \frac{|q_1| \cdot |q_2|}{r^2} \qquad (5.1)$$

whereas $\epsilon_0 = 8.854187812 \cdot 10^{-12} \frac{As}{Vm}$ symbolizes the absolute dielectric vacuum permittivity, a physical constant. The Coulomb force $|\mathbf{F}_Q|$ is directed along the line from the central point of one ion to its counterpart from the other. If both ions are oppositely charged, their Coulomb forces are attracting to each other. In case of correspondent charge, the Coulomb forces have a push-away effect. To do so, Coulomb forces can accelerate both incorporated ions since

$$|\mathbf{F}_Q| = m \cdot |\mathbf{a}| \qquad (5.2)$$

holds with m representing ion's mass and $|\mathbf{a}|$ its acceleration. The acceleration increases the speed $|\mathbf{v}|$ of the ion over time step Δt by $|\mathbf{v}| = |\mathbf{a}| \cdot \Delta t$. During motion, the distance r between the ions changes again which in turn results in a modified Coulomb force. The larger the distance r, the weaker is its effect and vice versa.

Since a vessel can contain many ions (much more than two), all pairwise interactions between them caused by Coulomb forces need to be calculated and superpositioned (added) for each single ion in order to obtain the entire effect. Here, it is more convenient to utilize a vector-based mathematical formulation. Let us assume that the central point of each ion i is represented by a three-dimensional vector $\mathbf{r}_i$. Another ion k is located at $\mathbf{r}_k$. The Coulomb force vector $\mathbf{F}_{ik}(\mathbf{r}_i)$ affecting ion i by k can be formulated by:

$$\mathbf{F}_{ik}(\mathbf{r}_i) = \frac{q_i \cdot q_k}{4 \cdot \pi \cdot \epsilon_0} \cdot \frac{1}{|\mathbf{r}_i - \mathbf{r}_k|^3} \cdot (\mathbf{r}_i - \mathbf{r}_k) \tag{5.3}$$

For the resulting total Coulomb force $\mathbf{F}_i(\mathbf{r}_i)$ affecting ion i, all forces $\mathbf{F}_{ik}(\mathbf{r}_i)$ have to be vectorially summed up over k by:

$$\mathbf{F}_i(\mathbf{r}_i) = \mathbf{F}_{i1}(\mathbf{r}_i) + \mathbf{F}_{i2}(\mathbf{r}_i) + \ldots + \mathbf{F}_{ik}(\mathbf{r}_i) = \sum_k \mathbf{F}_{ik}(\mathbf{r}_i) \tag{5.4}$$

Ion i's total acceleration $\mathbf{a}_i(\mathbf{r}_i)$ constitutes $\mathbf{a}_i(\mathbf{r}_i) = \frac{1}{m_i} \cdot \mathbf{F}_i(\mathbf{r}_i)$. Within one time step Δt, the velocity $\mathbf{v}_i(\mathbf{r}_i)$ of ion i incrementally changes by $\Delta \mathbf{v}_i(\mathbf{r}_i) = \mathbf{a}_i(\mathbf{r}_i) \cdot \Delta t$ updating its speed vector.

Molecules

A compound formed either by a number of atoms or by a mixture of atoms and ions or even exclusively by ions is called *molecule*. A molecule might consist of a multiplicity of one chemical element. Alternatively, it can be composed of a variety of chemical elements as well. All molecules have in common that the number of underlying atoms and/or ions is finite. At least two are required, but biomolecules are able to reach up to several thousands of them. Each molecule is characterized by its three-dimensional typically static spatial structure in which all incorporated atoms and/or ions are placed. Chemical bonds in concert with electrostatic forces cause the spatial structure of a molecule.

A *chemical bond* that links two atoms or one atom with one ion mainly results from an electron pair and is said to be *covalent*. Here, electrons residing in the outermost orbitals of either atoms interact with each other. Each atom and each ion tend to completely fill its outermost orbital with electrons exhausting its capacity due to the comparatively lower level of inner energy necessary to maintain this configuration. Atoms from chemical elements whose outermost orbital is completely filled a priori (inert gases like helium) are unable to contribute to molecules. All other atoms and most of the ions can act as components of molecules. In order to set a single covalent bond, two atoms or one atom and one ion need to approximate to each other in a way that both outermost orbitals interfere. An electron from the one orbital and its counterpart from the other one develop an electron pair. Both orbitals share this electron pair which in turn increases the number of electrons in each of the orbitals by one. In consequence, both orbitals are a bit more filled than before existence of the electron pair. Since an outermost orbital might contain more than one electron, an atom or ion can be involved in more than one electron pair with one or with several adjacent atoms or ions and hence set up more than one covalent chemical bond. The spatial distance between the central points of two atoms or of an atom and an ion linked by a covalent chemical bond is called *bond length*. Typically, it ranges between around 70 pm and 250 pm. Moreover, each covalent chemical bond exhibits an individual *binding energy*. It is defined as the amount of energy necessary to break (destroy) the underlying bond. The higher the binding energy, the stronger is the chemical bond. Binding energies of single covalent chemical bonds among atoms vary in a magnitude of several hundred kilojoule per mol, mostly between 150 $\frac{kJ}{mol}$ and 600 $\frac{kJ}{mol}$.

A compound exclusively built from ions can persist nearly without covalent chemical bonds, but instead, the ions mainly stick together by electrostatic forces forming an *ion lattice*. As a whole, it can be seen as a molecule in the broader sense even if no electron pair is present. An ion lattice describes a spatial structure of ions. In an alternating manner, positively charged and negatively charged ions attract to each other by Coulomb forces induced in the central point of each involved ion. Two ions of opposite electric charge are linked by ionic bonding. In the lattice structure, neighbored ions can come close to each other until their distance is equal to the sum of both radiuses. Corresponding lengths of ionic bondings are in a range from approximately 150 pm to 400 pm. The strength of an ionic bonding might be even higher than those of a single covalent chemical bond since its binding energy typically exceeds 170 $\frac{kJ}{mol}$ and can reach up to 1500 $\frac{kJ}{mol}$.

For later simulation and processing, we need to create a *data record* of the spatial structure of each molecule together with its chemical bonds. All copies of a molecule present in the entire vessel system share this data record. The basis of each molecule's data record is a three-dimensional Cartesian coordinate system in picometer scale. Inspired by the notion of a space-filling model (calotte model), each atom and ion incorporated into a molecule is considered to be a sphere able to intersect with others. We manually assign a three-dimensional *position vector* to any central point of the atoms and ions. Geometry and orientation of the resulting spatial structure provide the anchor points for the molecular skeleton. In addition to the position vector, each atom and ion is marked by its identifier (chemical symbol) which enables access to the corresponding data sets taken from the periodic table. In order to complete a molecular data record, all chemical bonds have to be included as well. A chemical bond is parameterized by both of its linked atoms or ions complemented by the binding energy and by the information whether it is a covalent bond, an ionic bonding, or a mixture of both forms. The bond length directly results from the Euclidean distance of either underlying atoms or ions.

Having finalized the data contributing to a molecular data record, a schematic representation of the described molecule for visualization is required. Here, we decided to virtually circumscribe each molecule by a *spheric cover* whose radius is determined by the spatial dimension of the molecule. The advantage of utilizing a spheric cover is the fact that the spatial orientation of the molecule does not matter and can be ignored when running a simulation. The radius of the spheric cover is figured out by the largest distention of the molecule regarding x-, y-, and

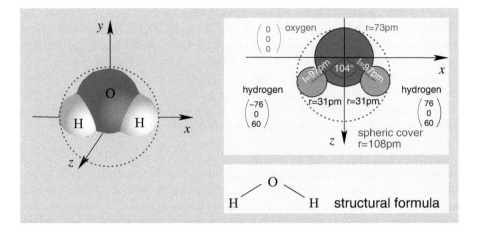

Fig. 5.4 A *water* molecule (H_2O) is composed of three atoms: one atom from the chemical element oxygen (O) linked with two atoms of hydrogen (H) by two separate single covalent chemical bonds. The oxygen atom has a radius of 73 pm, each hydrogen atom 31 pm, respectively. The outermost orbital of the oxygen hosts 6 out of 8 possible electrons while each hydrogen's orbital carries 1 electron having a capacity of 2. So two electron pairs arise. In consequence, all outermost orbitals have been completely filled. Each of both electron pairs originates a single covalent chemical bond whose length is 97 pm with a binding energy of 463 $\frac{kJ}{mol}$. The angle between both bonds constitutes $104°$. Within a three-dimensional Cartesian coordinate system in picometer scale, we denote central point's coordinates of all atoms complemented by the parameters of all chemical bonds. Finally, the entire molecule gets circumscribed by a spheric cover (indicated by a dotted shape) whose radius $r = 108pm$ results from the spatial dimension of the molecule

z coordinate axes. Figure 5.4 illustrates the composition of a water molecule by its atoms and their spatial positions together with all further parameters.

Particles
Explicitly defined atoms, ions, and molecules have been assumed to be individually moveable in space within a liquid environment inspired by the compartment's ingredients of a biological cell or by a test tube contents. When considering biological systems as a whole on the one hand and in vitro setups like electrophoresis gels on the other, some kind of *solid spatial structures* residing inside a vessel are needed. Solid structures aim to be resistant against Brownian motion. They keep fixed positions within the three-dimensional space of the underlying vessel, and they reflect moveable constituents in case of an impact with low speed.

Nevertheless, solid structures might be involved in chemical reactions in case of collisions with moveable atoms, ions, or molecules which in turn could knock out parts of the solid structure. Then, these parts dissolve away and become moveable. Vice versa, colliding atoms, ions, or molecules can also stick to the solid structure strengthening its shape. Another behavioral scenario of a solid structure might resemble a biological receptor embedded into a cell membrane. A receptor has an affinity to specific types of molecules or ions. When colliding with one of those exemplars, a messenger molecule at the opposite side of the receptor gets released indicating perception and initiating a signalling cascade. A solid structure formed like a tunnel and equipped with controllable electric charges placed at dedicated positions is able to act in terms of an ion channel.

We expect solid spatial structures to be exclusively composed of *solid particles*. A solid particle is an abstract *box-shaped building block* generally marked with an individual identifier and with the size of the box (length, width, height) in a picometer scale. We provide two possibilities in order to define a solid particle. Firstly, its contents can be given by a single atom, ion, or molecule to be incorporated into the solid particle. Here, the box is represented by a cube whose size is quantified in a way that the volume of the cube equals the volume of the underlying sphere obtained from the atom, ion, or molecule (see Fig. 5.5a). Secondly, a solid particle is allowed to be freely configured without any constitutional template by assigning a mass together with length, width, and height of the box and—if necessary—positions and variable quantities of electric point charges within the box as shown in Fig. 5.5b.

Freely configurable particles embody a modelling instrument to cope with different *levels of abstraction*. Partially unknown molecular structures, for instance, evident in some proteins or complex organic macromolecules, can be simply included in a model, and they might interact with other constituents of the molecular system under study according to predefined chemical reaction rules.

When we conceived the JENA approach, particles primarily have been introduced to exclusively maintain an immoveable behavior at fixed positions within

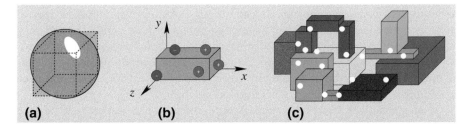

Fig. 5.5 (**a**) A solid (immoveable) particle has been visualized by a box whose volume equals the volume of the underlying sphere symbolizing the incorporated atom, ion, molecule, or moveable particle. (**b**) A box representing a solid particle is placed in a picometer-scaled three-dimensional Cartesian coordinate system oriented in parallel to the coordinate axes with freely configurable length, width, and height. Inside a box, electric point charges might be set at arbitrary positions if necessary to indicate Coulomb forces. (**c**) Example of a compound exclusively made from solid particles sticked to each other. For simplicity, all boxes forming a compound have the same orientation parallel or orthogonal to each other. A linkage (bond) within a compound connects two neighbored boxes that typically share a common plane or at least a common point. The coordinates of this point denoted in the coordinate systems of either boxes specify the position of the linkage and hence the placement of the boxes related to each other. All boxes in a compound need to be connected, and loose boxes are not allowed. In case a compound made from solid particles migrates to a moveable state, a sphere with the same volume as all boxes in total is generated

solid structures. Later on, it turned out to be advantageous to manage particles in a more flexible way. So a particle is allowed to change its status from solid (*immoveable*) to *moveable* and vice versa by chemical or processing rules. When dissolved away from a solid structure by means of auxiliary substances, a particle becomes moveable and starts to follow the Brownian motion throughout the liquid environment of the hosting vessel. In contrast, a moveable particle can hit a solid structure and sticks to it by chemical binding. Hence, its status migrates from moveable to immoveable. In consequence, each particle comes with the variable attribute whether it is treated to be solid (immoveable) or not. For visualization, we depict immoveable particles by a box and moveable particles by a sphere, whereas a particle keeps its spatial volume when transformed from a box to a sphere or back.

Furthermore, the concept of freely configurable moveable particles enables integration of abstract reaction models within the JENA simulation software typically managed in membrane computing or artificial chemistries. Nucleotides found in strands of deoxyribonucleic acid (DNA) or ribonucleic acid (RNA) or other monomeric units represent typical examples to be captured by particles.

A productive feature of particles is its ability to form *compounds* among each other. To this end, particles can attach and bind to each other. Their boxes or spheres get glued together at the plane and position they touch (see Fig. 5.5c). A linkage between two neighbored particles can be seen as a chemical bond in the broader sense. Since its bond length is implicitly set by the size of either boxes or spheres, we restrict ourselves to parameterize the binding energy if available. Having in mind that the binding energy in solid material like crystal can reach more than the fourfold of those found in ionic bondings, values of $6000 \frac{kJ}{mol}$ or even more express a high stability. This mechanical robustness can guarantee a persistence of solid molecular structures acting as support elements which cannot be destroyed by impacts from colliding atoms, ions, or molecules. However, special enzymes with catalytic activity are capable of breaking those bonds. An arbitrary number of particles might connect to form a compound from boxes or from spheres. All particles subsumed by a compound need to be uniformly marked either to be moveable or to be immoveable in a freely configurable manner. The rules for creation of a compound contain this information.

Compounds made from solid (immoveable) particles can successively emerge by an assembly effect of chemical reactions with colliding constituents. In this way, even growing compounds of solid particles are able to link together to form a common compound containing all particle boxes and linkages from its predecessors, but a (nested) hierarchy of compounds is not managed.

A definition of compounds from solid particles ab initio is supported by the JENA simulation software. This feature can be used among other things for creation of permeable membranes placed in a vessel or for description of filaments or backbone structures. We are aware of the fact that a composition of boxes, all of them placed with the same orientation, merely provides restricted facilities in order to model complex surface structures. Nevertheless, the concept of particles together with their flexibility to toggle between a moveable and immoveable state and equipped with the capability of forming and decomposing compounds is a strong and expressive instrument.

5.2.2   Vessels and Delimiters

We demand chemical reactions and physical processes among atoms, ions, molecules, and particles to take place within a *vessel*. A vessel defines the spatial dimension of a molecular system and confines its constituents from the environment. Generally, a vessel is intended to symbolize a compartment of a biological cell or a test tube for in vitro techniques. We regard a vessel to be a freely configurable box-shaped *cuboid* placed in a three-dimensional Cartesian coordinate system in a way that one of the corners coincides with the point of origin. For simplicity, the cuboid needs to be oriented in parallel to the coordinate axes (see Fig. 5.6a). The size of a vessel (length, width, and height) might vary within a range of few nanometers (10^{-9} m) up to some millimeters (10^{-3} m). Once stipulated, the size of a vessel cannot be modified afterward. The computation time and effort for emulation of system's dynamics typically increase along with ascendingly declared volume of a vessel. When initially set up, the outer walls of a vessel act as barriers impermeable for any constituents and for material but able to apply or to dissipate heat in the form of thermal energy.

The inner space of a vessel might be separated into disjoint nonoverlapping *chambers*. To this end, an arbitrary number of *delimiters* might be placed across a vessel. A delimiter is a barrier exhibited by a plane located in parallel to two of the underlying coordinate system's axes as exemplified in Fig. 5.6b. For implementation, a delimiter consists of an oversized immoveable particle ranging throughout the whole dimension of the vessel. Technically, the delimiter particle

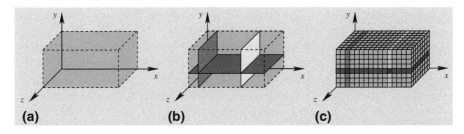

(a)   **(b)**   **(c)**

Fig. 5.6 (**a**) Definition of a vessel as a freely configurable cuboid placed in a three-dimensional Cartesian coordinate system oriented in parallel to the coordinate axes. One of the cuboid's corners coincides with the point of origin. (**b**) Placement of delimiters in order to separate a vessel into disjoint chambers. Three delimiters, each of them forming a plane in parallel to a plane spanned by two of the coordinate system axes, divide the vessel into six box-shaped chambers with different volumes. A delimiter is made from an oversized immoveable particle. (**c**) Representation of a vessel by means of voxels, a three-dimensional grid pattern of small cube-shaped volume elements discretizing the space inside the vessel. Some voxels are occupied by parts of the delimiters

comes with a local coordinate system whose point of origin maps to a point within the coordinate system of the vessel. This point called anchor point marks the position of the delimiter. The main advantage of delimiters lies in their flexible nature when acting over time. At arbitrary points in time during simulation or in consequence of predefined conditions, a delimiter can be created inside or removed from a vessel. This feature allows definition of separate reaction chambers with initially different reaction conditions to get unified after certain product molecules have been appeared which in turn can further assemble in progress.

For technical modelling of a vessel with its constituting atoms, ions, molecules, moveable and immoveable particles, and delimiters, we consider a vessel to be composed of a plethora of small *volume elements*, so-called *voxels* illustrated in Fig. 5.6c. A voxel is a small virtual cube whose side length is set per default to 500 pm but can be freely configured with a fixed value according to the needs of the system under study. The voxels represent the smallest distinguishable locations and positions within a vessel. A voxel is either occupied by one or several atoms, ions, molecules, moveable particles on the one hand, or it is captured by an immoveable particle, a part of an immoveable particle, or a part of a delimiter. The voxels determine the underlying spatial granularity of the molecular system under study since they form a three-dimensional lattice for placement and positioning of all system's constituents at any points in time. The resulting *discretization of space* enables a more efficient algorithmic handling of simulation issues.

Having the grid pattern of the voxels for the whole vessel available, all delimiters and immoveable particles can be set. To do so, the corresponding voxels have been estimated and marked as occupied. During this preprocessing step, a huge data structure emerges containing all voxels. For each voxel, its spatial position together with the information whether it is empty or occupied and in case of occupied, by which immoveable particle or delimiter, need to be figured out. A vessel can be composed of up to several hundred million voxels which implies a notable computation time. The next preprocessing step is dedicated to identification of the individual chambers within the vessel. For this purpose, we utilize the *method of growing bubbles*. Out of many randomly selected spatially distributed starting voxels marked as empty, we let bubbles grow by taking into account all neighbors of each starting voxel. If also marked as empty, they belong to the same chamber. As soon as two growing bubbles start to intersect, they become unified and marked to be part of the same chamber as well. Please note that permeable membranes composed of immoveable particles and exhibiting holes, channels, or pores do not separate distinct chambers. Instead, these membranes have been interpreted as solid structures residing inside a chamber. After the first preprocessing step is done, all chambers should have been identified by the containing empty voxels. For each chamber s, its spatial volume V_s is obtained by counting the number of containing voxels. The knowledge about the underlying volume of a chamber plays an important role for filling in with atoms, ions, molecules, and moveable particles.

For each vessel, its initial *temperature T* needs to be set. The temperature subsumes the average kinetic energy of all moveable particles, molecules, ions, and atoms residing in the vessel. Hence, their velocities of motion are strongly influenced by the temperature. The initial value of temperature can be freely configured either at a Kelvin scale (K) or by degrees centigrade (°C) having in mind that $0K = -273.15°C$ which characterizes the absolute zero point of the smallest possible temperature. Setting this or even lower temperatures is permitted since the motion of moveable constituents gets stopped then. The user is responsible to select a temperature that causes a liquid state of aggregation inside the vessel.

Now, the initial placement of atoms, ions, molecules, and moveable particles into the chambers of the vessel can be done by the JENA tool. To this end, the user specifies for each sort of atoms, ions, molecules, and moveable particles their initial *abundance n* (number of copies) or, alternatively, their initial *concentration c*. The abundance can be given by the absolute number of copies, but it can also be set by mol having in mind that 1mol stands for $6.02214076 \cdot 10^{23}$ molecules or moveable particles expressed by Avogadro's constant. Let A be the identifier of an unbound atom, unbound ion, molecule, or moveable particle available in n_A copies. A is called a *species*. Its concentration c_A, also denoted as $[A]$, is defined by

$$c_A = [A] = \frac{n_A}{V_s} \tag{5.5}$$

whereas V_s indicates the volume of the hosting chamber inside the vessel. Since the volume of each chamber is finite, there exists a maximal abundance and hence a maximal concentration for each species which cannot be exceeded in order to guarantee movability in terms of a liquid.

For each species initially present in the vessel, the user specifies the *"point of injection"* by x, y, and z coordinates of the vessel's coordinate system located inside the vessel. The point of injection identifies a certain chamber. In case that no chambers exist, the point of injection has no meaning. The desired number of copies for the species is then generated and homogeneously distributed in approximated spatial equipartition inside the chamber (or inside the whole vessel if no chambers have been declared). The placement results in marking corresponding voxels to be occupied by an exemplar of the species. The initial placement is separately done for all species defined by the user.

Now, the contents of each chamber is automatically complemented by additional *water molecules*. In a liquid, the average distance of adjacent unbound atoms, unbound ions, molecules, and moveable particles should be in the magnitude of their size. This density assures the properties of a liquid like flexibility in shape and almost no compressibility. Water molecules get added until the final density is reached. Eventually, a number of voxels is marked to be occupied by water molecules. The number of inserted water molecules might vary across the chambers subject to their enrichment with species. In the unlikely case of an overdensed species concentration in which no water molecules can be added, the JENA tool produces an error message and stops further processing.

Before the *Brownian motion* can start, an individual direction of movement and a speed have to be assigned to each unbound atom, unbound ion, molecule, and moveable particle including all water molecules. This is done by a *speed vector* at time $t = 0$ denoted $\mathbf{v}(0) = (v_x(0), v_y(0), v_z(0))$ and attached to each exemplar of each species and to all water molecules. The direction of movement has been randomly chosen by two angles interpreted as spherical coordinates (latitude α with $0 \leq \alpha \leq \pi$ and longitude β with $0 \leq \beta \leq 2\pi$, respectively).

According to the laws of thermodynamics, the *absolute speed values* $|\mathbf{v}|$ for each unbound atom, unbound ion, molecule, and moveable particle of the same species follow the *Maxwell-Boltzmann distribution* valid for gases and liquids and described by the probability density function

$$
\mathrm{p}(|\mathbf{v}|) = 4 \cdot \pi \cdot \left(\frac{m}{2 \cdot \pi \cdot k_B \cdot T} \right)^{\frac{3}{2}} \cdot |\mathbf{v}|^2 \cdot e^{-\frac{m \cdot |\mathbf{v}|^2}{2 \cdot k_B \cdot T}} \tag{5.6}
$$

in which m represents the individual mass, T the Kelvin temperature, and $k_B = 1.380649 \cdot 10^{-23} \frac{\mathrm{J}}{\mathrm{K}}$ the Boltzmann constant. $\mathrm{p}(|\mathbf{v}|)$ provides the probability of the absolute speed value $|\mathbf{v}|$ for an unbound atom, unbound ion, molecule, or moveable particle with mass m at temperature T (see Fig. 5.7).

The Maxwell-Boltzmann distribution turns out to be asymmetric stating that very few exemplars of a species have a very low speed, most exemplars a low up to medium speed, and some exemplars a high or very high speed. Typically, the average speed constitutes several hundred meters per second. The Maxwell-Boltzmann distribution is based on the observation that molecules sharing the same kinetic energy $E_{\mathrm{kin}} = \frac{m}{2} \cdot |\mathbf{v}|^2$ and hence having the same mass m and the same speed value $|\mathbf{v}|$ arrange when ascendingly sorted by speed to form a spherical orbital with radius $|\mathbf{v}|$ whose spherical surface $4 \cdot \pi \cdot |\mathbf{v}|^2$ gets filled.

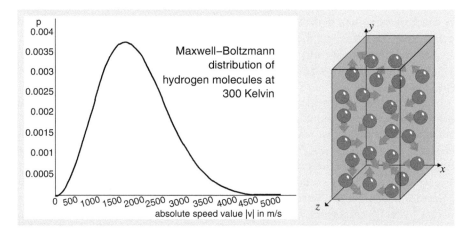

Fig. 5.7 Maxwell-Boltzmann distribution $\mathrm{p}(|\mathbf{v}|)$ of hydrogen molecules (H_2) at temperature $T = 300\mathrm{K}$ revealing the portion of molecules with absolute speed value $|\mathbf{v}|$ from 0 to 5000 $\frac{\mathrm{m}}{\mathrm{s}}$. The directions of movement for the molecules are randomly set within a homogeneous environment. A resulting individual speed vector at time $t = 0$ denoted $\mathbf{v}(0) = (v_x(0), v_y(0), v_z(0))$ has been assigned to each molecule present in the vessel

For each unbound atom, unbound ion, molecule, and moveable particle present in the vessel, we randomly assign an absolute speed value $|\mathbf{v}|$ in a way that the Maxwell-Boltzmann distribution is held over all exemplars of each species. Now, all individual speed vectors $\mathbf{v}(0)$ at time $t = 0$ can be obtained by

$$\mathbf{v}(0) = \begin{pmatrix} v_x(0) \\ v_y(0) \\ v_z(0) \end{pmatrix} = \begin{pmatrix} |\mathbf{v}| \cdot \sin(\alpha) \cdot \sin(\beta) \\ |\mathbf{v}| \cdot \cos(\alpha) \\ |\mathbf{v}| \cdot \sin(\alpha) \cdot \cos(\beta) \end{pmatrix} \tag{5.7}$$

After having all speed vectors initialized, the molecular system is ready to start simulation of Brownian motion and observation of the interactions among system's constituents. For all speed vectors at any point in time t including $t = 0$, the law $|\mathbf{v}| = |\mathbf{v}(t)| = \sqrt{v_x(t)^2 + v_y(t)^2 + v_z(t)^2}$ is valid disclosing the relation between the absolute value of speed and the corresponding vector components.

5.2.3   Brownian Motion and Thermodynamics

Each unbound atom, unbound ion, molecule, and moveable particle present in the vessel and its chambers is equipped with two individual vectors. The *position vector* $\mathbf{x} = (x, y, z)$ records the current position in the vessel expressed by its coordinates. In addition, the *speed vector* $\mathbf{v} = (v_x, v_y, v_z)$ determines the direction and the velocity of movement within the vessel.

For simulation of *Brownian motion*, we discretize the course of time into equidistant *time steps* symbolized by Δt. The duration of every time step is globally set for the whole molecular system inside the vessel under study. Since the *voxels* represent the smallest distinguishable unit of space and spatial position, the time step should be configured in a way that most of the moveable system's constituents migrate from their current voxel to another one in order to bridge a measurable distance. Taking this requirement into account, the time step Δt typically ranges between 1 ns (10^{-9}s) and several μs (10^{-6}s) and can be freely configured whereas 50 ns have been set as default.

Now, the update scheme can be formulated. To this end, we consider the position vector $\mathbf{x}$ and the speed vector $\mathbf{v}$ as functions over time t whose initial values at $t = 0$ have been given. Assuming a uniform motion, the update of each position vector by pure Brownian motion reads as follows:

$$\mathbf{x}(t + \Delta t) = \mathbf{x}(t) + \Delta t \cdot \mathbf{v}(t) = \begin{pmatrix} x(t) + \Delta t \cdot v_x(t) \\ y(t) + \Delta t \cdot v_y(t) \\ z(t) + \Delta t \cdot v_z(t) \end{pmatrix} \tag{5.8}$$

Furthermore, the new position of electrically charged ions, molecules, and moveable particles has been influenced by *Coulomb forces* induced by other electrically charged constituents. Additionally, explicitly defined external electrical and/or mechanical forces will also have an effect on the updated position. Since an arbitrary *force* expressed by a vector $\mathbf{F}$ causes an acceleration $\mathbf{a} = -\frac{1}{m} \cdot \mathbf{F}$ of the moveable constituent with mass m in case of *attractive* forces and $\mathbf{a} = \frac{1}{m} \cdot \mathbf{F}$ in case of *repulsive* ones, an increment $\Delta \mathbf{x} = \frac{1}{2} \cdot (\Delta t)^2 \cdot \mathbf{a}$ is made to the position with respect to each relevant source of force present in the system adjusting the new position by $\mathbf{x}(t + \Delta t) = \mathbf{x}(t) + \Delta t \cdot \mathbf{v}(t) + \sum(\Delta \mathbf{x})$. Since an acceleration $\mathbf{a}$ caused by a force $\mathbf{F}$ also affects the velocity of moveable constituents, their speed vectors necessitate an update as well which is done by $\mathbf{v}(t + \Delta t) = \mathbf{v}(t) + \Delta t \cdot \mathbf{a}$. The modification of speed can also mean a slowdown in case of $\mathbf{a}$ is directed oppositely or nearly oppositely in comparison to $\mathbf{v}$.

The new position $\mathbf{x}(t + \Delta t)$ of each unbound atom, unbound ion, molecule, and moveable particle should result in a new voxel defined within the space of the underlying vessel. Successively, each moveable constituent gets removed from its previous voxel and attached to the new one according to the new position.

In rare cases, it might happen that a moveable constituent located near an outer wall of the vessel gets an updated position outside the vessel which is impermissible. Here, the closest voxel inside the vessel needs to be identified, and the position vector $\mathbf{x}(t)$ is set to these coordinates. Then, a *reflection* at the wall of collision will be done. To do so, the speed vector becomes modified for the next time steps. Reflection at a wall in parallel to the plane spanned by the x and z axes results in $v_y(t + \Delta t) = -v_y(t)$. Respectively, a reflection at a wall in parallel to the plane spanned by the x and y axes implies $v_z(t + \Delta t) = -v_z(t)$, and finally, a reflection at a wall in parallel to the plane spanned by the y and z axes leads to $v_x(t + \Delta t) = -v_x(t)$.

Beyond reflection at an outer wall, the new position $\mathbf{x}(t + \Delta t)$ of each moveable constituent might identify voxels whose state decides about different scenarios. The simplest case is a previously empty voxel. Here, the unbound atom, unbound ion, molecule, or moveable particle occupies the empty voxel and that's it. The situation becomes more complicated if the new voxel has been already marked by other system's constituents residing there and is not empty. This indicates a *collision*.

The new voxel might be occupied by a part of a delimiter or by a part of a solid (immoveable) particle the considered moveable constituent collided with. The subsequent collision behavior depends on the existence (presence or absence) of a *chemical reaction rule* mentioning all collision partners as substrates. If no matching reaction rule is defined, the collision is treated as a *reflection*. The colliding moveable constituent rebounds from the solid structure. This is done by an update of moveable constituent's speed vector in the same way like a reflection at an outer wall. Solid structures inside a vessel are always assumed to be oriented in parallel to the vessel's coordinate system axes.

The presence of a matching reaction rule leads to evaluation whether or not a reaction occurs. To this end, the *kinetic energy* of the collided moveable constituent with mass m is obtained by $E_{kin} = \frac{m}{2} \cdot |\mathbf{v}(t)|^2$. Each reaction rule comes with a predefined *activation energy* E_a necessary to conduct the reaction. So it is checked whether or not $E_{kin} \geq E_a$. If not, the amount of energy is too low to run the reaction, and the scenario results again in a reflection as described before. In case the kinetic energy reaches or exceeds the required activation energy, the reaction occurs as defined in the reaction rule. There are three options: (1) The moveable constituent could be *absorbed* by the solid structure becoming a part of it. Therefore, the moveable constituent gets fixed at its position and marked to be immoveable from now on. Its speed vector is set to the zero vector and deleted. Neighbored voxels might be marked as occupied as well since the solid structure has grown. (2) Alternatively, a reaction rule can instruct a behavior in which the solid (immoveable) particle at the position of collision gets *knocked out* from its solid structure becoming moveable from now on. A new random speed vector is created for this new moveable constituent in accordance with the Maxwell-Boltzmann distribution as described before. The moveable constituent that initiated the collision on its own undergoes a reflection by corresponding update of its speed vector. (3) The moveable constituent could be *transformed* into other unbound atoms, unbound ions, molecules, or moveable particles leaving intact the solid structure collided with. Here, the solid structure acts as a kind of catalyst. All resulting new moveable constituents need to be initialized with speed vectors randomly equipped with direction and absolute speed value coinciding with the Maxwell-Boltzmann distribution. Cases (2) and (3) can be combined by knocking out a part of the solid structure and getting transformed despite this (Fig. 5.8).

A collision can exclusively involve moveable constituents. This becomes apparent if and only if the corresponding voxel is marked by several moveable constituents which in turn have to be assumed to collide as a whole.

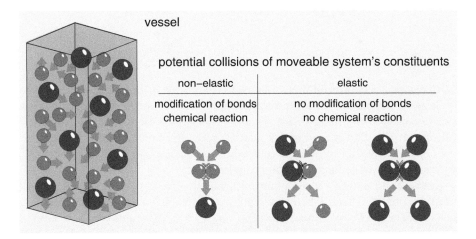

Fig. 5.8 Illustration of elastic and nonelastic collisions that might occur among moveable constituents of a vessel or a chamber. Elastic collisions keep the total kinetic energy following the conservation of momentum. The constituents stay intact but change their speed and direction of movement. A nonelastic collision indicates a chemical reaction in which the inner structure of constituents gets modified by breaking and/or creation of chemical bonds. Resulting reaction products emerge as new moveable constituents and start their Brownian motion

In principle, the number of moveable constituents colliding with each other and placed within the same new voxel could be arbitrarily high. In practice, most of the molecular collisions take place with two objects. Seldomly, three or four objects hit to each other. Collisions with a larger number of objects than four are practically impossible. In accordance with the rules of thermodynamics and molecular mechanics, a collision might exhibit either an *elastic* or a *nonelastic* behavior. In order to decide about this, the total kinetic energy of all constituents involved in the collision has to be calculated based on their masses and speed vectors. One constituent with mass m and speed vector $\mathbf{v}(t)$ contributes a portion of $E_{\text{kin}} = \frac{1}{2} \cdot m \cdot |\mathbf{v}(t)|^2$ to the total kinetic energy $E_{\text{kin\_total}} = \sum E_{\text{kin}}$.

In case there is no chemical reaction rule defined having all collided constituents as substrates or the total kinetic energy is lower than the activation energy E_{a} of a matching chemical reaction ($E_{\text{kin\_total}} < E_{\text{a}}$), the collision is treated to be *elastic*. Here, the *momentum conservation* holds which means that all kinetic energy from the colliding constituents is kept forming the kinetic energy of the same constituents after collision spreading out in different directions with different velocities. More or less, all colliding constituents reflect to each other, and they stay intact without modification of their inner structure or mass. Moreover, we assume for simplicity that each elastic collision is carried out in a *central* manner in which the spheres hit to each other in a way that both radiuses at the point of collision form a common line. Let us consider two elastically colliding constituents called i and k with their masses m_i and m_k and with their speed vectors $\mathbf{v}_i(t)$ and $\mathbf{v}_k(t)$, respectively. The elastic collision results in updated speed vectors by the scheme:

$$\mathbf{v}_i(t + \Delta t) = \frac{m_i - m_k}{m_i + m_k} \cdot \mathbf{v}_i(t) + \frac{2 \cdot m_k}{m_i + m_k} \cdot \mathbf{v}_k(t) \qquad (5.9)$$

$$\mathbf{v}_k(t + \Delta t) = \frac{m_k - m_i}{m_i + m_k} \cdot \mathbf{v}_k(t) + \frac{2 \cdot m_i}{m_i + m_k} \cdot \mathbf{v}_i(t)$$

An elastic collision with more than two constituents is divided into a sequence of elastic collisions with two constituents each. Let us assume for illustration a collision of three objects named A, B, and C. This scenario is split into an elastic collision A with B, a second one B with C, and a third one A with C. In case of four objects elastically colliding to each other, a sequence of six collisions with two objects each has to be figured out and handled.

Whenever a chemical reaction rule exists mentioning all collided constituents as substrates and their total kinetic energy $E_{\text{kin\_total}}$ reaches or exceeds the required activation energy E_{a} of the reaction ($E_{\text{kin\_total}} \geq E_{\text{a}}$), the reaction will be carried out as described in the reaction rule. A part of the total kinetic energy is used to break chemical bonds and/or to create new chemical bonds transforming the substrates into reaction products, and the momentum conservation is not valid any more. Instead, the collision is treated to be *nonelastic*. Let i and k be two collided constituents with masses m_i and m_k and speed vectors $\mathbf{v}_i(t)$ and $\mathbf{v}_k(t)$ binding to each other and forming the reaction product p (due to a reaction rule of the form

$i + k \longrightarrow p$). We obtain the following scheme for the mass m_p and for the speed vector $\mathbf{v}_p(t + \Delta t)$ having in mind that the previous constituents i and k do not exist anymore after nonelastic collision:

$$m_p = m_i + m_k \tag{5.10}$$

$$\mathbf{v}_p(t + \Delta t) = \frac{m_i}{m_i + m_k} \cdot \mathbf{v}_i(t) + \frac{m_k}{m_i + m_k} \cdot \mathbf{v}_k(t)$$

A nonelastic collision is called *effective* because of conduction of a chemical reaction.

A chemical reaction might have more than two substrates colliding to each other. Let A, B, and C again be identifiers of constituents. A reaction rule of the form $A + A + B \longrightarrow C$ or $A + B + C \longrightarrow ABC$ identifies three substrates. Reactions with four substrates can also occur while more than four substrates are unrealistic. For treatment of nonelastic collisions in chemical reactions with more than two substrates, we split the corresponding reaction rule into a sequence of reaction rules, each with two substrates. A reaction of the form $A + B + C \longrightarrow ABC$ is split into $A + B \longrightarrow AB$ and $AB + C \longrightarrow ABC$. In case of a reaction with more than one reaction product, we also split the reaction in a number of reactions, one for each reaction product. Let us add D and E as substances acting as reaction products in a reaction $A + B \longrightarrow D + E$. We consider two separate partial reactions $A + B \longrightarrow D$ and $A + B \longrightarrow E$ instead, whereas $m_A + m_B = m_D + m_E$. More complex reactions will be split accordingly like $A + B + C \longrightarrow D + E$ which results in three partial reactions $A + B \longrightarrow AB$, $AB + C \longrightarrow D$, and $AB + C \longrightarrow E$, respectively.

5.2.4   Chemical Reactions by Effective Collisions and by Spontaneous Decay

Chemical reactions have in common that at least one chemical bond or ionic bonding among involved substances becomes modified in order to generate new connection structures between atoms and/or ions. *Substances* are transformed into *reaction products* by means of a chemical reaction. According to the Billiard model of Brownian motion, containing constituents like unbound atoms, unbound ions, molecules, and particles present within the vessel can collide with each other. Whenever a collision occurs, all colliding constituents form the substances for a potential reaction.

Breaking an existing chemical bond or ionic bonding as well as creation of a new bond consumes energy which in turn is provided by the kinetic energy of the collided constituents. The amount of energy necessary to trigger a chemical reaction is called *activation energy* E_a. Each combination of substances able to react with each other defines a chemical reaction with an individual activation energy. Typically, the mandatory activation energy of a chemical reaction ranges between approximately $30 \frac{kJ}{mol}$ and $100 \frac{kJ}{mol}$. Biochemical reactions often share an activation energy around 67 $\frac{kJ}{mol}$. It becomes apparent that the activation energy is commonly much lower than the binding energy among atoms or ions. Since the binding energy is defined as the amount of energy needed to break the bond, the question arises why an activation energy of around 25% of the binding energy or even less suffices. The answer lies in the nature of an electron pair representing a bond. Argued in a simplified way, the electron pair can migrate to the position of a newly generated chemical bond staying intact. Other unpaired electrons fill the gap vice versa. So the rearrangement and modification of a chemical bond might happen with a low activation energy. The situation becomes different in case of a chemical bond to be broken without generation of a new bond at another position inside the molecule. Here, the activation energy turns out to be higher and equals the binding energy of the affected bond.

Whenever the total kinetic energy of colliding substrate constituents reaches or exceeds the activation energy, the collision is said to be *effective*, and the chemical reaction occurs transforming the substrates into reaction products. Thermodynamically, a nonelastic collision is made. Directions of movement and speed vectors of reaction products result from that. The same chemical reaction can simultaneously take place at different locations inside the vessel since the substrate constituents might collide independently from each other. Typically, at the beginning of the time course, a chemical reaction runs quite intensely because of many effective collisions inside the vessel or chamber. Gradually, the number of reactive substrate constituents decreases while more and more reaction products are available. Over time, many reactions become weaker and weaker since less and less substrate constituents effectively collide.

We denote a chemical reaction by a *reaction rule* mentioning the identifiers of involved substrate constituents and the identifiers of resulting reaction products together with the activation energy of the reaction. All substrate constituents and reaction products need to be predefined as atoms, ions, molecules, or particles in the JENA tool. A reaction rule refers to their identifiers. For instance, a reaction rule of the form $A + A + B \longrightarrow C + D$ with $E_a = x$ involves the substrate constituents A and B generating reaction products C and D consuming x units of activation energy. Two exemplars A and one exemplar B need to effectively collide in order to produce one exemplar C and one exemplar D. A multiplicity of exemplars from the same constituent can be expressed by a so-called *stoichiometric factor*, here two exemplars of A. Using stoichiometric factors, the reaction rule reads $2A + B \longrightarrow C + D$; $E_a = x$. Exclusively natural numbers act as stoichiometric factors, whereas 0 is permitted indicating that the corresponding species is not needed and not involved. A stoichiometric factor 1 needs not to be written explicitly.

Now, we can introduce a general scheme in order to capture all chemical reactions defined in a vessel or chamber. Let us assume S_1 to S_p be the identifiers of all atoms, ions, molecules, and particles present or expected to appear, and let the optional coordinates (x_k, y_k, z_k) mark a position in the vessel's coordinate system to identify the corresponding chamber within the vessel where reaction k is defined. The scheme of reaction rules has the form

$$(x_1, y_1, z_1): a_{1,1}S_1 + a_{2,1}S_2 + \ldots + a_{p,1}S_p \longrightarrow b_{1,1}S_1 + \ldots + b_{p,1}S_p; \quad E_{a,1}$$

$$(x_2, y_2, z_2): a_{1,2}S_1 + a_{2,2}S_2 + \ldots + a_{p,2}S_p \longrightarrow b_{1,2}S_1 + \ldots + b_{p,2}S_p; \quad E_{a,2}$$

$$\vdots$$

$$(x_r, y_r, z_r): a_{1,r}S_1 + a_{2,r}S_2 + \ldots + a_{p,r}S_p \longrightarrow b_{1,r}S_1 + \ldots + b_{p,r}S_p; \quad E_{a,r}$$

in which p is the number of distinct species, r the number of reactions (number of reaction rules), $a_{i,k} \in \mathbb{N}$ with $i = 1, \ldots, p$ and $k = 1, \ldots, r$ the stoichiometric factors of the substrate constituents, and $b_{i,k} \in \mathbb{N}$ with $i = 1, \ldots, p$ and $k = 1, \ldots, r$ the stoichiometric factors of the reaction products. Each reaction rule comes with an individual activation energy $E_{a,k}$ with $k = 1, \ldots, r$.

Each chemical reaction follows the law of *mass conservation*. The total mass of all substrate constituents exactly coincides with the total mass of the resulting reaction products. Having a reaction rule $a_{1,k}S_1 + a_{2,k}S_2 + \ldots + a_{p,k}S_p \longrightarrow b_{1,k}S_1 + b_{2,k}S_2 + \ldots + b_{p,k}S_p; \quad E_{a,k}$ at hand, it holds:

$$\sum_{i=1}^{p} (a_{i,k} \cdot m_{S_i}) = \sum_{i=1}^{p} (b_{i,k} \cdot m_{S_i}) \qquad \forall k = 1, \ldots, r \tag{5.11}$$

The law of mass conservation emerges from the observation that atoms and ions forming substrate constituents and reaction products stay intact. Merely, their spatial arrangement and their bonds to each other can change by chemical reactions. That's why no mass gets lost, and no additional mass can appear.

A crucial parameter that controls the course of a chemical reaction is *temperature*. The Kelvin temperature T inside a vessel and its chambers results from the *average kinetic energy* $\overline{E_{kin}}$ of all unbound atoms, unbound ions, molecules, and moveable particles. The thermodynamical law $\overline{E_{kin}} = \frac{3}{2} \cdot k_B \cdot T$ with the Boltzmann constant $k_B = 1.380649 \cdot 10^{-23} \frac{J}{K}$ expresses this relation. The higher the temperature, the faster the chemical reactions run due to a higher speed of the moveable constituents which leads to a larger number of effective collisions per time step. When increasing the environmental temperature by 10 K, the affected chemical reactions commonly get accelerated two- until threefold. The current temperature T is calculated based on the speed vectors of all moveable constituents present in the vessel.

It might happen that the temperature inside a vessel is too low in order to enable a chemical reaction defined as reaction rule, especially in case of a high activation energy. There are two strategies for operating those reactions: (1) Utilization of a *catalyst* able to significantly drop the activation energy. The catalyst, mostly an enzyme (protein molecule), acts as an additional substrate, promotes the interplay of other substrates, and finally emerges unchanged from the reaction. Particularly, in biochemical reactions, catalysts are the first choice to accelerate a reaction. (2) Increase of temperature by heating. In this way, further energy is transmitted to the reaction system which in turn leads to a higher average speed of its moveable constituents, and hence, a higher reactivity is obtained. Biomolecules are often prone to higher temperatures since they tend to lose their spatial structure by degradation. Many biomolecules fail to be robust against temperatures greater than approximately 40°C.

Interestingly, the course of a chemical reaction might either consume or release thermal energy that implies a modification of the temperature inside the vessel. The reason for that is based on the *endothermic* or *exothermic* nature of a chemical reaction. The chemical bonds and ionic bondings in the substrate molecules store an amount of *inner energy*. Whenever the outermost orbital of an atom is completely filled with electrons by incorporation of electron pairs, it is said to be saturated, and its inner energy reaches a minimum value. In contrast, unsaturated atoms possess more inner energy necessary to maintain this configuration. Each chemical reaction starts with a certain level of the total inner energy of all involved substrates. In order to initiate a reaction, the barrier set by the activation energy has to be overcome. Eventually, the total inner energy of the reaction products might deviate from those of the substrates (see Fig. 5.9). In case it becomes higher, the reaction permanently consumes energy. Thermal energy needs to be applied continuously to keep alive the reaction which is called endothermic. Contrarily, the total inner energy of the reaction products can be lower than the substrates. Here, thermal energy is released into the environment, and the reaction runs autonomously. It is called to be exothermic.

What stands out is that the temperature inside a vessel can change while chemical reactions take place. Sometimes, heating or cooling is required in order to control the temperature. To this end, we establish a *temperature management* in the JENA tool. At arbitrary points in time, a freely configurable temperature can be set by *instruction*, or the current temperature can be incremented or decremented. A

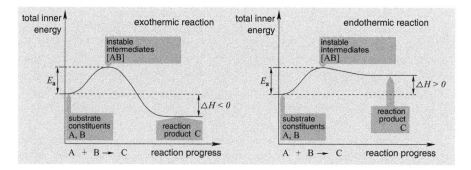

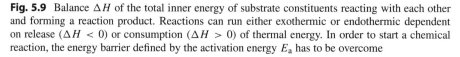

Fig. 5.9 Balance ΔH of the total inner energy of substrate constituents reacting with each other and forming a reaction product. Reactions can run either exothermic or endothermic dependent on release ($\Delta H < 0$) or consumption ($\Delta H > 0$) of thermal energy. In order to start a chemical reaction, the energy barrier defined by the activation energy E_a has to be overcome

change of temperature will affect the speed vectors of all moveable constituents in the vessel. Their absolute speed values undergo an update in conformity with the Maxwell-Boltzmann distribution. Since many moveable constituents have to be taken into account, a temperature update might consume some computation time for simulation.

Our implementation combines the Billiard model of thermodynamics with the characteristics of chemical reactions and reaction kinetics at a fine-grained level of abstraction. We neglect possible effects of the spatial orientation of colliding substrate constituents. There are a number of reactions especially in biochemistry in which the orientation of colliding molecules matters to decide whether or not they react. Except from this feature, we are able to reconstruct abstract reaction parameters like rate constants and Arrhenius terms from the simulation of a reaction system over time. Abstract reaction parameters can be used in mass-action kinetics, and they are a part of ordinary differential equations approximating the time course of species concentrations.

Particles handled in the reaction system have been marked either to be moveable or solid (immoveable). This attribute can be used when formulating reaction rules. Each substrate constituent or reaction product representing a particle might be freely configurable attached in reaction rules with the superscript symbol "m" for moveable or "s" for solid (immoveable) to express the corresponding behavior. Let, for instance, P be the identifier of a particle. A reaction rule $P^s + A \longrightarrow P^m + A$ describes the knocking out of a particle from a solid structure with the help of a catalyst molecule A. It selects immoveable particles P ignoring moveable exemplars. We are aware of the fact that status transformations between moveable and solid change the overall mass of the moveable constituents in the vessel which can slightly affect the average kinetic energy and hence the temperature.

The number of reaction rules defined in a vessel or chamber is not limited. It might happen that the same or a subset combination of substrate constituents is specified in several reaction rules. These rules compete with each other when detecting a corresponding collision. An example is given by the rules $A + B \longrightarrow C + D$ and $A + B \longrightarrow E$. In case of a collision between A and B, the decision must be made which of the matching reaction rules will be applied. To this end, we evaluate the individual activation energies $E_{a,k}$ attached to each reaction rule k. Based on the activation energy, we determine the *simplified Arrhenius equation* by the term $e^{-\frac{E_{a,k}}{R \cdot T}}$ with the universal gas constant $R = 8.314462618 \, \frac{\text{kg·m}^2}{\text{s}^2 \cdot \text{mol·K}}$ and the Kelvin temperature T. The portion of this term in relation to the sum of the terms from all competing reaction rules determines a *probability* used for a *weighted random selection* of the reaction rule to be applied.

There is a special class of chemical reactions called *spontaneous decay*. They have in common that merely one substrate constituent is specified which is typically decomposed into several reaction products. For instance, a reaction rule of the form $A \longrightarrow B + C$ stands for a spontaneous decay of A producing its components B and C. A characteristic feature of a spontaneous decay is the absence of any effective collision. This makes the technical handling within a Billiard model more complicated since the points in time have to be estimated in which an exemplar of the species to decay will "spontaneously" react without any collision partner. For this purpose, we consult the activation energy $E_{a,k}$ of the spontaneous decay's reaction rule k. By means of the term $[A] \cdot e^{-\frac{E_{a,k}}{R \cdot T}} \cdot \Delta t$ whereas $[A]$ is the concentration of the species A to decay in the chamber or vessel, we obtain an index measure of the decay velocity indicating how many individual decays of A need to take place within the vessel or chamber in the current time step Δt. Then, the exemplars of A to decay are chosen randomly and treated according to the spontaneous decay's reaction rule. The implementation of spontaneous decay is geared to the time-discretized law of mass-action reaction kinetics.

5.2.5   Applying External Forces

Beyond chemical reactions, *physical processes* play a major role for modelling and simulation of principles for biological information processing. In this context, physical processes become manifest in exposure to *external forces* affecting a vessel and its constituents. We distinguish two kinds of external forces, namely, *mechanical* and *electrical* ones. External forces in general influence the movement of moveable constituents whereas both properties—direction and speed—might undergo a variation. Chemical bonds and ionic bondings remain unchanged by the effect of external forces. Instead, external forces aim to harmonize or to control the movement of individual unbound atoms, unbound ions, molecules, and moveable particles present in the vessel. Their Brownian motion starts to interfere with the directed acceleration induced by the sum of all external forces taken into account. In consequence, the disordered motion of moveable constituents gets gradually replaced by a regular *flow* or *stream* throughout the chambers of a vessel. This physical process can be organized in a way that a successive *spatial separation* of moveable constituents by their mass or by their electric charge is made which in turn is the basis for a plethora of biological methods and laboratory techniques. Not seldom, chemical reactions and external forces act together, for instance, by release of reaction products or by bringing together suitably selected substrate constituents. For application of external forces, we consider the vessel with its coordinate system as a whole without any distinction of chambers. In other words, external forces have been understood to represent *global quantities* the entire reaction system with all of its chambers is faced with.

For modelling of external forces, we employ the technique of *vector fields*. A vector field assigns each voxel (x, y, z). The vessel is composed of a *force vector* $\mathbf{F}$ whose direction and value can be dynamically configured by means of a mathematical term. Beyond the position (x, y, z) within the vessel, each individual vector symbolizing an external force within the field might be dependent on the current point in time t. Altogether, the vector field for an arbitrary external force has the general form

$$F(x, y, z, t) = \begin{pmatrix} F_x(x, y, z, t) \\ F_y(x, y, z, t) \\ F_z(x, y, z, t) \end{pmatrix} \tag{5.12}$$

whereas the components F_x, F_y, and F_z express the portions of the force applied in x, y, and z-dimension, respectively. The absolute value arises from:

$$|F(x, y, z, t)| = \sqrt{F_x(x, y, z, t)^2 + F_y(x, y, z, t)^2 + F_z(x, y, z, t)^2}$$

A force $F(x, y, z, t)$ present at the position (x, y, z) at the point in time t accelerates each moveable constituent with mass m residing at (x, y, z) by $a = \frac{1}{m} \cdot F(x, y, z, t)$ which influences the corresponding speed vector by the increment $\Delta t \cdot a$, whereas the effects of all external forces vectorially sum up.

Mechanical External Forces
Mechanical external forces have an effect on all kinds of moveable constituents by affecting the movement of unbound atoms, unbound ions, molecules, and moveable particles. Mechanical external forces define a three-dimensional force field which incorporates the space of the whole vessel under study. Application of *pressure* or mechanical power like *stirring*, *pumping*, or *vortexing* are typical causes for generation of mechanical external forces.

Let us illustrate a force field that emerges from a constant pressure applied to the liquid in the vessel. Pressure p is defined to express the quantity of force $|F|$ vertically affecting an area A which becomes apparent by the equation $p = \frac{|F|}{A}$. The area A can be specified as a *plane* placed in the three-dimensional coordinate system of the vessel. For instance, the arbitrarily chosen implicit equation $3 \cdot x - 4 \cdot y + 2 \cdot z = 5$ stands for a plane oriented in an inclined manner (see Fig. 5.10a). Its normal vector $n = (3, -4, 2)$ with $|n| = \sqrt{3^2 + (-4)^2 + 2^2} = \sqrt{29}$ determines the direction of vertically impacting force vectors. Let $f > 0$ be the constant intensity of force. The resulting force field reads:

$$F(x, y, z, t) = \frac{f}{\sqrt{3} \cdot |n|} \cdot n = \begin{pmatrix} \frac{f}{\sqrt{3} \cdot \sqrt{29}} \cdot 3 \\ \frac{f}{\sqrt{3} \cdot \sqrt{29}} \cdot (-4) \\ \frac{f}{\sqrt{3} \cdot \sqrt{29}} \cdot 2 \end{pmatrix} \tag{5.13}$$

The force field turns out to be *constant* throughout the entire vessel (Fig. 5.10b). Since liquids are almost incompressible, a constant pressure merely implies a slight compression of the liquid's moveable constituents which start to enrich at the outer walls of the vessel opposite to the plane where they undergo a higher number of elastic collisions among each other. A permanent liquid stream cannot be modelled in this way.

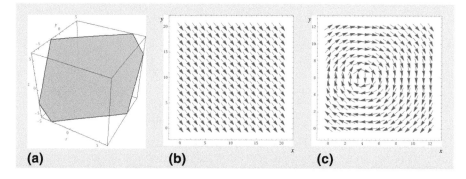

Fig. 5.10 (a) Inclined plane placed into the vessel's coordinate system to symbolixe the area vertically attacked by forces in order to emulate pressure. (b) xy projection of the resulting homogeneous and unidirectional force field. (c) Cylindrical mechanical force field (swirl) whose longitudinal axis goes through the central point with $a = 4$ and $b = 6$. Cylinder's longitudinal axis takes course in parallel to the z axis. Intensity of forces is homogeneous throughout the whole field

More interesting from a physical point of view is a *swirl* able to rotate the moveable constituents of the liquid inside the vessel. Let the mechanical external force field be spatially organized like a *cylinder* whose longitudinal axis is located in parallel to the z axis and goes through the point $(a, b, 0)$ (see Fig. 5.10c). The intensity f of the forces ($f > 0$) is homogeneous within the whole field. The resulting definition of the force field reads:

$$\mathbf{F}(x, y, z, t) = \frac{f}{\sqrt{2}} \cdot \begin{pmatrix} \frac{y-b}{\sqrt{(x-a)^2+(y-b)^2}} \\ -\frac{x-a}{\sqrt{(x-a)^2+(y-b)^2}} \\ 0 \end{pmatrix} \tag{5.14}$$

Electrical External Forces

Electrical external forces exclusively affect electrically charged moveable constituents of the vessel, namely, unbound ions, molecules incorporating ions, and moveable particles marked with electric charges. All other constituents perceive no influence by electrical external forces. In general, an electric external force field can either result from a *point charge* placed at an arbitrary spatial position, or it can be induced by an *electric field* that emerges from an external voltage supply source and pervades the entire vessel. An electric field might have a constant (direct current, DC) nature, or it can pulse over time (alternating current, AC) with a fixed or even variable frequency.

We declare an electric force field to be directed from the *positive pole* (source) toward the *negative pole* (sink) which coincides with the technical definition of the direction of electric current. An electrical force accelerates an oppositely charged moveable constituent (plus-minus or minus-plus) in an attracting manner, while

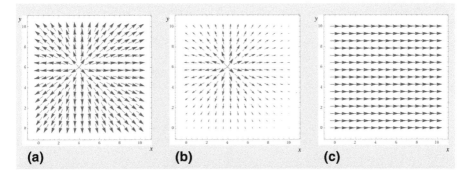

Fig. 5.11 (**a**) xy projection of the first stage of modelling an electric force field spherically spread out by a point charge placed at $a = 4, b = 6, c = 3$. (**b**) Force field after consideration of diminishing intensity of force with ascending distance to the central point. (**c**) Snapshot of a pulse field directed in parallel to the x axis (xy projection)

equally charged moveable constituents (plus-plus or minus-minus) are pushed away from each other. Hence, the direction of acceleration turns from **a** to $-$**a**.

Let us first consider an example in which a *positive point charge* is located at the position (a, b, c) of the vessel. Starting from this central point, the forces spatially spread out in a radial (star-shaped) way. Although the intensity of the forces diminishes with increasing distance to the central point, we begin the force field modelling with constant intensity $f > 0$ (see Fig. 5.11a). In this case, the vector field has the form:

$$\mathbf{F}(x, y, z, t) = \frac{f}{\sqrt{3}} \cdot \begin{pmatrix} \frac{x-a}{\sqrt{(x-a)^2+(y-b)^2+(z-c)^2}} \\ \frac{y-b}{\sqrt{(x-a)^2+(y-b)^2+(z-c)^2}} \\ \frac{z-c}{\sqrt{(x-a)^2+(y-b)^2+(z-c)^2}} \end{pmatrix} \tag{5.15}$$

Now, we can add the effect of diminishing intensity with ascending distance $r = \sqrt{(x-a)^2 + (y-b)^2 + (z-c)^2}$ to the central point (a, b, c). Due to *Coulomb's law*, the force value behaves proportional to $\frac{1}{r^2}$. When introducing a proportionality factor D, we obtain the equation for an electric force field spherically distributed around a point charge as depicted in Fig. 5.11b:

$$\mathbf{F}(x, y, z, t) = \frac{f}{\sqrt{3}} \cdot \begin{pmatrix} D \cdot \frac{x-a}{(\sqrt{(x-a)^2+(y-b)^2+(z-c)^2})^3} \\ D \cdot \frac{y-b}{(\sqrt{(x-a)^2+(y-b)^2+(z-c)^2})^3} \\ D \cdot \frac{z-c}{(\sqrt{(x-a)^2+(y-b)^2+(z-c)^2})^3} \end{pmatrix} \tag{5.16}$$

While an electric force field generated by a point charge remains unchanged over time, a pulse field exhibits a time-dependent oscillatory nature. In order to model this kind of behavior, we exemplify a vector field oriented in parallel to the x axis. We assume a sinusoidal oscillation of the force intensity with a constant amplitude $f > 0$. For simplicity, we choose a period length in parity with τ time units. The resulting pulse field has the form:

$$\mathbf{F}(x, y, z, t) = f \cdot \begin{pmatrix} \cos\left(\frac{2 \cdot \pi}{\tau} \cdot t\right) \\ 0 \\ 0 \end{pmatrix} \tag{5.17}$$

Figure 5.11c shows the pulse field at the points in time $t = 0, \tau, 2 \cdot \tau, \ldots$. Within each period, the polarity of the pulse field alternates twice.

The modelling approach of vector fields provides a powerful and expressive instrument for description of external forces applied to the vessel under study. The vector field might be adapted to physical laws and equipped with suitable parameters. Several force fields can act simultaneously and independent of each other by vectorial addition of their portions to obtain the total effect.

5.2.6   Active Membranes and Dynamical Delimiters

Sometimes, emulation and control of chemical reactions and physical processes active within a vessel require additional instruments beyond Brownian motion, reaction rules, and external forces. Particularly, static structures and fixed elements can benefit from a possibility in order to make them dynamic which gives a greater flexibility in modelling of complex and interwoven processing schemes. A first step toward dynamical structures has been defined by toggling the state of particles between moveable and solid (immoveable) by means of corresponding reaction rules. In principle, this instrument is sufficient to simulate the behavior of *active membranes* by dedicated creation or dissolution of delimiters or membrane structures composed of solid particles. The only way to do so discussed up to now consists in a set of reaction rules in which a "seed particle" can be set, and further particles might attach mediated by auxiliary substances. Creation or complete dissolution of a large membrane using this strategy turns out to be a demanding and time-consuming task and lacks any attempts in which complex spatial structures enter a cell as a whole like endocytosis.

Aiming at incorporation of a broader spectrum of *environmental stimuli*, we allow pre-definition of so-called *instructions*. Each instruction comes with a previously set *point in time t* or a *condition*. As soon as the point in time is reached or the condition is fulfilled for the first time, the instruction gets executed. In case of a fulfilled condition, the instruction can be configured to be performed immediately or with a definable delay given by a number of time steps. A condition can evaluate the current *temperature T* whether it is below, equals, or exceeds a configurable threshold. Alternatively, a condition might express whether or not a *species concentration* is below, equals, or exceeds a certain value. The instruction consists of an *action* performed within the vessel under study. At the current stage of the JENA tool, six types of actions are available for configuration of instructions:

Set temperature: The Kelvin temperature inside the vessel can be set to an arbitrary value $T > 0$. In consequence, the individual speed vectors of all moveable constituents present within the vessel have been recalculated. While the directions of movement remain unchanged, the speed values undergo an acceleration (in case of ascending temperature) or a slowdown (when cooling down) in accordance with keeping the Maxwell-Boltzmann distribution. We act on the assumption that the temperature is homogeneous and almost equal within the whole vessel.

Increment or decrement of temperature: Based on the current temperature present in the vessel, an increment or decrement given in Kelvin can be made. The resulting temperature must not reach 0K or below since the instruction will be ignored in this case. Oppositely, there is no upper limit defined for temperature. Moreover, phase transformations (e.g., from liquid to gas or from liquid to ice) haven't been taken into consideration up to now. The increment or decrement of temperature is an instrument to model effects of heating or cooling which is sometimes necessary to control reactions and assure their desired behavior. Analogously to the "set temperature" instruction, the speed vectors of all moveable constituents will be updated.

Set new solid particle or new delimiter: Many processes in biology come with creation or dissolution of membranes in order to restructure reaction spaces, compartments, or vesicles during the life cycle of a cell. We reflect this aspect by an instruction able to set a new solid (immoveable) particle or a new delimiter. The new particle or delimiter has to be predefined and specified and is accessed then by its identifier. The position for placement within the vessel's coordinate system is needed to be given as well. All voxels occupied by the new particle or delimiter have been estimated and checked whether or not other immoveable constituents compete against space. If so, the new particle or delimiter fails to be placed, and the instruction terminates without any effect. In case of vacancy, the corresponding voxels will be emptied by removal of all moveable constituents including water molecules from the vessel. These unbound atoms, unbound ions, molecules, or moveable particles will be lost from the system whose total mass of moveable constituents diminishes. Instead, the new particle or delimiter starts to reside in this space, and the voxels have been marked to be occupied in this way. Setting a new solid particle or delimiter can divide a chamber into several chambers. The reaction rules will be copied for each chamber that emerges.

Remove solid particle or delimiter: Unification of previously separate reaction chambers and biological processes like exocytosis come with the demand to eliminate solid structures from a vessel. To this end, we introduce an according instruction. The solid (immoveable) particle or delimiter to be removed has to be addressed by its identifier and/or position with regard to the vessel's coordinate system. The voxels previously occupied by the particle or delimiter will be filled with new water molecules in order to perpetuate the thermodynamic properties of a liquid. Their speed vectors get initialized to meet the Maxwell-Boltzmann distribution. The new water molecules increase the total mass of moveable constituents collected in the vessel. Furthermore, removal of a solid particle or delimiter might imply a unification of previously separate chambers into one common reaction space. The reaction rules from all involved chambers will be available in the unified chamber except for copies.

Inject moveable constituents: This instruction allows injection of additional moveable constituents (unbound atoms, unbound ions, molecules, or moveable particles) from the same type at a freely configurable point in time. The injection comes with a position with regard to the coordinate system of the vessel. A given number of moveable constituent's copies gets placed and distributed in the corresponding chamber or in the whole vessel in case no chambers exist. A number of water molecules in parity to the number of inserted copies are removed from the chamber or vessel.

Activate or deactivate reaction rule: It might happen that a chemical reaction needs massless triggers like light or radiation to become active, for instance, light-dependent reactions in photosynthesis. What stands out is the usefulness of an instruction able to activate or deactivate a specific reaction rule in a freely configurable way. We accommodate this request by a corresponding instruction marking a reaction rule as "on" or "off'.' Especially in combination with setting or removal of delimiters which modifies the number of chambers, activation and deactivation of reaction rules turn out to be helpful for achieving appropriate process specifications.

We are aware of the fact that instructions represent a more or less artificial but useful instrument to influence the progress of chemical reactions and physical processes. Coping with dynamical spatial structures is a crucial aspect in membrane computing and a major feature of biological information processing.

5.2.7 Simulation, Monitoring, Logging, and Analyses

The operation of the JENA tool is based on *input* and *output files*. Each input file is prepared by the user in advance. It contains all necessary data in order to initialize the system and to run the simulation. For specification of all data collected in an input file, a specific syntax is required. The given input file becomes read by the tool and checked for consistency and plausibility. Afterward, the simulation run starts with generation of constituents, filling the vessel(s), allocation of voxels, identification of chambers, and application of external forces. Organized by discrete time steps, the configuration of the system with the positions of all currently existing constituents except water molecules gets logged time step by time step or after a number of time steps when tracing the behavior including evaluation of instructions. Finally, a large logfile is available as output ready to get further analyzed and visualized.

An *input file* is written in plain text divided into a number of mandatory and optional *sections*. The sections of an input file widely correspond to the previous subsections of this chapter. It makes sense to start with the #constituents section. Here, the data on predefined types of atoms, ions, molecules, and particles including delimiters need to be configured. The mandatory section named #vessels is dedicated to collect all data for description of one vessel or several vessels independent from each other. A vessel is characterized by its unique identifier, its dimensions, its coordinate system, the granularity of voxels, and its initial temperature. Moreover, the initial placement of solid particles and delimiters and the initial points of injection for moveable constituents need to be declared. Another section called #reactions contains the reaction rules defined for each vessel, whereas each reaction rule is assigned to a vessel and a chamber within the vessel if configured. All reaction rules refer to the globally specified types of atoms, ions, molecules, and particles mentioned in the corresponding section. In case that several vessels exist, each vessel might have its individual set of reaction rules. A finite number of superpositioned external forces can be formulated in the section #forces. Again, each vessel is allowed to have its specific set of external forces. The section #instructions enables setup of instructions separately for all vessels available. Finally, a mandatory #simulation section covers all information needed to control the course of simulation uniformly for all vessels. The duration of a time step Δt and the point in time to terminate the simulation have been captured. In addition, the detailedness of the output file collecting the simulation results can be specified here.

A minimal input file is restricted to a single vessel merely containing a #vessels section without constituents, reactions, external forces, and instructions complemented by a #simulation section. This setting will lead to a vessel automatically filled with water molecules which in turn perform a Brownian motion. A multiplicity of vessels is suitable to simultaneously compare different experimental conditions varied among the vessels. For future JENA versions, we plan additional kinds of instructions able to manage an exchange of moveable constituents among vessels.

While the simulation runs, the corresponding output file is successively produced. In its simplest form, an output file lists the abundance (absolute number of copies) of each moveable constituent in each vessel except water molecules at a number of equidistant time steps. Additionally, global parameters like temperature, existence of chambers, and volumes of chambers have been included. According to the settings made in the input file's #simulation section, species abundance can be logged separately per chamber and by monitoring the species concentrations. More in detail, the spatiotemporal trace of selected or all individual moveable constituents except water molecules might be inserted into the output file. Occurrences of reactions (effective collisions) can be marked to enrich the trace information (Fig. 5.12).

The output file is the basis for subsequent analyses and visualizations. Since an output file is written in plain text as well, it can be evaluated in a flexible way with the JENA tool but also with other tools like R for statistical examinations. The

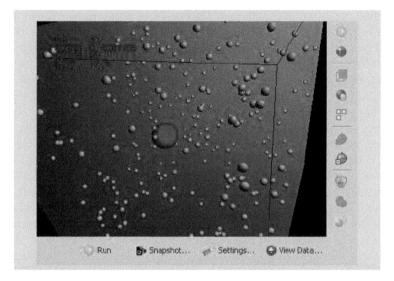

Fig. 5.12 Example of a perspective view of a vessel with its moveable constituents except water molecules at a configurable point in time. The perspective of the external observer is variable and enables an imagination of the spatial distribution of vessel's contents

JENA tool at its present stage of development comes with a couple of analysis and visualization features:

Abundance or species concentration of selected or all moveable constituents over time per chamber or in a whole vessel: The resulting diagram plots the course of species concentrations or species abundance subject to the discrete points in time logged in the output file. The diagram might refer either to an entire vessel or to a single chamber situated inside a vessel.

Histogram of chamber or vessel contents over time: In contrast to the aforementioned diagram, the courses are placed on top of each other. In this way, the portions of species in relation to all moveable constituents become easily visible.

Perspective view of a vessel with its contents at a configurable point in time: The box of a vessel is depicted from the perspective of an external observer. The spheres of all moveable constituents together with the cuboids of all immoveable constituents present in the vessel at a configurable point in time are shown.

Spatial trace view of an arbitrarily selectable moveable constituent over time: Again, the box of a vessel is depicted from the perspective of an external observer. For one selectable individual moveable constituent, its spatial trace throughout the vessel during simulation gets illustrated. Positions in which reactions occur by effective collisions have been marked.

View of a layer in a vessel located in parallel to two of the coordinate system axes: This visualization takes into consideration a box-shaped thin slice across the vessel in parallel to two of the coordinate system axes. All moveable and immoveable constituents except water molecules located in the slice at a freely configurable point in time have been depicted. The resulting figure can be interpreted as a cross section of the vessel and gives insight into the spatial distribution of constituents.

Cumulative view of all layers in a vessel (vessel view from top or from a side wall): Here, all slices throughout the vessel placed on top of each other have been summed up producing a cumulative view of the moveable and immoveable constituents except water molecules present in a vessel at a freely configurable point in time.

Frequency of effective collisions in a vessel over time: For this type of diagram, a constituent (type of unbound atom, unbound ion, molecule, or particle) has been chosen that acts as a substrate in at least one reaction rule. The diagram displays the points in time of effective collisions (chemical reactions) incorporating the selected substrate. Based on these data, the average frequency of effective collisions over simulation time is calculated.

Course of temperature in a vessel over time: The temperature in a vessel might vary during simulation due to the reaction's balance of energy and due to possible heating or cooling effects expressed by instructions. The resulting diagram shows the course of temperature over simulation time based on the kinetic energies of all moveable constituents in the vessel under study.

Beyond visualizations and diagrams, simulation results exhibit a basis for subsequent analyses. The most popular application consists in parameter fitting, especially estimation of rate constants of chemical reactions and further abstract parameters employed for process modelling by means of differential equation systems.

5.3   JENA Source Code Design

The first idea for the JENA tool dates back to 2017. In early 2018, we started with software development. In the meantime, the JENA project currently comprises more than 400,000 lines of Java source code spread into around 80 classes with approximately 1500 methods and functions in total. Up to now, 35 students participated in software development, testing, debugging, and employment. We coordinate the JENA tool at Friedrich Schiller University Jena, Germany. It is planned to persist as an ongoing long-term project. After the software will have reached its beta state, we are going to make it available for download including all source code via the research platform at www.molecular-computing.de.

Students attending the one-semester master courses "Molecular Algorithms" and "Foundations of Object-Oriented Programming" contribute to JENA by producing a piece of source code addressing a phenomenon or a process found in biology or biochemistry. Accompanied by an exhaustive literature search, the phenomenon or process gets described at a low level of abstraction. To this end, suitable data structures and data types need to be created in order to capture all details of interest. Furthermore, we make use of parameters for control of randomized or predetermined effects that might occur. Parameters can also include probability distributions based on empirical studies or derived from natural laws. Attention is paid to the objective that as many effects as possible have been integrated into the corresponding Java source code. Simultaneously, another group of students is searching for abstract models of biocomputing reflecting the phenomenon or process under study. So the Java source code can be complemented by one or more formal representations. In consequence, we successively obtain a collection of varying implementations, all dedicated to the same phenomenon or process but widely spread in their level of abstraction. We are aware of the fact that our JENA tool primarily serves as an experimental workbench directed to "play" with models and implementations and to learn about their advantages and disadvantages which facilitate an evaluation from a practical perspective.

The JENA software architecture is organized to be composed of five main module packages dedicated to their employment for *data management, simulation engine, visualization, user interface,* and *application kernel.* Following a strict object-oriented approach, the classes defined in the packages communicate to each other by well-defined interfaces.

The main challenge within the domain of data management consists in coping with the huge amount of data capturing the positions and speed vectors of all constituents (atoms, ions, molecules, particles) present in the vessel(s) under study. The number of constituents can reach several hundred millions of them including all water molecules. We made the decision of discretization of space in order to divide the vessel into a grid of small boxes (volume elements) called voxels. It turns out that the spatial arrangement of voxels forming the vessel remains static since the vessel proportions cannot change during simulation. So it gives advantage to implement a huge *hash table* that links a *list* of constituent's records to each voxel. The anchor address of each list can be directly derived from the x, y, and z coordinates of the corresponding voxel which enable a fast and effective access. The contents of each list have been handled in a dynamical manner since the presence of constituents in a voxel typically changes over simulation time. The hash table as a whole might consume a total amount up to several terabytes for storage in memory. Therefore, we use to handle simulation of large molecular systems at a central server while small systems up to few million constituents can be managed at a commercially available personal computer.

The simulation engine unites all procedures and algorithmic techniques necessary for progression of all constituents in space and over time. Especially the updates of speed vectors represent a demanding task due to the fact that recalculation of speed vector components is computationally expensive. On the one hand, complex mathematical operations like trigonometric functions are needed. On the other hand, accelerations caused by many other constituents from the environment and from possible external forces can sum up from thousands of portions to be individually estimated and considered. Accelerations affect the speed vector. Here, we decided to implement a kind of lazy evaluation neglecting marginal influences below a threshold of around 0.01%. For computation of trigonometric functions, we utilize prefabricated numerical tables with fast access instead of Taylor approximation. The granularity of vector fields defined by external forces has been spatially discretized as well with respect to the voxels. The same holds for reaction rules.

Visualization is based on simulation outputs collected within an output file. Perspective views of a vessel have been obtained from a vanishing point projection in which hidden regions are excluded from further evaluation. From former software projects in bioinformatics by our JENA research group, we have the freely available visualization package of SRSim [11] at hand able to depict a three-dimensional arrangement of colored spheres with light effects. We have integrated the corresponding routines into JENA.

Currently, the user interface of the JENA tool is held spartan since it is mainly restricted to the input file provided by the user prior to starting the simulation. The input file contains all information about initialization of the molecular system and for simulation of its behavior. This avoids a variety of dialogue windows and icons but transfers the responsibility for correctness of all configurations made in the input file to the user. Some but not all potentially possible inconsistencies have been checked automatically before starting the simulation.

The application kernel controls the interplay of all other modules and defines the processing steps in the desired manner. Here, schemata of successive actions have been identified and specified, for instance, a sequence of steps to be done for execution of an instruction.

The JENA software is a product of many team members and contributors aimed at achievement of functionality rather than aesthetics and perfectionism from a theoretical point of view in software construction. Following the notion of an experimental system, JENA is thought to explore ideas, their implementation, and their integration into an entire workbench to be completed in an ongoing long-term project.

5.4   Selection of JENA Case Studies

By means of four dedicated modelling and simulation case studies, we demonstrate the practicability of the JENA tool. Each study addresses an individual aspect of biological information processing carried out either inside a biological cell or employed as a laboratory technique. The case studies aim at a fine-grained emulation of physical processes and/or chemical reactions operating in concert. We start with the *chemical Lotka-Volterra oscillator* able to maintain a stable oscillatory behavior by merely three reactions. The second study is focused on *electrophoresis*, a technique for spatial separation of electrically charged biomolecules like DNA by their mass corresponding to DNA strand length. *Centrifugation* as a well-established method for separation of a mixture of liquids by their components with different mass densities is considered in the third study, while the final one models a *neural signal transduction across the synaptic cleft*.

5.4.1   Chemical Lotka-Volterra Oscillator

Oscillatory signals represent an important instrument for biological information processing since generation and maintenance of biological rhythms rely on stable oscillations. They act as clock signals, as triggers for periodic activities, and for exhibition of anticipating behavioral patterns.

The chemical Lotka-Volterra oscillator [24] is an artificial chemistry consisting of a minimalist reaction scheme composed of merely three reactions. Positive feedback loops among autocatalytic reactions enable a sustained oscillation in terms of a predator-prey relationship between abstract molecular species called X and Y. In addition, a supply species called A is needed. Its concentration should be kept constant or nearly constant over time in order to push the oscillation forward by permanent inflow. A waste species named B collects by-products. The reaction rules read:

$$A + X \longrightarrow 2X; \quad E_{a,1} = 67\text{kJ/mol} \tag{5.18}$$

$$X + Y \longrightarrow 2Y; \quad E_{a,2} = 67\text{kJ/mol} \tag{5.19}$$

$$Y \longrightarrow B; \quad E_{a,3} = 67\text{kJ/mol} \tag{5.20}$$

Positive feedback loops imply a self-amplifying effect combined with a delay. At the beginning, the "prey" species X undergoes an exponential duplication (reproduction) promoted by supplier A in which the number of moveable constituents of the type X grows faster and faster due to reaction 5.18. After a while, the exponential growth of X collapses since the "predator" Y consumes more and more exemplars of X in order to promote its own duplication expressed by reaction 5.19. In consequence, the number of X exemplars dramatically diminishes and reaches a low base level. A short time later, the growth of the Y population stops as well due to lack of X necessary to "feed" Y for reproduction. Now, the number of Y exemplars sinks down which in turn allows species X to exponentially reproduce again starting a new oscillation cycle. It stands out that a spike-shaped oscillatory waveform emerges in which the peaks of Y follow the peaks of X with a short delay. The period length of the limit cycle oscillation is mainly determined by the velocity of the degradation reaction 5.20. The faster this reaction runs, the shorter the resulting period length gets adjusted. The degradation reaction can be accelerated by decrease of its activation energy $E_{a,3}$. Technically, this reaction is treated as a spontaneous decay without taking into account effective collisions because of the only substrate Y. In the simulation scenario, we uniformly assign an activation energy of $67\ \frac{\text{kJ}}{\text{mol}}$ to all three reactions.

For the JENA simulation study, we define a cubical vessel whose dimension is 100 nm along the x, y, and z axes. Its volume constitutes $10^6\ \text{nm}^3$. The vessel contains no solid structures and no delimiters. The species of types A, X, Y, and B have been specified to embody moveable particles with uniform mass of $m = 10^{-24}\ \text{kg}$ and without inner structure. Initially, 5,000,000 exemplars of A,

3,000,000 exemplars of X, and 1,000,000 exemplars of Y have been injected and homogeneously distributed inside the vessel enriched by a number of water molecules. The initial temperature is set to $T = 300$ K. We plan to simulate the reaction system's behavior for 200 s model time with a discrete time step of $\Delta t = 50$ ns by logging all species abundance every 1000 ns. Since the number of particles from type A needs to be (almost) constant over time to act as a supplier and to conduct a permanent inflow, we add instructions into the input file to make sure that every 2 s an amount of 381,270 new particles of type A will be inserted into the system to exactly compensate for consumption of A which pushes the oscillation.

Figure 5.13 shows the simulation results put into graphs. Here, the abundance courses of the species A, X, and Y over simulation time become visible. Waste species B linearly accumulates over time and is skipped in the diagram. The depicted abundance courses have been smoothed by a moving average filter to eliminate a slight noise. The oscillatory behavior exhibiting a spike-shaped waveform with exponential growth and reduction becomes apparent. The transient phase at the beginning of the oscillatory process is short and passes into a limit cycle. The study illustrates that the JENA tool is able to manage a multiple particle system containing several million moveable constituents. A high number of particles are necessary to obtain a sustained oscillation. In case of reducing the number of

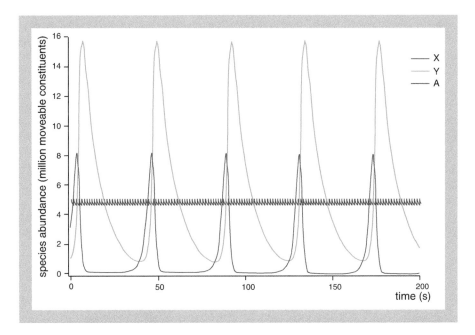

Fig. 5.13 Simulation of a chemical Lotka-Volterra oscillator using a minimalist reaction system. Species A acts as supplier kept at a nearly constant level of particle abundance. Species abundance X and Y oscillate exhibiting a spike-shaped waveform typical for the predator-prey relationship of the system

particles to a few thousands, the oscillation course becomes more instable or chaotic, and one of the species X or Y might extinct, terminating the oscillation.

5.4.2 Electrophoresis

Electrophoresis subsumes a physical technique able to spatially separate electrically charged molecules by their weights [19]. Particularly, DNA (negatively charged) and many naturally originated proteins (twisted and folded chains of amino acids whose electric charge is mainly determined by outer amino acid side chains) are beneficial candidates for widespread applications in molecular biology and chemical analysis [35].

Mostly, electrophoresis takes place within a special physical medium like a *gel* which carries and steers the molecules during the separation process. To do so, the gel is prepared in a way to be equipped with numerous *pores* forming woven channels or tunnels sufficiently sized to allow passage of charged sample molecules. For instance, *agarose* is commonly used to compose a gel suitable for electrophoresis on DNA. The fiber structure of agarose enables pores whose diameter usually varies between 150 and 500 nanometers while a DNA strand (in biologically prevalent B-DNA conformation) diametrically consumes merely 2 nanometers, but its length can reach several hundred nanometers [13]. The ready-made gel, typically between 10 and 30 centimeters in length or width and up to 5 millimeters thick, is embedded in a gel *chamber* filled up with a buffer solution in order to adjust an appropriate pH environment. The gel chamber comes with two electrodes, a negative one and a positive one, placed at the opposite boundaries of the gel (see Fig. 5.14).

Subsequently, the sample mixture of DNA strands to be separated becomes injected into the gel close to the negative electrode. Now, an electrical DC voltage, provided by an external power supply and mostly chosen between 80 and 120 volts, is applied to the electrodes. Driven by the external electrical force, the negatively charged molecules begin to run toward the positive electrode along a lane through the pores of the gel. In order to mobilize, each molecule has to overcome its friction notable in both forms, with the gel on the one hand and inherently on the other.

Interestingly, the resulting velocity of movement strongly depends on the mass (weight) of the individual molecules. Since small and light molecules induce a low

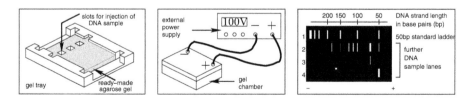

Fig. 5.14 Sketching technical instruments and outcome of agarose gel electrophoresis

friction, they run faster than heavier exemplars. This distinction finally affects the resulting spatial separation according to the weights of involved charged molecules. The process of electrophoresis is stopped by switching off the voltage shortly before the smallest molecules have reached the opposite end of the gel. For an easier visualization of this process, the molecular mixture initially becomes enriched by a weakly binding dye whose velocity converges in compliance with the smallest sample molecules [35].

In addition, the DNA sample molecules had been stained using a fluorescence marker like *ethidium bromide* [30]. This substance loosely binds to the hydrogen bonds of double-stranded DNA and persists at the DNA during the electrophoresis run. Ethidium bromide attached to DNA fluoresces under ultraviolet (UV) light making the DNA visible inside the gel. Typically, the DNA after electrophoresis is arranged in so-called *bands* (sustained bar-shaped blots) along the underlying lane. Normally, these bands appear in light-gray up to white colors on a dark gel background. The color's intensity gives a raw information on the absolute number of molecules of almost the same mass accumulated within each band.

In a first and mostly sufficient approximation, gel electrophoresis can be modelled by a parity balance of forces. The electrical force F_E needs to overcome the friction F_R. Movement of charged molecules starts up if and only if both forces equal to each other:

$$F_E = F_R \tag{5.21}$$

Now, we can resolve both forces by formulating its strength using a couple of dedicated parameters. The electrical force is defined as the product of the molecular electric charge q with the electric field E which in turn can be expressed by the quotient of the voltage U and the distance h between the electrodes: $F_E = q \cdot E = q \cdot \frac{U}{h}$. In contrast, the friction in accordance with *Stokes' law* reads $F_R = 6 \cdot \pi \cdot \eta \cdot r \cdot v$, assuming movement of a sphere where r denotes the radius, v symbolizes its velocity, and η stands for the viscosity of the medium, mainly reflecting the average size of the pores. The velocity can be assumed to remain almost constant after a short acceleration phase in conjunction with switching on the electric voltage. Putting everything together reveals:

$$v = \frac{q \cdot E}{6 \cdot \pi \cdot \eta \cdot r} \tag{5.22}$$

The only indetermined parameter is the radius r of the imagined sphere representing the moving charged molecule. In order to cope with that, we can presume that the volume $V_{molecule}$ of the charged molecule resembles the volume V_{sphere} of the imagined sphere. Having this in mind, we can write $V_{molecule} = \frac{m}{\rho}$ with m denoting the mass (weight) of the molecule and ρ its density. Moreover, $V_{sphere} = \frac{4}{3} \cdot \pi \cdot r^3$.

From that, we obtain:

$$r = \left(\frac{3}{4 \cdot \pi} \cdot \frac{m}{\rho} \right)^{\frac{1}{3}} \tag{5.23}$$

Let us now compose a resulting function s : $\mathbb{R}^2 \longrightarrow \mathbb{R}$ which describes the distance moved by a charged molecule with mass m after an elapsed time t:

$$s(m, t) = v \cdot t \tag{5.24}$$

$$= \frac{q \cdot E}{6 \cdot \pi \cdot \eta \left(\frac{3 \cdot m}{4 \cdot \pi \cdot \rho} \right)^{\frac{1}{3}}} \cdot t \tag{5.25}$$

$$= \underbrace{\frac{q}{6 \cdot \pi \cdot \left(\frac{3}{4 \cdot \pi \cdot \rho} \right)^{\frac{1}{3}}}}_{\text{taken as global parameter } G} \cdot \frac{E}{\eta} \cdot \frac{1}{m^{\frac{1}{3}}} \cdot t \tag{5.26}$$

$$= G \cdot \frac{E}{\eta} \cdot \frac{1}{m^{\frac{1}{3}}} \cdot t \tag{5.27}$$

For DNA agarose gel electrophoresis, the electric field E frequently constitutes between $400 \frac{V}{m}$ and $500 \frac{V}{m}$ while the viscosity commonly differs from $0.001 \frac{kg}{m \cdot s}$ (consistency like water in large-pored gels) up to $0.02 \frac{kg}{m \cdot s}$ in small-meshed gels enhancing the friction along with producing heat. When employing the molecule mass m in kg along with elapsed time t in s and remembering that $1 VAs = 1 \frac{kg \cdot m^2}{s^3}$, the final value of the function s is returned in meters.

In order to disclose the relation between mass of a DNA double strand and its length in base pairs, we need to consider the average mass of a nucleotide. Indeed, there are slight mass deviations between single nucleotides A (adenine, $\approx 5.467 \cdot 10^{-25}$ kg), C (cytosine, $\approx 5.234 \cdot 10^{-25}$ kg), G (guanine, $\approx 5.732 \cdot 10^{-25}$ kg), and T (thymine, $\approx 5.301 \cdot 10^{-25}$ kg). Each nucleotide mass comprises the chemical base together with its section of the sugar-phosphate backbone. In average, we obtain $\approx 5.4335 \cdot 10^{-25}$ kg per nucleotide or $\approx 1.0867 \cdot 10^{-24}$ kg per base pair. Marginal influences of dye and ethidium bromide are neglected.

When observing gel electrophoresis on DNA in practice, we witness the occurrence of undesired side effects resulting in some misplaced DNA strands. It might happen that short DNA strands run slower than expected due to its supercoiled spatial structure which increases the friction. Several DNA strands of different mass can be spatially interwoven in a way that the electrical force used to move the strands does not suffice to ungarble the DNA cluster. What stands out is a certain fuzziness regarding the masses of DNA strands enriched in the same band.

Having the formalization of gel electrophoresis in terms of a parameterized process on a pool of DNA strands at hand, we can implement a corresponding model. The main motivation to do so lies in the necessity to figure out the abstract global parameter G by an appropriate value according to the specificity of the utilized gel. Moreover, a JENA model should be able to illustrate the process of gel electrophoresis and some of its undesired side effects like fuzziness of bands and its intensity. For setup of the experimental study, we model a pool of $90,000$ linear DNA double strands as moveable particles without inner structure since the nucleotide sequence does not matter for separation by length using gel electrophoresis. Inspired by a so-called *ladder*, a DNA size marker composed of a mix of DNA strands with varying lengths obtained from a cleaved plasmid, we create 13 types of moveable particles. They correspond to DNA double strands with lengths of $100, 200, 300, 400, 500, 600, 700, 800, 900, 1000, 1200, 1500,$ and 3000 base pairs (bp). We assume an average mass of $m = 1.0867 \cdot 10^{-24}$ kg per base pair. DNA strand particles with lengths of 500 and 1000 base pairs have been generated in 12,000 copies, all other lengths in 6000 copies each. Since each DNA strand particle gets symbolized by a sphere, its radius increases with ascending mass and strand length. Each DNA strand particle is equipped with an electrically negative charge. The corresponding point charge of $q = 2 \cdot n \cdot e$ with n expressing the number of base pairs and e the elementary charge of an electron is assigned to the central point of the sphere symbolizing a DNA strand particle.

The cuboid vessel for carrying out the gel electrophoresis becomes sized 10 cm in x dimension (lane length), 1 cm in y dimension (lane width), and 0.5 cm in z dimension (height). At the position $x = 1\mu m$, we initially place a delimiter in parallel to the yz plane in order to model the injection slot by a chamber for placement of the DNA strand particles prior to starting the electrophoresis process. The delimiter separates the vessel into two disjoint chambers. One of them forms the slot, and the other one stands for the electrophoresis gel. We presume a 1.5% agarose gel whose filaments surround pores for passage of particles and imply a certain viscosity of the medium. The gel chamber with a volume of nearly 5 cm^3 contains the agarose and water, both with similar mass density of around $1 \frac{g}{cm^3}$. So the entire agarose gel filled with water has a mass of approximately 5 g which means that 75 mg pure agarose powder have been used. In the model, we distribute this mass to 100,000 small solid particles in micrometer scale randomly placed in the gel chamber in spatial equipartition in order to mimic the friction effect of the agarose filaments.

Now, we can inject the moveable DNA strand particles into the slot and fill both chambers with additional water molecules to emulate the behavior of a liquid. We set an initial temperature of $T = 300$ K for the Brownian motion. To start the electrophoresis process, an external electric force field is applied directed in parallel to the x axis with a constant field intensity of $500 \frac{V}{m}$. The time step Δt is set to 1 μs. At the point in time $t = \Delta t$, we remove by instruction the delimiter to release the DNA strand particles from the slot which enter the gel and pass toward its opposite side. The less the mass of a DNA strand particle, the faster it can move by the external electrical force. The electrical force pushing the particles forward through the gel is larger than counter-effects of the Brownian motion causing a slight individual slowdown. When elastically colliding with solid particles of agarose

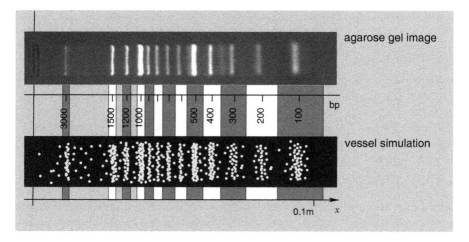

Fig. 5.15 Agarose gel image from a 100bp ladder of DNA double strands (upper part) and corresponding simulation result of the electrophoresis process by a JENA model described in the text. The lower part shows a $10\,\mu m$ thick layer of the virtual gel. White dots mark the final positions of DNA strand particles

filaments, the DNA strand particles get reflected and redirected which also might diminish their speed toward the opposite side of the gel. In consequence, DNA strand particles with the same mass slightly spread by their speed of movement in parallel to the x axis, causing a certain fuzziness.

We run the electrophoresis simulation for a model time of 30 min. After the corresponding number of time steps has elapsed, the external electric force field gets deactivated. Figure 5.15 shows in its lower part a resulting spatial distribution of approximately 700 DNA strand particles within a section of the gel by depicting a layer in parallel to the xz plane at the height $y = 2.5$ mm and $10\,\mu m$ thick. For better visibility, the diameters of the spheres representing the DNA strand particles (white dots) have been enlarged up to 10,000-fold. A high degree of similarity between the simulation result and a real-world agarose gel with a 100 bp ladder becomes apparent. In order to obtain this result, we did several simulation runs with varying size, granularity, and spatial distribution of solid particles at fixed positions inside the gel modelling agarose filaments. These solid particles are responsible for the effect of friction by causing elastic collisions with the DNA strand particles which perturb their motion along the direction of the electric field. It turns out that a certain amount of "disorder" and "irregularity" in spatial placement of the solid particles seems to be essential. Few DNA strand particles "stick" at some solid particles unable to leave this position.

After successive adjustment and verification of the JENA model for electrophoresis, it can be employed for parameter fitting in formula 5.27 to obtain an appropriate approximation of G. This formula provides a simple and easy-to-use formalization of electrophoresis with linear DNA double strands using 1.5% agarose gel (viscosity

$\eta = 0.01 \frac{\text{kg}}{\text{m·s}}$) as a physical process for spatial DNA separation by strand length. For parameter fitting of G, we first identify spatial clusters of DNA strand particles forming the bands in the JENA model. For each band and hence for each available strand length and strand mass, an average position at the x axis has been calculated. These data act as a reference and target for parameter fitting. Now, formula 5.27 might be assigned with a randomly chosen initial value for G and applied. We estimate the cumulated error by weighted summation of the deviations of all bands. Using a *hill climbing* heuristic approach, G becomes incremented or decremented a bit, and the formula is employed again. After a number of several thousand iterations, a finally optimized value of G comes out. We fitted a constant average value of approx. $6.794 \cdot 10^{-4} \frac{\text{A·s·kg}^{\frac{1}{3}}}{\text{m}}$ for G in agarose gel electrophoresis on linear double-stranded non-denaturing DNA with 1.5% agarose and $E = 500 \frac{\text{V}}{\text{m}}$. Different compositions of the gel and different electric field intensities might imply other best-fit values of G disclosing a functional relationship.

5.4.3 Centrifugation

Centrifugation belongs to well-established and frequently utilized laboratory techniques for spatial separation of particles embedded in a liquid (suspension or dispersion) by their different mass densities. Another usage of centrifugation consists in spatial separation of a mixture of liquids (emulsion) into its components.

A typical application scenario of centrifugation is the recovery of DNA strands out of a band after agarose gel electrophoresis. Here, the band becomes excised from the gel using a scalpel. The resulting gel block contains the desired DNA strands but additionally many agarose filaments, encapsulated water molecules, and not seldomly rests of proteins from previous operations on DNA. A test tube gets prepared by filling in a liquid able to break up the agarose filaments. The gel block has been immerged after what the filaments decay and dissolve. Encapsulated water gets released. Now, a mix of different types of particles embedded in a liquid persists in the test tube.

Separation of particles by centrifugation makes use of *external mechanical forces*. To this end, a device called *centrifuge* is set into operation. Its central component is a *rotor*, a revolvable cylinder equipped with a ring of conical slots for placement and locking of test tubes. All test tubes prepared for centrifugation need to be inserted into the slots of the ring in an equally offset manner in order to avoid imbalances. Afterward, the test tubes have been arranged radially with their bottoms located outward in the rotor. Eventually, the rotor is set into a fast rotation around its central axis for some seconds (short spin) up to few minutes (long spin). The speed might reach up to several thousand rotations per minute (rpm) using standard laboratory centrifuges on a table.

Along with the fast rotation of the rotor, *centrifugal forces* have been induced directed radially outward from the rotation axis. The centrifugal forces cause an additional acceleration of the moveable constituents present in each centrifugated test tube toward its bottom. The acceleration value $|\mathbf{a}|$ increases with ascending distance r to the rotation axis (radius) expressed by the equation

$$|\mathbf{a}| = 4 \cdot \pi^2 \cdot r \cdot n^2 \tag{5.28}$$

in which n symbolizes the revolution speed typically set in the unit s^{-1} or $\min^{-1}$. The resulting centrifugal force affecting a particle with mass m has the value $|\mathbf{F_C}| = m \cdot |\mathbf{a}|$.

By getting accelerated more and more toward the bottom of the test tube, the moveable constituents begin to heavily collide in an elastic manner. Particles with a large mass will move rather straight toward the bottom while particles with lower mass get redirected by collisions with heavier particles. So lightweight particles have been more and more displaced from the bottom. In consequence of the strong elastic collisions, they are forced to move toward the rotation axis and start to enrich there. The inertia of the heavier particles to straightly move toward the bottom and their resistance against low-mass particles when elastically colliding implies the effect of spatial separation. Ideally, the process of centrifugation lasts until most of the heaviest and densest particles have reached the bottom and enriched there. Along the longitudinal axis of each centrifugated test tube, a spatial separation of the containing moveable particles can be observed with ascending density $\rho = \frac{m}{V}$ (m, particle mass; V, particle volume) from the top downward to the bottom. In many cases, several colored *phases* (layers) become visible, whereas a phase stands for an enrichment of particles of the same type.

When carefully removed from its rotor slot, a test tube with all separate phases is available for postprocessing. The phases might be successively pipetted and transferred to other vessels. Sometimes, the densest particles residing at the test tube bottom form a solid or powdery phase which is called *pellet*. For instance, this is the case when recovering DNA from an agarose gel. After centrifugation, the containing DNA gets concentrated in a pellet. All other phases, composed of liquids and agarose fragments, need to be eliminated by pipetting before the remaining pellet can be diluted with high-purity water to be proceeded as a DNA solution.

A JENA model intends to illustrate the process of centrifugation. To this end, we define a vessel with a squarish base area at the xz plane of the underlying coordinate system. The point in which both diagonals intersect coincides with the central point of the centrifuge's rotor. Having in mind a minicentrifuge, we assign a rotor diameter of 35 mm. The rotation axis of the rotor is covered by an immoveable particle placed in parallel to the y dimension of the coordinate system. This barrier prevents moveable particles from entering the rotation axis. Furthermore, we place four equally shaped large-sized cuboid delimiters into the corners of the square that exhibits a cross section of the rotor (see left part of Fig. 5.16). Radially from the central point, four orthogonal slots between the delimiters persist which in turn act as test tubes. Their bottoms are located outward and oppositely to the central point. Each of the four slots has a length of 15 mm and a width of 5 mm.

In the JENA model, we plan to initially insert all moveable particles for centrifugation near the rotation axis of the rotor. To do so, four auxiliary delimiters

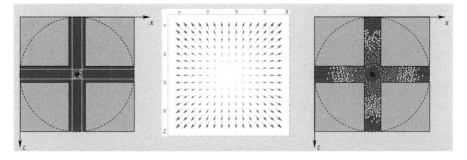

Fig. 5.16 Schematic illustration of the modelling setup for centrifugation and its results. The vessel with delimiters acting as rotor and initial placement of moveable particles is shown in the left part. The vector field of acceleration resulting from centrifugal forces radially to the rotation axis is depicted in the middle part. Final spatial separation of moveable particles arranged in three phases in each of the four slots after centrifugation becomes visible in the right part

are necessary, marked by white lines across the rotor in the left part of Fig. 5.16. They confine the initial spatial area available for the moveable particles prior to centrifugation, avoiding a disordered homogeneous distribution throughout the whole slots. After the first time step of centrifugation simulation, these four delimiters will be removed by instruction. Three types of moveable particles have been configured with uniform spheric volume V and masses m of 10^{-26} kg (green), 10^{-24} kg (white), and 10^{-22} kg (magenta). *Fiftythousand* exemplars of each particle type are generated and placed near the rotation axis. The initial temperature for Brownian motion is set to $T = 300$ K.

The effect of centrifugal forces radially accelerating the moveable particles into the slots has been emulated by external mechanical forces. For this purpose, we create a three-dimensional force field cylindrically oriented around the rotation axis of the rotor with regard to the vessel's coordinate system. Let $(a, b, c) \in \mathbb{R}^3$ represent a central point and the line (a, s, c) for all $s \in \mathbb{R}$ the rotation axis. A vector field radially oriented at the rotation axis and with uniform values throughout space can be defined by $\mathbf{F}_{\text{uniform}}(x, y, z) = (\frac{x-a}{\sqrt{(x-a)^2+(z-c)^2}}, 0, \frac{z-c}{\sqrt{(x-a)^2+(z-c)^2}})$ whereas the term $\sqrt{(x-a)^2 + (z-c)^2}$ stands for the distance of a point (x, y, z) from the rotation axis. Now, we can formulate the vector field of the centrifugal forces whose values follow Eq. (5.28). Having in mind that the radius $r = \sqrt{(x-a)^2 + (z-c)^2}$ coincides with the distance to the rotation axis, the resulting expression can be simplified to the form:

$$\mathbf{F}_{\text{centrifugal}}(x, y, z, t) = \frac{4 \cdot \pi^2 \cdot n^2 \cdot m(x, y, z, t)}{\sqrt{2}} \cdot \begin{pmatrix} x - a \\ 0 \\ z - c \end{pmatrix} \quad (5.29)$$

The term $m(x, y, z, t)$ symbolizes the mass located in position (x, y, z) at the point in time t. The variable n stands for the revolution speed. The acceleration **a** affecting each moveable particle is given by the vector field $\mathbf{a}(x, y, z, t) = \frac{1}{m(x,y,z,t)} \cdot \mathbf{F}_{\text{centrifugal}}(x, y, z, t)$. The middle part of Fig. 5.16 shows a sectional view of a vector field of accelerations with the central point at $a = 17.5$ and $c = 17.5$. Please note that the acceleration is independent from each moveable particle's mass.

For the simulation study, we run the centrifugation for 30 s with a revolution speed of 3000 rpm which corresponds to $n = 50\,\text{s}^{-1}$. The time step Δt is set to 1 μs. The right part of Fig. 5.16 gives a schematic illustration of the final separation of moveable particles, making cognizable three phases in each of the four test tube slots. The colored moveable particles have been enlarged up to 100-fold for better visibility.

5.4.4   Neural Signal Transduction Across Synaptic Cleft

The capability of appropriate response to environmental stimuli has been identified to be a common feature of all living organisms and hence a crucial general property of life. *Sensory perception* and *cognition* come along with generation and evaluation of a plethora of signals expressing an imagination of the environment and its relevant issues. In addition, the response of an organism by *behavioral activities* requires control and monitoring of actuators, appendages, limbs, or extremities which necessitates induction and propagation of corresponding instructions encoded by dedicated signal sequences. Furthermore, higher organisms equipped with a brain or central nervous system manage a lot of inherent signals giving information about the physical constitution and the internal state of organs and body functions. It turns out that coping with manifold signals, their transduction and processing are essential for keeping alive.

Vertebrates possess a network of interwoven and connected *neurons* reaching all components of the body responsible for most tasks of signal processing. A neuron is a specialized type of a biological cell for weighted summation and transduction of neural signals. Figure 5.17 gives an overview of the neuron structure and its most relevant components. The cell *nucleus* contains the genomic DNA and is surrounded by *dendrites*, a treelike structure with multiple branches. Each of them is spatially connected with a synapse of a predecessor neuron, or it is linked with a sensor as signal generator for reception and perception. Signals enter the dendrites by sequences of *spikes* made of a surge of *cations*, most of them natrium (sodium) ions denoted as Na^+. Via microtubules—molecular hoses composed of protein complexes—the spikes pass the dendrites toward the nucleus and become accumulated by summing up. The frequency and duration of a spike sequence might vary among the single branches within the dendrites. Beyond, spike sequences from frequently used branches get a higher weight when summed up in comparison to those with a sparse signal intensity. What stands out is that in the nucleus, a stream of cations over time arrives and gets blocked in the first instance. Whenever an individual threshold of cation concentration is reached or exceeded, the neuron starts

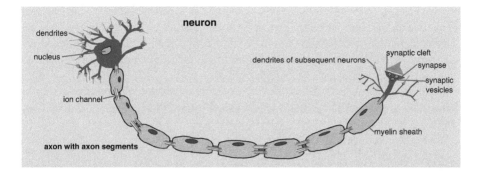

Fig. 5.17 Structure of a neuron with its main components for signal processing found in vertebrates

to *fire* what means that a subsequent stream of spikes is released into the *axon* of the neuron, a cascade of *axon segments* coupled to each other by *ion channels*.

Each axon segment comes with one or more *microtubules* operating like a wire. By means of an electric field produced by delimiting membrane proteins and their electric charges (*membrane potential*),, the spikes of cations get directed throughout the axon segment. Its opposite end provides ion channels bridging an axon segment with its successor. An ion channel controls passage of the cation spikes. Additionally, a signal refresh is done by amplification and reshaping. The spikes flattened and weakened along the microtubular wire. Each axon segment has been wrapped by a *myelin sheath* acting as an isolator against the local environment that contributes the cation spikes to be protected from perturbations and interferences with other electrical signals. Since an axon with its segments can reach a total length up to approximately 1 m, maintenance of a high quality of signal transduction is crucial for keeping frequency and waveform of each operated spike sequence.

The axon on its own ends up in one or more *synapses* placed in a branched manner. A synapse is responsible to forward the information encoded by the sequence of spikes to the next neuron. To this end, the electrical signal is transformed into a chemical representation. For this functionality, each synapse accommodates a number of *synaptic vesicles*. Having a nearly spheric form, a synaptic vesicle contains an individual combination of *neurotransmitters* enclosed by a membrane. Presence of cations temporarily accumulated in a synapse from arriving spikes initiates a chemical signalling cascade at the outer face of synaptic vesicles. Subject to the amount of cations attachable to a vesicle, it defines an individual threshold to become activated. After the needed amount of cations has been reached, the vesicle moves toward the outer face of the synapse and releases its neurotransmitters by *exocytosis* into the *synaptic cleft*, a thin gap to the next neuron. Neurotransmitters are a collection of messenger molecules able to enter the nearest dendrite of the adjacent neuron to get received again. This is done by a variety of receptors available at the dendrite's surface. Each of these receptors is coupled with another ion channel. As soon as the receptor gets activated by a suitable neurotransmitter, its ion channel opens for a short while in order to release a new spike of cations starting to pass the neuron processed in the same way as in its predecessor neuron. Since many receptor-controlled ion channels exist in a dendrite operating simultaneously, many cation spikes arise forming a sequence. Spiking signals feature by a high specificity and by a low amount of energy necessary for generation, transduction, and processing in comparison to sinusoidal oscillations because of the small average signal level over time.

We realize that neural signal processing is based on a complex interplay of numerous electrical, mechanical, and chemical processes complementing each other to achieve the entire functionality. This biological scenario emphasizes the usefulness of a modelling and simulation tool able to cope with a multiplicity of natural principles found in physics and chemistry and their cooperative bundling.

Before the modelling part of the case study can start, we pay attention to a deeper understanding of the *functioning of ion channels* as fundamental elements of neural signal processing.

Neural signal transduction is based on presence of movable electrically charged particles, especially *cations*. This complements the observation that a majority of complex intracellular molecules exhibits a negative electric charge such as RNA, DNA, and most proteins. Hence, an axon segment as a whole acts as a negative electrical potential surrounded by free or loosely bound cations like calcium (Ca^{2+}), natrium (Na^+), or potassium (K^+). Originated from environmental minerals, they reside at the outer face of the membrane surrounding an axon segment.

A neural signal cascade throughout the axon of a neuron is made of a sequence of *ion channels*, whereas each ion channel consists of a large protein placed throughout the outer membranes of adjacent axon segments (see Fig. 5.18). An ion channel allows a group of ions to pass together into the next axon segment driven by an electrochemical gradient [9]. To this end, the channel temporarily opens by deblocking a molecular gate. This gate, formed by an amino acid chain as a part of the underlying large protein, is controlled by electrical forces between the opposite ends of the channel. Whenever the resulting voltage exceeds a certain threshold, a so-called action potential has built up, the molecular gate becomes open, and a group of ions quickly runs into the body of the axon segment inducing a spike-shaped electrical signal. Afterward, the voltage between the opposite ends of the channel is nearly zero due to compensation of electric charges which implies closing the gate by adjusting the corresponding amino acid chain. It takes some time until enough cations accumulate at the outer end of the ion channel in order to open the gate again. Finally, the ion channel exhibits a spiking oscillatory behavior over time regarding the concentration course of entering cations. Inside the axon segment, these cations propagate alongside the microtubule, initiating wave patterns and triggering downstream processes.

Beneficially, the permeability of ion channels in each axon segment is sensitive to neural activity. Along with increasing activity, the required electrical force to open the molecular gate becomes diminished. This leads to a higher frequency (or shorter periodicity, respectively) of the spiking oscillation. From a systems biology point of

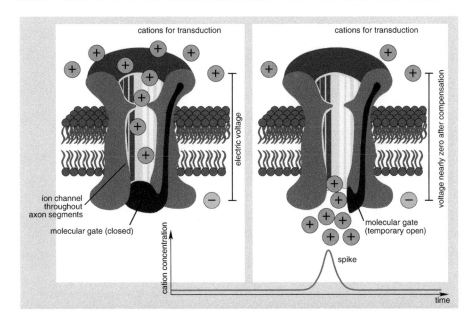

Fig. 5.18 Schematic representation of an ion channel and its functional principle. Cations $(+)$ accumulate at the outer face of the membrane surrounding an axon segment (**left**). After their amount has reached a certain threshold, the electric voltage with respect to the negatively charged inner part of the axon segment $(-)$ induces an electrical force which in turn temporarily opens a molecular gate. A group of cations passes this gate together which results in a spiking signal (**right**). Afterward, the voltage is nearly zero due to compensation of electric charges, and the molecular gate becomes closed again

view, a neural signal cascade based on ion channels primarily performs a frequency encoding of the input signal comparable with frequency modulation in engineering.

For the modelling study, we select an axon of a neuron with its segments, a synapse containing vesicles filled with neurotransmitters, and the synaptic cleft. The study aims at achievement of a spatiotemporal emulation of the behavioral patterns of cations, spike sequences, vesicles, and neurotransmitters for illustration of the holistic processing scheme from a general point of view. Later, a successive refinement might incorporate more and more details toward a quantifiable model capable of parameter fitting and disclosing underlying laws between frequency or duration of spike sequences and patterns of neurotransmitter release.

Figure 5.19 illustrates the initial modelling setup and the propagation phases of cation spikes throughout the axon segments together with subsequent release of neurotransmitters from a synaptic vesicle into the synaptic cleft. Let us describe a general formalization of the molecular system whose behavior coincides with biological knowledge. A later fine-tuning of the model can help to figure out process parameter values and underlying macroscopic laws from microscopic interactions. (**1**) A common elongated vessel ($1 \, \text{mm} \times 1 \, \mu\text{m} \times 1 \, \mu\text{m}$) is defined to incorporate all relevant system components separated by delimiters. The leftmost chamber stands

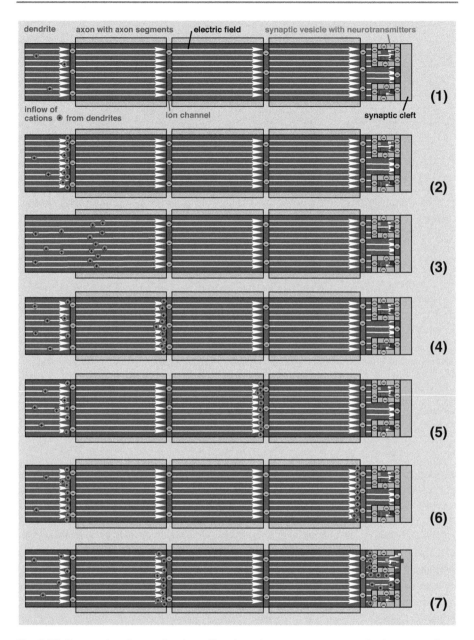

Fig. 5.19 Propagation phases of cation spikes throughout axon segments and subsequent release of neurotransmitters from synaptic vesicles into synaptic cleft

for the transit region from the nucleus into the axon supplied by an inflow of cations from the dendrites as soon as the neuron is firing. The inflow is implemented by instructions creating and setting new cations every few time steps. Downstream ion channels symbolized by solid particles with negative point charges divide the axon into three consecutive segments. Behind the axon, the right end of the vessel contains the synapse with some synaptic vesicles. Each vesicle is embedded into six surface areas acting as boundaries. They have been modelled as solid particles with negative point charges. Neurotransmitters represented by small solid particles have been attached at the inner faces of these delimiters. In total, the rightmost delimiters of the synapse demarcate a small outer chamber having the function of the synaptic cleft. The membrane potential present in the axon generates an electric field directed along and in parallel of the longitudinal axis. Its effect has been included by external electrical forces that steer the cations on their route through the axon. **(2)** More and more cations accumulate and enrich in the leftmost chamber stopped by the first ion channel still blocked by the presence of the corresponding delimiter. Over time, the number of cations increases continuously. Successively, they loosely bind to the delimiter of the first ion channel. **(3)** Immediately after the number of loosely bound cations has reached a predefined threshold, the ion channel temporarily opens which is done by a conditional instruction for removal of its delimiter. Now, a spike of cations continues with passing on its route entering the first axon segment. During passage, some cations out of the spike are slightly faster than others due to influences of Brownian motion and elastic collisions with water molecules. In consequence, the spike begins to disperse and becomes weaker. **(4)** A predefined time span after opening the first ion channel, the spike has completely moved into the first axon segment which in turn compensates the action potential, and the first ion channel needs to close again. This is done by another instruction set into operation with a delay. A fixed configurable number of time steps after opening the ion channel by conditional instruction, the delimiter is placed again preventing further cations from penetration of the first axon segment. Meanwhile, the spike of cations inside the first axon segment arrives at its opposite end marked with the next blocked ion channel. The cations need to accumulate at its entry what refreshes and restores the shape of the spike. **(5)** The second ion channel temporarily opens by conditional instruction, allows passage of a spike of cations, and closes again shortly after by delayed instruction. The cations move across the second axon segment and collect at the entry of the third ion channel. **(6)** After the predefined threshold of loosely bound cations is reached, the third ion channel temporarily opens, releasing the spike of cations into the third axon segment, and closes again by delayed instruction. The cations pass the third axon segment and wait in front of the rightmost ion channel terminating the third axon segment in front of the synapse. Simultaneously, a next collection of cations from the dendrites has been accumulated ready to enter the first axon segment forming the next spike. **(7)** Now, the original spike arrived at the synapse after the rightmost ion channel has temporarily opened and closed again. The cations traverse the synapse and bind to the outer faces (delimiters) of synaptic vesicles. Since the surface of each synaptic vesicle varies in its size, the number of cations able to bind there might deviate as well. By means of a chemical reaction (reaction rule) taking into account the number of bound ions to the compound of solid particles symbolizing the vesicle, it opens by elimination of the outer boundary solid particle. Moreover, the neurotransmitters are transformed from solid particles into moveable ones which models their release. For simplicity, we define the reaction in a way that the cations finally disappear along with release of neurotransmitters. By means of Brownian motion as main driving force for diffusion, the neurotransmitter particles migrate into the synaptic cleft depicted by the rightmost chamber. Simultaneously, the next spike has reached and passed the first axon segment.

The modelling case study can reproduce the desired behavior by the instruments available within the JENA tool. The interplay of physical processes and chemical reactions becomes obvious. Nevertheless, we are aware of the fact that the model at its present level is rather abstract and artificial without refinement and without fitting of parameters for a configuration in accordance with quantifiable measures. Configuration of cation abundance, thresholds, time delays, electric field properties, and proportions of the neuron's components to act in concert for obtaining an expected average spike periodicity of approximately 100 ms and a medium signal transduction speed of around $140 \frac{m}{s}$ requires an extension of the model system from a three-stage axon to several hundreds of axon segments and a more precise description of all dynamical structures including their regeneration.

5.5   Conclusions and Prospectives

We believe that the JENA tool in its present form contains a variety of useful, expressive, powerful, and elegant concepts and methods for modelling and simulation of biological information processing over time and in space at a medium abstraction level of molecules, particles, and their interplay. The tool mainly benefits from the combination of chemical reactions with physical processes since this feature facilitates formulation of many complex and interwoven biological principles like neural signal transduction. We envisage description, emulation, and analysis of a freely configurable molecular system in terms of a virtual cell or a virtual laboratory in which liquids and solid structures dynamically act, react, and interact.

The assumption of a vessel filled with atoms, ions, molecules, and moveable particles that perform a Brownian motion coincides with the well-established thermodynamical notion of composition found in liquids. Additional solid (immoveable) particles might form delimiters, permeable membranes, microtubules, or other three-dimensional spatial structures able to separate a vessel into chambers, compartments, or entities like vesicles, trabecular bone structures, or agarose gel filaments.

We allow specification of an individual set of reaction rules attached to an arbitrary reaction space (chamber) completely enclosed by solid particles or outer walls of the vessel. This setting enables definition of independent sets of reaction rules executed in parallel within different parts of the underlying vessel. Moreover, reaction rules might incorporate transformations of particles between a moveable and solid state, making them an instrument for successive assembly or decomposition of compounds and hence able to cope with dynamical structures. Following the intention of the so-called Billiard model, a chemical reaction emerges from an effective collision of its substrate molecules or particles with enough kinetic energy to overcome the activation energy. An exception is given by decay reactions in which merely one substrate spontaneously degenerates. We allow for this by determination of points in time for molecular decay.

Many physical processes rely on the effect of varying forces influencing the motion of molecules and particles. Since electrical and mechanical forces are most relevant, corresponding force fields can be defined by means of interfering three-dimensional vector fields. This feature turns out to be a powerful instrument because many laboratory techniques and biological processes make use of external forces. Examples are centrifugation, electrophoresis, ion channels, osmosis, filters, and pumps.

Complementing the aforementioned modelling concepts for an autonomous system's behavior without any controlling intervention from outside, we provide the instrument of instructions in order to enable directed modifications of the molecular system either at predefined points in time or subject to fulfillment of conditions like exceeding a minimum particle concentration. Particularly for modelling of abstract issues or environmental stimuli, instructions are the first choice. They can create or eliminate solid particles, inject new moveable constituents, change the temperature, and add or remove reaction rules which implies a high flexibility for exploration of case studies.

Currently, the JENA tool has reached its alpha state prior to be made available for all interested users. After a couple of tests and improvements will be finalized, the software package can be downloaded for free from our research platform at www.molecular-computing.de.

Despite the JENA tool is not far away from the first level of maturation, there are many ideas for further improvements and extensions. Future work is planned whose next steps address following open problems, questions, and wishes.

Although a multiplicity of vessels can be managed, these vessels have been considered to be isolated from each other so far. It would give a higher descriptive convenience to connect several vessels inspired by a tissue, by a united cell structure, or by a distributed multipurpose laboratory equipment. To do so, we need to find a way to make outer vessel boundaries permeable for exchange of atoms, ions, and moveable particles. The connectivity of vessels on their own should be handled in a dynamical manner as well, for instance, by suitable new types of instructions able to link or to disconnect vessels and capable of regulation of outer wall's selective or time-dependent permeability.

Due to the discretization of space by voxels (small-volume elements), elastic and nonelastic collisions have been treated to run in a central manner which means that both colliding molecules or particles move along a course frontally faced to each other. This assumption brings a high degree of idealization, increasing the level of abstraction since most collisions have a peripheral or decentral nature whose mathematical modelling is more complex, consumes more computational resources, but gives more realistic results.

Convincing visualization has been identified to be a challenging task. This is mainly due to the fact that atoms, ions, and molecules turn out to be rather small in comparison to the dimensions of a vessel. When depicted in its original proportions, many constituents are simply invisible since they occupy less than one pixel. In contrast, there might exist a high number up to several billion constituents, especially in case that water molecules are included in a visualization. Here, we are seeking for new and complementing approaches.

JENA in its entirety is conceived of an ongoing long-term project with many facets, fascinating case studies, a growing pool of models, and amazing applications also in teaching and education. From a scientific point of view, the JENA tool is envisioned for helping to turn empirical bioinformatics knowledge into systematic knowledge derivable and explainable based on natural laws and promoted by membrane computing.

References

1. A. Bejan, *Advanced Engineering of Thermodynamics*, 4th edn. (Wiley, New York, 2016)
2. D.A. Case, T.E. Cheatham, T. Darden, H. Gohlke, R. Luo, K.M. Merz, Jr., A. Onufriev, C. Simmerling, B. Wang, R. Woods, The Amber biomolecular simulation programs. J. Comput. Chem. **26**, 1668–1688 (2005). https://doi.org/10.1002/jcc.20290.
3. T. Clark, *A Handbook of Computational Chemistry: A Practical Guide to Chemical Structure and Energy Calculations* (Wiley-Interscience, New York, 1985)
4. K.A. Connors, *Chemical Kinetics: The Study of Reaction Rates in Solution* (VCH Publishers, New York, 1990)
5. L.G. Davis, M.D. Dibner, J.F. Battey, *Basic Methods in Molecular Biology* (Elsevier, Amsterdam, 2006)
6. P. Dayan, L. Abbott, *Theoretical Neuroscience: Computational and Mathematical Modeling of Neural Systems* (MIT Press, Cambridge, 2001)
7. D. Flanagan, *Java in a Nutshell* (O'Reilly, New York, 2005)
8. M. García-Quismondo, R. Gutiérrez-Escudero, I. Pérez-Hurtado, M.J. Pérez-Jiménez, A. Riscos-Núñez, An overview of P-Lingua 2.0, in *Membrane Computing (WMC 2009)*, ed. by Gh. Păun, M.J. Pérez-Jiménez, A. Riscos, G. Rozenberg, A. Salomaa. Lecture Notes in Computer Science, vol. 5957 (2010), pp. 264–288. https://doi.org/10.1007/978-3-642-11467-0_20
9. R. Glaser, *Biophysics: An Introduction* (Springer, Berlin, 2012)
10. P. Greengard, The neurobiology of slow synaptic transmission. Science **294**(5544), 1024–1030 (2001). https://doi.org/10.1126/science.294.5544.1024
11. G. Grünert, B. Ibrahim, T. Lenser, M. Lohel, T. Hinze, P. Dittrich, Rule-based spatial modeling with diffusing, geometrically constrained molecules. BMC Bioinf. **11**, 307 (2010). https://doi.org/0.1186/1471-2105-11-307
12. S.R. Hameroff, *Ultimate Computing. Biomolecular Consciousness and Nanotechnology* (North-Holland/Elsevier, Amsterdam, 1987)
13. D. Hames, N. Hooper, *Biochemistry*, 3rd edn. (Taylor and Francis, London, 2005)
14. R.A. Harvey, P.C. Champe, *Biochemistry* (Lippincott Williams and Wilkins, Baltimore, 2005)

15. T. Hinze, The Java Environment for Nature-inspired Approaches (JENA): a workbench for bioComputing and bioModelling enthusiasts, in *Enjoying Natural Computing, Series Lecture Notes in Computer Science*, vol. 11270, ed. by C. Graciani, A. Riscos-Núñez, Gh. Păun, G. Rozenberg, A. Salomaa (2018), pp. 155–169. https://doi.org/10.1007/978-3-030-00265-7_13

16. T. Hinze, J. Behre, C. Bodenstein, G. Escuela, G. Grünert, P. Hofstedt, P. Sauer, S. Hayat, P. Dittrich, Membrane systems and tools combining dynamical structures with reaction kinetics for applications in chronobiology, in *Applications of Membrane Computing in Systems and Synthetic Biology*, ed. by P. Frisco, M. Gheorghe, M.J. Pérez-Jiménez. Series Emergence, Complexity, and Computation, vol. 7 (Springer, Berlin, 2014), pp. 133–173. https://doi.org/10.1007/978-3-319-03191-0_5

17. W. Hoppe, W. Lohmann, H. Markl, H. Ziegler, *Biophysics* (Springer, Berlin, 1983)

18. P.A. Iglesias, B.P. Ingalls. *Control Theory and Systems Biology* (MIT Press, New York, 2010)

19. B.G. Johannson, Agarose gel electrophoresis. Scand. J. Clin. Lab. Invest. **29**(s124), 7–19 (1972). https://doi.org/10.3109/00365517209102747.

20. H. Kitano, Computational systems biology. Nature **420**, 206–210 (2002). https://doi.org/10.1038/nature01254

21. E. Klipp, R. Herwig, A. Kowald, C. Wierling, H. Lehrach, *Systems Biology in Practics* (Wiley VCH, New York, 2005)

22. C. Koch, *Biophysics of Computation. Information Processing in Single Neurons* (Oxford University, Oxford, 1999)

23. Z.L. Kruk, C.J. Pycock, *Neurotransmitters and Drugs* (Croom Helm, London, 2007)

24. A.J. Lotka, Contribution to the theory of periodic reactions. J. Phys. Chem. **14**(3), 271–274 (1910). https://doi.org/10.1021/j150111a004

25. P. Mörters, Y. Peres, *Brownian Motion* (Cambridge University, Cambridge, 2010)

26. Gh. Păun, G. Rozenberg, A. Salomaa *The Oxford Handbook of Membrane Computing* (Oxford University, Oxford, 2010)

27. I. Pérez-Hurtado, D. Orellana-Martín, G. Zhang, M.J. Pérez-Jiménez, P-lingua in two steps: flexibility and efficiency. J. Membr. Comput. **1**(2), 93–102 (2019). https://doi.org/10.1007/s41965-019-00014-1

28. T.D. Pollard, W.C. Earnshaw, J. Lippincott-Schwartz, G.T. Johnson, *Cell Biology*, 3rd edn. (Elsevier, Amsterdam, 2017)

29. A.K. Rappe, C.J. Casewit, K.S. Colwell, W.A. Goddard, W.M. Skiff, UFF, a full periodic table force field for molecular mechanics and molecular dynamics simulations. J Am. Chem. Soc. **114**(25), 10024–10035 (1992). https://doi.org/10.1021/ja00051a040

30. R.W. Sabnis, *Handbook of Biological Dyes and Stains: Synthesis and Industrial Application* (Wiley-VCH, New York, 2010)

31. R. Salomon-Ferrer, D.A. Case, R.C. Walker, An overview of the Amber biomolecular simulation package. WIREs Comput. Mol. Sci. **3**, 198–210 (2013). https://doi.org/10.1002/wcms.1121

32. T.C. Südhof, J. Rizo, Synaptic vesicle exocytosis. Cold Spring Harbor Perspect. Biol. **3**(12), 1–15 (2011). https://doi.org/10.1101/cshperspect.a005637

33. G.I. Taylor, Diffusion by continuous movements. Proc. London Math. Soc. **2**(1), 196–212 (1922). First published. https://doi.org//10.1112/plms/s2-20.1.196

34. G.J. van Wylen, R.E. Sonntag, *Fundamentals of Classical Thermodynamics* (Wiley, New York, 1985)

35. R. Westermeier, *Electrophoresis in Practice* (Wiley-VCH, New York, 2005)

36. M. Weissbluth, *Atoms and Molecules* (Academic Press, New York, 2008)

P Systems Implementation on GPUs

6

6.1 Introduction

The development of P system simulators is usually driven by the importance of certain models. Usually, these simulators are implemented in a flexible way, allowing not only to simulate a wide variety of P systems but also to help construct simulators for other models. An example of this flexibility is P-Lingua framework[13]. However, for certain applications and models, efficient simulation tools are required. For instance, the simulation of population dynamics P systems is crucial for model validation of real ecosystems and for virtual experimentation. In this case, the faster the simulation tool, the shorter the time to construct a valid model. Another interest behind the development of efficient tools is also for analyzing theoretical aspects of P systems (parallelism, non-determinism, etc.) and how to bridge them with today, *in-silico* technology [48].

There are several ways to accelerate the simulation of P systems: changing the technology where to implement the simulators (e.g., from interpreted languages like Java to compiled ones like C++), increasing the power of the processors where to run the simulations (e.g., increasing the clock frequency, the memory bandwidth and clock, etc.), or using high performance computing (HPC) technologies to implement real parallelism. The main trend when developing efficient simulators has been the last one: taking advantage of the inherent parallelism of the models and mapping it into parallel platforms such as clusters, supercomputers, accelerators, etc.

According to [15], we can define high performance computing (HPC) as *"the practice of aggregating computing power in a way that delivers much higher performance than one could get out of a typical desktop computer or workstation in order to solve large problem instances in science, engineering, or business"*. This is usually accomplished by means of parallelism, since it is the basis for the acceleration of large and complex real-world applications. The maximum exponent of HPC is known as supercomputing, where the computing power of current technology is being continuously pushed. A ranking of the most powerful

© The Author(s), under exclusive license to Springer Nature Singapore Pte Ltd. 2021   163
G. Zhang et al., *Membrane Computing Models: Implementations*,
https://doi.org/10.1007/978-981-16-1566-5_6

supercomputers can be consulted at Top500 website [46]. To the time of writing, most of the top 10 supercomputers are based on nodes extended with accelerators.

HPC accelerators are dedicated chips that serve as co-processors, extending in this way the computing power. Examples of accelerators are FPGAs and GPUs. The latter refers to the processors inside the graphics cards, which take over the task of graphics generation in computers. However, with the increasing demand in 3D rendering for gaming and video, and as foreseen by Elster [12] and others, GPUs (Graphics Processing Units) have evolved to a massively parallel processor that is suitable for parallel computing. Today, GPUs are the enabling technology for trending areas such as Deep Learning, Data Science, physics simulation, real-time ray tracing graphics, etc.

Concerning P systems and their applications, GPUs have been shown to be an alternative for accelerating simulations. In [4], the double parallelism of P systems were mapped over the double parallelism inside GPUs. This idea has been refined over the time, in such a way that the simulators are now better adapted to GPU parallelism. We can identify three types of simulators: those developed for very specific P systems or family of P systems (specific simulators) and developed for a wide range of P systems inside a variant (generic simulators) and a hybrid simulator that receives high-level information to be better adapted (adaptive simulators).

In this chapter, we will introduce all the concepts related with GPU computing and its applications. Later, we will go through some P system simulators depending on their type: specific, generic, or hybrid. Finally, we will provide some guidelines on how to develop new simulators for P systems on GPUs.

6.2   GPU Computing

In this section, we will introduce the main concepts of GPU computing, including CUDA and modern GPU architecture. This will provide the required background to understand the design of P system simulators on GPUs.

6.2.1   The Graphics Processing Unit

The first Graphics Processing Units (GPUs) were introduced back in 1999 [11], in order to overcome the bottleneck created by the CPU when generating real-time graphics, such as in videogames and in 3D rendering. Since then, every graphics card has integrated such kind of specific processors. Usually, we refer to GPU and graphics card as synonyms. It is important to remark the place where the GPU is located on a computer. The GPU is connected with the CPU through a data bridge (Northbridge), which is also used to access the main memory (RAM). Currently, modern GPUs are connected through the so called PCI Express bus, which runs at more than 64GB/s (when using 16-lane configuration).

GPUs, since they were born, install processor cores that are specialized for graphics (pixel colorization, etc.). Thus, these processors are able to include more cores than usual CPUs because they are more specific and, so, lightweight. This GPU architecture has evolved over the time, being both more parallel and flexible. The former means that it included more and more computing cores, and the latter means that these cores were more programmable. In fact, since 2002, the graphics pipeline implemented in GPU hardware became programmable through small programs called shaders. Programming languages such as Cg, GLSL, DirectX Shading languages, etc. are employed for shaders. There were two types of shaders (for vertices and fragments), but in 2007 they were unified (e.g., the U of CUDA stands for Unified).

The evolution of shaders led to a new area called GPGPU (general purpose computing on the GPU), whose name was coined by Mark Harris in 2002. The target of this research area is to develop parallel methodologies to program GPUs for other purposes rather than graphics, such as scientific computing. Today, this is more known as GPU computing and has been settled as an alternative within HPC. That is, GPUs are nowadays an HPC accelerator that can be found in the most powerful supercomputers. GPUs are good at data parallelism. More specifically, they are based on SPMD programming model (Single Program Multiple Data): the GPU processes many independent elements in parallel using the same program [35].

Currently, GPU computing is also a heterogeneous computing system [17], where the GPU is known as device and the CPU is known as host. The host has a role of a master, which takes over the execution and manages the different devices that can be in the system. Devices are co-processors that help to accelerate the algorithms by executing code in a parallel fashion, reducing in this way the overhead on the host. This trend is being consolidated with OpenCL [31], the first free, open standard for multi-platform, heterogeneous parallel programming of modern processors found in PCs, servers, and embedded devices. OpenCL is being used not only for GPUs but also for FPGAs, multicore CPUs, etc. However, the drivers and compilers developed by each manufacturer of chips (NVIDIA, Intel, AMD...) are not up to date and lack full support. This is why a new standard, called SYCL, is being conceived, but it is still experimental (to date).

GPUs can be programmed with both OpenCL and SYCL [44]. Moreover, NVIDIA GPUs can be also programmed with CUDA [32], which is a proprietary technology that is very mature and has lot of functionality. By having a quick look to the literature, it is possible to see that CUDA is the most used platform for GPU computing. On the other side, AMD GPUs can be also programmed with a CUDA-like environment called HIP [34], which is based on RoCm. This allows programmers to translate easily CUDA code to AMD technology. Other standard languages and platforms to program GPUs are based on the graphics pipeline, such as OpenGL, GLSL, and Vulkan [47]. They can also be used for GPU computing in a not very complex way.

In short, GPU computing poses a highly parallel architecture with thousands of lightweight processor cores and high-bandwidth memory that can be programmed with several standard languages. The most evolved one is CUDA, but it works only for NVIDIA GPUs. Since the introduction of CUDA in 2007, many scientific applications have used GPU computing. Their low cost compared to the performance offered has made GPUs an attractive alternative. In fact, currently they are the enabling technology (i.e., if you want to tackle these problems, you should be using GPUs) for Deep Learning [18], nanopore DNA sequencing, and high-energy particle trajectory reconstruction in LHCb HLT 1.

6.2.2   CUDA Programming Model

In this chapter, we will be focusing on CUDA [32, 33], since, as mentioned, it is the most widely technology for GPU computing, and on top of that, the majority of P system simulators have been developed with CUDA. Let us recall that CUDA, as usual in GPU computing, offers a heterogeneous system to the user, where the CPU is known as the host, and the GPU is the device. The execution flow in a CUDA program is like in any common program; it starts with the CPU main function. At some points, the CPU asks the GPU to allocate memory, transfer memory, launch computation, retrieve results, etc.

CUDA devices take advantage of data-parallel program sections and accelerate their execution. A CUDA program therefore consists of one or more phases that are executed either in the host or in device. Sequential and control phases are implemented in the host code, while phases which exhibit a large amount of data parallelism are implemented in the device code. A CUDA program is also a unified source code covering both sides.

We call kernels to those functions executed by the device (GPU). When they are requested to be executed by the host, they allocate an execution grid on device. A grid typically populates a large number of execution threads that work in SPMD fashion: they execute the same piece of code (the kernel function) to probably different portions of data. Actually, a kernel is written as a usual function in a programming language (so far, only C++, Fortran or Python) but using special keywords given by the CUDA API. These keywords, such as the thread identifier, might take different values at different threads in run time, so that they can have index different data elements, or even take different execution path (although this is not optimal). CUDA threads are much lighter than CPU threads. A CUDA programmer can assume that these threads take a few cycles to be generated and scheduled. This contrasts with the threads of the CPU, which normally require thousands of clock cycles to be managed.

Threads within a grid are arranged in a two-level hierarchy. At the higher level, each grid consists of a two-dimensional array of *thread blocks*. At the lower level, each block is organized as a three-dimensional array of threads. All blocks in a grid have the same number and organization of threads. Moreover, each block is identified by a two-dimensional identifier and each thread within its block by a three-dimensional identifier. To date, a thread block can contain, at most, 1024 threads. Threads within a block can easily cooperate through a special fast memory (see below) and special warp-wide operations (see next section) and be synchronized with a barrier operation.

One kernel is executed by just one grid that, has mentioned, arranges an array of thread blocks, each with the same configuration of threads. It is also possible to launch several kernels at the same time on a GPU with different grids. This is allowed by the so-called CUDA streams. They are concepts similar to lanes, where kernels get executed. As long as there are available resources on the GPU, the kernel executions can be done simultaneously. CUDA streams also allow to overlap execution with memory transfers, designing in this way full computing pipelines.

CUDA programmers also have to explicitly manage the memory layout and hierarchy. GPUs offer different memory spaces arranged in a hierarchy where to store the data of a parallel program. In CUDA, the host and the devices have separate memory spaces (as it is in the real hardware). In order to run a kernel on the device, the data has to be there. Hence, enough memory should be first allocated, and later the relevant data has to be transferred from host to device. Similarly, after the execution of the kernels on the device, the resulting data has to be copied from device to host memory, and finally the allocated device memory should be released. From this point of view, we can assume that CUDA uses static memory allocations. Dynamic memory is already supported at the kernels, but there are restrictions, and it drastically downgrades the performance.

The memory that serves as communication channel between the host and the device is called global (or device) memory. The host can allocate memory and copy memory, and CUDA threads can access it and make modifications. However, this memory is the slowest in the GPU, but the largest one. The best performance is achieved when contiguous threads (according to their identifiers) access contiguous positions of data, in what is called coalesced memory access. This helps to maximize the utilization of the memory bandwidth.

Threads can use a common memory space when they are in the same thread block, which is called shared memory. Accesses to shared memory are very fast when done in a coalesced way. However, it is a small space of up to just kilobytes. On the other side, we can find cached memories. They are memories that automatically speedup the access to repeated data through a cache. Examples of them are constant and texture memories. They are read-only memories for the GPU, and the CPU can just copy data in there, under certain restrictions. Moreover, modern GPUs have two levels of cache memory for accesses to global memory, but this is completely transparent to the code.

In summary, algorithms implemented in CUDA are structured as follows [17]:

1. The host initializes the program, reading the input data.
2. The host allocate enough memory space in global memory for input and auxiliary data.
3. The host copies the input and auxiliary data to the device.
4. The host launches a kernel to the device, with the following syntax: `kernelName <<< numBlocks, numThreads, streamId, sharedMemory >>> (param1, param2,...)`

5. When a kernel is executed, at the device side:
    (a) The threads of each block read its corresponding data portion from global memory to shared memory or to internal variables (also called registers, see next section).
    (b) Threads work with the data directly on the shared memory or with their registers.
    (c) Threads copy these data back to global memory.
6. The host might call more kernels, copy more data, retrieve data, etc.
7. When the algorithm is done, the host copies back the results from global memory of the device.

As mentioned before, threads from different blocks cannot cooperate directly, but only through the global memory and using a special set of atomic operations. These operations are implemented by implicit locks, so that accesses to desired data elements can be efficiently synchronized through them. However, this is restricted to the use of a small set of operations.

6.2.3 GPU Architecture

A modern GPU architecture [19] consists of a processor array which has hundreds (even thousands) of *SP* (streaming processor) cores organized in *SM* (streaming multiprocessor). In this sense, every SM contains the following units: SP arithmetic cores, SFU single-precision floating point units (for specific operations such as sine, cosine, reciprocal square root, etc.), double precision units, instruction cache, read only constant cache, read/write shared memory and L1 cache memory, a set of 32-bit registers, and access to the off-chip memory (device/local memory). The arithmetic units are capable to execute several instructions per clock cycle, and they are fully pipelined, running at frequencies around 1 GHz (depending on the GPU). The amount of cores, floating point units, shared memory, etc. depends on the GPU itself.

SMs is able to manage and execute thousands of threads in hardware with zero scheduling overhead. Each thread has its own thread execution state and can execute an independent code path. This execution is done in a *SIMT (Single-Instruction Multiple-Thread)* fashion [19], where threads execute the same instruction on different piece of data. SMs create, manage, schedule, and execute threads in groups of 32 threads (of the same thread block). This set of 32 threads is called *warp*. Each SM can handle several warps. Individual threads of the same warp must be of the same type and start together at the same program address in order to be scheduled simultaneously, but they are free to branch (e.g., an if then else clause) and execute independently at the cost of serialization.

When a grid is created to execute a kernel, the thread blocks are created and assigned to SMs. An SM can handle several thread blocks, but a thread block is assigned only to one SM. Then, the thread block is split into warps and they are scheduled. When a warp is selected, its threads are executed on SPs as long as the threads are synchronized in the same execution flow of the code. If the threads of a warp diverge, the warp serially executes each taken branch path, disabling threads that are not on that path. When all the paths complete, the threads re-converge to the original execution path.

As shown by the CUDA programming model [17], the GPU contains several memory spaces. First of all, both the GPU and the CPU have separated memory spaces. They are connected through a bus that can be PCI Express ×16 bus standard. Global memory is the largest (up to several gigabytes) but the slowest one. Although there is a two-level cache memory system to speedup repeated access to same data, an access to global memory is around 400 times slower than accessing on-chip memory spaces (such as shared memory or registers). Moreover, in order to fulfill the memory bandwidth, threads should make coalesced accesses.

As mentioned, inside each SM we can find a memory space called shared memory. Its size is measured in kilobytes, but its access is very fast, even close to the accesses to registers. This memory space is also split into shared memory and L1 cache memory. The latter is transparent to CUDA programs, while shared memory is manually managed (one can allocate space and let threads to copy and modify data). There are also many other units for cached memory which is read only for the cores. Finally, SMs incorporate a large amount of registers, whose access is the fastest since they are next to the cores. They are used to allocate the values of single variables declared in the code (e.g., iterators, auxiliary variables, etc.).

6.2.4 Good Practices

CUDA is supported by a wide range of tools [33], including a compiler (called nvcc), the driver for the GPU, libraries, and examples. They are freely available at their website. There is also a vast amount of documentation, books, and literature in this respect. CUDA is not only the most mature platform for GPU computing but also the one with the largest community and support. It is important to know the compiler options for automatic optimizations (like -O3) and to understand and use the libraries (e.g., CuRAND for random number generation, CuSPARSE for sparse matrix representations and operations, etc.).

It is also a good practice to start developing a reference program in sequential C/C++ before starting implementing in CUDA. This is critical in order to first understand the algorithm, secondly to validate the parallel version, and also to run benchmarks and performance analysis.

Finally, let us introduce four ways to accelerate the execution of a program on a GPU with CUDA [35]. They will help to understand the designs of GPU-based P system simulators:

- *Emphasize parallelism*: GPUs prefer to run thousands of lightweight threads. Thus, the algorithms should permit dividing the computation into many independent pieces by decreasing the resources assigned to each thread and avoiding synchronization.

- *Minimize branch divergence*: if a warp is broken because divergence in the path executed by the threads, then there is no real parallelism.
- *Maximize arithmetic intensity*: computation is relatively cheap for today's GPUs, but bandwidth is precious. It is better to maximize the computational operations per memory transaction. Shared memory or registers can help for this purpose.
- *Exploit streaming bandwidth*: on the other side, GPUs and their on-board memory have a peak bandwidth much faster than in CPUs. It is achieved by streaming memory access patterns: coalesced access to aligned memory positions. A good way to maximize the bandwidth in an algorithm is by the scatter/gather strategy.

6.3   Generic Simulations

In this section, we will introduce a type of simulation of P systems, which is called generic simulation [22, 25]. We will describe how to implement this kind of simulators in CUDA and provide two illustrative examples.

6.3.1   Definition

When implementing a P system simulator, it is important to understand what type of P systems we want to simulate before starting the development. We will say that a generic simulator is a simulator developed for a wide range of P systems belonging to the same variant. If the simulator is able to handle a large variety of P systems (with very distinct rules and alphabets, even designed to solve different problems), then it is generic. Sometimes the types of P systems are restricted somehow for the sake of simplicity, but as long as the simulator accepts P systems from different families (but for the same variant), we will say it is generic and not specific.

In this scenario, it is not possible to know what can happen in the computation at a certain transition step. Therefore, it has to be prepared for any situation, so we need to cover worst-case scenarios when developing such kind of simulators. For example, we need to provide an upper bound of existing objects at a certain step, in order to avoid memory overflows. Furthermore, in principle, all rules might be selected for execution at a certain step (until their applicability is checked). The rules must be stored in memory since we do not know them until the P system model is parsed. As mentioned in Chap. 2, simulators are usually defined by three modules: input parser, simulation engine, and output module. Generic simulators can be designed to reproduce either a single computation or all computations of the input P system.

The memory layout is also an essential part of a simulator, since P system simulators have been demonstrated to be memory and memory bandwidth bound. When storing the information of P system configuration, we can use either [25]:

- *Sparse representation*: using a large array to store multiplicities, with a position per each possible object (all objects defined in the alphabet). The access is direct since the object identifier is the index where to access the array. However, if many objects are not present at a certain moment, the array will be full of zeroes.
- *Dense representation*: using a double array with a component for the object identifier and the other for multiplicity. We need to search for the object, unless we track them and we know exactly where they are store at any moment. This can help to drastically reduce the size because objects with multiplicity zero can be discarded.

Generic simulators usually use sparse representations, since, in this way, they can identify objects very efficiently, in $O(1)$. The object identifier is employed as the index to access the array where storing the multisets, and by representing the whole alphabet, we make sure of an upper bound for the worst-case scenario.

6.3.2 Simulating P Systems with Active Membranes

In this section we will depict the very first GPU simulator for P systems ever developed. It was a generic simulator and helped to understand how to better map the parallelism of P systems on the parallelism on GPUs. The simulated models were of the variant P systems with active membranes and elementary division.

The original work is published in [4, 21, 22]. The full framework of simulators for P systems with active membranes, including the sequential, fast sequential, and CUDA parallel simulators, is called *PCUDA*. It is a subproject of the PMCGPU project and can be downloaded from the official website http://sourceforge.net/p/pmcgpu [45] or the repository https://github.com/RGNC/pcuda.

6.3.2.1 Recognizer P Systems with Active Membranes
Families of cell-like P systems whose membrane structures does not grow, that is, there is no rules producing new membranes in the system, only can solve in polynomial time and uniform way, problems in class **P**. Therefore, new ingredients are needed in order to be able to provide efficient solutions of computationally hard problems by making use of an exponential workspace, expressed in terms of number of membranes and number of objects, created in linear time. In [36], a new computing model, called *P system with active membranes*, was introduced. In these systems, the membranes have associated with electrical charges and make use of *division rules*, inspired from the *mitosis* and *meiosis* processes, as a mechanism to generate in linear time, an exponential workspace. Polynomial time and uniform solutions to **NP**-complete problems were given by using families of the new computing model.

Next, P systems with active membranes and division rules only for elementary division are formally defined.

Definition 6.1. A P system with active membranes of degree $q \geq 1$ is a tuple $\Pi = (\Gamma, H, \mu, \mathcal{M}_1, \ldots, \mathcal{M}_q, \mathcal{R}, i_{out})$, where:

1. Γ and H are finite alphabets such that $\Gamma \cap H = \emptyset$;
2. μ is a rooted tree with q nodes labeled by elements from H (the root is labeled by $i_s \in H$);
3. $\mathcal{M}_1, \ldots, \mathcal{M}_q$ belongs to $M(\Gamma)$, that is, all of them are multisets over Γ;
4. $\mathcal{R}$ is a finite set of rules, of the following forms:
   (a) $[a \rightarrow u]_h^\alpha$, for $h \in H, \alpha \in \{+, -, 0\}, a \in \Gamma, u \in M(\Gamma)$ (object evolution rules);
   (b) $a [\ ]_h^{\alpha_1} \rightarrow [b]_h^{\alpha_2}$, for $h \in H \setminus \{i_s\}, \alpha_1, \alpha_2 \in \{+, -, 0\}, a, b \in \Gamma$ (send-in rules);
   (c) $[a]_h^{\alpha_1} \rightarrow b [\ ]_h^{\alpha_2}$, for $h \in H, \alpha_1, \alpha_2 \in \{+, -, 0\}, a, b \in \Gamma$ (send-out rules);
   (d) $[a]_h^\alpha \rightarrow b$, for $h \in H \setminus \{i_s, i_{out}\}, \alpha \in \{+, -, 0\}, a, b \in \Gamma$ (dissolution rules);
   (e) $[a]_h^{\alpha_1} \rightarrow [b]_h^{\alpha_2} [c]_h^{\alpha_3}$, for $h \in H \setminus \{i_s, i_{out}\}, \alpha_1, \alpha_2, \alpha_3 \in \{+, -, 0\}, a, b, c \in \Gamma$ (division rules for elementary membranes);
5. $i_{out} \in H \cup \{env\}$, where $env \notin \Gamma \cup H$.

A P system with active membranes of degree $q \geq 1$, $\Pi = (\Gamma, H, \mu, \mathcal{M}_1, \ldots, \mathcal{M}_q, \mathcal{R}, i_{out})$, can be viewed as a set of q membranes, injectively labeled by elements of H, arranged in a hierarchical structure μ given by a labeled rooted tree (called *membrane structure*) whose root is called the *skin membrane* (labeled by i_s), such that (a) each membrane has associated with it an electrical charge from the set $\{+, -, 0\}$; (b) $\mathcal{M}_1, \ldots, \mathcal{M}_p$ represent the finite multisets of *objects* (symbols of the working alphabet Γ) initially placed in the q membranes of the system; (c) $\mathcal{R}$ is a finite set of rules over Γ associated with the labels; and (d) $i_{out} \in H \cup \{env\}$ indicates the output zone. We use the term *zone i* to refer to membrane i in the case $i \in H$ and to refer to the "environment" of the system in the case $i = env$. The leaves of μ are called *elementary membranes*.

Next, the semantics of the new computing model is described. A *configuration* (or *instantaneous description*) C_t at an instant t of a P system with active membranes is described by the following elements: (a) the membrane structure at instant t and (b) all multisets of objects over Γ associated with all the membranes present in the system at that moment.

An *object evolution rule* $[a \rightarrow u]_h^\alpha$ is *applicable* to a configuration C_t at an instant t, if there exists a membrane labeled by h with electrical charge α, in C_t, such that contains object a. When applying such a rule to such a membrane, one object a is consumed and objects from the multiset u is produced in that membrane.

A *send-in communication rule* $a [\ ]_h^{\alpha_1} \rightarrow [b]_h^{\alpha_2}$ is *applicable* to a configuration C_t at an instant t, if there exists a membrane labeled by h with electrical charge α_1, in C_t such that h is not the label of the root of μ and its parent membrane contains object a. When applying such a rule to such a membrane, one object a is consumed from the parent membrane, and object b is produced in the corresponding membrane labeled by h. Besides, the charge α_1 of that membrane h is replaced by α_2.

A *send-out communication rule* $[\, a \,]_h^{\alpha_1} \rightarrow b \,[\ \ ]_h^{\alpha_2}$ is *applicable* to a configuration C_t at an instant t, if there exists a membrane labeled by h with electrical charge α_1, in C_t such that it contains object a. When applying such a rule to such a membrane, one object a is consumed from such membrane h, and object b is produced in the parent of such membrane (in the case that such membrane is the skin, then object b is produced in the environment). Besides, the charge α_1 of that membrane h is replaced by α_2.

A *dissolution rule* $[\, a \,]_h^{\alpha} \rightarrow b$ is *applicable* to a configuration C_t at an instant t, if there exists a membrane labeled by h with electrical charge α, in C_t, different from the skin membrane and the output zone, such that it contains object a. When applying such a rule to such a membrane, one object a is consumed, membrane h is dissolved, and one object b and the remaining objects of the membrane where the rule is applied are sent to its parent (or the first ancestor that has not been dissolved).

A *division rule for elementary membrane* $[\, a \,]_h^{\alpha_1} \rightarrow [\, b \,]_h^{\alpha_2} \, [\, c \,]_h^{\alpha_3}$ is *applicable* to a configuration C_t at an instant t, if there exists an elementary membrane labeled by h with electrical charge α_1, in C_t, different from the skin membrane and the output zone, such that it contains object a. When applying such a rule to such a membrane, the membrane with label h is divided into two membranes with the same label; in the first copy, one object a is replaced by one object b; in the second one, one object a is replaced by one object c; all the other objects are replicated and copies of them are placed in the two new membranes. Besides, the charge α_1 of the first created membrane h is replaced by α_2, and the charge α_1 of the second created membrane h is replaced by α_3.

In P systems with active membranes, the rules are applied according to the following principles:

- At one transition step: (i) one object and one membrane can be used by only one rule, selected in a non-deterministic way, and (ii) at most a rule of types (b)–(e), selected in a non-deterministic way, can be applied to a membrane, and then it is applied once.
- Object evolution rules can be simultaneously applied to a membrane with one rule of types (b)–(e). If it is the case, object evolution rules will be applied in a maximally parallel manner.
- If an object evolution rule and a division rule are applied to a membrane at the same transition step, then we suppose that first the evolution rule is applied, and then the division is produced. Of course, this process takes only one transition step.
- The skin membrane and the output membrane, if any, can never get divided nor dissolved.

Given a P system with active membranes, $\Pi = (\Gamma, H, \mu, \mathcal{M}_1, \ldots, \mathcal{M}_q, \mathcal{R}, i_{out})$, the *initial configuration* of Π is $C_0 = (\mathcal{M}_1, \cdots, \mathcal{M}_q)$. A configuration is a *halting configuration* if no rule of the system is applicable to it. We say that configuration

C_1 yields configuration C_2 in one *transition step*, denoted $C_1 \Rightarrow_\Pi C_2$, if we can pass from C_1 to C_2 by applying the rules from $\mathcal{R}$ following the previous remarks. A *computation* of Π is a (finite or infinite) sequence of configurations such that:

1. The first term of the sequence is the initial configuration of the system.
2. Each non-initial configuration of the sequence is obtained from the previous configuration in one transition step
3. If the sequence is finite (called *halting computation*), then the last term of the sequence is a halting configuration.

All computations start from an initial configuration and proceed as stated above; only halting computations give a result, which is encoded by the objects present in the output zone i_{out} in the halting configuration.

Let us notice that these P systems have some important features: (a) They use three electrical charges; (b) the polarization of a membrane can be modified by the application of a rule; (c) the label of a membrane cannot be modified by the application of a rule; and (d) they do not use cooperation neither priorities.

Decision problems are associated with languages in such manner that *solving* a decision problem is defined by *recognizing* the language associated with it. For that, *recognizer membrane systems* were introduced in [41] (called *decision P systems*), and complexity classes associated with these systems were introduced in [40]. Over the last few years, the previous methodology for addressing the **P** *versus* **NP** problem has been applied in the framework of *Membrane Computing*.

A computing model in the paradigm of Membrane Computing (generically called *membrane system*) is said to be a *recognizer system* if it has the following syntactic and semantic peculiarities: (a) the working alphabet has two distinguished objects (yes and no); (b) there exist an input alphabet strictly contained in the working alphabet and an *input membrane*; (c) the initial content of each compartment is a multiset of objects from the working alphabet not belonging to the input alphabet; (d) all computations of the system are halt; and (e) for each computation, either object yes or object no (but not both) must have been released to the environment and only at its last step. Recognizer membrane systems have the ability to accept or reject multisets over the input alphabet. Specifically, given a recognizer membrane system Π, for each multiset m over the input alphabet, a new initial configuration is obtained by adding the multiset m to the content of the input compartment at the initial configuration of Π (the system Π with this new initial configuration associated with m is denoted by $\Pi + m$). Then, we say that system Π *accepts* (respectively, *reject*) the input multiset m if and only if all computations of the system $\Pi + m$ answer yes (resp. no).

Unlike a Turing machine where there is an infinite tape, all the elements that make up a recognizer membrane system have a finite description. Therefore, while a decision problem (with an infinite set of instances) can be solved by a single Turing machine, an infinite family of recognizer membrane systems is necessary to solve it.

Following [40], we say that a family $\mathbf{\Pi} = \{\Pi(n) \mid n \in \mathbb{N}\}$ of recognizer membrane systems solves a decision problem X in *polynomial time and uniform way* if the following holds: (i) the family Π can be generated by a deterministic Turing machine working in polynomial time; and (ii) there exists a pair (cod, s) of polynomial-time computable functions (over the set of instances of X) such that (a) for each instance $u \in I_X$, $s(u)$ is a natural number and $cod(u)$ is an input multiset of the system $\Pi(s(u))$; (b) for each $n \in \mathbb{N}$, the set $s^{-1}(\{n\})$ is a finite set; and (c) the family Π is *polynomially bounded*, *sound*, and *complete* with regard to (X, cod, s) (see [40] for details).

Given a computing model $\mathcal{R}$ of recognizer membrane systems, $\mathbf{PMC}_{\mathcal{R}}$ denotes the set of decision problems solvable by families from $\mathcal{R}$ in polynomial time and uniform way. This complexity class is closed under complement and under polynomial-time reduction [40]. Hence, if X is a complete problem for a complexity class $\mathcal{K}$ and $X \in \mathbf{PMC}_{\mathcal{R}}$, then we deduce that $\mathcal{K} \cup \text{co-}\mathcal{K} \subseteq \mathbf{PMC}_{\mathcal{R}}$.

P systems with active membranes (without dissolution and using division rules only for elementary membranes) have been successfully used to design polynomial time solutions to (weak and strong) **NP**-complete problems (e.g., SAT [42], Subset Sum [38], Knapsack [39], Partition [14], etc.). It is important to note that some of these solutions only make use of two polarizations in their design.

6.3.2.2 Simulation Algorithm

The simulator is based on the sequential simulator for P systems with active membranes provided in pLinguaCore [13]. In this design, the simulation process is a loop divided into two stages: *selection stage* and *execution stage*. The selection stage consists in the search for rules to be executed in each membrane of a given configuration. The selected rules are executed at the execution stage, what finalizes the simulation of a computation step (or transition).

The input data for the selection stage contains the description of the membranes with their multisets (strings over the working alphabet of objects, labels associated with the membrane, etc.) and the set of defined rules. The output data of this stage are the multisets of selected rules. Only the execution stage changes the information of the configuration. It is the reason why execution stage needs synchronization when accessing to the membrane structure and the multisets.

At the end of the execution stage, the simulation process restarts the selection stage in an iterative way until a halting configuration is reached. This stop condition is twofold: a certain number of iterations or a final configuration is reached. On one hand, we define a maximum number of iterations at the beginning of the simulation. On the other hand, a halting configuration is obtained when there are no more rules to select at selection stage. As previously explained, the halting configuration is always reached since it is a simulator for recognizer P systems.

Non-determinism affects the selection stage, since it is possible to have more than one selectable rule but only one can be executed. For example, two evolution rules can be executed using the same object, a division rule and a send-in rule that can be selected in the same membrane at the same time. In order to avoid non-determinism somehow, the simulator assumes only confluent P systems. Thus, instead of working with the entire tree of possible computations, the simulator selects and simulates only one computation path, since all paths are guaranteed to give the same answer.

We can take advantage of this property by selecting path using the lowest cost rules. We will measure this cost in number of membranes and synchronization operations. These are the conditions that could damage the simulation performance the most. In this context, we introduce the following priorities among rules in the selection stage:

1. *Dissolution rules*: they decrease the number of membranes (highest priority).
2. *Evolution rules*: they do not need any communication among membranes (which avoids synchronization).
3. *Send-out rules*: they do need communication between the given membrane and its parent (adding one object to its parent).
4. *Send-in rules*: they do need communication between the given membrane and its parent (reserving one object from its parent and adding the object to itself).
5. *Division rules*: they increase the number of membranes (lowest priority).

During the execution stage, the information of the system can vary by including new objects inside membranes, dissolving membranes, dividing membranes, etc., obtaining a new configuration. This new configuration will be the input data for the selection stage of the next iteration.

Finally, note that this two-staged algorithm allows to keep a coherence in the simulation. If we perform selection and execution of rules, one by one, it would be difficult to ensure the semantic constraints of the system. Moreover, the selected and executed rules in a step of the simulator may not correspond to the rules applied in a computing step of the theoretical model. An alternative solution might be to take two copies of the configuration, one to be updated with the right-hand sides of the rules and another to select rules (subtracting the left-hand sides of rules). As this involves a bigger use of memory, the simulator uses the two stages and a temporary data structure to store information of the selection of rules.

6.3.2.3 Sequential Simulator

As previously mentioned, CUDA programming model [33] is based on the C/C++ language [16]. Therefore, the first recommended step when developing applications in CUDA is to start from a baseline algorithm written in C++, identifying the parts that can be susceptible to be parallelized on the GPU. In this work, we have based on the simulator for P systems with active membranes developed in pLinguaCore [13]. This sequential (or single-threaded) simulator is programmed in JAVA, so the first step was to translate the code to C++.

The first version of the sequential simulator implements the structure of membranes by using C++ pointers and dynamic memory allocations. Each membrane stores a pointer to its parent, a pointer to the first of its children, another pointer to one of its brothers (having the same parent membrane), the charge, and the multiset of objects. The multiset of objects is also implemented by a (dynamic) linked list based on pointers. Each object in the multiset stores its multiplicity (if zero, it is deleted to save memory space) and a pointer to the next object. Therefore, memory spaces for membranes and objects are created and deleted "on demand." The rules of the system are statically stored, so that we can easily access to the rules associated to each membrane, by using its label and charge. Furthermore, the multiset of selected rules is also implemented using a dynamic linked list. However, we found that this drastically slowdown the simulation, since objects get created and consumed at every step, and hence, we are continually allocating and destroying memory, what is very time consuming.

Therefore, a simulator using static structures that get allocated at the beginning of the simulator was developed and shown to be 160 times faster than the first version [21]. These structures are the same also for the parallel simulator, so they are replicated at both sides in order to achieve fair comparisons. In summary, the memory layout to represent the P system is based on the following data structures:

- *Multisets*: an array storing the multisets of the objects using a sparse representation. Since, for simplicity, it is assumed that the simulated P system can contain only two levels in the memory hierarchy (a skin membrane and elementary membranes), the representation of the environment, skin, and elementary membranes are separated. The amount of elementary membranes is set initially by the user.
- *Charges*: an array storing the charge of each membrane.
- *Rule sets*: an array storing rules information. It is indexed by using a membrane label, a charge, and finally an object index. Given that it is possible to have more than one rule associated to the same object, and assuming that the P system is confluent, only one rule of each type is stored.

One major problem to overcome is the competition for objects between different membranes. In this case, internal membranes applying send-in rules are competing for the objects in the parent. We loop the tree from the top to the bottom, so the top level membranes have more priority using its objects than internal membranes using send-in rules.

The input of the simulator (the P system with active membranes to simulate) is given by a binary file. It is a file whose information is encoded in Bytes and bits (not understandable by humans like plain text), which is suitable for compressing data. This binary file contains all the information of the P system (alphabet, labels, rules, etc.) which is the input of the simulator. The format is depicted in [21]. pLinguaCore 2.0 [13] is able to translate a P system written in P-Lingua language into a binary file. First, we define the P system into P-Lingua. pLinguaCore translates it to a binary file, which is used as the input of the simulator. The output is a plain text generated with a format similar to the one provided in pLinguaCore.

6.3.2.4 Parallel Simulation on CUDA

Whenever we design algorithms in the CUDA programming model, the main effort is dividing the required work into processing pieces, which have to be processed by TB thread blocks of T threads each. Using a thread block size of $T = 256$, it is empirically determined to obtain the overall best performance on the Tesla C1060 [43]. Each thread block accesses to one different set of input data and assigns a single or small constant number of input elements to each thread.

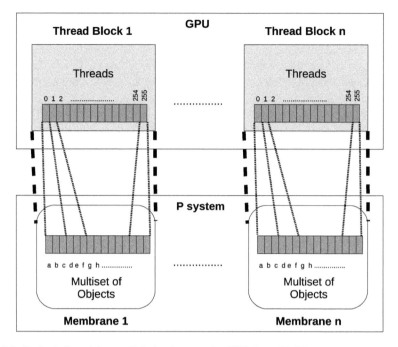

Fig. 6.1 Basic design of the parallel simulator on the GPU. From [4, 21]

Each thread block can be considered independent to the other, and it is at this level at which internal communication (among threads) is cheap using explicit barriers to synchronize, and external communication (among blocks) becomes expensive, since global synchronization can only be achieved by the barrier implicit between successive kernel calls. The need of global synchronization in the designs requires successive kernel calls even to the same kernel.

Figure 6.1 shows the overall design of the simulator on the GPU [4]. Thread blocks and threads are distributed as follows. Each membrane of the simulated P system is attributed to each thread block. In this way, the parallelism between membranes by using the parallelism between thread blocks is identified. However, this is tricky. Membranes can communicate accordingly to the hierarchical tree structure, while thread blocks are all independent. Communication through send-out and dissolution rules (down-up direction) is controlled by globally synchronizing the selection and execution stages. This is implemented by using different kernels. However, send-in rules (up-down direction in the tree) are more complicated to control. In this case, different membranes can compete for single objects. The sequential simulator controls this issue by looping the tree from the top to the bottom. However, the parallel simulator has to run all the membranes in parallel. Therefore, for the sake of simplicity, the parallel simulator can handle only two levels of membrane hierarchy: the skin (controlled by the host) and the rest of elementary membranes (controlled by the thread blocks in device). This is the tree structure we can find in the literature for the majority of solutions based on P systems with active membranes (note that division rules enlarge the tree width-wise) [40].

Furthermore, each individual thread is assigned to each object within a membrane (corresponding to its thread block). It is responsible for identifying the rules that can be executed using the corresponding object, that is, rules that have that object in their left-hand sides. Since all blocks must have the same number of threads, and each membrane can contain a different multiset of objects in every time step, we identify as common for all membranes the whole alphabet. Note that threads can work with many objects that do not really exist in the membrane, as all the alphabet of objects is usually not present within a membrane at a given instant. In fact, the simulator assigns multiple objects to the same thread for not restricting the number of objects in the alphabet. However, the number of objects in the alphabet must be divisible by a number smaller than 512 (the maximum number of threads per thread block), in order to equally distribute the objects among the threads.

The simulator contains five kernels to implement the selection and execution stages [21]. The first kernel implements the selection stage and also the execution stage for evolution rules. The other four kernels implement the other execution rules (dissolution, division, send-out, and send-in rules). All the kernels follow this basic design. The selection kernel starts with the selection stage. After the selection stage, we also execute in this kernel the evolution rules. These rules are executed inside this kernel for three main reasons: the evolution rules do not imply communication (and therefore, synchronization) among membranes; they are executed in a maximal way, and this decision allows us to use less global memory because it is not necessary to store the selected evolution rules for the execution stage. The rest of the rules to be applied are executed in four different kernels, one kernel per each kind of rule (dissolution, division, send-out, and send-in).

Algorithm 2 shows the pseudo-code of the simulator. First of all, the data needed for the computation is moved to the GPU. Then, the code calls the selection kernel which returns the selected rules for the current configuration of the P system. Among the possible selected rules, there will be different kinds of rules to be executed. Therefore, the type of those rules is identified for launching only the required kernels to accomplish the execution stage. As explained before, this process iterates until the maximum number of steps is reached or the system returns an answer. Finally, the result data is copied back to the CPU.

6.3.2.5 Performance Comparative Analysis

In this section, the performance of the developed simulators is compared. This is done by a very simple example, with the aim of studying the behavior of the CUDA kernels. In order to evaluate the performance of the simulator, a family of P systems was designed, named test P system, where it is easy to vary the number of membranes as well as the number of objects [4]. This test P system also fits the behavior of the GPU since only evolution and division rules are defined (without communication and dissolution rules), and every object in every membrane will

---

Algorithm 2: Parallel simulator of P systems on the GPU, from [21]

```
 1: configuration ← initialConfiguration
 2: selectedRules ← Ø
 3: step ← 0
 4: isFinalConfiguration ← false
 5: CopyDataFromCPUtoGPU(configuration)
 6: CopyDataFromCPUtoGPU(rules)
 7: while step < maxStep ∧ NOT isFinalConfiguration do
 8:     kernelSelection(rules,configuration,selectedRules)
 9:     if DISSOLUTION ∈ selectedRules then
10:         kernelDissolution(rules,configuration,selectedRules)
11:     end if
12:     if DIVISION ∈ selectedRules then
13:         kernelDivision(rules,configuration,selectedRules)
14:     end if
15:     if SEND-OUT ∈ selectedRules then
16:         kernelSendOut(rules,configuration,selectedRules)
17:     end if
18:     if SEND-IN ∈ selectedRules then
19:         kernelSendIn(rules,configuration,selectedRules)
20:     end if
21:     step ← step + 1
22:     isFinalConfiguration ← checkFinalConfiguration(configuration)
23: end while
24: CopyDataFromGPUtoCPU(configuration)
```

---

evolve according to a given rule. The defined P system is of the following form $\Pi = (O, H, \mu, \omega_1, \omega_2, R)$, where:

- $O = \{d, o_i \ / \ 0 \leq i \leq n\}$,
- $H = 1, 2$,
- $\mu = [[\,]_2]_2$,
- $\omega_1 = \emptyset, \omega_2 = O$,
- $R =$

    (i) Evolution rules: $[o_i \rightarrow o_i]_2^0, 0 <= i < n$
    (ii) Division rule: $[d]_2^0 \rightarrow [d]_2^0[d]_2^0$

Thus, the test P system allows us to take control of the number of objects in the system by modifying the n parameter. Furthermore, the number of rules changes along with the number of objects, and the number of membranes in every step of the computation is equal to 2^s, where s is the step number. Lastly, the number of evolution rules selected and executed per membrane in every step is invariable, since they are defined one per object and all the objects of the alphabet are presented in every membrane labeled with 2.

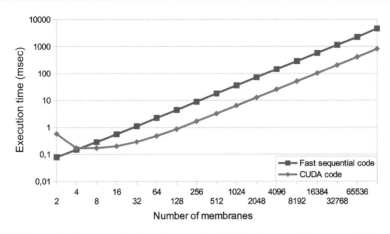

Fig. 6.2 Comparing the execution time for one step of the fast sequential and parallel simulators, by increasing the number of membranes in the system and using a total of 2560 objects in the alphabet. From [4, 21]

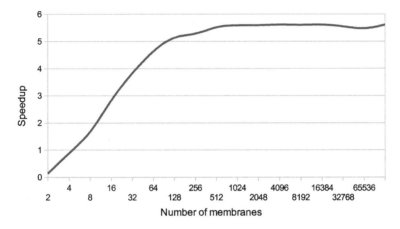

Fig. 6.3 Comparing the speedup for one step of the fast sequential and parallel simulators, by increasing the number of membranes in the system and using a total of 2560 objects in the alphabet. From [4, 21]

Figures 6.2 and 6.3 show the results obtained for the parallel simulator versus the sequential version. Notice that in both graphs the Y-axis is also represented in a logarithmic form. The benchmark covers the parallelism between membranes by exponentially increasing the number of membranes. It can be seen that the CPU simulator also increases its time exponentially from the beginning (with four membranes) until reaching the final configuration (with 32768 membranes). The CUDA simulator, which assigns 256 threads per block (each thread handles 10 elements per membrane), also increases its execution time in a near exponential way, but the performance difference is about 5.7×, and this difference enlarges with the number of membranes (from 1024), because the resources of the GPU are fully utilized.

6.3.3   Simulating Population Dynamics P Systems

In this section, a simulator for Population Dynamics P (PDP) systems is revisited. It is a generic simulator implementing the DCBA algorithm for PDP systems.

The original work is published in [21, 22, 24, 28]. The framework of generic simulators for PDP systems on GPU is called *ABCDGPU*. It is a subproject of the PMCGPU project and can be downloaded from the official website http://sourceforge.net/p/pmcgpu [45] or the repository https://github.com/RGNC/abcd-gpu.

6.3.3.1 Population Dynamics P Systems

Population Dynamics P systems are a variant of *multienvironment P systems with active membranes* [6–8]. The model consists of a directed graph of environments, each of them containing a P system where electrical charges are associated with membranes. All P systems share the same *skeleton*, in the sense that they have the same working alphabet, the same membrane structure, and the same set of rules. Nevertheless, in this framework each rule has associated a probability function which can vary for each environment.

Definition 6.2. A Population Dynamics P system (PDP) of degree (q, m), $q, m \geq 1$, taking $T \geq 1$ time units, is a tuple

$$\Pi = (G, \Gamma, \Sigma, T, \mathcal{R}_E, \mu, \mathcal{R}, \{f_{r,j} : r \in \mathcal{R}, 1 \leq j \leq m\}, \{\mathcal{M}_{i,j} : 1 \leq i \leq q, 1 \leq j \leq m\})$$

where:

- $G = (V, S)$ is a directed graph. Let $V = \{e_1, \ldots, e_m\}$.
- Γ and Σ are alphabets such that $\Sigma \subsetneq \Gamma$.
- T is a natural number.
- $\mathcal{R}_E$ is a finite set of rules of the form $(x)_{e_j} \xrightarrow{p_r} (y_1)_{e_{j_1}} \cdots (y_h)_{e_{j_h}}$, where $x, y_1, \ldots, y_h \in \Sigma$, $(e_j, e_{j_l}) \in S$, $1 \leq l \leq h$, and $p_r : \{1, \ldots, T\} \longrightarrow [0, 1]$ is a computable function such that for each $e_j \in V$ and $x \in \Sigma$, the sum of functions associated with the rules of the type $(x)_{e_j} \xrightarrow{p_r} (y_1)_{e_{j_1}} \cdots (y_h)_{e_{j_h}}$ is the constant function 1.
- μ is a rooted tree labeled by $1 \leq i \leq q$, and by symbols from the set $EC = \{0, +, -\}$.
- $\mathcal{R}$ is a finite set of rules of the form $u[v]_i^\alpha \rightarrow u'[v']_i^{\alpha'}$, where $u, v, u', v' \in M_f(\Gamma)$, $u + v \neq \emptyset$, $1 \leq i \leq q$ and $\alpha, \alpha' \in \{0, +, -\}$, such that there is no rules $(x)_{e_j} \xrightarrow{p_r} (y_1)_{e_{j_1}} \cdots (y_h)_{e_{j_h}}$ and $u[v]_i^\alpha \rightarrow u'[v']_i^{\alpha'}$ having $x \in u$.

- For each $r \in \mathcal{R}$ and $1 \leq j \leq m$, $f_{r,j} : \{1, \ldots, T\} \longrightarrow [0, 1]$ is a computable function such that for each $u, v \in M_f(\Gamma)$, $1 \leq i \leq q$, $\alpha, \alpha' \in \{0, +, -\}$ and $1 \leq j \leq m$, the sum of functions $f_{r,j}$ with $r \equiv u[v]_i^\alpha \rightarrow u'[v']_i^{\alpha'}$, is the constant function 1.
- For each i, j $(1 \leq i \leq q, 1 \leq j \leq m)$, $\mathcal{M}_{i,j}$ is a finite multiset over Γ.

A Population Dynamics P system defined as above can be viewed as a set of m environments $e_1, \ldots, e_m$ interlinked by the edges from the directed graph G. Each environment e_j only can contain symbols from the alphabet Σ, and all of them also contain a P system skeleton, $\Pi_j = (\Gamma, \mu, \mathcal{M}_{1,j}, \ldots, \mathcal{M}_{q,j}, \mathcal{R})$, of degree q, where:

(a) Γ is the working alphabet whose elements are called objects.
(b) μ is a rooted tree which describes a membrane structure consisting of q membranes injectively labeled by $1, \ldots, q$. The skin membrane (the root of the tree) is labeled by 1. We also associate electrical charges from the set $\{0, +, -\}$ with membranes.
(c) $\mathcal{M}_{1,j}, \ldots, \mathcal{M}_{q,j}$ are finite multisets over Γ, describing the objects initially placed in the q regions of μ, within the environment e_j.
(d) $\mathcal{R}$ is the set of evolution rules of each P system. Every rule $r \in \mathcal{R}$ in Π_j has a computable function $f_{r,j}$ associated with it. For each environment e_j, we denote by $\mathcal{R}_{\Pi_j}$ the set of rules with probabilities obtained by coupling each $r \in \mathcal{R}$ with the corresponding function $f_{r,j}$.

Therefore, there is a set $\mathcal{R}_E$ of communication rules between environments, and the natural number T represents the simulation time of the system. The set of rules of the whole system is $\bigcup_{j=1}^{m} \mathcal{R}_{\Pi_j} \cup \mathcal{R}_E$.

The *semantics* of Population Dynamics P systems is defined through a non-deterministic and synchronous model (in the sense that a global clock is assumed). Next, we describe some semantics aspects of these systems.

An evolution rule $r \in \mathcal{R}$, of the form $u[v]_i^\alpha \rightarrow u'[v']_i^{\alpha'}$, is applicable to each membrane labeled by i, whose electrical charge is α, and it contains the multiset v, and its parent contains the multiset u. When such rule is applied, the objects of the multisets v and u are removed from membrane i and from its parent membrane, respectively. Simultaneously, the objects of the multiset u' are added to the parent membrane i, and objects of multiset v' are introduced in membrane i. The application also replaces the charge of membrane i to α'. In each environment e_j, the rule r has associated a probability function $f_{r,j}$ that provides an index of the applicability when several rules compete for objects. In this model, the cooperation degree is given by $|u| + |v|$.

A rule $r \in \mathcal{R}_E$, of the form $(x)_{e_j} \xrightarrow{p_r} (y_1)_{e_{j_1}} \ldots (y_h)_{e_{j_h}}$, is applicable to the environment e_j if it contains object x. When such rule is applied, object x passes from e_j to $e_{j_1}, \ldots, e_{j_h}$ possibly modified into objects $y_1, \ldots, y_h$ respectively. At any moment t $(1 \leq t \leq T)$ for each object x in environment e_j, if there exist communication rules of the type $(x)_{e_j} \xrightarrow{p_r} (y_1)_{e_{j_1}} \ldots (y_h)_{e_{j_h}}$, then one of these rules will be applied. If more than one such a rule can be applied to an object at a given instant, the system selects one randomly, according to their probability which is given by $p_r(t)$.

For each j $(1 \leq j \leq m)$, there is just one further restriction, concerning the consistency of charges: in order to simultaneously apply several rules of $\mathcal{R}_{\Pi_j}$ to the same membrane, all the rules must produce the same electrical charge in the membrane in which to be applied. Thus, we will say that the rules of the system, in this computational framework, are applied in a *non-deterministic, maximally consistent*, and *parallel* way.

An *instantaneous description* or *configuration* of the system at any instant t is a tuple of multisets of objects present in the m environments and at each of the regions of each Π_j, together with the polarizations of the membranes in each P system. We assume that all environments are initially empty and that all membranes initially have a neutral polarization. We assume a global clock exists, synchronizing all membranes and the application of all the rules (from $\mathcal{R}_E$ and from $\mathcal{R}_{\Pi_j}$ in all environments).

In each time unit, we can transform a given configuration in another configuration by using the rules from the whole system as follows: at each transition step, the rules to be applied are selected in a non-deterministic way according to the probabilities assigned to them, and all applicable rules are simultaneously applied in a maximal way. In this way, we get *transitions* from one configuration of the system to the next one.

A *computation* is a sequence of configurations such that the first term of the sequence is the initial configuration of the system, and each non-initial configuration of the sequence is obtained from the previous configuration by applying rules of the system in a maximally consistent and parallel manner with the restrictions previously mentioned.

6.3.3.2 Simulation Algorithm

The simulation algorithms for PDP systems called BBB and DCBA [21, 27] are based on the grouping of rules into blocks. These groups are constructed by looking the left-hand side. Note that rules having the same left-hand side must have associated probabilities summing 1. Specifically, DCBA works using a refined definition of block, called consistent block [21, 27], as shown in Definition 6.3. DNDP [21, 30] does not use the concept of blocks, but it selects rules by a random loop instead.

Definition 6.3. Rules from R and R_E are classified into consistent blocks by either of the following:

(a) The rule block associated with $(i, \alpha, \alpha', u, v)$ is $B_{i,\alpha,\alpha',u,v} = \{r \in R : LHS(r) = (i, \alpha, u, v) \wedge charge(RHS(r)) = \alpha'\}$
(b) The rule block associated with (e_j, x) is $B_{e_j,x} = \{r \in R_E : LHS(r) = (e_j, x)\}$.

The selection of rules in BBB and DCBA relies always first on selecting blocks, calculating a multinomial random variate, and therefore obtaining a selection of rules within each block. In this sense, we can say that rules within a block will not compete among objects when using BBB and DCBA, because they are selected altogether. This, again, does not hold in DNDP, where rules are selected individually according to the probabilities. Block competition takes place whenever two blocks have distinct but overlapping left-hand sides.

DCBA tackles the resource competition issue by performing a proportional distribution of objects among competing blocks. This is done by using the *distribution table*, which is a system-wide time having blocks per columns and pairs (object,region) per rows. Algorithm 3 shows a summary of the algorithm, which can be depicted in [27]. It can be seen that, as usual, each loop iteration is made by two stages: selection and execution. Selection stage consists of three phases: phase 1 distributes objects to the blocks in a certain proportional way, phase 2 ensures *maximality* by checking the maximal number of applications of each block, and phase 3 translates from block to rule applications by calculating random numbers using a multinomial distribution. Finally, execution stage (or phase 4) generates the right-hand side of rules.

Algorithm 3: Sketch of DCBA algorithm for PDP systems

1: Initialization of the algorithm: *static distribution table* (**columns:** blocks, **Rows:** (objects,membrane))
2: **for** $t \leftarrow 0 \ldots T$ **do**
3:     **Selection** stage:
4:         **Phase 1** (Distribution of objects among rule blocks)
5:         **Phase 2** (Maximality selection of rule blocks)
6:         **Phase 3** (Probabilistic distribution, blocks to rules)
7:     **Execution** stage
8: **end for**

The proportional distribution of objects along the blocks is carried out through a table which implements the relations between blocks (columns) and objects in membranes (rows). We always start with a static (general) table, and depending on the current configuration of the PDP system, the table is dynamically modified by deleting columns related to non-applicable blocks. Note that after phase 1, we have to assure that the maximality condition still holds. This is normally conveyed by a random loop over the remaining blocks.

Finally, DCBA also handles the consistency of rules by defining the concept of consistent blocks [21, 27]: rules within a block have the same left-hand side and the same charge in the right-hand side. There is a further restriction within phase 1: if two non-consistent blocks (having different associated right-hand charge) can be selected in a configuration, the simulation algorithm will return an error, or optionally non-deterministically choose a subset of consistent blocks.

6.3.3.3 Design of the Parallel Simulator

Normally, the end user (i.e., ecological experts and model designers) runs many simulations on each set of parameters to extract statistical information of the probabilistic model. This can be automated by adding an outermost loop for simulations in the main procedure of the DCBA, which is easily parallelized.

At first glance, these two levels of parallelism (simulations and environments [23]) could fit the double parallelism of the CUDA architecture (thread blocks and threads). For example, we could assign each simulation to a block of threads and each environment to a thread (since they require synchronization at each time step). However, the number of environments depends inherently on the model. Typically, 2 to 20 environments are considered, which is not enough for fulfilling the GPU resources. Number of simulations typically range from 50 to 100, which is sufficient for thread blocks, but still a poor number compared to the several hundred cores available on modern GPUs.

Thus, the selection of rule blocks (phase 1) and rules (phase 2 and 3) is further parallelized. Hence, the simulator can utilize a huge number of thread blocks by distributing simulations (parallel simulations, as memory can store them) and environments in each one and process each rule block by each thread. Since there are normally more rule blocks (thousand of them) than threads per thread block (up to 512), 256 threads are created, which iterate over the rule blocks in tiles. This design is graphically shown on Fig. 6.4. Each phase of the algorithm has been designed following the general CUDA design explained above and implemented separately as individual kernels. Thus, simulations and environments are synchronized by the successive calls to the kernels.

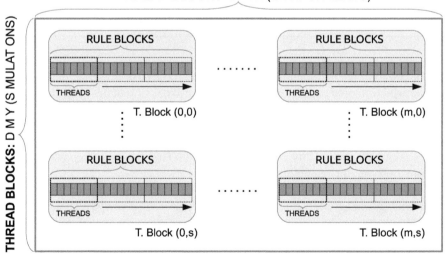

Fig. 6.4 General design of the CUDA-based simulator: 2D grid and 1D thread blocks. Threads loop the rule blocks in tiles. From [21, 28]

6.3.3.4 GPU Implementation of the DCBA Phases

The main challenge at phase 1 is the expanded static table $\mathcal{T}_j$ construction. The size of this table is of order $O(|B| \cdot |\Gamma| \cdot (q + 1))$, where $|B|$ is the number of rule blocks, $|\Gamma|$ is the size of the alphabet (total amount of different objects), and $q + 1$ corresponds to the number of membranes plus the space for the environment. A full implementation of $\mathcal{T}_j$ can be expensive for large systems and very sparse: competitions for one object appears for a relatively small number of blocks. Thus the expanded static table is implemented by a *virtual table*, which is similar but based on the information of the rules:

- Operations over columns: they can be transformed to operations for each rule block and their left-hand sides.
- Operations over rows: they can be transformed to operations over the left-hand sides of rule blocks and storing the partial results into a global array (one position per row).

Further auxiliary data structures are used to virtually simulate the table [23]:

- *activationVector*: the information of filtered blocks is stored here as Boolean values.
- *addition*: the total sums of the rows are stored using this global vector, one per each pair object and region.
- *MinN*: the minimum numbers per column are stored here.
- *BlockSel*: the total number of applications for each block is stored here.
- *RuleSel*: the total number of applications for each rule is stored here.

The implementation of phase 1 is actually done by means of three kernels, executing one after the other and using the same grid configuration as mentioned in Fig. 6.4. The second and third kernels are executed several times according to parameter A (accuracy) of DCBA [28]:

1. Kernel for Filters: FILTERS 1 and 2 are implemented here.
2. Kernel for Normalization: the two parts (row additions and minimum calculations) of the normalization step is implemented in a kernel. The two parts are synchronized by *synchtreads* CUDA instruction. The work assigned to threads is divergent, that is, each thread works with one rule block, but writes information for each object appearing in the LHS. Therefore, the writes to *addition* are carried out by atomic operations.
3. Kernel for Updating and FILTER 2. As before, the work of each thread is divergent. Thus, the update of the configuration is also implemented with atomic operations. Moreover, the *BlockSel* gets updated with the new distribution of selection.

Phase 2 is the most challenging part when parallelizing by blocks. The selection of blocks is performed in an inherently sequential way: we need to know how much a block can consume before checking the next one. At least, phase 2 can be run simultaneously to each environment and simulation. For this phase, a special version of this kernel was designed. This kernel dynamically calculates the competition of blocks, so that the dependencies of blocks are pre-calculated in order to know which blocks can be selected independently of each other, and everything is done in shared memory. *BlockSel* gets updated with the last selections, and the configuration is also updated to prevent other blocks from being selected.

Phase 3 requires a random number generation system for multinomial distributions that was not existing for CUDA. A dedicated implementation was done, called *CURAND_BINOMIAL*, and it is based on the accelerated uniform and normal random variate generation in CUDA with *CuRAND* and the BINV algorithm. This is therefore used to calculate multinomial distributions per rule block and write to *RuleSel*.

Finally, for phase 4, the rule selection *RuleSel* is used to generate the right-hand side, by using atomic operations over the configuration. The parallelization is done by using a similar grid configuration as shown in Fig. 6.4, but looping over rules instead of rule blocks.

6.3.3.5 Performance Results of the Simulator

In order to test the performance of the simulators, a random generator of PDP systems was designed (designated *pdps-rand*). These randomly created PDP systems have no biological meaning. The purpose is to stress the simulator in order to analyze the implemented designs with different topologies. *pdps-rand* is parametrized in such a way that it can create PDP systems of a desired size.

The parallel simulator on the GPU (*pdp-gpu-sim*) and a parallel simulator on multicore CPUs (*pdp-omp-sim*, for 1 (sequential), 2 and 4 cores) are compared. All experiments were run on a GPU server: Linux 64-bit server, with a 4-core (2 GHz) dual socket Intel i5 Xeon Nehalem processor, 12 GBytes of DDR3 RAM, and two NVIDIA Tesla C1060 graphics cards (240 cores at 1.30 GHz, 4 GBytes of memory). GPU cores are typically slower than CPU cores.

The test analyses the performance when increasing the parallelism level of the CUDA threads within thread blocks, that is, the number of rule blocks. The speedup achieved by *pdp-gpu-sim* versus *pdp-omp-sim* is shown in Fig. 6.5. The number of simulations is fixed to 50 and the environments to 20 (hence, a total of 1000 thread blocks). The number of objects is proportionally increased together with the number of rule blocks, in such a way that the ratio for number of rule blocks and number of objects is always 2. The mean LHS length is 1.5 (this is normal value for many real ecosystem models, as seen in the literature). The speedup gets stable to around $7\times$ on the number of rule blocks for the GPU versus CPU. For the multicore versions with 2 and 4 CPUs, the speedups are maintained to $4.3\times$ and $3\times$, respectively. In the experiments, this number is also achieved when running with 10^6 rule blocks.

As stated in [23], parallelizing by simulations yields the largest speedups on multicore platforms. In order to test the efficiency of the simulator when

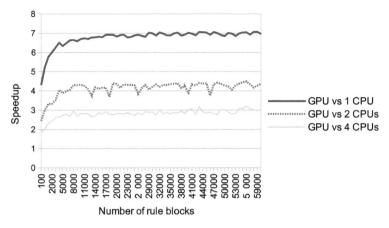

Fig. 6.5 Scalability of the simulators when increasing the number of rule blocks, from [21, 28]

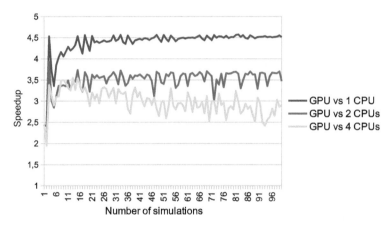

Fig. 6.6 Scalability of the simulators when increasing the number of simulations, from [21, 28]

increasing the number of simulations, rule blocks are fixed to 50000, environments to 20, objects to 5000, and mean LHS length to 1.5. As shown in Fig. 6.6, the GPU achieves better runtime than the multicore implementations. The speedup is maintained to 4.5× using one core, 3.5× for 2 cores, and 2.7× for 4 cores.

6.4 Specific Simulations

In this section, we will introduce a type of simulation of P systems, which is called specific simulation [25]. We will describe how to implement this kind of simulators in CUDA and provide two major examples.

6.4.1   Definition

When implementing a P system simulator, it is important to understand what type of P systems we want to simulate before starting the development. We will say that a specific simulator is any simulator developed for just a certain P system or family of P systems. In other words, if we focus on just one P system or a parametrized definition of P systems forming a family, then we need a specific simulator. On the one hand, this is a restricted version of a simulator, since it can handle a reduced variety of P systems, but it also helps to adjust better the simulator to parallel architectures.

Basically, restricting the P systems to be simulated helps us to take a better control of the algorithm by predicting when certain things will happen. On the one hand, by just focusing on a P system variant, we will know which kind of rules and what semantics apply. On the other hand, by knowing exactly the P systems to simulate, we can develop tailored code to certain parts of the model. For example, we can see in the literature that when developing solutions to certain problems, it is very useful to design it by making a scheme of the computation. This means that the computation tree of the designed P system is usually bound and can be divided into stages. For example, in SAT solutions, there is usually a stage where an exponential amount of membranes is generated by applying division rules, and it is known at which moment the stage starts and ends, because it is part of the design of the solution. By making an exhaustive analysis, it would be even possible to predict which objects can appear in which membranes and when.

Therefore, specific simulators can take advantage of that information in order to adapt the code and the data structures. Specific functions and kernels can be written for each stage, and the memory layout to store the P system information can be drastically reduced. In fact, the information of rules (left and right-hand sides) can be encoded in the source code, instead of storing them in memory, because we know the rules.

The memory layout is also an essential part of a simulator, since P system simulators have been demonstrated to be memory and memory bandwidth bound. When storing the information of P system configuration, we can use either of the following[25]:

- *Sparse representation*: using a large array to store multiplicities, with a position per each possible object (all objects defined in the alphabet). The access is direct since the object identifier is the index where to access the array. However, if many objects are not present at a certain moment, the array will be full of zeroes.
- *Dense representation*: using a double array with a component for the object identifier and the other for multiplicity. We need to search for the object, unless we track them and we know exactly where they are store at any moment. This can help to drastically reduce the size because objects with multiplicity zero can be discarded.

Specific simulators can use dense representation, if we can know where each object is at every transition step, so that the rules can access them directly. Moreover, there are many objects that work as counters, for example o_i, $0 \le i \le n$. They are distinct objects but at the end they are related. If we know that o_i and o_j, with $i \ne j$ will not be present at the same time, then we can use just one position, or even use a variable (register) to store the subindex.

Finally, it is important to remark that specific simulators must keep being full simulators; that is, if the simulator goes beyond the P system model and skips representing the P system features, then we are simulating something else. In other words, we will say that a program is simulating a P system if we can ask the program, at any transition step, any piece of information of the state of the P system (configuration, rules applied, etc.). Thus, a specific simulator should be developed in such a way that we could extract from it the configuration of the P system or the rules that have been applied.

6.4.2 Simulating a SAT Solution with Active Membrane P Systems

The first specific simulator implemented in CUDA was a family of recognizer P systems with active membranes designed to solve the SAT problem in linear time (but with exponential workspace). In this section, we will discuss the design of this simulator and its performance achieved with CUDA.

The original work is published in [3, 5, 21, 22]. The framework of all these simulators is named *PCUDASAT*, and it can be downloaded from the official website http://sourceforge.net/p/pmcgpu [45] or the repository https://github.com/RGNC/pcudasat.

6.4.2.1 SAT Solution with Active Membranes

Let $\varphi = C_1 \wedge \cdots \wedge C_m$ be a propositional formula in **CNF** such that the set of variables of the formula is $Var(\varphi) = \{x_1, \ldots, x_n\}$, consisting of m *clauses* $C_i = y_{i,1} \vee \cdots \vee y_{i,k_i}$, $1 \le i \le m$, where $y_{i,i'} \in \{x_j, \neg x_j : 1 \le j \le n\}$ are the literals of φ. We can assume that the formula is in simplified expression, i.e., no clause contains two occurrences of the same literal, and no clause can contain, simultaneously, a literal and its negation. The SAT problem is defined as follows: given a Boolean formula in conjunctive normal form (CNF), to determine whether or not there exists a truth assignment to its variables on which the formula evaluates true.

The solution to SAT based on recognizer P system with active membranes is defined as $\Pi_{am-SAT}(\langle m, n \rangle) = (\Gamma, \Sigma, \mu, \mathcal{M}_1, \mathcal{M}_2, \mathcal{R}, 2)$ of degree 2, for each pair of natural numbers $m, n \in \mathcal{N}$. Specifically:

- The input alphabet is $\Sigma = \{x_{i,j}, \overline{x}_{i,j} | 1 \le i \le m, 1 \le j \le n\}$.
- The working alphabet is

$$\Gamma = \Sigma \cup \{c_k | 1 \le k \le m + 2\} \cup \{d_k | 1 \le k \le 3n + 2m + 3\} \cup$$
$$\cup \{r_{i,k} | 0 \le i \le m, 1 \le k \le 2n\} \cup \{e, t\} \cup n\{Yes, No\}$$

- The set of labels is $\{1, 2\}$.
- The initial structure of membranes is $\mu = [\,[\,]_2\,]_1$.
- The initial multisets associated with the membranes are $\mathcal{M}_1 = \emptyset$ y $\mathcal{M}_2 = \{d_1\}$.
- The input membrane is the one labeled by 2.
- The set $\mathcal{R}$ consists of the following rules:

(a) $[d_k]_2^0 \rightarrow [d_k]_2^+[d_k]_2^-$, for $1 \le k \le n$.

(b) $[x_{i,1} \rightarrow r_{i,1}]_2^+$, $[\,\overline{x}_{i,1} \rightarrow r_{i,1}]_2^-$, for $1 \le i \le m$.
$[x_{i,1} \rightarrow \lambda]_2^-$, $[\overline{x}_{i,1} \rightarrow \lambda]_2^+$, for $1 \le i \le m$.

(c) $[x_{i,j} \rightarrow x_{i,j-1}]_2^+$, $[x_{i,j} \rightarrow x_{i,j-1}]_2^-$, for $1 \le i \le m$, $2 \le j \le n$. $[\,\overline{x}_{i,j} \rightarrow \overline{x}_{i,j-1}]_2^+$, $[\,\overline{x}_{i,j} \rightarrow \overline{x}_{i,j-1}]_2^-$, for $1 \le i \le m$, $2 \le j \le n$.

(d) $[d_k]_2^+ \rightarrow [\,]_2^0 d_k$, , $[d_k]_2^- \rightarrow [\,]_2^0 d_k$, for $1 \le k \le n$.
$d_k[\,]_2^0 \rightarrow [d_{k+1}]_2^0$, for $1 \le k \le n - 1\}$.

(e) $[r_{i,k} \rightarrow r_{i,k+1}]_2^0$, for $1 \le i \le m$, $1 \le k \le 2n - 1$.

(f) $[d_k \rightarrow d_{k+1}]_1^0$, for $n \le k \le 3n - 3$; $[d_{3n-2} \rightarrow d_{3n-1}e]_1^0$.

(g) $e[\,]_2^0 \rightarrow [c_1]_2^+$; $[d_{3n-1} \rightarrow d_{3n}]_1^0$.

(h) $[d_k \rightarrow d_{k+1}]_1^0$, for $3n \le k \le 3n + 2m + 2$.

(i) $[r_{1,2n}]_2^+ \rightarrow [\,]_2^- r_{1,2n}$.

(j) $[r_{i,2n} \rightarrow r_{i-1,2n}]_2^-$, for $1 \le i \le m$.

(k) $r_{1,2n}[\,]_2^- \rightarrow [r_{0,2n}]_2^+$.

(l) $[c_k \rightarrow c_{k+1}]_2^-$, for $1 \le k \le m$.

(m) $[c_{m+1}]_2^+ \rightarrow [\,]_2^0 c_{m+1}$.

(n) $[c_{m+1} \rightarrow c_{m+2}t]_1^0$.

(o) $[t\,]_1^0 \rightarrow [\,]_1^+ t$.

(p) $[c_{m+2}]_1^+ \rightarrow [\,]_1^- Yes$.

(q) $[d_{3n+2m+3}]_1^0 \rightarrow [\,]_1^+ No$.

We also consider a polynomial encoding (cod, s) of the SAT problem in the family $\mathbf{\Pi_{am-SAT}} = \{\Pi_{am-SAT}(t) \mid t \in \mathcal{N}\}$. The function cod associates to the previously described propositional formula φ (an instance of SAT with n variables and m clauses), the following multiset of objects

$$cod(\varphi) = \bigcup_{i=1}^{m} \{x_{i,j} | x_j \in C_i\} \cup \{\overline{x}_{i,j} | \neg x_j \in C_i\}$$

In this case, object $x_{i,j}$ represents that variable x_j in clause C_i.

The *size* function, s, is defined as follows $s(\varphi) = \langle m, n \rangle = \frac{(m+n) \cdot (m+n+1)}{2} + m$. Then, $cod(\varphi)$ is an input multiset of the system $\Pi_{am-SAT}(s(\varphi))$ and the pair (cod, s) is therefore a polynomial encoding of the SAT problem in the family $\mathbf{\Pi_{am-SAT}}$. Thus, the system of the family $\mathbf{\Pi_{am-SAT}}$ processing the instance φ will be the P system with active membranes $\Pi_{am-SAT}(s(\varphi))$ with input multiset $cod(\varphi)$.

The system $\Pi_{am-SAT}(s(\varphi))$ with input $cod(\varphi)$ is confluent, and its computation is structured in four phases as follows:

- *Generation phase*: all possible relevant truth assignment is generated for the set of variables of the formula $\{x_1, \ldots, x_n\}$. It is achieved by using division rules in the internal membranes (labeled by 2). This will allow the generation of 2^n membranes that will encode all possible assignments. Nevertheless, in this phase, while the valuations are being generated, the clauses that are true by the encoded valuation in each internal membrane are checked. This idea is implemented through a very sophisticated process by which only the truth values 1 and 0 are given to the variable 1. This variable 1 corresponds to the variable x_1 in the first loop step, but by a set of indices, the variable 1 corresponds to the variable x_2 in the second loop step, and so on. This phase is executed in $3n - 1$ computation steps, and only the rules (a), (b), (c), (d) and (e) are applied.
- *Synchronization phase*: it prepares the system for the checking phase synchronizing the execution of the system by unifying certain sub-indices of some objects. The execution of this phase consumes $2n$ computation steps, and only rules (e), (f) and (g) are executed.
- *Check-out phase*: in this phase, it is determined how many clauses are true for each truth assignment encoded by the internal membranes. This is done using the objects c_k $(k > 1)$, whose appearance in a membrane means that exactly $k - 1$ clauses are made true by the encoded valuation in that membrane. This phase is executed in $2m$ steps, and rules (h), (i), (j), (k) and (l) are applied.
- *Output phase*: in this phase the system provides the corresponding output depending on the analysis of the check-out phase. That is, this step performs a search of the internal membranes encoding a solution (i.e., containing object c_{m+1}). If a membrane satisfies the above condition, the object *Yes* is sent to the environment, and the system stops. Otherwise, the object *No* is sent to the environment and the system stops. The execution of this phase is done in 4 steps and the used rules are (m), (n), (o), (p) and (q).

6.4.2.2 Sequential Simulator and Data Structures

The sequential simulator design is based on the four main phases of a P system computation from Π_{am-SAT}: generation, synchronization, check-out, and output. Thus, the computation of the P system to simulate (from the family Π_{am-SAT}) is reproduced by sequentially executing these phases. Firstly, the generation phase is executed, generating 2^n membranes by dividing each one in n steps, where n is the number of variables of the input CNF formula. Since we know the value of n, the simulator knows the amount of membranes to generate before starting the simulation. After that, the simulator executes the synchronization phase which evolves the objects following the rules previously explained. The check-out phase determines the membranes that codify a solution of the SAT instance, and finally the output phase sends out the correct answer to the environment.

It is important to remark that the semantics of the P system is reproduced by the simulation algorithm, so the simulator is specific for this solution. Thus, the only input for the simulator is the CNF formula provided in DIMACS CNF format. We can assume therefore that the simulator behaves as a SAT solver, receiving a propositional formula and giving the corresponding answer. However, this solver is implemented following a solution by means of P systems.

The first challenge is to decrease the sparsity of the data structures storing the configuration of the P system. After an exhaustive analysis of the computation, the upper bound of number of distinct objects appearing in a membrane can be fixed to the size of the input multiset (the number of literals in the input propositional formula). Indeed, one can observe that the size of the right-hand side of evolution rules is always 1. Thus, every object in the input multiset always evolves to either another or disappears. By definition, send-in, send-out, and division rules do not generate more than one object in the right-hand side.

Hence, the representation of the P system is made by an array storing the multisets of objects for every membrane labeled by 2. The amount of elements per membrane equals to, as mentioned above, the size of the input multiset (total number of literals in the formula, $|cod(\varphi)|$). This array is initially allocated for the maximum amount of membranes 2 that the P system will create, which is 2^n (note that n is defined in the input file). Only the first one is initialized by storing the full input multiset. Division rules will initialize each membrane later on.

The encoding of objects for the input multiset can be made at a bit-level within integers of 32 bits. Each integer stores the following (8 bits for each field):

1. The name of the object (x or $\overline{x}$)
2. Reserved space.
3. Variable (subindex i).
4. Clause (subindex j).

It is noteworthy that the membrane charges are not stored, since we can observe from the computation that a partition of membranes having positive and negative charges can be done over the array. In other words, the first half of membranes are positive, and the other half (new ones) negative. The skin membrane is not represented, since its purpose is to store objects sent out from membranes, those which are sent in to the same membranes in the next step. This process is therefore simulated within each membrane, avoiding to store the information for the skin membrane. Other objects, such as yes, no, and c counter, are also placed as variables encoded directly in source code.

6.4.2.3 Design of the GPU Simulator

The parallel simulator on the GPU was designed to take over the most demanding phases on the computation of $\Pi_{\mathbf{am-SAT}}$, which are the first three phases. The last one (output phase) is developed on the CPU. In order to map the parallelism into the GPU, the simulator assigns a thread block to each membrane, as shown in Fig. 6.7. In this way, the parallelism among membranes is represented. Moreover, each thread is assigned to each object of the input multiset, which is a literal of the input formula (with the exception of object d_1). This mapping is common to all the defined kernels.

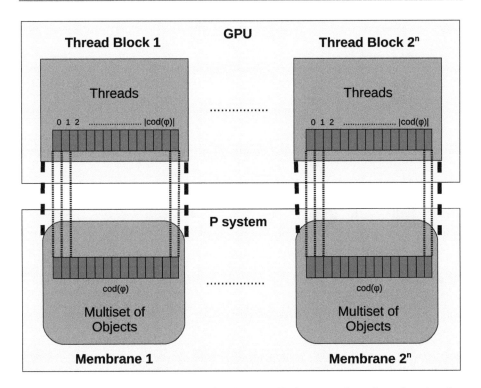

Fig. 6.7 Design of the parallel simulator for $\Pi_{\mathrm{am-SAT}}$. Each generated membrane is assigned to a thread block, and each object (initially, the input multiset) is assigned to a thread. From [3, 21]

Algorithm 4 shows the pseudocode for the host side the simulator. The generation phase is simulated by using three kernels which execute the rules in this phase. This is an iterative process of n steps where the kernels are called n times. A tailored kernel for division is designed to make copies of all membranes executing division rules, whose behavior is shown in Fig. 6.8. There is a double parallelism in the division, as shown in the figure; threads within a block are in charge of making the copies for the new membrane and changing just the corresponding object. But this is also repeated for each thread block. In each iteration, the simulator adjusts the number of thread blocks before calling the kernel, since new membranes are created. That is, the membranes are distributed along the two-dimensional grid of thread blocks.

When the exponential amount of membranes is created, synchronization and check-out phases are executed. This is simulated within just one kernel for both phases, in parallel for each membrane. Global synchronization is not necessary because there is no communication among the internal membranes at these phases. Finally, the output phase is developed on the CPU, checking the conditions and launching the result of the computation.

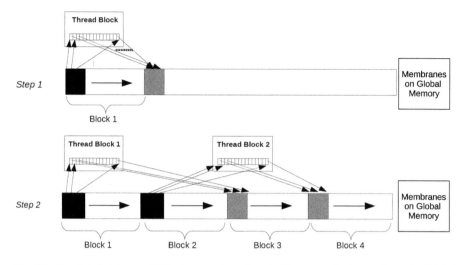

Fig. 6.8 Parallel division on GPU at generation phase in Π_{am-SAT}. Each membrane is divided by a thread block, which copies the objects also in parallel by using several threads. If the number of objects is larger than 256, the thread block repeats the process until covering all the objects. From [5]

Algorithm 4: Parallel Simulator of Π_{am-SAT}, at host side. From [3, 21]

1: {Initialization}
2: $Threads \leftarrow |cod(\varphi)|$ {The number of literals in the CNF formula}
3: $Blocks \leftarrow (1, 1)$ {One block in the 2-dimensional grid}
4: $d \leftarrow 0$ {A counter}
5: $numMembranes \leftarrow 1$ {Number of membranes}
6: $psystem \leftarrow allocateGPUMemory(2^n)$ {Allocate enough memory to represent the P system}

7: {Generation phase}
8: **repeat**
9:     $Division\_kernel <<< Blocks, Threads >>> (psystem, numMembranes)$
10:    $numMembranes \leftarrow numMembranes \times 2$
11:    $Blocks \leftarrow AdjustBlocks(psystem, numMembranes)$ {Distribute membranes among blocks}
12:    $Send\_out\_kernel <<< Blocks, Threads >>> (psystem, numMembranes)$
13:    $Send\_in\_kernel <<< Blocks, Threads >>> (psystem, numMembranes)$
14:    $d \leftarrow d + 1$
15: **until** $d < n$ {Repeat n times (number of variables)}

16: {Synchronization and Check-out phases}
17: $Syn\_Check\_kernel <<< Blocks, Threads >>> (psystem, numMembranes)$

18: {Output phase (executed on the CPU)}
19: $Output(psystem, numMembranes)$

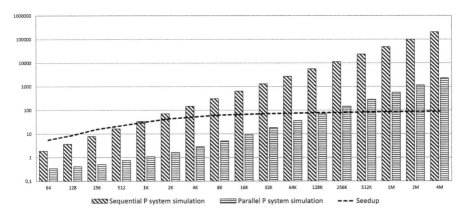

Fig. 6.9 Simulation performance for *am-sat-gpu* vs *am-sat-seq* when increasing the number of membranes (x-axis). From [3, 21]

6.4.2.4 Performance Analysis

Next, we analyze the performance of the simulators above described for Π_{am-SAT}: the sequential simulator developed in C++ (from now, *am-sat-seq*) and the GPU parallel simulator on CUDA (*am-sat-gpu*). The experimental results were obtained using a Tesla C1060 GPU.

Figure 6.9 shows the experimental performance of the cell-like simulators (in a log scale) when increasing the number of membranes in the P system (and hence, the number of blocks in the GPU and also the variables in the CNF formula) until reaching 2^{12} membranes. The number of simulated membranes is restricted by the available memory of the system. The number of literals in the formula is fixed to 256, which means 256 threads per block.

It can be seen that once the GPU resources have been fully occupied, the execution time increases linearly with the number of blocks. In this case, we report up to 94× of speedup between *am-sat-seq* and *am-sat-gpu*. However, Fig. 6.9 shows the speedup becomes a constant number of 100× when the number of membranes is greater than 128 K.[1] This is the number of blocks launched in the grid of the GPU.

We finalize the performance analysis by also considering the data management (allocation and transfer) time of the GPU. This is also very important, because it is part of the solution. Figure 6.10 shows the speedup achieved by comparing *am-sat-gpu* (with data management) and *am-sat-seq*. We can see that for small amounts of membranes, the speedup is below 1, what means a worst performance. However, after 32 K membranes, the speedup is 1.23×, and it is increased along with the number of membranes until 64× for 4 M membranes. This is caused by the decrease in the kernels time, and the time of handling the data is almost constant for any

---

[1] Note that we use here "K" and "M" for binary prefixes "kilo" and "mega", respectively. Therefore, $128\,K = 2^{17} = 131072$.

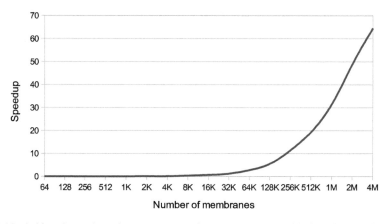

Fig. 6.10 Achieved speedup of *am-sat-gpu* against *am-sat-seq* considering also the GPU data management, when increasing the number of membranes (x-axis). From [3, 21]

size. Note that the data management performed by *am-sat-gpu* is the following: data allocation, initial configuration (only 1 membrane) transfer, and answer (object yes or not) transfer. The information of the P system during the computation is always kept on the GPU memory.

6.4.3   Simulating a SAT Solution with Tissue P Systems

In this section, we depict a specific simulator for the family of recognizer tissue P systems with cell division. We first explain the data structures and the phases that compound the simulation algorithm, then the sequential version, and after that the parallel one based on CUDA, describing the different optimizations taken for each phase of the simulator.

The original work is published in [21, 22, 26]. This simulation framework is named *TSPCUDASAT*, and it can be downloaded from the official website http://sourceforge.net/p/pmcgpu [45] or the repository https://github.com/RGNC/tspcudasat.

6.4.3.1 Recognizer Tissue P System with Cell Division
In the paradigm of membrane computing, a new computing model (*tissue P system with cell division*) is introduced by using the biological membranes placed in the nodes of a directed graph, inspired from the cell inter-communication in tissues [20]. Besides, cell division is an elegant process that enables organisms to grow and reproduce. Mitosis is a process of cell division which results in the production of two daughter cells from a single parent cell. Daughter cells are identical to one another and to the original parent cell. Through a sequence of steps, the replicated genetic material in a parent cell is equally distributed to two daughter cells. While there are some subtle differences, mitosis is remarkably similar across organisms.

Definition 6.4. A *tissue P system with cell division* of degree $q \geq 1$, is a tuple $\Pi = (\Gamma, \mathcal{E}, \mathcal{M}_1, \ldots, \mathcal{M}_q, \mathcal{R}, i_{out})$, where:

1. Γ is a finite *alphabet*:
2. $\mathcal{E} \subsetneq \Gamma$;
3. $\mathcal{M}_1, \ldots, \mathcal{M}_q$ are finite multisets over Γ;
4. $\mathcal{R}$ is a finite set of communication rules of the following forms:
   (a) Communication rules: $(i, u/v, j)$, for $i, j \in \{0, 1, 2, \ldots, q\}, i \neq j, u, v \in M(\Gamma), |u| + |v| > 0$;
   (b) Division rules: $[a]_i \rightarrow [b]_i [c]_i$, where $i \in \{1, 2, \ldots, q\}, i \neq i_{out}$ and $a, b, c \in \Gamma$.
5. $i_{out} \in \{0, 1, \ldots, q\}$.

A *tissue P system with cell division* $\Pi = (\Gamma, \mathcal{E}, \mathcal{M}_1, \ldots, \mathcal{M}_q, \mathcal{R}, i_{out})$ of degree $q \geq 1$, can be viewed as a set of q *cells*, labeled by $1, \ldots, q$, with an *environment* labeled by 0 such that (a) $\mathcal{M}_1, \ldots, \mathcal{M}_q$ represent the finite multisets of *objects* (symbols of the working alphabet Γ) initially placed in the q cells of the system; (b) $\mathcal{E}$ is the set of objects initially located in the environment of the system, all of them available in an arbitrary number of copies; (c) $\mathcal{R}$ is a finite set of rules over Γ associated with the cells and the environment; and (d) $i_{out} \in \{0, 1, \ldots, q\}$ indicates the output zone. We use the term *zone i* to refer to cell i, in the case $1 \leq i \leq q$ and to refer the environment in the case $i = 0$.

A communication rule $(i, u/v, j)$ is called a *symport rule* if $u = \lambda$ or $v = \lambda$. A symport rule $(i, u/\lambda, j)$ provides a virtual arc from zone i to zone j. A communication rule $(i, u/v, j)$ is called an *antiport rule* if $u \neq \lambda$ and $v \neq \lambda$. An antiport rule $(i, u/v, j)$ provides two arcs: one from zone i to zone j and another one from zone j to zone i. Therefore, every tissue P system has an underlying directed graph whose nodes are the zones (cells and the environment) of the system and the arcs are obtained from communication rules.

A *configuration* (or *instantaneous description*) C_t at an instant t of a tissue P system Π is a tuple whose components are the multisets over Γ associated with each cell present in the system at moment t and the multiset over $\Gamma \setminus \mathcal{E}$ associated with the environment at moment t.

A communication rule $(i, u/v, j)$ is applicable to zones i, j to a configuration C_t at instant t, if in that configuration the multiset u is contained in one zone i and multiset v is contained in one zone j. When applying such a communication rule to such zones, the objects of the multiset represented by u are sent from zone i to zone j, and simultaneously, the objects of multiset v are sent from zone j to zone i. The *length* of communication rule $(i, u/v, j)$ is defined as $|u| + |v|$.

A division rule $[a]_i \rightarrow [b]_i[c]_i$ is applicable to a configuration at an instant t, if one cell i belongs to that configuration containing object a. When applying a division rule $[a]_i \rightarrow [b]_i[c]_i$ to such a cell i, under the influence of object a, that cell is divided into two cells with the same label i; in the first copy, object a is replaced by object b, in the second one, object a is replaced by object c; all the other objects residing in such a cell i are replicated, and copies of them are placed in the two new cells. The output cell i_{out} and any cell with input degree equal to zero cannot be divided.

The rules of a tissue P system with cell division are applied as follows: communication rules will be applied in a non-deterministic maximally parallel manner as it is customary in membrane computing but with the following important remark: if a cell divides, then the division rule is the only one which is applied for that cell at that step; the objects inside that cell do not evolve by means of communication rules. In other words, before division a cell interrupts all its communication channels with the other cells and with the environment. The new cells resulting from division will interact with other cells or with the environment only at the next step—providing that they do not divide once again. The label of a cell precisely identifies the rules which can be applied to it.

Given a tissue P system with cell division, $\Pi = (\Gamma, \mathcal{E}, \mathcal{M}_1, \ldots, \mathcal{M}_q, \mathcal{R}, i_{out})$, the *initial configuration* of Π is $C_0 = (\mathcal{M}_1, \cdots, \mathcal{M}_q; \emptyset)$. A configuration is a *halting configuration* if no rule of the system is applicable to it. We say that configuration C_1 yields configuration C_2 in one *transition step*, denoted $C_1 \Rightarrow_\Pi C_2$, if we can pass from C_1 to C_2 by applying the rules from $\mathcal{R}$ following the previous remarks. In tissue P systems with cell division, the concepts of *computation, recognizer system,* and *polynomial time and uniform solution* to a decision problem are introduced in a similar way than in P systems with active membranes.

6.4.3.2 SAT Solution with Tissue P Systems

This section presents an efficient solution to SAT problem by means of family of recognizer tissue P systems with cell division. Let $\varphi = C_1 \wedge \cdots \wedge C_m$ be a propositional formula in **CNF** such that the set of variables of the formula is $Var(\varphi) = \{x_1, \ldots, x_n\}$ and consists of m *clauses* $C_j = y_{j,1} \vee \cdots \vee y_{j,k_j}, 1 \leq i \leq m$, where $y_{j,j'} \in \{x_i, \neg x_i : 1 \leq i \leq n\}$ are the literals of φ. Without loss of generality, we can assume that the formula is in simplified expression.

For each pair of natural numbers $m, n \in \mathbf{N}$, we will consider the recognizer tissue P system with cell division $\Pi_{tsp-SAT}(\langle m, n \rangle) = (\Gamma, \Sigma, \mu, \mathcal{M}_1, \mathcal{M}_2, R, 2)$ of degree 2, defined as follows:

- The input alphabet is $\Sigma = \{x_{i,j}, \overline{x}_{i,j} \mid 1 \leq i \leq n, \ 1 \leq j \leq m\}$
- The working alphabet is

$$\begin{aligned}
\Gamma = \ & \Sigma \cup \{a_i, t_i, f_i \mid 1 \leq i \leq n\} \cup \{r_i \mid 1 \leq i \leq m\} \cup \\
& \cup \{T_i, F_i \mid 1 \leq i \leq n\} \cup \{T_{i,j}, F_{i,j} \mid 1 \leq i \leq n, 1 \leq j \leq m+1\} \cup \\
& \cup \{b_i \mid 1 \leq i \leq 2n+m+1\} \cup \{c_i \mid 1 \leq i \leq n+1\} \cup \\
& \cup \{d_i \mid 1 \leq i \leq 2n+2m+nm+1\} \cup \\
& \cup \{e_i \mid 1 \leq i \leq 2n+2m+nm+3\} \cup \{f, g, \text{yes}, \text{no}\}
\end{aligned}$$

- The environment alphabet is $\mathcal{E} = \Gamma - \{\text{yes}, \text{no}\}$.
- The set of labels is $\{1, 2\}$.

- The initial multisets associated with the cells are $\mathcal{M}_1 = \{\text{yes}, \text{no}, b_1, c_1, d_1, e_1\}$ and $\mathcal{M}_2 = \{f, g, a_1, a_2, \ldots, a_n\}$.
- The input cell is the one labeled by 2, and the output region is the environment.
- The set $\mathcal{R}$ is formed by the following rules:

1. **Division rule:**
   (a) $[a_i]_2 \rightarrow [T_i]_2 [F_i]_2$, for $i = 1, 2, \ldots, n$.
2. **Communication rules:**
   (b) $(1, b_i / b_{i+1}^2, 0)$, for $i = 1, \ldots, n$.
   (c) $(1, c_i / c_{i+1}^2, 0)$, for $i = 1, \ldots, n$.
   (d) $(1, d_i / d_{i+1}^2, 0)$, for $i = 1, \ldots, n$.
   (e) $(1, e_i / e_{i+1}, 0)$, for $i = 1, \ldots, 2n + 2m + nm + 2$.
   (f) $(1, b_{n+1} c_{n+1} / f, 2)$.
   (g) $(1, d_{n+1} / g, 2)$.
   (h*) $(1, f^2 / f, 0)$.
   (h) $(2, c_{n+1} T_i / c_{n+1} T_{i,1}, 0)$, for $i = 1, \ldots, n$.
   (i) $(2, c_{n+1} F_i / c_{n+1} F_{i,1}, 0)$, for $i = 1, \ldots, n$.
   (j) $(2, T_{i,j} / t_i T_{i,j+1}, 0)$, for $i = 1, \ldots, n$ and $j = 1, \ldots, m$.
   (k) $(2, F_{i,j} / f_i F_{i,j+1}, 0)$, for $i = 1, \ldots, n$ and $j = 1, \ldots, m$.
   (l) $(2, b_i / b_{i+1}, 0)$.
   (m) $(2, d_i / d_{i+1}, 0)$, for $i = n + 1, \ldots, 2n + m$.
   (n) $(2, b_{2n+m+1} t_i x_{i,j} / b_{2n+m+1} r_j, 0)$.
   (o) $(2, b_{2n+m+1} f_i \overline{x}_{i,j} / b_{2n+m+1} r_j, 0)$, for $1 \le i \le n$ and $1 \le j \le m$.
   (p) $(2, d_i / d_{i+1}, 0)$, for $i = 2n + m + 1, \ldots, 2n + m + nm$.
   (q) $(2, d_{2n+m+nm+j} r_j / d_{2n+m+nm+j+1}, 0)$, for $j = 1, \ldots, m$.
   (r) $(2, d_{2n+2m+nm+1} / f \text{ yes}, 1)$.
   (s) $(2, \text{yes} / \lambda, 0)$.
   (t) $(1, e_{2n+2m+nm+3} f \text{ no} / \lambda, 0)$.

Next, we consider a polynomial encoding (cod, s) of the SAT problem in the family $\mathbf{\Pi}_{\text{tsp-SAT}} = \{\Pi_{tsp-SAT}(t) \mid t \in \mathbb{N}\}$. The function cod associates to the previously described propositional formula φ that is an instance of SAT with parameters n (number of variables) and m (number of clauses), with the following multiset of objects

$$cod(\varphi) = \bigcup_{i=1}^{m} \{x_{i,j} \mid x_i \in C_j\} \cup \{\overline{x}_{i,j} \mid \neg x_i \in C_j\}$$

In this case, object $x_{i,j}$ represents that variable x_i belongs to clause C_j. The *size* function, s, is defined as follows $s(\varphi) = \langle m, n \rangle = \frac{(m+n) \cdot (m+n+1)}{2} + m$. The system of the family $\mathbf{\Pi}_{\text{tsp-SAT}}$ to process the instance φ will be the tissue P system $\Pi_{tsp-SAT}(s(\varphi))$ with input multiset $cod(\varphi)$.

The execution of the system $\Pi_{tsp-SAT}(s(\varphi))$ with input $cod(\varphi)$ is structured in six phases:

- *Valuations generation phase*: in this phase all the possible relevant truth valuations are generated for the set of variables of the formula $\{x_1, \ldots, x_n\}$. This is accomplished by using division rules (a), whereby each object x_i produces two new cells, one having the object T_i that codifies the true value of the variable x_i, y and the other having the object T_i that codifies the false value of the variable x_i. Thus, 2^n cells are obtained in n computation steps. These cells are labeled by 2, and each one codifies each possible truth valuation of the set of variables $\{x_1, \ldots, x_n\}$. Meanwhile, the objects f, g are replicated in each created cell. This phase spends n computation steps.
- *Counter generation phase*: simultaneously, and using the rules (b), (c), (d), and (e), the counters b_i, c_i, d_i, e_i of the cell labeled by 1 are evolving such that in each computation step the number of objects in each one is doubling. Thereby, through this process and after n steps, we get 2^n copies of the objects b_{n+1}, c_{n+1}, and d_{n+1}. Objects $b's$ will be used to check which clauses are satisfied for each truth valuation. Objects $c's$ are used to obtain a sufficient number of copies of t_i, f_i (namely, m). Objects $d's$ will be used to check if there is at least one valuation satisfying all clauses. Finally, objects $e's$ will be used to produced, in its case, the object no at the end of the computation.
- *Checking preparation phase*: this phase aims at preparing the system for checking clauses. For this, at step $n + 1$ of the computation, and by the application of the rules (f) and (g), the counters b_{n+1}, c_{n+1}, d_{n+1} of the cell 1 are exchanged for the objects f and g of the 2^n cell 2. Thus, after this step, each cell labeled by two has a copy of the objects b_{n+1}, c_{n+1}, d_{n+1}, while cell 1 has 2 copies of the objects f and g.

    Subsequently, the presence of an object c_{n+1} in each one of the 2^n cells labeled by 2 allows to generate the objects $T_{i,1}$ and $F_{i,1}$. By the application of rules (j) and (k), these objects allow the emergence of m copies of t_i and m copies of f_i, according to the values of truth or falsity that a cell 2 assigns to a variable x_i. This process spends $n + m$ steps since there is only one object c_{n+1} in each cell 2, and moreover, for each $i = 1, \ldots, n$, the rules (j) and (k) are applied exactly m consecutively times. Simultaneously, in the first steps of this process, the application of the rule (h^*) makes the cell labeled by 1 to appear only one copy of the object yes. Simultaneously in this phase, the counters b_i, d_i and e_i are evolving by the applications of the corresponding rules.
- *Checking clauses phase*: in this phase it is determined which clauses are true for every truth valuation encoded by a cell labeled by 2. This phase starts at the computation step $(n + 1) + (n + m) + 1 = 2n + m + 2$. Using the rules (n) and (o), the true clauses are checked for each valuation encoded by a cell, so that the appearance of an object r_j in a cell 2 means that the corresponding valuation makes true the clause C_j. Bearing in mind that a single copy of the object b_{2n+m+1} is in each cell, the phase takes nm computation steps.

Thus, the configuration $C_{2n+m+nm+1}$ is characterized by the following:

- It contains exactly 2^n cells labeled by 2. Each one contains the object $d_{2n+m+nm+1}$, and copies of objects r_j for each clause C_j are made true by the encoded valuation in the cell.
- It contains a unique cell labeled by 1, containing a copy of objects yes, no, f, g and the counter $e_{2n+m+nm+2}$.

This phase consumes m computation steps.

- *Formula checking phase*: in this phase it is determined if there exists any valuation making true the m clauses of the formula. For this, the rules of type (q) are used, analyzing in an ordered way (first the clause C_1, after that clause C_2, and so on) if the clauses of the formula are being satisfied by the represented valuation in the corresponding cell labeled by 2. For example, from counter $d_{2n+m+nm+1}$ appearing in every cell 2, the appearance of the object r_1 (the valuation makes true clause C_1) permits to generate in that cell the object $d_{2n+m+nm+2}$. This object, in turn, permits to evolve object $d_{2n+m+nm+3}$ if in that cell appears the object r_2. In this manner, a valuation represented by a cell labeled by 2 makes true the formula φ if and only if the object $d_{2n+m+nm+m+1}$ appears in the content of that cell in the configuration $C_{2n+m+nm+m+1}$.

- *Output phase*: in this phase, the system will provide the corresponding output, depending on the analysis in the formula checking phase.

  If the formula φ is satisfiable, then there is some cell in the configuration $C_{2n+m+nm+m+1}$ that contains an object $d_{2n+m+nm+m+1}$. In this case, the application of rule (r) sends an object f and the object yes to the cell 1. The object yes therefore disappears from cell 1, and consequently, rule (t) cannot be applied. In the next computation step, the application of the rule (s) produces an object yes in the environment (for the first time during the whole computation) and the process ends.

  If the formula φ is not satisfiable, then there no exist any cell in the configuration $C_{2n+m+nm+m+1}$ containing an object $d_{2n+m+nm+m+1}$. In this case, the rule (r) is not applicable, and in the next computation step, the counter e_i evolves, providing an object $e_{2n+m+nm+m+3}$ in cell 1. This object permits the application of rule (t), since the objects no and f remain in cell 1. In this way, the object no is sent in the next computation step, and the computation finalizes.

6.4.3.3 Sequential Simulation and Data Structure

For an easier implementation, the simulation algorithm has been divided into five (simulation) phases, instead of the six phases in $\Pi_{\text{tsp-SAT}}$ since we merge some of them. Each of these simulation phases are implemented in code as separated functions whenever is possible. They corresponds to the application of certain rules, as explained below:

- *Generation phase*: it performs the application of rules from (a) to (e) of systems from $\Pi_{\text{tsp-SAT}}$. Therefore, it comprises the two first phases of the theoretical model: valuations generation phase and counters generation phase.

- *Exchange phase*: it simulates the application of rules (f) and (g). It comprises the first part of the checking preparation phase.
- *Synchronization phase*: it applies the rules from (h) to (m), so comprising the second part of the checking preparation phase.
- *Checking phase*: it performs the application of rules from (n) to (p). Thus, it is the checking clauses phase we identified in the theoretical model.
- *Output phase*: it applies rules from (q) to (t). It then performs both the formula checking phase and the output phase identified in the theoretical model.

The sequential simulator implements these five simulation phases directly in code. The input of the simulator is the same than the one used in the simulator for the cell-like solution Π_{am-SAT}. A DIMACS CNF file is provided, and the simulator outputs the response of the computation. Therefore, it acts merely as a SAT solver, but the implementation follows the computation of the systems from the family $\Pi_{tsp-SAT}$.

Furthermore, we have adopted a set of optimizations to improve the performance of the sequential simulator. After several tests, we show that the best optimizations are as follows [21]:

- As the exchange phase is very simple, it is then implemented after the generation phase loop, within the same function.
- The full synchronization phase is applied to one cell before going to the next one. This allows to exploit data locality in cache memories.
- In the checking phase, the objects r_j, for $1 \leq j \leq m$, are inserted in order in the corresponding array whenever they are created. Thus, the output phase can be easily performed, in such a way that it is not necessary to loop all the objects coming from the input multiset (literals). Now it is enough to check if there exists the m objects r_j.

For this solution, the memory layout for the representation of the tissue P system differentiates between cells labeled 1 and 2, having a different data structure representing each type of cell in the system.

First, cell 1 is represented as an array having a maximum dimension of five elements. That is, the multiset for cell 1 has the maximum amount of five objects. These five objects are the three counters, b, c, and d (which are initially in this cell), and the two objects *yes* and *no* (that will final answer to the problem). Note that the size of the array for cell 1 is always constant, as it is independent of the input parameters of the simulator.

Second, the cells labeled by 2 are also represented by a one-dimensional array. All of them are stored inside this large array, since it is initially allocated to store the maximum amount of cells (2^n). By studying a computation of the systems

$\Pi_{\text{tsp}-\text{SAT}}$, we conclude that the maximum number of objects appearing in a cell 2 is $(2n) + 4 + |cod(\varphi)|$, where:

- $|cod(\varphi)|$ elements for the initial multiset,
- n elements for objects $T_{i,j}$ and $F_{i,j}$, for $1 \le i \le n$ and $1 \le j \le m$. Note that an object $T_{i,j}$ and an object $F_{i,j}$, for any i, cannot be simultaneously placed within a cell 2. Moreover, the index j is used sequentially in the computation steps of the system, i.e., replacing objects in the evolution process of incrementing the second index. For all of this, n elements are enough to store those objects.
- n elements for objects t_i and f_i, for $1 \le i \le n$. Note that objects f_i and t_j, for $i = j$, cannot be simultaneously placed within a cell 2, so n elements are enough to store those objects.
- 4 elements for counter objects a, b, c, and d. They will be replaced for counter objects f and g.

The objects are represented similarly to the simulator for $\Pi_{\text{am}-\text{SAT}}$. In this case, we recover the reserved space utilized to store the multiplicity of the object, inasmuch as it exceeds 1. In summary, they are encoded at bit-level within integers of 32 bits that store the following (8 bits for each field):

1. The name of the object (x or $\overline{x}$)
2. Multiplicity of the object. As there are objects whose multiplicity can exceed 2^8, this field can eventually be joined to the next one (variable).
3. Variable (subindex i).
4. Clause (subindex j).

6.4.3.4 Design of the Parallel Simulator

The design of this parallel simulator is driven by the same structure of phases we have used for the sequential one. Separated CUDA kernels are utilized to speedup the execution of each phase.

The general assignment of work for threads and thread blocks is summarized in Fig. 6.11. Each thread block corresponds to each cell labeled by 2 created in the system. However, unlike the previous simulator for the cell-like solution, we do not assign a thread per literal. The assignment of each thread, this time, is different for each simulation phase. The work mapping per phase is therefore as follows:

- *Generation phase*: the number of thread blocks is iteratively increased together with the amount of cells created in each computation step. We distribute cells along the two-dimensional grid through successive kernel calls. Each thread block contains $(2n) + 4 + |cod(\varphi)|$ threads. That is, the amount of elements assigned to each cell in the global array storing multisets. Threads are then used to copy each individual elements of the corresponding cell when it is divided.
- *Exchange phase*: it is executed at the kernel for generation phase, using the same amount of thread blocks, but only the corresponding threads perform the exchange.

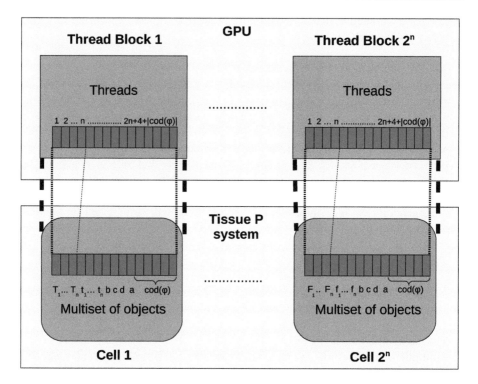

Fig. 6.11 General design of the parallel simulator for $\Pi_{tsp-SAT}$. From [21, 26]

- *Synchronization phase*: the thread blocks are assigned to the cells labeled by 2, like in the last step of the generation phase. For this phase, the number of threads is n (number of variables). If we use the same amount of threads than in generation phase, most of them will be idle. So it is preferred to launch less threads, but performing effective work. We have experimentally corroborated this fact.
- *Checking phase*: the number of thread blocks is again assigned to be the number of cells labeled by 2. However, for this phase we use a block size of $|cod(\varphi)|$. That is, each thread is used to execute, in parallel, rules of type (n) and (o). The result at the SAT problem resolution level, each thread checks if the corresponding literal makes true its clause, depending on the truth assignment encoded by the cell assigned to the thread block.
- *Output phase*: rules of type (q) are sequentially executed in a separate kernel, again using $|cod(\varphi)|$ threads per block and 2^n thread blocks (2^n is the number of cells labeled by 2).

For this solution, we have applied a small set of optimizations, focused on the GPU implementation, to improve the performance of the parallel simulator. We identify that the simulator runs twice faster than the simulator without these optimizations. We will use the optimized version of the parallel simulator to perform the comparisons. These optimizations are oriented to improve two performance aspects of GPU computing, what leads us to consider two kind of optimizations. The first one is to *emphasize the parallelism*. This optimization aims to increase the number of threads per block (to the recommended amount from 64 to 256), so it allows to fulfill warps and hide latency. The second is to *exploit streaming bandwidth*. To do this, the data is loaded first to the shared memory, and operated there, avoiding global memory (expensive) accesses. Next, we show the specific optimizations we have carried out for each phase:

- *Generation phase*: no optimizations were implemented here, since the implementation already satisfies the first optimization type. The second type will require a more sophisticated implementation, like the one presented in Sect. 6.4.2.
- *Exchange phase*: this phase, as it is joined with the generation phase, has no optimizations.
- *Synchronization phase*: the two optimization types are implemented here. The second optimization type is carried out by using shared memory to avoid global memory accesses. The first type is performed by increasing the number of threads per block. For the simulator, we can assume that n (number of variables, and the number of threads per block) is a small number, since the number of cells grows exponentially with respect to it. For example, let $n = 32$. Then, 2^{32} cells will be created, what require $2^{32}(68 + |cod(\varphi)|)$ bytes (in gigabytes: $272 + 4|cod(\varphi)|$). This number obviously exceeds the amount of available device memory. We therefore need to increase the number of threads per block, since $n < 32$ means to not fulfil a CUDA warp. A solution here is to assign more than one cell to each thread block. This amount is $\frac{256}{n}$, being 256 the optimum number of threads per block. It allows us to reach a number of threads close to the optimum one. However, we have to take care also of having enough shared memory to load the data of every assigned cell.
- *Checking phase*: since $|cod(\varphi)|$ can be greater than 32, we then keep this number as the number of threads per block. However, we use shared memory to speedup the accesses to the elements of the array.
- *Output phase*: as in the previous phase, we also use shared memory, and the number of threads per block is kept to $|cod(\varphi)|$.

6.4.3.5 Performance Analysis

In this subsection, we analyze the performance of the two simulators developed for the family of tissue-like P systems $\Pi_{\text{tsp-SAT}}$: the sequential simulator developed in C++ (from now, *tsp-sat-seq*) and the parallel simulator on the GPU (*tsp-sat-gpu*).

Figure 6.12 shows the results for both simulators when increasing the number of cells (by increasing the number of variables in the input CNF formulas), considering only kernel runtime for *tsp-sat-gpu*. For this case, we can observe that again the kernels of *tsp-sat-gpu* run faster than *tsp-sat-seq*. However, the performance gain is increased with the amount of cell 2 created by the system. For 64 membranes, the speedup is of 2×, but for 2 M cells it is of 8.3×.

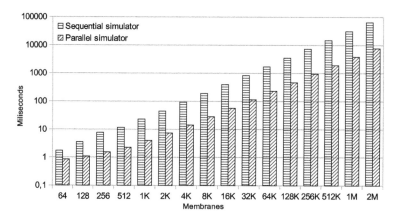

Fig. 6.12 Simulation performance for *tsp-sat-seq* and *tsp-sat-gpu* when increasing the number of membranes (x-axis). From [21, 26]

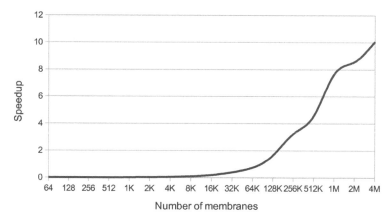

Fig. 6.13 Speedup achieved running Test 2 (256 Objects/Cell) for *tsp-sat-gpu* and *tsp-sat-seq* considering also the GPU data management, when increasing the number of membranes (x-axis). From [21, 26]

Finally, we show the speedup achieved by the simulator *tsp-sat-gpu*, taking into account also the amount of time consumed by the data management (allocation and transfer). It is observed that, since the data management time is fixed for all the sizes (copy the initial multiset and retrieve the final answer), the speedup exceeds 1 only after 128 K membranes. Systems with smaller number of cells are executed slower than in the CPU, because of the data management. However, for very large systems, the speedup is as large as with only kernels. The maximum speedup we report for this simulator is given for 4 M cells, up to 10× (Fig. 6.13).

6.5   Adaptive Simulations

In this section, we will introduce a third type of simulation of P systems, which is called adaptive simulation.

6.5.1   Definition

We have discussed the difference between generic and specific simulators. In this section, we will discuss a hybrid type, which is called adaptative, or simply adaptive, simulation. A simulator of this kind is initially a generic simulator, which is designed to simulate a wide range of P systems within a variant. However, the simulator is provided with high-level information that can be either discarded (then remaining as generic) or used to adapt the simulation to improve its efficiency.

In this sense, an adaptative simulator has the goal of getting closer to specific simulators without losing generality; that is, they are generic simulators with improved performance by taking advantage of extra information provided directly by designers (e.g., modules). For example, if the algorithm scheme of the computation is known by the designer (as it is, as discussed for the specific simulators), then it can be given to the simulator in order to be able to discard rules at selection stage (because the algorithm scheme is known).

Next, we will overview the first adaptive simulator for P systems implemented so far, which is published in [29]. This simulation framework is implemented within *ABCD-GPU*, and it can be downloaded from the official website http://sourceforge.net/p/pmcgpu [45] or the repository https://github.com/RGNC/abcd-gpu/tree/adaptative.

6.5.2   Simulating Population Dynamics P Systems

The idea of adaptative simulators was introduced and analyzed in [29]. It is inspired in the way directives work in common programming languages. They are special syntactic elements that tell extra information to the compiler, allowing to better adapt the code for some purposes if the compiler accepts it (e.g., in OpenMP, one call can easily ask to parallelize the iterations of a loop). This way, a P system model designer can also provide very useful information to the simulator, rather than just the syntactic and/or semantic elements of the P system to simulate, such as the algorithmic scheme of the computation.

Specifically in PDP systems, ecosystem modelers often use algorithmic schemes for their models [6]. This is given as cycle that is repeated (per year, per season, etc.). A cycle in the model is a fixed amount of transition steps where a sequence of modules take place. These modules reproduce certain processes such as reproduction of species, feeding, migration, etc. Moreover, these modules consist of certain rules that are carefully designed to model the corresponding process. Therefore, we can say that somehow the model designer already knows which rules can be executed in each time step. Thus, if they are able to provide that information, the simulator can take advantage of this to dismiss rules automatically at each step.

The PDP system simulator was turned into adaptative. First, the model designer is able to provide the information of the modules they are defining by using the new P-Lingua 5 software [37]. This new version now includes new syntax elements called *features*. They are written as @featureName = featureValue and can be defined globally (for the whole system) or locally (for individual rules). ABCD-GPU takes this information to organize the rules by modules. If the simulator does not recognize the information provided by the features, it can proceed and simulate the system without problems.

In summary, there are two main pieces of information that has to be declared in order to define modules:

1. Information about the modular structure of the model. This includes module names and their temporal relation. The latter indicates when a module starts inside a cycle and which modules will follow a given one.
2. Information about distribution of rules in modules. That is, which module each rule belongs to.

The simulator precomputes which modules are active in each step within the cycle before starting the simulation. In this way, this information can be used to easily identify the rules that might be applicable at each transition step. For this purpose, the rule blocks and the rules are sorted in order to compact them into modules; rules belonging to the same module are put one after the other. The kernels of ABCD-GPU are expanded to accept extra indexes indicating the modules and where the rules of the modules are. In this way, the threads as distributed in Fig. 6.4 will have a shorter loop, because the rule blocks (and rules) are just those from the module being active. Furthermore, if the solution has parallel modules in a cycle, then they can also run in parallel thanks to CUDA streams. We can launch the kernels for phase 1 also in parallel at different streams, one per module. As for environments and simulations, the behavior remains as before.

6.5.2.1 Analysis of Performance Results

Next, the behavior and performance of the adaptative PDP system simulators for GPU and OpenMP are analyzed. The model employed as benchmark is based on the tritrophic interactions presented in [9, 10]. This is a virtual ecosystem that was defined to illustrate PDP systems as a modeling framework. In this model, three trophic levels are represented: grass, herbivores, and carnivores. These species interact with each other, reproduce, and move along the 10 environments when no food is encountered. Rule block competitions take place. For instance, all herbivores compete for grass that is represented by a single object, G.

For benchmarking purposes, the model has been generalized so that the number of species can be changed. The corresponding parameters (probabilities, amount of copies eaten per species, etc.) are generated randomly. This was possible thanks to the ability of P-Lingua 5 to incorporate calls from the model to random number generation functions. Moreover, the modules of the model are identified by P-Lingua 5 features.

In this section, the benchmark carried out to the adaptative PDP systems simulator is analyzed. The two versions of the simulator are compared: generic and adaptive versions of ABCD-GPU. The extended tritrophic model is used as input. In all experiments, 20 years of the virtual ecosystem are simulated (corresponding to 180 transition steps of the PDP systems). The *A* parameter of DCBA is set to 2. No output was asked, so only the simulation runtimes were measured. The scalability of the simulators is analyzed by increasing the number of species. Specifically, 7 will be used to denote the *base* model, which has in fact 7 species. In order to have an idea of the dimensions of the model, the ratio of rule blocks per species is approximately 22: 21985 rule blocks are generated for 1000 species, being 9990 communication rule blocks and 11,995 skeleton rule blocks. Another parameter affecting scalability is the amount of simulations running in parallel. For this reason, 50 simulations were launched for the tests. The following two configurations of CPU and GPU hardware were used to run the simulations (short names are provided in bold):

- **(i7)** Intel i7-8700 CPU at 3.20 GHz, having 12 logical cores (6 physical)
- **(P100)** Tesla P100 GPU, having 3584 cores at 1.33 GHz

A cross comparison of runtimes and speedups achieved by GPU compared to CPU is shown in Fig. 6.14, which corresponds to the speedups reached by the above simulation times. The GPU is faster, in both *adaptive* and *generic* versions, than the multicore counterparts when handling middle and large models. Only for the

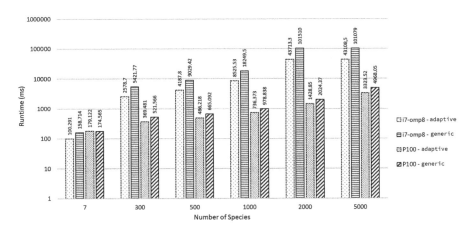

Fig. 6.14 Comparison of P100 versus i7 with 8 threads, for both generic and adaptive versions of *abcd-gpu* tested for different number of species in the model. It shows the corresponding speedups of P100 against i7 for both version. 50 simulations were run. Bar plots use logarithmic scale for y-axis. From [29]

small base model, the GPU is a bit slower (above $0.9\times$). Speedups are higher with larger models, being around $30\times$ and $50\times$ for *adaptive* and *generic* simulators, respectively, and for 2000 species. When simulating hundreds of species, $6\times$ and $10\times$ accelerations were obtained for *adaptive* and *generic* versions. Finally, the speedup of the GPU is lower when using the *adaptive* version, given that the impact of the *modular* scheme is better for the CPU than for the GPU.

We can conclude that this design helped to improve the performance by $2.5\times$ extra when using a P100 GPU [29].

6.6   Conclusions

GPUs have been established as a massively parallel processor and an enabling technology where programmers currently accelerate scientific applications. They provide a good parallel platform to simulate P systems due to the double parallel nature that both GPUs and P systems present. Their shared memory system also helps to efficiently synchronize the simulation of the models. Moreover, they are a cheap and scalable parallel architecture that can be seen in current HPC solutions.

However, the results in the literature [22, 48] show that P systems simulations are memory bandwidth bound: they spend more time accessing and updating data (multisets) than executing computation. The main cause is that simulating P systems requires a high synchronization degree (e.g., the global clock of the models, rule cooperation, rules competition, etc.), and the number of operations to execute per memory access is very small (P systems execute rewriting rules). This restricts the design of parallel simulators. A parallel simulator designer has to be careful with the representation and management of each P system ingredient. A bad step taken on GPU programming can easily break parallelism and, so, performance.

We can identify a taxonomy of simulators developed so far. Generic parallel simulators are intended to be flexible enough to simulate a wide range of P systems within a variant. They also take advantage of P systems parallelism to speedup the simulation. However, when working with highly flexible simulators, the P systems design has to be reconsidered to achieve performance, in such a way that they execute as many rules as possible in each computation step. Some variants simulated by generic simulators are P systems with active membranes and elementary division and Population Dynamic P systems. Other related works also include spiking neural P systems variants [1, 2].

On the other hand, specific simulators are designed for just certain P systems within a solution or family. This way, the simulator can be designed adapting all parts to the P systems, since their scheme is known at developing time. The performance achieved in these simulators are much higher, but it comes at restricting the P systems to simulate. For example, one cannot define new rules to simulate, since they are already predetermined. In the middle term, we have a new type of simulation called adaptive. Basically, it is a generic simulator but that includes high level information that can be either discarded by the simulator (going generic) or used to adapt the simulation and achieve better performance (adaptive).

We can identify some challenges for the future. For example, concerning the memory bandwidth limit, one challenge is to design P system variants where the model contains a higher computational intensity. Moreover, memory accesses can be partially reduced by improving data structures using a compacted, dense, and well-ordered memory representation of P systems. A challenge is to use a dense representation in an effective way in generic simulators. Finally, a P system model with cooperation in the LHS usually leads to this issue, making it more difficult when the cooperation is larger.

References

1. J.P. Carandang, F.G.C. Cabarle, H.N. Adorna, N.H.S. Hernandez, M.A. Martínez-del-Amor, Handling non-determinism in spiking neural P systems: algorithms and simulations. Fundam. Inf. **164**(2–3), 139–155 (2019). https://doi.org/10.3233/FI-2019-1759
2. J.P. Carandang, J.M.B. Villaflores, F.G.C. Cabarle, H.N. Adorna, M.A. Martínez-del-Amor, CuSNP: spiking neural P systems simulators in CUDA. Rom. J Inf Sci Technol. **20**(1), 57–70 (2017)
3. J.M. Cecilia, J.M. García, G.D. Guerrero, M.A. Martínez-del-Amor, I. Pérez-Hurtado, M.J. Pérez-Jiménez, Simulating a P system based efficient solution to SAT by using GPUs. J Logic Algebraic Program. **79**(6), 317–325 (2010). https://doi.org/10.1016/j.jlap.2010.03.008
4. J.M. Cecilia, J.M. García, G.D. Guerrero, M.A. Martínez-del-Amor, I. Pérez-Hurtado, M.J. Pérez-Jiménez, Simulation of P systems with active membranes on CUDA. Briefings in Bioinf. **11**(3), 313–322 (2010). https://doi.org/10.1093/bib/bbp064
5. J.M. Cecilia, J.M. García, G.D. Guerrero, M.A. Martínez-del-Amor, M.J. Pérez-Jiménez, M. Ujaldón, The GPU on the simulation of cellular computing models. Soft Comput. **16**(2), 231–246 (2012). https://doi.org/10.1007/s00500-011-0716-1
6. M.A. Colomer, A. Margalida, M.J. Pérez-Jiménez, Population Dynamics P system (PDP) models: a standardized protocol for describing and applying novel bio-inspired computing tools. PLOS ONE **8**(5), e60698 (2013). https://doi.org/10.1371/journal.pone.0060698
7. M.A. Colomer, A. Margalida, D. Sanuy, M.J. Pérez-Jiménez, A bio-inspired computing model as a new tool for modeling ecosystems: the avian scavengers as a case study. Ecol. Model. **222**(1), 33–47 (2011). https://doi.org/10.1016/j.ecolmodel.2010.09.012
8. M.A. Colomer, A. Margalida, L. Valencia, A. Palau, Application of a computational model for complex fluvial ecosystems: the population dynamics of zebra mussel Dreissena polymorpha as a case study. Ecol. Complexity **20**, 116–126 (2014). https://doi.org/10.1016/j.ecocom.2014.09.006
9. M.A. Colomer, I. Pérez-Hurtado, M.J. Pérez-Jiménez, A. Riscos-Núñez. Comparing simulation algorithms for multienvironment probabilistic P systems over a standard virtual ecosystem, in *IEEE Fifth International Conference on Bio-Inspired Computing: Theories and Applications (BIC-TA 2010)*, vol. 1 (2010). https://doi.org/10.1109/BICTA.2010.5645258
10. M.A. Colomer, I. Pérez-Hurtado, M.J. Pérez-Jiménez, A. Riscos-Núñez, Comparing simulation algorithms for multienvironment probabilistic P systems over a standard virtual ecosystem. Nat. Comput. **11**(3), 369–379 (2012). https://doi.org/10.1007/s11047-011-9289-2
11. T.S. Crow, Evolution of the graphical processing unit. Master's thesis, University of Nevada Reno (2004). http://www.cse.unr.edu/~fredh/papers/thesis/023-crow/GPUFinal.pdf
12. A.C. Elster, High-Performance Computing: past, present, and future, in *Applied Parallel Computing, Lecture Notes in Computer Science*, ed. by J. Fagerholm, J. Haataja, J. Järvinen, M. Lyly, P. Raback, V. Savolainen, vol. 2367 (2006), pp. 433–444. https://doi.org/10.1007/3-540-48051-X_43

13. M. García-Quismondo, R. Gutiérrez-Escudero, M.A. Martínez-del-Amor, E. Orejuela-Pinedo, I. Pérez-Hurtado, P-Lingua 2.0: A software framework for cell-like P systems. Int. J. Comput. Commun. Control **4**(3), 234–243 (2009). https://doi.org/10.15837/ijccc.2009.3.2431
14. M.A. Gutiérrez-Naranjo, M.J. Pérez-Jiménez, A. Riscos-Núñez, A fast P system for finding a balanced 2-partition. Soft Comput. **9**, 673–678 (2005). https://doi.org/10.1007/s00500-004-0397-0
15. Inside HPC blog. http://insidehpc.org
16. B.W. Kernighan, D. Ritchie. *The C Programming Language*, 2nd edn. (Prentice Hall, Englewood Cliffs 1988)
17. D.B. Kirk, W.W. Hwu, *Programming Massively Parallel Processors: A Hands-on Approach*, 3rd edn. (Morgan Kaufmann, San Francisco, 2016). https://www.sciencedirect.com/science/book/9780128119860
18. A. Krizhevsky, I. Sutskever, G.E. Hinton, Imagenet classification with deep convolutional neural networks. Adv. Neural Inf. Process. Syst. **25**(2) (2012). https://doi.org/10.1145/3065386
19. E. Lindholm, J. Nickolls, S. Oberman, J. Montrym, NVIDIA Tesla: a unified graphics and computing architecture. IEEE Micro **28**(2), 39–55 (2008). https://doi.org/10.1109/MM.2008.31
20. C. Martín-Vide, Gh. Păun, J. Pazos, A. Rodríguez-Patón, Tissue P systems. Theor. Comput. Sci. **296**(2), 295–326 (2003). https://doi.org/10.1016/S0304-3975(02)00659-X
21. M.A. Martínez-del-Amor, *Accelerating Membrane Systems Simulators Using High Performance Computing with GPU*. Ph.D. Thesis, Universidad de Sevilla, 2013. http://hdl.handle.net/11441/15644
22. M.A. Martínez-del-Amor, M. García-Quismondo, L.F. Macías-Ramos, L. Valencia-Cabrera, A. Riscos-Núñez, M.J. Pérez-Jiménez, Simulating P systems on GPU devices: a survey. Fundam. Inf. **136**(3), 269–284 (2015). https://doi.org/10.3233/FI-2015-1157
23. M.A. Martínez-del-Amor, I. Karlin, R.E. Jensen, M.J. Pérez-Jiménez, A.C. Elster, Parallel simulation of probabilistic P systems on multicore platforms, in *Proceedings of the Tenth Brainstorming Week on Membrane Computing*, ed. by M. García-Quismondo, L.F. Macías-Ramos, Gh. Păun, L. Valencia-Cabrera, vol. II (Fénix Editora, 2012), pp. 17–26
24. M.A. Martínez-del-Amor, L.F. Macías-Ramos, L. Valencia-Cabrera, M.J. Pérez-Jiménez, Parallel simulation of Population Dynamics P systems: updates and roadmap. Nat. Comput. **15**(4), 565–573 (2015). https://doi.org/10.1007/s11047-016-9566-1
25. M.A. Martínez-del Amor, D. Orellana-Martín, I. Pérez-Hurtado, L. Valencia-Cabrera, A. Riscos-Núñez, M.J. Pérez-Jiménez, Design of specific P systems simulators on GPUs, in *Membrane Computing. CMC 2018*, ed. by T. Hinze, G. Rozenberg, A. Salomaa, C. Zandron. Lecture Notes in Computer Science, vol. 11399 (2019), pp. 202–207. https://doi.org/10.1007/978-3-030-12797-8_14
26. M.A. Martínez-del-Amor, J. Pérez-Carrasco, M.J. Pérez-Jiménez, Characterizing the parallel simulation of P systems on the GPU. Int. J. Unconv. Comput. **9**(5–6), 405–424 (2013)
27. M.A. Martínez-del-Amor, I. Pérez-Hurtado, M. García-Quismondo, L.F. Macías-Ramos, L. Valencia-Cabrera, A. Romero-Jiménez, C. Graciani-Díaz, A. Riscos-Núñez., M.A. Colomer, M.J. Pérez-Jiménez, DCBA: simulating Population Dynamics P Systems with proportional object distribution, in *Membrane Computing. CMC 2012*, ed. by E. Csuhaj-Varjú, M. Gheorghe, G. Rozenberg, A. Salomaa, G. Vaszil. Lecture Notes in Computer Science, vol. 7762 (2012), pp. 291–310. https://doi.org/10.1007/978-3-642-36751-9_18
28. M.A. Martínez-del-Amor, I. Pérez-Hurtado, A. Gastalver-Rubio, A.C. Elster, M.J. Pérez-Jiménez, Population Dynamics P Systems on CUDA, in *Computational Methods in Systems Biology*, ed. by D. Gilbert, M. Heiner. Lecture Notes in Computer Science, vol. 7605 (2012), pp. 247–266. https://doi.org/10.1007/978-3-642-33636-2_15
29. M.A. Martínez-del-Amor, I. Pérez-Hurtado, D. Orellana-Martín, M.J. Pérez-Jiménez, Adaptive parallel simulators for bioinspired computing models. Future Gener. Comput. Syst. **107**, 469–484 (2020). https://doi.org/10.1016/j.future.2020.02.012

30. M.A. Martínez-del-Amor, I. Pérez-Hurtado, M.J. Pérez-Jiménez, A. Riscos-Núñez, M.A. Colomer, A new simulation algorithm for multienvironment probabilistic P systems, in *2010 IEEE Fifth International Conference on Bio-Inspired Computing: Theories and Applications (BIC-TA)*, Changsha, 2010, vol. 1 (2010), pp. 59–68. https://doi.org/10.1109/BICTA.2010.5645352
31. A. Munshi, B.R. Gaster, T.G. Mattson, J. Fung, D. Ginsburg, *OpenCL Programming Guide*, 1st edn. (Addison-Wesley, Reading, 2011)
32. J. Nickolls, I. Buck, M. Garland, K. Skadron, Scalable parallel programming with CUDA: is CUDA the parallel programming model that application developers have been waiting for? Queue **6**(2), 40–53 (2008). https://doi.org/10.1145/1365490.1365500
33. NVIDIA CUDA C Programming Guide. https://docs.nvidia.com/cuda/cuda-c-programming-guide/index.html. Accessed June 2019
34. N. Otterness, J. Anderson, AMD GPUs as an alternative to NVIDIA for supporting real-time workloads, in *Proceedings of the 32nd Euromicro Conference on Real-Time Systems*, (2020), pp. 10:1–10:23. https://doi.org/10.4230/LIPIcs.ECRTS.2020.10
35. J.D. Owens, M. Houston, D. Luebke, S. Green, J.E. Stone, J.C. Phillips, GPU computing. Proc. IEEE **96**(5), 879–899 (2008). https://doi.org/10.1109/JPROC.2008.917757
36. Gh. Păun, P systems with active membranes: attacking NP-complete problems. J. Autom. Lang. Comb. **6**, 75–90 (1999)
37. I. Pérez-Hurtado, D. Orellana-Martín, G. Zhang, M.J. Pérez-Jiménez, P-lingua in two steps: flexibility and efficiency. J. Membr. Comput. **1**(2), 93–102 (2019). https://doi.org/10.1007/s41965-019-00014-1
38. M.J. Pérez-Jiménez, A. Riscos-Núñez, Solving the Subset-Sum problem by P systems with active membranes. N. Gener. Comput. **23**(4), 339–356 (2005). https://doi.org/10.1007/BF03037637
39. M.J. Pérez-Jiménez, A. Riscos-Núñez, A linear-time solution for the knapsack problem with active membranes, in *Membrane Computing. WMC 2003*, ed. by C. Martín-Vide, G. Mauri, Gh. Păun, G. Rozenberg, A. Salomaa. Lecture Notes in Computer Science, vol. 2933 (2004), pp. 250–268. https://doi.org/10.1007/b95207
40. M.J. Pérez-Jiménez, A. Romero-Jiménez, F. Sancho-Caparrini, Complexity classes in models of cellular computing with membranes. Nat. Comput. **2**(3), 265–285 (2003). https://doi.org/10.1023/A:1025449224520
41. M.J. Pérez-Jiménez, A. Romero-Jiménez, F. Sancho-Caparrini, Decision P systems and the $P \neq NP$ conjecture, in *Membrane Computing. WMC 2002*, ed. by Gh. Păun, G. Rozenberg, A. Salomaa, C. Zandron. Lecture Notes in Computer Science, vol. 2597 (2003), pp. 388–399. https://doi.org/10.1007/3-540-36490-0_27
42. M.J. Pérez-Jiménez, A. Romero-Jiménez, F. Sancho-Caparrini, A polynomial complexity class in P systems using membrane division. J. Autom. Lang. Comb. **11**, 423–434 (2006)
43. N. Satish, M. Harris, M. Garland, Designing efficient sorting algorithms for manycore GPUs, in *Proceedings of the 2009 IEEE International Symposium on Parallel & Distributed Processing (IPDPS '09)*, Rome, 2009 (IEEE Computer Society, Silver Spring, 2009), pp. 1–10. https://doi.org/10.1109/IPDPS.2009.5161005
44. W. Shin, K.H. Yoo, N. Baek, Large-scale data computing performance comparisons on SYCL heterogeneous parallel processing layer implementations. Appl. Sci. **10**, 1656 (2020). https://doi.org/10.3390/app10051656
45. The PMCGPU (Parallel simulators for Membrane Computing on the GPU) project website. http://sourceforge.net/p/pmcgpu. Accessed June 2019
46. The top 500 supercomputer site. http://www.top500.org
47. A. Torres-Moríño, M.A. Martínez-del-Amor, F. Sancho-Caparrini, GPU-parallel crowd simulation with Vulkan, in *Proceedings of the 18th High Performance Computing & Simulation (HPCS 2020)*. (2020, in press)
48. G. Zhang, Z. Shang, S. Verlan, M.A. Martínez-del-Amor, C. Yuan, L. Valencia-Cabrera, M.J. Pérez-Jiménez, An overview of hardware implementation of Membrane Computing models. ACM Comput. Surv. **53**(4), 90 (2020). https://doi.org/10.1145/3402456

7 P Systems Implementation on FPGA

7.1 Introduction

P systems feature a highly distributed heterogeneous parallel computation governed by a global clock. They are a very tempting candidate for parallel algorithms description, and there are several such attempts in the literature [1, 3, 11, 18]. However, these investigations remain purely theoretical, as any simulation of P systems on traditional computers is more-or-less sequential, as the parallelism should be broken because current-day CPUs have a low number of cores. Even using graphical processing unit (GPU) hardware featuring thousands of computational cores does not solve the problem, as it is tailored for single instruction multiple data (SIMD) computations that are mostly homogeneous. In contrast, most algorithms developed using P systems are not homogeneous and have different types of instructions to be executed in parallel.

In contrast, sequential digital circuits (which are the basic building block of any today digital device) consist of many different computational cores distributed all over the chip and synchronized by a global clock signal. While not a requirement, it is important to have a local interaction between cores, as long-distance signal transmission cannot happen at high clock speeds. Field-programmed gate array (FPGA) is a reconfigurable hardware that allows to implement such type of circuits. Because of the reconfigurability, it is possible to use FPGA for quick prototyping as they allow a fast hardware development cycle.

P systems correspond well to the computing specificity exhibited by sequential digital circuits. So, several implementations of different variants of P systems were done using FPGAs. It should be noted that in contrast to the software simulation on a CPU or GPU, a unique hardware design should be used for each concrete P system. More precisely, in the first case a software program is written, and each concrete P system, as well as its corresponding initial parameters or input values, is fed to this program as input. The program then simulates the execution of each step of the considered P system and provides the necessary output. Unfortunately, using such approach for FPGA implementations would take too much time and effort to be implemented, and it is not clear whether it would give any advantage over software implementations, as in this case it is not easy to keep a large-scale parallelism. So, from the beginning, FPGA implementations chose a different strategy by providing for each concrete system a unique hardware design, thus allowing to exploit the maximum parallel performance of the underlying hardware. In order to be able to consider more than a single example, most of the projects considered software generators that starting from the description of a P system and of its initial conditions generate a hardware design implementing the given description. Unfortunately, there is still a need for manual touch-ups, so hardware design skills are needed in order to use such implementations.

Early attempts were concentrated on the simulation of the functioning of some variant of P systems on FPGA [15–17, 26, 28, 33]. An overview of these results is given in Sect. 7.5. They show the feasibility of the approach and feature quite important speed-ups of order greater than 10^4 with respect to best software (or GPU-based) simulations. While important as proof of concept, the usability difficulties and the required hardware design skills make these implementations difficult to be used by large public for practical problems.

Recently, a different approach emerged in hardware simulation of P systems. It started from the observation that several ingredients of the model are not well adapted to FPGA and are extremely difficult to implement in a parallel manner, e.g., the computation of the set of rules for the maximally parallel evolution. Also, the multiset data structure is not sufficiently efficient for many real-world applications because of the unary encoding. Based on these observations, a particular model of P systems, called generalized numerical P systems (GNPS), was designed allowing efficient implementations in FPGA [29, 30], achieving speedups of order 10^6. This model is based on an older notion of numerical P systems (NPS) [21], a P systems model that was introduced to model economical processes. Numerical P systems and their extension enzymatic numerical P systems (ENPS) [23] were used in practical applications for the design of robot controllers [24, 25] using a software simulator connected to the robot microcontroller. Using GNPS, a similar application is targeted, but based on an FPGA implementation [30]. The definition of GNPS and the implementation details of the corresponding applications are given in Sects. 7.3, 7.4, and 8.3, 8.4.

7.2   FPGA Hardware

In this chapter, we will consider the FPGA structure and we will use the FPGA-related terminology as provided by Xilinx [37], the company which was at the origin of this technology. Other FPGA vendors may use a slightly different structure and terminology, but the main concepts are similar.

The FPGA is a reconfigurable hardware used to prototype digital circuits. The basic unit of an FPGA is a *slice* that is mainly composed of several look-up tables (LUTs), flip-flops (FFs), multiplexers (MX), and fast carry chain(s). For Xilinx

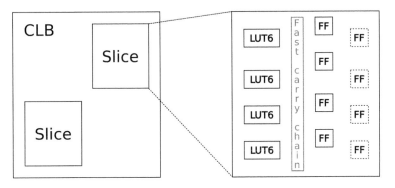

Fig. 7.1 Internal structure of FPGA. Each configurable logic block (CLB) is composed of two slices. Each slice contains 4 6-lookup tables (LUT6), 8 flip-flops (FFs) and a fast carry chain, interconnected by several muxes that are not shown for readability. Dotted FFs can be connected to any LUT

7 series devices, a slice is composed of 4 LUTs and 8 FFs [36]; see Fig. 7.1. For other vendors and older Xilinx devices, these numbers may vary. LUTs are used to implement different combinatorial circuits such as logic gates, multiplexers, adders, encoders, and decoders. The flip-flop is a sequential logic component acting as a 1-bit memory element in the circuit.

Technically, a LUT defines a Boolean function having up to n inputs. At the moment of writing, the most common value for n is 6 (the corresponding type of LUT is named as LUT6). Another popular value is 4, which is also used in the virtual generic unit *logic cell* (LC) that corresponds to a LUT4 combined with two flip-flops. The notion of LC is used mostly to compare the computational capabilities of FPGA devices, especially from different vendors. However, we note that it is not possible to interconnect any LUT to any FF in a slice; commonly, a LUT can be easily connected to two associated FFs [36]. This is why sometimes LC is presented as a base unit instead of slice.

Slices are grouped into *configurable logic blocks* (CLBs). A CLB on Xilinx 7 series devices contains 2 slices [35, 36]; other vendors and devices may use up to 4 slices per CLB. All CLBs on a device are organized in a matrix form and have configurable interconnections, i.e., it is possible to interconnect any block with any other block; see Fig. 7.2. It should be clear that it is important to group connected blocks physically in close locations because long interconnection paths induce additional propagation delay and slow down the computation. The process of placement and interconnection (called *routing*) is highly specific for each device, and it is automatized by vendor tools, so the user does not interact with it directly.

Besides CLBs and interconnect matrix, an FPGA device contains input/output blocs used for external communication, a quartz clock oscillator generating a stable clock signal, and a clock distribution tree allowing to distribute the clock signal all over device with a minimum delay. A clock cycle is the time interval between two rising (going from low to high level) edges of the clock oscillator. An FPGA

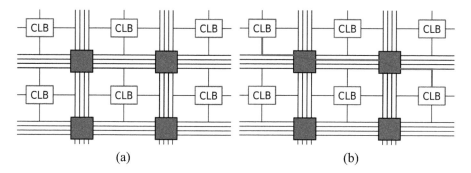

Fig. 7.2 Internal structure of FPGA. Configurable logic blocks (CLBs) are inlaid in the matrix of interconnects (**a**). Two distant configurable logic blocks (CLBs) can be interconnected by a path using the matrix of interconnects (**b**)

may also contain on-device memory of different types, analog/digital converters, and digital signal processing (DSP) blocks. The latter ones are particularly useful in implementations as they can be used to perform fast arithmetical operations (addition, subtraction, and multiplication) for multi-bit integer values (typically 48-bit).

The design of the circuit for an FPGA device is performed using a hardware description language (HDL). The most common HDLs are VHDL and Verilog. The design can be performed on several levels of abstraction, ranging from the switch/transistor level until the behavioral level, corresponding to a Mealy machine [12]. Usually, the design is performed at this latter level, unless there is a requirement for specific optimizations, or high-speed execution. An HDL design looks like a program; however, it is not executed but rather *synthesized* using vendor tools. This results in a register-transfer level (RTL) description of the circuit. Next, this description is mapped to the actual FPGA device's CLBs and interconnects using *place and route* step. If there are no errors during these steps, then the *bitstream* is generated, which contains all necessary information for the FPGA programming (values of LUT tables and positions of interconnect switches). Finally, this bitstream is transferred to FPGA that is reprogrammed according to it. This programming is volatile and should be renewed each time the device powers on; so usually, the bitstream is stored on additional flash memory, and a special microcontroller charges it at each FPGA boot. A typical problem arising during the place and route step are timing violations—the total delay of several operations and/or the delay of the interconnection between CLBs is more than the system clock cycle. Such problems should be solved (using different methods); otherwise the design would not function on FPGA device.

Since the whole process described above is time consuming and since it is very difficult to capture errors on the device running at 50–100 MHz clock speed, several *simulation* steps are usually performed before going to synthesis. During the simulation phase, the design as well as its external inputs are simulated stepwise using a software simulator. Verilog and VHDL provide language constructs and simulators to seamlessly perform this task. However, different tools can also be used, e.g., Verilator that compiles Verilog code to C++ in order to achieve a better performance.

7.3 Generalized Numerical P Systems (GNPS)

The model of (generalized) numerical P systems ((G)NPS) is very different from the classical models of membrane computing. While still having a structural relation and compartments, (G)NPS consider real-valued variables instead of multisets in each cell/compartment. Consequently, the evolution rules, called *programs*, do not correspond to multiset rewriting anymore and have a more complex semantics. Another key difference is how the result of the computation is considered. When using (G)NPS, the main interest is not the value of a variable at some time moment (e.g., after halting), but rather the dynamics of variables' evolution. So, in some sense the value of each variable at each time step is the output of the system, although we may be interested only in a subset of them. This naturally leads to the inclusion of the concept of dedicated input and output variables. The functioning of the system supposes that input variables are read-only and can be updated by an external entity at each step. The output variables are write-only, and an external entity may use their values at each step. Such a definition allows to effectively build controllers based on GNPS, without using any additional tools or mechanisms to pass the values and start/stop the computation. Moreover, properties of GNPS discussed above map well to the structure and the functioning of an FPGA design.

7.3.1 Formal Definition

We give below the formal definition of GNPS following [30].

Definition 7.1. A generalized numerical P system is the following tuple

$$\Pi = (m, V, I, O, (Var_1, Var_1(0)), \ldots, (Var_m, Var_m(0)), Pr),$$

where

- $m > 0$ is the number of cells/membranes,
- V is an alphabet of variables,
- $I \subseteq V$ is the set of input variables, $I \cap O = \emptyset$,
- $O \subseteq V$ is the set of output variables, $I \cap O = \emptyset$,
- $Var_i \subseteq V$ is the list of internal variables for cell i; we may use the notation where variables are labeled with two indices, the second one indicating their location, i.e., $Var_i = \{x_{1i}, \ldots, x_{k_i i}\}$,
- $Var_i(0)$ is the vector of initial values for variables internal to cell i,

- Pr is the set of rules of the system (see their description below).

A program (rule) $r \in Pr$ has the following form:

$$P(x_{1i}, \ldots, x_{ki}; E_1, \ldots, E_l); F(x_{1i}, \ldots, x_{ki}) \to c_1|v_1, \ldots, c_n|v_n, \qquad (7.1)$$

where

- $\{x_{1i}, \ldots, x_{ki}\} \subseteq Var_i$ for some i, $1 \le i \le m$, are variables located altogether in the same cell i,
- $\{E_1, \ldots, E_l\} \cap Var_i = \emptyset$ are variables not located in cell i above,
- $\{v_1, \ldots, v_n\} \subseteq V$ are any variables of the system,
- $c_j \in \mathbb{N}$, $1 \le j \le n$ are repartition coefficients that together with variables v_j form the *repartition protocol*,
- P is the *applicability condition*, which is a decidable predicate over indicated variables,
- F is the *production function*, which is a computable function.

In the definitions above, the values of variables are considered to be real. Then it is clear that the predicate P should be decidable and the function F should be computable on reals. In the case of an always true predicate, it can be omitted.

We remark that the definition above considers GNPS to be composed from a certain number of cells each of them containing one or several variables, so each variable has a unique associated cell it is contained in. Because of this property, it becomes clear that the set of rules Pr induces a structural relation between cells whose variables are involved in the same rule (in the predicate, in the function, or in the repartition protocol). Since there are no particular restrictions, this dependency induces a hypergraph, in the general case. Of course, special topologies like trees or graphs are of a particular interest for the membrane computing, and in the former case, we will use a Venn diagram notation and place rules and variables in corresponding cells. Abstracting from concrete details, GNPS use a structural abstraction intermediate between a tree-based structure and a flattened system, being the equivalent of the network of cells [6] in NPS. This allows to have the notion of the locality (useful for hardware implementation as it can trigger the use of neighbor cells), but does not impose the strong restriction of a tree structure like in classical variants of P systems and NPS—some examples of robot controllers based on NPS spend an enormous amount of time for data propagation because of the imposed tree structure.

In order to apply a rule r as described above, first its applicability condition is checked. If predicate P is true, then the rule is called *applicable*, and it is applied as follows [21, 30]. First the value of the production function is computed, based on current values of the variables. Second, each variable v_j, $1 \le j \le n$ from the repartition protocol part receives the fraction $\dfrac{c_j}{\sum_{t=1}^{n} c_t}$ of the computed production function value. If there are several applicable rules, then all of them are applied. If several rules update the same variable, then the corresponding amounts are added. Finally, the value of a variable at the beginning of each new step is reset to 0 if it was used in a computation of some production function. If more than one applicable rule is present, then all of them are applied at the same time.

Example 7.1. Consider the following GNPS

$$Pi = (1, \{a, b\}, \emptyset, \emptyset, (\{a, b\}, (1, 2)), Pr),$$

where the set of rules Pr contains the following rules:

$r_1 : a < b; 3(b + 1) \rightarrow 2|a, 1|b$

$r_2 : b < a; 3(a + 1) \rightarrow 1|a, 2|b$

$r_3 : a + b \rightarrow 1|a, 2|b$

At step 0, only rules r_1 and r_3 are applicable (the latter one is always applicable, as the corresponding predicate is always true). The value of the production function F for r_1 is equal to $3(b(0) + 1) = 3(2 + 1) = 9$. This value is then redistributed according to the repartition protocol. $\frac{2}{2+1} = \frac{2}{3}$ of this value ($=6$) will be added to $a(1)$, while $\frac{1}{3}$ of this value ($=3$) will be added to $b(1)$. A similar computation for rule r_3 gives the value 1 (resp. 2) to be added to $a(1)$ (resp. $b(1)$). Since both a and b were used to compute the production functions for r_1 and r_3, their values are reset to zero before step 1. So, finally we obtain that $a(1) = 0 + 6 + 1 = 7$ and $b(1) = 0 + 3 + 2 = 5$. Proceeding similarly, we compute $a(2) = 12$ and $b(2) = 24$ (this time rules r_2 and r_3 are applicable).

By examining the explanation above, it results that the evolution of the system can be described by the following discrete time series (we suppose that r is described as in (7.1)):

$$x_{ls}(t + 1) = \sum_{\substack{r \in Pr \text{ and } r \text{ is applicable} \\ r \text{ has } x_{ls} \text{ in rhs as } v_j}} F(x_{1i}(t), \ldots, x_{ki}(t)) \frac{c_j}{\sum_{t=1}^{n} c_t} + \bar{x}_{ls}(t), \quad (7.2)$$

where $\bar{x}_{ls}(t) = \begin{cases} x_{ls}(t) & \text{if } x_{ls} \text{ does not appear in any production function } F \\ & \text{of an applicable rule,} \\ 0 & \text{otherwise.} \end{cases}$

We recall that the initial values (at time 0) of variables from membrane i are given by the set $Var_i(0)$.

Example 7.2. Consider the following GNPS

$$\Pi = (3, V, I, O, (Var_1, Var_1(0)), (Var_2, Var_2(0)), (Var_3, Var_3(0)), Pr),$$

where

- $V = \{a, b, c, d, e\}, I = \{d\}, O = \{a\},$
- $Var_1 = \{a, b\}, Var_1(0) = (0, 0),$
- $Var_2 = \{d, e\}, Var_2(0) = (-, 0),$
- $Var_3 = \{c\}, Var_3(0) = (0).$
- The set of rules Pr is defined as follows

$r_1 : b < e; \ 2b + 1 \rightarrow 1|a,$

$r_2 : 0 < e; \ e - 1 \rightarrow 1|e,$

$r_3 : \neg(0 < e) \wedge \neg(0 < c); \ 2d \rightarrow 1|e,$

$r_4 : c < e; \ 2(c + 1) \rightarrow 1|c, 1|b.$

The rules above induce the following structure of Π (a circular graph):

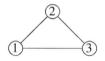

To understand the functioning of the system, we will rewrite it in terms of time series. In order to do this, we shall first consider the individual rule contributions to each variable of the distribution protocol. For example, rule r_4 is equivalent to the following two rules:

$$r_{4a} : c < e; \ c + 1 \rightarrow 1|c,$$

$$r_{4b} : c < e; \ c + 1 \rightarrow 1|b.$$

Hence, this rule updates variables b and c with the value of $c + 1$, under the assumption that $c < e$.

By decomposing rules' contribution and then summing on all possibilities for each variable, we obtain that the evolution of the system can be described by the following system of equations:

$$a(t + 1) = \text{if } b(t) < e(t) \text{ then } 2b(t) + 1 \text{ else } a(t)$$

$$b(t + 1) = \text{if } c(t) < e(t) \text{ then } c(t) + 1 \text{ else } b(t)$$

$$c(t + 1) = \text{if } c(t) < e(t) \text{ then } c(t) + 1 \text{ else } c(t)$$

$$e(t + 1) = \text{if not } 0 < e(t) \text{ and not } 0 < c(t) \text{ then } 2d(t) \text{ else } e(t) - 1$$

$$a(0) = 0, \quad b(0) = 0, \quad c(0) = 0, \quad e(0) = 0$$

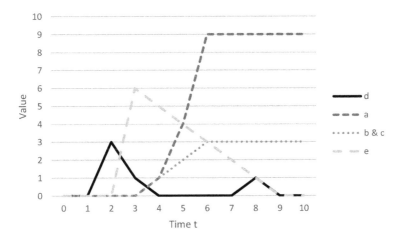

Fig. 7.3 The dynamics of system from Example 7.2 for the input $d = 3$ at time $t = 2$. The output a stabilizes at $3^2 = 9$ after $3 + 1 = 4$ steps from the first change of d. Subsequent variations of the value of d are ignored

During the first step, only rule r_3 is applicable (all other conditions are initially false). If the value of d is zero, then there is no change in the system. When the value of d becomes $n > 0$ at step t', e receives the double of this value $2n$ on the next time step ($t' + 1$). At this moment, rules r_1, r_2, and r_3 become applicable. It is easy to observe that in this case $a(t' + 1 + k) = \sum_{b=0}^{k} 2b + 1 = k^2$ (for $k \leq n$). At time $t' + 1 + n$, the value of e becomes equal to the value of c and b; hence rules r_1 and r_4 are not applicable anymore, and since $c > 0$, rule r_3 can never be applied as well. Hence, the value of the output a remains stable and equal to n^2. To conclude, the system waits for a non-zero input d. Starting from this moment, the squares of numbers from 1 to d are output at each step, after what the system permanently outputs d^2. Only the first change of value of d is taken into account; all other changes of d are ignored. An example of dynamics of Π for $d = 3$ at time $t = 2$ is shown on Fig. 7.3.

7.3.2 Basic Variant

For practical applications, it is reasonable to limit the values of variables to be integer, or even natural. The main reason for this is that the representation of real numbers in digital form is an approximation based on their floating-point or fixed-point encodings using unsigned integer values. Hence, it possible to assume that the implementation always uses integer numbers (and maybe different arithmetic functions). Moreover, the representation of negative numbers is usually done using the 2^n complement, so they can be considered as positive integers too. Of course, the arithmetic operations like addition and the comparison relation should be defined a bit differently with this assumption.

Another important limitation for practical applications are the restrictions on the type of predicates P and functions F in the rules. For example, NPS considers always true predicates only, by definition. Also in the case of NPS, generally, functions F in rules are polynomials. For FPGA implementation reasons, it is interesting to limit P and F to be linear, somehow similar to Presburger definability. We recall that the Presburger arithmetic is the first-order theory of natural numbers with addition and equality, i.e., one can use comparisons, Boolean operations, additions, subtractions, and constant multiplications in expressions. Since GNPS model allows negative and real values, it is not correct to say that P and F are Presburger-definable, because the domain is different. However, it can be argued as above that all cited operations can be reduced to some particular operations on natural numbers having properties identical to those of Presburger arithmetic, more precisely being semi-linear over corresponding domains [9]. So, we will use the notion of Presburger-definable expression also in the case of GNPS (with real or integer values).

The above remarks motivate to consider a *basic* variant of GNPS where all rules have predicates and functions defined using only the operations of addition, subtraction, constant multiplication, integer comparison, and Boolean operators. The system from Example 7.2 is of such type. To accommodate functions that cannot be defined in this manner, an algebraic signature is added to the definition collecting corresponding symbols. Hence, such a system can be defined as the tuple

$$\Pi = (m, V, I, O, (Var_1, Var_1(0)), \ldots, (Var_m, Var_m(0)), Pr, \sigma),$$

where all components except σ are defined in the same manner as in Definition 7.1. The finite algebraic signature σ contains the list of additional functions used in Π with respect to the addition/subtraction and constant multiplication. The rules of Π have the same form as in Eq. (7.1); however, it is required for P to be a predicate over indicated variables written in Presburger arithmetic enhanced with the signature σ. Similarly, it is required for F to be a function written in Presburger arithmetic enhanced with the signature σ from the definition of Π; see Example 7.3.

Example 7.3. We can consider the following predicate for a rule

$$P(x, y, z; E, F) = \neg E < x \wedge (F < 2y + 3z).$$

If we consider an algebraic signature containing the ordinary multiplication operation ($\sigma = \{\times\}$), then it would be possible to write the following predicate

$$P(x, y, z; E, F) = \neg E < x \wedge ((F < 2y + 3z) \vee (E + F < x \times y + z)).$$

Finally, we remark that by taking σ to be a full signature (containing both functional and relational symbols), the definition above can replace Definition 7.1. Indeed, in the case of real or integer numbers, appropriate relations and functions can be added to σ in order to ensure the definability of functions and predicates in rules.

We illustrate the usage of the signature by the following example.

Example 7.4. Consider the following GNPS $\Pi = (1, V, I, O, (Var_1, Var_1(0)), Pr, \sigma)$, where

- $V = \{a, b, in_1, in_2, out_1, out_2\}$, $I = \{in_1, in_2\}$, $O = \{out_1, out_2\}$,
- $Var_0 = V$, $Var_1(0) = (0, 0, -, -, 0, 0)$,
- $\sigma = \{| \cdot |, \sqrt{\cdot}\}$.
- The set of rules Pr is defined as follows:

$$r_1 : \sqrt{\frac{in_1 + in_2}{2}} \rightarrow 1|a,$$

$$r_2 : 2a \rightarrow 1|b, 1|out_1$$

$$r_3 : |a - b| < 0.001;\ 0 \rightarrow 1|out_2,$$

$$r_4 : \neg(|a - b| < 0.001);\ 1 \rightarrow 1|out_2.$$

This system has a single cell and two input, two output, and two internal variables.

The set of equations corresponding to this system is the following:

$$a(t + 1) = \sqrt{\frac{in_1(t) + in_2(t)}{2}} \qquad\qquad a(0) = 0$$

$$b(t + 1) = a(t) \qquad\qquad b(0) = 0$$

$$out_1(t + 1) = a(t) \qquad\qquad out_1(0) = 0$$

$$out_2(t + 1) = \text{if } |a(t) - b(t)| < 0.001 \text{ then } 0 \text{ else } 1 \qquad\qquad out_2(0) = 0$$

By looking at equations above, it is clear that the system computes the square root of the average value of its inputs with a two-step delay and also indicates if this value changed by more than 0.1% on the previous step. We recall that all rules are executed in parallel and that the modulo function is defined in the signature.

According to [30], NPS (but also GNPS) allow an interesting normal form.

Definition 7.2. A GNPS is said to be in the binary normal form if all rules are of form

$$P(x_{1i}, \ldots, x_{ki}; E_1, \ldots, E_m); F(x_{1i}, \ldots, x_{ki}) \rightarrow c|v, L|\lambda,$$

for some $i, m, k > 0$; $c, L \geq 0$ and where $v \in V$ and λ is a special dummy variable.

Moreover, if the condition that variables of the production function should be from the same membrane is relaxed, then it is possible to obtain a stronger result by combining all rules related to a single variable into one rule by choosing appropriate coefficients and predicates, yielding rules of following form:

$$P(x_1, \ldots, x_n); F(y_1, \ldots, y_m) \rightarrow 1|v,$$

where $x_i, y_j, v \in V, 1 \le i \le n, 1 \le j \le m$.

Such special (G)NPS having only rules of the above type are said to be in *unary normal form*. As shown in [30], the corresponding time series are identical to those described by Eq. (7.2).

7.3.3 Historical Remarks

We conclude this section by pointing out the difference between GNPS and previous models of NPS and ENPS. First of all, the structure of (E)NPS is always a tree, so variables present in predicates and the repartition protocol are either from the child or parent cells/membranes.

Next, in the case of NPS, all predicates P from any rule are always true, so all rules are always applicable. The rules of NPS are grouped by cell, depending on the origin of variables from their production function (we recall that they are all from the same cell). The standard semantics of NPS allows to apply a single rule per cell and requires a non-deterministic choice if there are several rules in the same cell. A variant of NPS using the *all-parallel* derivation mode [10] applies all rules, even if there are several rules per cell.

For the sake of completeness, we give below the traditional notation used for NPS; see [21, 22]. There is a slight difference in syntax with respect to Definition 7.1; however, semantically, all elements have the same meaning.

Definition 7.3. A numerical P system (NPS) is the following tuple

$$\Pi = (m, \mu, (Var_1, Var_1(0), Pr_1), \ldots, (Var_m, Var_m(0), Pr_m)),$$

where

- $m > 0$ is the number of membranes,
- μ is the membrane structure,
- $Var_i \subseteq V$ is the list of internal variables for membrane i; by convention variables are labeled with two indices, the second one indicating their location, i.e., $Var_i = \{x_{1i}, \ldots, x_{k_i i}\}$,
- $Var_i(0)$ is the vector of initial values for variables internal to membrane i,
- Pr_i is the set of rules located in membrane i.
  They are of form $F(x_{1i}, \ldots, x_{ki}) \rightarrow c_1|v_1 + \ldots + c_n|v_n$.

In the case of ENPS, the applicability predicate has always the same form, comparing a value of a variable e with the smallest value of other variables from the production function: $P(x_{1i}, \ldots, x_{ni}; e) \equiv e > \min(x_{1i}, \ldots, x_{ni})$.

This definition is the most common one [23]. Unfortunately, there are also different definitions with the same syntax, but a different semantics: $e > \min(|x_{1i}|, \ldots, |x_{ni}|)$ in [25] and $e > \min(c(x_{1i}), \ldots, c(x_{ni}))$ in [23], with $c(x)$ being the concentration of x in the biological sense, which may induce in confusion. For the rule execution semantics, generally all rules that are applicable are applied; however, the first papers on ENPS also considered the same mode of a single non-deterministic rule application, like in the case of NPS.

Like above, for the sake of completeness, we give below the traditional notation used for ENPS; see [23, 24]. Again, there is a slight difference in syntax with respect to Definition 7.1; however, semantically, all elements have the same meaning.

Definition 7.4. An enzymatic numerical P system (ENPS) is the following tuple

$$\Pi = (m, \mu, (Var_1, Var_1(0), E_1, Pr_1), \ldots, (Var_m, Var_m(0), E_m, Pr_m)),$$

where

- $m > 0$ is the number of membranes,
- μ is the membrane structure,
- $Var_i \subseteq V$ is the list of internal variables for membrane i; by convention, variables are labeled with two indices, the second one indicating their location, i.e., $Var_i = \{x_{1i}, \ldots, x_{k_i i}\}$,
- $Var_i(0)$ is the vector of initial values for variables internal to membrane i,
- E_i is the set of *enzymatic* variables of membrane i, *i.e* variables that can be used in comparison operators,
- Pr_i is the set of rules located in membrane i. They are of form ($e_{si} \in E_i$):
  $F(x_{1i}, \ldots, x_{ki}) \rightarrow c_1|v_1 + \ldots + c_n|v_n$, or
  $F(x_{1i}, \ldots, x_{ki})(e_{si} \rightarrow)c_1|v_1 + \ldots + c_n|v_n$.

The second type of rules corresponds to rules with the comparison predicate. However, we recall that several different predicates are considered with the same rule notation, so it is important to read the details of each paper in order to understand which one is used. We recall that GNPS requires to explicitly indicate the predicate, eliminating any possible confusion.

In the case of NPS, the obtained time series do not use conditions, so sometimes they can be solved analytically as in the following example.

Example 7.5. Consider the following NPS:

$$\Pi = (2, V, I, O, (Var_1, Var_1(0)), (Var_2, Var_2(0)), Pr),$$

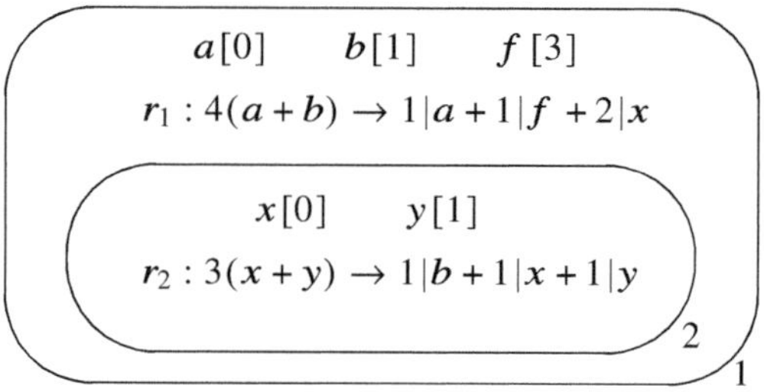

Fig. 7.4 Numerical P system from Example 7.5. The nested (membrane) structure is represented by a Venn diagram; the variables and the rules are placed in corresponding locations; the initial value of variables follow them in square brackets

where $I = \emptyset$, $O = \{f\}$, $Var_1 = \{a, b, f\}$, $Var_2 = \{x, y\}$, $Var_1(0) = (0, 1, 3)$, $Var_2(0) = (0, 1)$. The rules of the system are defined as follows:

$r_1 : 4(a + b) \rightarrow 1|a + 1|f + 2|x.$

$r_2 : 3(x + y) \rightarrow 1|b + 1|x + 1|y.$

The system has two cells that are connected, so they can be considered in a tree relation. Hence, it can be represented by a Venn diagram as depicted in Fig. 7.4.

It is not difficult to observe that the corresponding system can be rewritten as the following time series with initial conditions $a(0) = 0$, $b(0) = 1$, $f(0) = 3$, $x(0) = 0$, $y(0) = 1$.

$$\begin{cases} a(t + 1) = a(t) + b(t) \\ b(t + 1) = x(t) + y(t) \\ f(t + 1) = f(t) + a(t) + b(t) \\ x(t + 1) = x(t) + y(t) + 2(a(t) + b(t)) \\ y(t + 1) = x(t) + y(t) \end{cases} \qquad (7.3)$$

This system of recurrences can be solved analytically using standard methods. The analytical solution for system defined by Eq. (7.3) is given as follows:

$$a(t) = 2 \times 3^{t-2}, \qquad b(t) = 4 \times 3^{t-2}, \qquad f(t) = 3^{t-1} + 3,$$

$$x(t) = 8 \times 3^{t-2}, \qquad y(t) = 2 \times 3^{t-2} + 1, \qquad t > 1$$

7.4   Implementing GNPS on FPGA

The basic variant of GNPS admits quite a straightforward implementation in FPGA. To better explain the translation process, we will concentrate first on the NPS translation, i.e., supposing that all predicates are always true; hence all rules are applicable at each step. In this case, Eq. (7.2) can be rewritten as follows (where $X(t)$, $Y(t)$, and $Q(t)$ are the vectors of input, output. and internal variables, respectively, at time t):

$$Q(t + 1) = F(Q(t), X(t)) \tag{7.4}$$

$$Y(t + 1) = G(Q(t), X(t)) \tag{7.5}$$

These equations are the generalization (using real numbers instead of Boolean values) of equations used in switching algebra [31] for the definition of the concept of Mealy automaton [12], which together with Moore automaton [13] form the basis of modern synchronous circuit design. Since from the implementation point of view real numbers should be encoded, e.g., using a fixed-point encoding, it appears that NPS are equivalent to (bit) vector[1] Moore/Mealy machines. It should be noted that because we consider basic (G)NPS without signature, functions F and G from the above equation are linear. This in turn allows a straight implementation using hardware FPGA technology.

First we indicate how to handle the variables of the system. The main idea is to represent each of them by vectors of (bit) registers using a fixed-point encoding having a fixed bit size $WIDTH$ and the binary point position $BPOS$. We recall that a fixed-point encoding of real numbers uses $WIDTH - BPOS$ bits for the integer part of the number (using a standard binary encoding) and $BPOS$ bits for the fractional part indicating the coefficients of the negative powers of 2. For example, 3.5 in fixed-point encoding with $WIDTH = 5$ and $BPOS = 2$ is written as 01110.

Because the addition and subtraction in fixed-point encoding correspond to ordinary binary addition and subtraction, they can be directly represented as adders in FPGA. In Verilog terms, it is even more straightforward as it has $+$ and $-$ operators that synthesize to corresponding adders. The constant multiplication can be replaced by several additions, but this is impractical and time consuming as it would add a long combinatorial path in the circuit that would fail the timing constraints (it will be longer than the system clock cycle). It is possible to use Verilog $*$ operator, which is further replaced by a sequence of adders and bit shifts (when one operand is constant). Since such an operation requires the manipulation of numbers having the $2 * WIDTH$ bit size and then a right shift by $BPOS$, we introduce a helper function _mult handling this transparently. Finally, we remark that the implementation of the next time step value of variables is done using a non-blocking assignment (whose semantics is to update all values simultaneously at the end of the clock edge).

The whole NPS becomes a Verilog module (it is possible to further subdivide it in modules according to NPS cell/membrane structure). The input variables become input signals for the module, and the output variables become output registers for the module.

---

[1] An integer or fixed-point encoded real is a bit vector.

Example 7.6. Consider the NPS system from Example 7.5. It has 1 output variable f and two rules:

$$r_1 : 4(a + b) \rightarrow 1|a + 1|f + 2|x.$$

$$r_2 : 3(x + y) \rightarrow 1|b + 1|x + 1|y.$$

By applying the reasoning above, we obtain the following Verilog code:

```
1   module A #(parameter WIDTH = 32, parameter BPPOS = 12)
2   (    output reg [WIDTH−1:0] f = 32'h3000,  // 3.0 in fixed−point encoding
3        input clk
4   );
5        reg [WIDTH−1:0] a = 0;
6        reg [WIDTH−1:0] b = 32'h1000;  // 1.0 in fixed−point encoding
7        reg [WIDTH−1:0] x = 0;
8        reg [WIDTH−1:0] y = 32'h1000;  // 1.0 in fixed−point encoding
9
10  always @(posedge clk) begin
11       a <= a + b;
12       b <= x + y;
13       f <= f + a + b;
14       x <= x + y + _mult(a + b, 32'h2000);  // 2.0 in fixed−point encoding
15       y <= x + y;
16  end
17  endmodule
```

The synthesis of this circuit using Vivado 2020.1 tools uses 160 LUT6 and 128 registers (using a total of 41 slices), which is about 0.5% of those available on Digilent Basys-3 FPGA.

Now let us return to the general GNPS case. The main difficulty that should be taken into account is how to handle predicates associated to each rule. However, since we consider the basic case with an empty signature, these predicates are Presburger, i.e., expressions involving Boolean operators, comparison, and linear functions. Such conditions can be directly transferred to Verilog using the conditional if expression operator ?.

Example 7.7. We consider here a slightly modified version of Example 7.4, where we exclude the square root operator. We keep all parts of the system and use the following modified rules:

$$r_1 : 0.5(in_1 + in_2) \rightarrow 1|a,$$

$$r_2 : 2a \rightarrow 1|b, 1|out_1$$

$$r_3 : |a - b| < 0.001; \ 0 \rightarrow 1|out_2,$$

$$r_4 : \neg(|a - b| < 0.001); \ 1 \rightarrow 1|out_2.$$

We remark that the modulo function $| \cdot |$ is Presburger-definable, so it does not need to be handled in a special manner.

The translation to Verilog makes use of the conditional ? operator:

```
1   module B #(parameter WIDTH = 32, parameter BPPOS = 12)
2   (    output reg [WIDTH-1:0] out1 , output reg [WIDTH-1:0] out2 ,
3        input   [WIDTH-1:0] in1 , input   [WIDTH-1:0] in2 ,
4        input clk
5   );
6        reg [WIDTH-1:0] a = 0;
7        reg [WIDTH-1:0] b = 0;
8
9   always @(posedge clk) begin
10       a <= _mult(in1+in2 , 2048); // 0.5
11       b <= a;
12       out1 <= a;
13       out2 <= a-b < 4 && a-b > -4 ? 0 : 4096; // 0.001 and 1
14  end
15  endmodule
```

The synthesis of this circuit using Vivado 2020.1 tools uses 33 LUT6 and 94 registers, which is about 0.16% of those available on Digilent Basys-3 FPGA.

As it can be seen from the examples above, the translation of GNPS to Verilog is rather straightforward, but still tedious to do by hand. A compiler `FPNtoVerilog` was developed in order to assist in this translation [4,30]. As input, it takes the GNPS model in form of Eqs. (7.4) and (7.2) and produces as output behavioral Verilog code implementing the corresponding Mealy/Moore automaton.

The compiler performs the following steps:

1. Parse the input file.
2. Identify input and output symbols.
3. Flatten the obtained system.
4. Perform constant propagation.
5. Convert all constants to fixed-point real number representation.
6. Write Verilog output.

These steps are performed using standard compiling techniques. The last step is a transformation as described above. As a result, a file containing the synthesizable (in FPGA) Verilog module whose code simulates each step of the GNPS at each clock tick is generated.

Remark 7.1. In the basic case, an empty signature σ is considered as this allows a straight translation to Verilog. For more complex computations, corresponding functions should be implemented additionally as Verilog modules. This can induce a delay; as in many cases, it is not possible to compute corresponding functions in one clock step.

Remark 7.2. In the case of fixed-point encoding, it is possible to easily implement the multiplication operation working in one time step. This can be done either directly (by using multiplication code dependent on the width of the encoding) or using a special component of FPGA called *DSP block* (sometimes referred as

Table 7.1 A short overview of capacities of these boards

Board	FPGA type	Max/default clock speed	LUTs[a]	FFs	DSPs
Digilent Basys 3	Artix-7 35T	450/100 MHz	20,800	41,600	90
Digilent Arty A7-100	Artix-7 100T	450/100 MHz	63,400	126,800	240
Xilinx VC707	Virtex-7 X485	800/200 MHz	303,600	607,200	2800

[a]These devices use LUT6

DSP slice) that allows to perform multiplication operations in one step (up to 48-bit width).

Remark 7.3. Contrary to multiplication, it is not easy to implement the division operation in one time step. However, the division by a constant c can be seen as the multiplication by c^{-1}.

Besides examples above, several case studies were considered. Two of these cases concentrating on robot controller design and robot path-planning algorithm are detailed in Chap. 8. As hardware target, development board Digilent BASYS 3 was used. It is equipped with a Xilinx Artix-7 XC7A35-TCPG236C-1 FPGA as core component. Several tests were also performed on Digilent Arty A7-100 board, featuring also an Artrix-7 XC7A100TCSG324-1 FPGA. Finally, some tests were performed on a Xilinx VC707 board featuring a Virtex-7 FPGA XC7VX485-TFFG1761-2. Table 7.1 below gives a short overview of capacities of these boards:

The development was performed mainly using Xilinx Vivado 2019.1 developing environment.

7.5 FPGA Implementations of Other Models of P Systems

In this section, we present all existing FPGA implementations of P systems different from GNPS. At the end of the section, a short discussion highlighting the strong and weak points of each implementation is performed.

7.5.1 Petreska and Teuscher Implementation

The first FPGA implementation of P systems was done by Petreska and Teuscher [26]. The targeted model was transitional P systems with priorities; see e.g., [20, 22] for the definitions. Also membrane creation/dissolution extensions were considered.

The system is organized as follows. The (multiset) contents of each membrane is represented by a set of 8-bit registers corresponding to each symbol from the alphabet. It is possible to increase the width of registers to 16-bit. A similar representation is used for rules: for each of them, a multiset corresponding to its lhs and rhs is used (more precisely, the rhs part is split into 3 components, corresponding to *here*, *in*, and *out* targets). In addition to these 4 vectors of 8-bit registers, several additional 8-bit registers are used to store the priority information and the creation/dissolution details.

The communication between outer to inner membranes is performed by a shared bus. A message containing the multiset of objects to be sent and the id of the target are posted by the outer membrane to the bus, and the corresponding inner membrane (having the mentioned id) collects this information, while other membranes are ignoring it. The communication in the other direction (from inner to outer membranes) is done via a channel passing through all inner membranes. During the communication phase, a message is initiated and passed through all inner membranes that can append the multiset they would like to send out, or just pass through the message if no objects should be sent out.

The application of rules is deterministic—the rules are used in a predefined order in each membrane. Each rule in a sequence is applied exactly once (if possible); then this process is repeated until no more rules are applicable.

The dissolution of a membrane is performed by setting its Enable signal to 0. The application of rules and the communication is dependent on this signal; so if it is not set, then no rule application can happen, and also the membrane works like a passthrough for any inner to outer communication.

The hardware description of the system is generated by a Java program that inputs the desired P system description via a graphical interface and outputs corresponding VHDL files (as well as simulation scripts). After the simulation phase, these files are used for synthesis and then for the place and route phase. As target board, a Xilinx Virtex-II Pro 2VP50 FPGA7 is used, containing about 96000 LUT4 and the same amount of FFs.

As test bed several membrane systems having 10 or 20 membranes as well as 6 or 12 objects were considered. The results show that the system can run at about 200 MHz clock speed for the simplest cases (without any extension) and at about 30 MHz when using the creation of membranes. The resource usage is between 4.2% for the simplest case (10 membranes and an alphabet of 6 objects) and 33% (20 membranes and an alphabet of 12 objects).

7.5.2   Nguyen Implementation

Another important attempt to tackle the FPGA implementation of transitional and symport/antiport P systems was done by Nguyen [14–17]. She tried to approach the problem from different points of view and thus providing several designs having different characteristics.

The *rule-based* design places the rewriting rule as the central computational unit. Membrane contents are represented by an array of 8-bit registers corresponding to each membrane/symbol combination. Somehow, this corresponds to a flattened view of the system, where only one membrane is present; see [5, 32] for more details on this topic. The bit width is a parameter of the system and can be updated if necessary. Rules access directly to the symbols' array. Their execution is performed by first computing the maximal possible number of applications of each rule (using division or min-based approaches) and then by executing the corresponding rule that number of times. It might happen for several rules to compete for the same objects; hence all of them cannot be executed the maximum number of times. The solution proposed by Nguyen is to assume a *total* priority among such rules and apply the rule with the highest priority first, then the next one up to the remaining maximum, and so on. Therefore, this solution allows deterministic computations only, with the predefined rule application order.

In Petreska's implementation, rule execution is sequential (one after another). In Nguyen's design, all rules are applied at the same time. While this allows important performance (and resource) gain, a synchronization procedure should be employed when multisets are updated by several rules at the same time. Two strategies were used to tackle this problem. *Time-oriented* strategy inserted delays in the rule execution allowing to ensure that the rules are executed in the correct order (a rule with a lower priority would wait more time before being executed than a rule with higher priority). *Space-oriented* strategy uses duplicates of each corresponding multiset for each involved rule. Then a special component synchronizes the contents of all these duplicates to a single final destination register. It is clear that the first strategy is time-consuming, as delays should be inserted in the rule execution; however, it is more economic in resource usage than the second one, which takes more hardware resources (i.e., space on the device).

A different design called *region-based* is also proposed. It aims to physically highlight the membrane processing unit on the FPGA device. According to the author, it allows better extensibility. The multisets of objects are represented as arrays of registers in some particular place (corresponding to a region). The communication between membranes is implemented using message passing via a dedicated channel: whenever it is possible for objects to move from one region to another region, the implementation includes a channel connecting the region processing unit for the source region to the region processing unit for the destination region. There are several proposed implementations for these communication channels; we refer to [14] for more details.

In all above cases, the evolution of the obtained system is maximally parallel and deterministic. In order to deal with the non-determinism, Nguyen proposed a special procedure, called *Direct Non-deterministic Distribution* (DND) algorithm, which corresponds to the construction of specific Pareto-optimal solution for the multicriteria optimization problem specified by the maximality conditions; see [15, 34] for more details. By varying the initial conditions, e.g., by a pseudo-random number generator, different solutions are obtained (corresponding to a non-deterministic choice of rules to be executed). This procedure was conceptually tested in hardware and found to be feasible. However, it was not implemented as part of the above architectures.

As in Petreska case, the hardware description of the system is generated by a Java program, called *P Builder*, that inputs the desired P system description via a text file and outputs corresponding files of the design written in Handel-C HDL. These files can be used for simulation and for synthesis (and further for place and route phase).

As target board, a Xilinx Virtex-II XC2V6000-FF1152-4 is used, containing about 76000 LUT4 and the same amount of FFs.

Many examples were used to test the obtained designs. The largest P system tested for the rule-based design had 49 regions and 176 rules and used about 22% of the device resources. The clock speed was around 60–80 MHz. In the case of region-based design, the biggest considered system had 50 rules, 25 regions, and 200 objects. The obtained clock speed was around 60 MHz.

7.5.3   Quiros and Verlan Implementation

The implementation of Quiros and Verlan is different from the two above as from the beginning its main goal was to perform a true non-deterministic execution of the target P system. A generic variant of the model based on the formal framework for P systems and being equivalent to most models of P systems having a static (non-varying) structure was used [6, 32]. In order to achieve the design goal, a completely different strategy was used. Previous ideas for non-deterministic evolution implied the construction of one of Pareto-optimal solutions for the corresponding multi-criteria optimization problem [34]. However, this does not guarantee a non-deterministic evolution, as this supposes that at each moment all possible evolutions must have the same probability to be chosen. By using an algorithm (like DND) that constructs a concrete solution, there is no guarantee that all of them can be reached and also have the same probability. A simple solution would be to construct all (maximally) parallel rule sets and then chose one of them equiprobably. Unfortunately, such a construction requires an enormous amount of resources. A better approach consists in computing the number n of such rule sets and then choosing one value from 1 to n equiprobably and then constructing the corresponding rule set.

The implementation by Quiros and Verlan is using the above idea. First, a theoretical model was defined based on the notion of rule dependency, e.g., when two rules may compete for the same object. Next, it was shown that it is possible to implement the idea above if for each configuration it is possible to express all rule application possibilities in form of words of some length of some regular (or non-ambiguous context-free) language. The number of sets of rules that can be applied is then computed using the Chomsky–Schutzenberger theorem giving the number of words of size n, $n > 0$ for a non-ambiguous context free language [2]. Technically, this is performed by constructing the generating series for corresponding languages. In the case of regular languages, these series are equivalent to linear recurrences and can be easily solved analytically. As a consequence, it becomes possible to compute the number of (maximally) parallel sets of rules by just computing the result of a function. Moreover, since this function is defined by a recurrence relation, it becomes relatively easy to implement it on FPGA as only several previous values (which can be memorized) are used to compute the new value. Next, a random choice is performed using a uniform pseudo-random number generator. Then, based on the representation of rule sets in terms of words of a regular language, this number is converted to a set of rules by exploring the corresponding automata. We refer to [27, 28, 33] for more technical details of the algorithm.

From the hardware design point of view, an array of hardware registers is used to represent the current configuration of the system (which is a network of cells or a flattened P system). Several register sizes were used: 8, 16, and 32 bits. Rules are not represented directly. Instead, the algorithms for the number of applicable rule sets, the choice of a set, and the construction of the configuration difference with the previous step are implemented. Their resource usage is not dependent on the rule number, but rather on rules' dependencies (more complex dependencies need more resources). Because of the mathematical features of the algorithms, only five clock cycles were needed to simulate one step of a target P system.

As in previous cases, the hardware description of the system is generated by a Java program that inputs the desired P system description via a text file and outputs corresponding files of the design written in VHDL. These files can be used for simulation and for synthesis (and further for place and route phase). Three target boards from Xilinx were used featuring following FPGA core components: Virtex-5 FX70T (44,800 LUT6 and FFs, 128DSP), Virtex-6 LX240T (150,720 LUT6 and FFs, 768 DSP), and Virtex-7 VX485T (303,600 LUT6, 607,200 FFs, and 2,800 DSP).

Several types of examples were tested having 10–200 rules with different dependencies. The clock speed was around 130 MHz. Resource usage were up to 40% in terms of LUTs; however, a high number of DSP was used (up to 99%), due to the usage of many multiplication and division operations.

7.5.4   Comments

While Petreska and Teuscher implementation is important as the first attempt to implement P systems on FPGA hardware, it suffers from many drawbacks. First, the rule execution strategy does not correspond to maximal parallelism, or to any other common execution strategy in P systems. Next, it is completely deterministic, which cuts off possible non-deterministic evolutions very common in P systems area. Another weak point of this implementation is the communication strategy by message passing that is sequential and slows down the overall computation. Finally, the proposed approach requires a high number of hardware resources, limiting its applicability mostly to toy examples.

Nguyen's approach allows realistic implementations of small- to medium-size P systems. The main drawback resides however in the deterministic rule execution (although maximally parallel). The implementation of the DND algorithm is not integrated in designs, and the prototype of DND implementation exhibits a high resource consumption. The second issue related to Nguyen's implementation is related to low implementation speed—it reaches only 80 MHz clock rate and because several dozens of cycles are needed to perform all necessary computations; the final speedup is not very big: according to the author, it is of order 500 with respect to a software implementation [14].

Quiros and Verlan approach provides a non-deterministic evolution of the system. Moreover, due to the architecture of the design, each P system step is performed in 5 steps on FPGA, which guarantees a high-speed execution. According to authors [28], a speed of 2×10^7 computational steps per second is achieved, yielding a speedup of order 3×10^4 with respect to the reference software implementation. The main drawback of the method is that it is applicable only for particular classes of P systems (those where the set of rules to be chosen at each step can be described by a word in a regular language). The corresponding class of P systems is quite large and includes universal systems; however, it is not easy to show that a particular P system belongs to it. To facilitate this search, a special *set-maximal* derivation mode was introduced. In this mode and under some assumptions about rule structure, the corresponding regular languages can be easily deduced [28, 33]. Another drawback of the method is the high usage of DSP blocks that limits the number of handled rules to about 200. However, we note that corresponding operations can be performed using CLBs. Then, as trade-off, the number of clock cycles for a single step simulation is increased. According to authors [33], up to 1000 rules can be handled in this manner on modern FPGA architectures.

7.6   Discussion

As it can be seen, despite of numerous benefits, there are not many examples of implementation of P systems using FPGA hardware. The main reason for this is the necessity of skills related to hardware design, and this requires a high learning curve. Next, since each design is unique, often a long time is needed before an HDL generator for specific types of problems is produced. One of long-term aims of FPNtoVerilog project [4] is to explore the possibilities to provide a complete solution in software development style, where one has only to write the GNPS system description, chose input/output modules, and let the compiler to generate the bitstream suitable to be sent to the FPGA and that implements the desired behavior on the device. However, it should be clear that efficient designs exploiting to the maximum capacities of FPGA cannot be obtained in this manner.

At the same time, the basic variant of P systems is not well-suited for an FPGA implementation. Features like maximal parallelism or membrane division were shown to be hard to implement on such devices. The main reason is their theoretical unboundedness, which adds an overhead when handled on FPGA. It was shown in several works that the maximal parallelism is not the only ingredient allowing to reach the computational completeness and universality. Other mechanisms like bounded derivation modes [7, 19] or context conditions (promoters and inhibitors) [22] are as powerful as the maximal parallelism and at the same time are easier to implement in FPGA. Moreover, many examples of P systems, e.g., from the Handbook on Membrane Computing [22], are made in a way to bound the maximal parallelism application to a fixed predefined number. In our opinion, there are no cases that would justify the usage of the maximal parallelism for problem solving in practice. So, we expect that further implementation efforts would first select the features of P systems based on the easiness of their implementation, before actually starting it.

Another important point of FPGA implementations, which is often not mentioned, is the necessity to handle the input and the output. When using P systems for practical problem solving, it becomes important to have designs specific for classes of problems and then chose a concrete instance of the problem by considering an appropriate input. It is also important to read the result of the computation in some way. Most of the efforts for FPGA implementation of P systems are concentrated only on the design of the core computational unit, simulating some variant of a P system, leaving the input/output acquisition as an unimportant side problem. However, we think that it should be treated with great attention from the beginning, as our experience shows that most of the development time is related to it. Also, while the promised speedups are high (up to 10^6 times), in the reality the speed of the implementation is limited by the input/output throughput. Realizations described in Sect. 7.5 do not handle any input (the initial configuration is hardcoded in the design), and the output is not captured, but examined using the integrated logic analyzer (ILA), which is slow and feasible only for several values as its primary function is the debug. The implementation presented in Sect. 7.4, additionally to ILA, is considered an input/output over device pins and also over the serial port (Universal Asynchronous Receiver Transmitter (UART)). It is clear that the overall response time (from input till the corresponding output) cannot be faster than the selected speed for UART, so most of the time the design is idle, waiting for the input to arrive. Hence, it becomes important to associate the FPGA implementation of a P system with high-speed data transfer buses in order to benefit from the high computational speed.

7.7 Conclusion

As mentioned before, not every type of P system can be efficiently implemented on FPGA. Moreover, taking into account the overall time needed from the problem coding until the obtention of the result, a software implementation would be faster in most of the cases. However, we see two use cases when a hardware implementation would significantly outperform any software one. The first case are Monte-Carlo-like simulations, where, starting from same initial conditions, rules are applied based on probability, so different trajectories can be obtained. The computation is repeated many times, and as a result, some mean value of all these trajectories is considered. Since there is no input and only a single output, the system can run at the fastest possible speed (repeating the same cycle and using a good (pseudo-)random number generator). Even taking into account the delay needed to get the final result, one can expect tens or even hundreds of thousands rounds of computations per second, clearly outperforming any possible software (and GPU-based) implementation by 3–4 orders of magnitude.

The second case exploits the ability of the implementation to work at high-speed throughput. Data coming from a high-speed input is processed fast and then sent to a high-speed output. Typical examples would be a robot controller dealing with very fast sensors, image processing, and generally any differential equation-based transformation of the input signal. For these cases, it is also quite evident that the FPGA implementation would outperform any software one by several orders of magnitude. At the same time, we note that, at the moment, robot sensors reaction time is of order of milliseconds, while the designs proposed in Sect. 7.4 are running at nanosecond level; hence still a lot of time is wasted for the input acquisition. However, we expect that in the future faster sensors would appear, coming with a need for a fast processing unit that can be provided by FPGA-based designs.

A question arises: what advantages a design flow based on P systems can propose with respect to a traditional one. There are several strong points in its favor. First, traditional design flows are performed at a very low level of abstraction. Even behavioral designs are still done in terms of the Mealy/Moore machine. High-level synthesis (HLS) tools usually expect a microprocessor to be implemented in FPGA, so they are not perfect for dealing with the parallelism. Matlab/Simulink FPGA translation tends to produce very large designs. P systems abstraction is higher than the cited ones, and it allows to better concentrate on the problem solution, still yielding designs exploiting the large-scale parallelism. Another advantage of using P systems for hardware circuit design is the compartment structure that allows to localize interactions and possibly map them to close regions of the FPGA hardware. P systems having a matrix-like inner structure are particularly well-suited to fulfill this goal. Finally, another advantage of using a workflow based on P systems resides in the additional verification possibilities for the design. There exist many verification tools for different models of P systems [8] that can be used in conjunction with traditional verification flows based on low-level Verilog or System Verilog assertions.

References

1. C. Buiu, A.G. Florea, Membrane Computing models and robot controller design, current results and challenges. J. Membr. Comput. **1**(4), 262–269 (2019). https://doi.org/10.1007/s41965-019-00029-8
2. N. Chomsky, M. Schützenberger. The algebraic theory of context-free languages, in *Computer Programming and Formal Systems, Studies in Logic and the Foundations of Mathematics*, ed. by P. Braffort, D. Hirschberg, vol. 35 (1963), pp. 118–161
3. D. Díaz-Pernil, M.A. Gutiérrez-Naranjo, H. Peng, Membrane computing and image processing: a short survey. J. Membr. Comput. **1**(1), 58–73 (2019). https://doi.org/10.1007/s41965-018-00002-x
4. FPNtoVerilog GitHub repository. https://github.com/sverlan/FPNtoVerilog
5. R. Freund, A. Leporati, G. Mauri, A.E. Porreca, S. Verlan, C. Zandron, Flattening in (tissue) P systems, in *Membrane Computing. CMC 2013*, ed. by A. Alhazov, S. Cojocaru, M. Gheorghe, Y. Rogozhin, G. Rozenberg, A. Salomaa. Lecture Notes in Computer Science, vol. 8340, pp. 173–188 (2013). https://doi.org/10.1007/978-3-642-54239-8_13
6. R. Freund, S. Verlan. A formal framework for static (tissue) P systems, in *Membrane Computing. WMC 2007*, ed. by G. Eleftherakis, P. Kefalas, Gh. Păun, G. Rozenberg, A. Salomaa. Lecture Notes in Computer Science, vol. 4860 (2007), pp. 271–284. https://doi.org/10.1007/978-3-540-77312-2_17

7. R. Freund, S. Verlan, (tissue) P systems working in the k-restricted minimally or maximally parallel transition mode. Nat. Comput. **10**(2), 821–833 (2011). https://doi.org/10.1007/s11047-010-9215-z

8. M. Gheorghe, F. Ipate, R. Lefticaru, C. Dragomir, An integrated approach to P systems formal verification, in *Membrane Computing. CMC 2010*, ed. by M. Gheorghe, T. Hinze, Gh. Păun, G. Rozenberg, A. Salomaa. Lecture Notes in Computer Science, vol. 6501 (2010), pp. 226–239. https://doi.org/10.1007/978-3-642-18123-8_18

9. S. Ginsburg, E.H. Spanier, Semigroups, presburger formulas, and languages. Pac. J. Math. **16**(2), 285–296 (1966). https://projecteuclid.org/euclid.pjm/1102994974

10. A. Leporati, A.E. Porreca, C. Zandron, G. Mauri, Improved universality results for parallel enzymatic numerical P systems. Int. J. Unconv. Comput. **9**(5–6), 385–404 (2013)

11. B. Li, H. Peng, J. Wang, X. Huang, Multi-focus image fusion based on dynamic threshold neural P systems and surfacelet transform. Knowl. Based Syst. **196**, 105794 (2020). https://doi.org/10.1016/j.knosys.2020.105794

12. G.H. Mealy, A method for synthesizing sequential circuits. Bell Syst. Tech. J. **34**(5), 1045–1079 (1955). https://doi.org/10.1002/j.1538-7305.1955.tb03788.x

13. E.F. Moore, Gedanken-experiments on sequential machines, *Automata Studies*, ed. by C. E. Shannon, J. McCarthy. Annals of Mathematics Studies, vol. 34, litho-printed (Princeton University Press, Princeton 1956), pp. 129–153

14. V.T.T. Nguyen, *Implementation of the Parallelism, Distribution and Nondeterminism of Membrane Computing Models on Reconfigurable Hardware*. Ph.D. thesis

15. V.T.T. Nguyen, D. Kearney, G. Gioiosa, An algorithm for non-deterministic object distribution in P systems and its implementation in hardware, in *Membrane Computing. WMC 2008*, D.W. Corne, P. Frisco, Gh. Păun, G. Rozenberg, A. Salomaa. Lecture Notes in Computer Science, vol. 5391 (2008), pp. 325–354. https://doi.org/10.1007/978-3-540-95885-7_24

16. V.T.T. Nguyen, D. Kearney, G. Gioiosa, An implementation of membrane computing using reconfigurable hardware. Comput. Inf. **27**(3+), 551–569 (2008)

17. V.T.T. Nguyen, D. Kearney, G. Gioiosa, A region-oriented hardware implementation for Membrane Computing applications, in *Membrane Computing. WMC 2009*, ed. by Gh. Păun, M.J. Pérez-Jiménez, A. Riscos, G. Rozenberg, A. Salomaa. Lecture Notes in Computer Science, vol. 5957 (2010), pp. 385–409. https://doi.org/10.1007/978-3-642-11467-0_27

18. R. Nicolescu, Parallel and distributed algorithms in P systems, in *Membrane Computing. CMC 2011*, ed. by M. Gheorghe, Gh. Păun, G. Rozenberg, A. Salomaa, S. Verlan. Lecture Notes in Computer Science, vol. 7184 (2011), pp. 35–50. https://doi.org/10.1007/978-3-642-28024-5_4

19. L. Pan, Gh. Păun, B. Song, Flat maximal parallelism in P systems with promoters. Theor. Comput. Sci. **623**, 83–91 (2016). https://doi.org//10.1016/j.tcs.2015.10.027

20. Gh. Păun, *Membrane Computing: An Introduction* (Springer, Berlin, 2002)

21. Gh. Păun, R.A. Păun, Membrane computing and economics: numerical P systems. Fundam. Inf. **73**(1–2), 213–227 (2006)

22. Gh. Păun, G. Rozenberg, A. Salomaa (eds.), *The Oxford Handbook of Membrane Computing* (Oxford University Press, Oxford, 2010)

23. A.B. Pavel, O. Arsene, C. Buiu, Enzymatic numerical P systems: a new class of membrane computing systems, in *2010 IEEE Fifth International Conference on Bio-Inspired Computing: Theories and Applications, BIC-TA 2010*, Changsha, China, September 23–26 (2010), pp. 1331–1336. https://doi.org/10.1109/BICTA.2010.5645071

24. A.B. Pavel, C. Buiu, Using enzymatic numerical P systems for modeling mobile robot controllers. Nat. Comput. **11**(3), 387–393 (2012). https://doi.org/10.1007/s11047-011-9286-5

25. A.B. Pavel, C.I. Vasile, I. Dumitrache, Robot localization implemented with enzymatic numerical P systems, in *Biomimetic and Biohybrid Systems. Living Machines 2012*, ed. by T.J. Prescott, N.F. Lepora, A. Mura, P.F.M.J. Verschure. Lecture Notes in Computer Science, vol. 7375. Barcelona, Spain, July 9–12, 2012 (2012), pp. 204–215. https://doi.org/10.1007/978-3-642-31525-1_18

26. B. Petreska, C. Teuscher, A reconfigurable hardware membrane system, in *Membrane Computing. WMC 2003*, ed. by C. Martín-Vide, G. Mauri, Gh. Păun, G. Rozenberg, A. Salomaa. Lecture Notes in Computer Science, vol. 2933 (2003), pp. 269–285. https://doi.org/10.1007/978-3-540-24619-0_20

27. J. Quirós, *Implementación sobre hardware reconfigurable de una arquitectura no determinista, paralela y distribuida de alto rendimiento, basada en modelos de computación con membranas*. Ph.D. thesis, Universidad de Sevilla, 2015 (in Spanish). http://hdl.handle.net/11441/39088

28. J. Quirós, S. Verlan, J. Viejo, A. Millán, M.J. Bellido, Fast hardware implementations of static P systems. Comput. Inf. **35**(3), 687–718 (2016)

29. Z. Shang, S. Verlan, G. Zhang, Hardware implementation of numerical P systems, in *Proceedings of the 20th International Conference on Membrane Computing, CMC20*, ed. by Gh. Păun, August 5–8, 2019, Curtea de Arges, Romania (2019), pp. 463–474.

30. Z. Shang, S. Verlan, G. Zhang, H. Rong, FPGA implementation of numerical P systems. Int. J. Unconven. Comput. **16** (2021, in press)

31. C.E. Shannon, The synthesis of two-terminal switching circuits. Bell Syst. Tech. J. **28**(1), 59–98 (1949). https://doi.org/10.1002/j.1538-7305.1949.tb03624.x

32. S. Verlan, Using the formal framework for P systems, in *Membrane Computing. CMC 2013*, ed. by A. Alhazov, S. Cojocaru, M. Gheorghe, Y. Rogozhin, G. Rozenberg, A. Salomaa. Lecture Notes in Computer Science, vol. 8340 (2013), pp. 56–79. https://doi.org/10.1007/978-3-642-54239-8_6

33. S. Verlan, J. Quirós, Fast hardware implementations of P systems, in *Membrane Computing, CMC 2012*, ed. by E. Csuhaj-Varjú, M. Gheorghe, G. Rozenberg, A. Salomaa, G. Vaszil. Lecture Notes in Computer Science, vol. 7762 (2012), pp. 404–423. https://doi.org/10.1007/978-3-642-36751-9_27

34. G. Zhang, Z. Shang, S. Verlan, M.A. Martínez-del-Amor, C. Yuan, L. Valencia-Cabrera, M.J. Pérez-Jiménez, An overview of hardware implementation of membrane computing models. ACM Comput. Surv. **53**(4), 90 (2020). https://doi.org/10.1145/3402456

35. Xilinx 7 Series FPGAs Packaging and PinoutProduct Specification. https://www.xilinx.com/support/documentation/user_guides/ug475_7Series_Pkg_Pinout.pdf

36. Xilinx 7 Series FPGAs Configurable Logic Block User Guide. https://www.xilinx.com/support/documentation/user_guides/ug474_7Series_CLB.pdf

37. Xilinx web site. https://www.xilinx.com/

Applications of Hardware Implementation of P Systems

8

8.1   Introduction

The inherent large-scale parallelism of membrane computing has the profound potential for the progress of extreme data processing. An interesting topic is the implementation of P systems on contemporary silicon integrated circuits. This allows to exploit the desirable parallel computational capability of P systems to explore a new orientation for high performance computing (HPC). Hence, it is important to propose hardware implementations of P systems as specific architectures. There are two main directions for such research: using (1) field-programmable gate arrays (FPGA) and (2) graphical processing units (GPUs) relying on compute unified device architecture (CUDA) platform [30,31]. In the first case, a completely new parallel circuit is specially designed to implement some variants of P systems. In the second case, the pre-defined CUDA parallel platform [4–6, 10, 11] is used to simulate P systems. Achieved performance and model correspondence are lower in the second case, but the development effort is also lower relatively. So finally, it becomes a compromise between traditional computer simulations and ad hoc highly parallel circuits.

Chapter 7 presented methods of implementation of several variants of P systems on FPGA. As discussed, these implementations are not very suitable for practical problem solving, because the implementation of the maximal parallelism and the unary encoding of problems require more resources that the device possesses. It was suggested that the model of numerical P systems (NPS) is more suitable for an FPGA application, especially for engineering fields.

This chapter discusses the usage of FPGA implementations of several important problems. Sections 8.2 and 8.3 concentrate on implementations of solutions for robot control and path planning problems.

We refer to Chap. 7 for the description of FPGA hardware, as well as for definitions of numerical P systems (NPS), enzymatic numerical P systems (ENPS), and generalized numerical P systems (GNPS). We also refer to Chap. 6 for the definition of generic versus specific simulators [8, 13, 14, 16, 17] and also the definitions of P systems with active membranes [33, 39] and population dynamics P systems [34] and their implementations in generic simulators.

8.2   Robot Membrane Controllers with FPGA Implementation

Since 2011, adopting numerical P systems (NPS) and enzymatic numerical P systems (ENPS) to model autonomous mobile robots controllers has been one of the research highlight of P system applications. The first example of using NPS in real-life application is given in [2, 3], featuring three NPS models for controllers for Khepera III and e-puck robots to perform obstacle avoidance, wall following, and following leader behaviors. These three NPSs were simulated by a software called SNUPS, which is designed as Java servlet. During the run, the robot invokes the SNUPS engine via a communication channel, transmitting sensor values. After computation, the results are returned to the robot to control motors' speeds, performing specific behaviors. Both experiments on simulated robots and real robots were conducted to verify the control effect of NPS.

The first ENPS robot controller performing obstacle avoidance behavior was proposed in [35]. It is a general controller not targeting particular robots. The portability of NPS and ENPS robot controllers was validated in [48] by adapting the control law, the number and placement of sensors, and the dimension parameters of robots. ENPSs with different functionalities were developed later on, expanding the utilizing range of ENPS besides robot motion control. For instance, an ENPS doing the robot localization was presented in [36]. Robot trajectory tracking ENPS was designed in [52].

In this section, we show examples of robot obstacle avoidance membrane controllers based on (E)NPS and generalized numerical P systems (GNPS) implemented on FPGA. We provide the procedure and the methodology of FPGA implementation of NPS variants. We give in details the experiments and the performance comparison between the FPGA implementations and reference software simulations [43].

8.2.1   Numerical P Systems-Based Membrane Controllers on FPGA

As stated above, the first obstacle avoidance NPS controller was proposed in [2]. It was targeting e-puck robot, equipped by eight infrared sensors situated around the body. This controller was run by invoking the SNUPS engine at each step, so there was a lost in parallelism.

The obstacle avoidance control law is given by Eqs. (8.1) and (8.2). It is not too complex, so it was chosen as a starting point for the implementation. We will further refer to this control law as *control law 1*. The target robot of FPGA implementation research is Pioneer 3 DX with 16 sonar sensors arranged in 2 arrays, whose placements are shown in Fig. 8.1.

Fig. 8.1 Plan view of Pioneer 3 robot which is covered by a hinged deck on the top. The 16 rectangles in light blue are the sonar sensors surrounding the robot, just beneath the hinged deck. Sensors are arranged in two arrays in the front and in the rear. The layout of sensors in two arrays is identical, as shown explicitly. From [43]

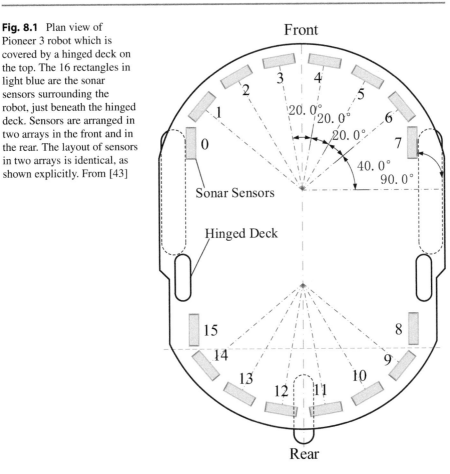

The obstacle avoidance NPS to be implemented is adapted on the basis of the first NPS in [2] according to the number of sensors of Pioneer 3 DX robot, since both the infrared sensors in e-puck and sonar sensors in Pioneer 3 DX return the distances between the robot and obstacles. The revised NPS to be implemented is illustrated in Fig. 8.2.

$$lw = CruiseSpeedLeft + \sum_{i=1}^{16} s_i * weithtLeft_i \qquad (8.1)$$

$$rw = CruiseSpeedRight + \sum_{i=1}^{16} s_i * weithtRight_i \qquad (8.2)$$

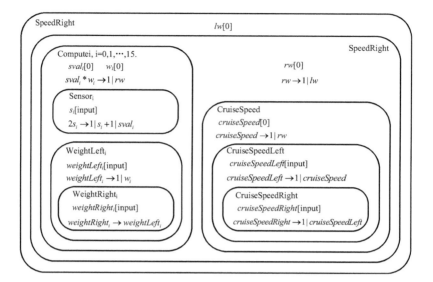

Fig. 8.2 The numerical P system NPS1. It derives from *Figure 7* in [2]. The 8 infrared sensors around the target robot are replaced by 16 sonar sensors. From [43]

In Eq. (8.1)

- *lw* is the speed value accepted by left motor as the required speed to follow.
- *CruiseSpeedLeft* is the cruise speed, the speed when no obstacles are detected.
- s_i is the *transformed* sensor readings.
- $weithtLeft_i$ are the weight values of sensors placed in the left-hand side of robot.

Variables in Eq. (8.2) are the counterparts of those from Eq. (8.1). *i* takes values from 0 to 15, corresponding to the numbers of sensors.

To easily distinguish variables, membranes, and Verilog modules described below, italics denote variables, boldfaced italics indicate membranes, and boldface signifies modules. In Fig. 8.2, variables $weightLeft_i$ and $weightRight_i$ ($i = 1, \ldots, 16$) are sensors' weights whose values reflect the influences of sensors on different positions to the speed of left and right wheel. Supposing an obstacle is detected on the left side, then the speed of the left wheel should be larger than the speed of the right wheel, so the robot can turn right to avoid this obstacle. Based on this assumption and taking Eq. (8.2) in account, the weight values of sensors 0, 1, 2, 3, and 15 should impose negative effects to right wheel speed in order to diminish its speed. At the same time, sensors 0, 1, 2, 3, and 15 should impose positive effects to the left wheel speed in order to raise its speed. Similarly, sensors 4, 5, 6, 7, and 8 impose negative effect to the left wheel but positive effect to the right wheel. Sensors located in the rear part of the robot are unhelpful for detecting obstacles in front, so their weight values are set to zero.

Table 8.1 Calibrated values of $weightLeft_i$ and $weightRight_i$, along with a set of sampled sensors readings used to verify the correctness of RTL translation

i	1	2	3	4	5	6	7	8
$weightLeft_i$	0.1	0.4	0.6	0.8	−0.8	−0.6	−0.4	−0.1
$weightRight_i$	−0.1	−0.4	−0.6	−0.8	0.8	0.6	0.4	0.1
s_i	277	0	0	0	0	0	17	208
i	9	10	11	12	13	14	15	16
$weightLeft_i$	−0.1	0	0	0	0	0	0	0.1
$weightRight_i$	0.1	0	0	0	0	0	0	−0.1
s_i	190	576	704	745	733	659	451	296

Consequently, the weight values of 16 sensors, namely, variables $weightLeft_i$ and $weightRight_i$, have inverse values to manifest the positive and negative effects. Pioneer 3 DX should be calibrated to determine the values of $weightLeft_i$ and $weightRight_i$. The general calibration process can be stated as follows: use control law given in Eqs. (8.1) and (8.2), assign some initial value to $weightLeft_i$ and $weightRight_i$, and then run Pioneer 3 DX robot. If it bumps into obstacles, alter initial values of these two arrays to some extent in line with the collision severity until it no longer hits any obstacles. The corresponding values of these two variable arrays are shown in Table 8.1.

Membranes of NPS1 can be classified into two types according to their functions: delivery membranes and computing membranes. ***WeightRight_i***, ***WeightLeft_i***, ***Sensor_i*** ($i = 1, \ldots, 16$), ***CruiseSpeedRight***, ***CruiseSpeedLeft***, and ***SpeedRight*** are delivery membranes whose role is to transmit values of one variable to another. For instance, values of variables $weightRight_i$ are sent to variables $weightLeft_i$, which are transferred to variables w_i that are used in membrane ***Compute_i*** furthermore. Membranes ***Compute_i*** ($i = 1, \ldots, 16$) and ***CruiseSpeed*** are computing membranes that compute new values of variable rw. Computations performed by computing membranes should be synchronized to reflect the parallelism of NPS. We recall that NPS1 should compute three steps to get results in such a cycle: after the first step finished, $rw = 0$, $lw = 0$; for the second step, rw obtained the left wheel speed value which will be assigned to lw in step 3 and $lw = 0$; in the next step, rw acquires the expected right wheel speed value and lw attains the second step value of rw. This process repeats as computing proceeds. The slowness of the process is related to delivery membranes that just delay the data transfer.

To coordinate the value transfer process in delivery membranes, counters are adopted aiming at this action. Taking the value transfer in ***WeightRight_i*** and ***WeightLeft_i*** as an example, the initial values of variables $weightRight_i$, $weightLeft_i$, and $counter$ are zeros. Variable $counter$ counts in a loop from 0 to 2, corresponding to computational step 1–3. The weight values from Table 8.1 are assigned to $weightRight_i$ and $weightLeft_i$. At the next step, the values of $weightRight_i$ become zero and remain such until the end of the third step, because their values are consumed by production functions and do not appear in any repartition protocols. The values of $weightRight_i$ loop in accordance with $counter$ value loop. The second step values of $weightRight_i$ are transferred to $weightLeft_i$ according to programs in membrane $\boldsymbol{WeightLeft_i}$. The third step values of $weightLeft_i$ become zero again. Timing diagrams below exhibit this behavior.

Membranes $\boldsymbol{Sensor_i}$ are omitted in the Verilog code, and programs $sval_i * w_i \rightarrow 1|rw$ in membrane $\boldsymbol{Compute_i}$ are substituted with $s_i * weightLeft_i \rightarrow 1|rw$. Because the effect of program $2s_i \rightarrow 1|s_i + 1|sval_i$ in $\boldsymbol{Sensor_i}$ is to assign sensors' readings to $sval_i$ and the effect of program $weightLeft_i \rightarrow 1|w_i$ in $\boldsymbol{WeightLeft_i}$ is to transfer values of $weightLeft_i$ to w_i, using $\boldsymbol{Sensor_i}$ modules would add 1 more clock cycle, which can be reduced by performing $s_i * weightLeft_i \rightarrow 1|rw$. Assuming that variables s_i have sonar sensors' readings as initial values, computing membranes ($\boldsymbol{Compute_i}$ and $\boldsymbol{CruiseSpeed}$) are triggered to compute rw at the next step. In the first clock cycle, $rw = 0$ and initial values of $weightLeft_i$ are zeros. In the second cycle, rw obtains the speed of the left wheel because $weightLeft_i$ got their exact values during the second cycle. In the third cycle, rw acquires the speed of the right wheel because $weightLeft_i$ got the values of $weightRight_i$ in the first cycle, which are transferred during the second cycle. Hence, NPS1 accurately computes in three steps to get results. The timing diagram of the mentioned process is depicted in Fig. 8.3.

Two types of Verilog modules are designed to carry out value transfer and computing operations described above. Module $\textbf{WeightRight}$ assigns right weight values (in Table 8.1) of sensors to variables $weightRight_i$, while module $\textbf{WeightLeft}$ assigns left weight values of sensors and transfers the values of $weightRight_i$ to $weightLeft_i$. Analogously, modules $\textbf{CruiseSpeedRight}$ and $\textbf{CruiseSpeedRight}$ perform a similar operation on variables $cruiseSpeedRight$ and $cruiseSpeedLeft$. Module $\textbf{CruiseSpeed}$ transfers the value of $cruiseSpeedLeft$ to $cruiseSpeed$. Module $\textbf{Compute}$ is designed to conduct parallel computations originated from $\boldsymbol{Compute_i}$. Module $\textbf{SpeedLeft}$ passes the value of rw to lw. No module corresponds to membrane $\boldsymbol{SpeedRight}$ because there are no programs within it. The value of $counter$ together with clock cycling guarantees the whole processes to be controlled accurately. Modules are connected to each other according to signals' input-output relationships, for example, the output of $\textbf{WeightRight}$ is the input of $\textbf{WeightLeft}$.

From Fig. 8.2, it is obvious that membranes are organized in nested structure. At the Verilog level, modules are not nested but independent from each other. Another difference is that the function of modules is not the same as the function of membranes; hence, there is no one-to-one correspondence. At the same time, the behavior of Verilog code and NPS1 is identical: at each computation step, the value of each variable and computing outcome are the same. The register transfer level (RTL) model is shown in Fig. 8.4, where input/output ports and their connection relationships are indicated as well.

As can be seen the third data line in Table 8.1, variables have real numbers as values. Since they cannot be represented in digital circuits directly, a fixed-point or a floating point integer encoding should be used. In this example, real numbers are encoded using a fixed-point encoding. To be specific, each variable is assigned a 24-bit register. The first 11 bits correspond to integer part and the following 13

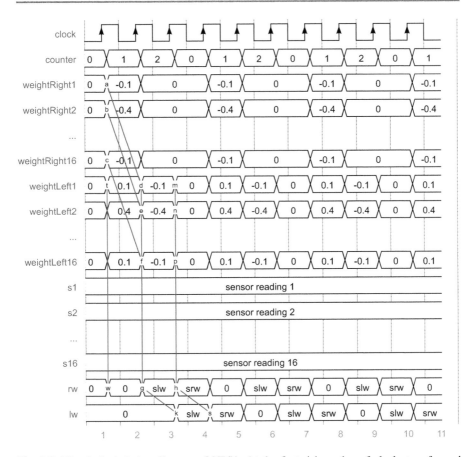

Fig. 8.3 The desired timing diagram of NPS1. At the first rising edge of clock, transfer and computation operations are triggered simultaneously. During the first clock cycle, $weightRight_i$ and $weightLeft_i$ obtain values given in Table 8.1. The outcomes obtained are 0s for the initial values of $weightLeft_i$, although sensor variables have readings. At the next clock cycle, rw gets the speed of the left wheel (denoted by "slw") for $weightLeft_i$ is delivered the left wheel weight values. It is the same reason why rw attains the speed of the right wheel (denoted by "srw") at the third clock cycle. Red lines indicate value transfers from $weightRight_i$ to $weightLeft_i$ and from rw to lw. Blue lines highlight parallel computing of programs in associated membranes. From [43]

bits to the fractional part of a variable value. This encoding allows to represent numbers in the range $[-2047, 1023]$, which includes the value range of sensors' reading $[0,1000]$.

In order to compute the speed-up of the hardware implementation, we use a reference implementation and simulation using the NPS simulator PeP. The host computer is a Dell *Latitude* equipped with a Intel Core i7-7820HQ and 16 GB RAM. Target FPGA of this research is Xilinx Artix-7 xc7a35t-1cpg236c which is the core part of BASYS 3 FPGA developing board; see Sect. 7.4 for more details. The development was done using Xilinx Vivado 2018.2 software.

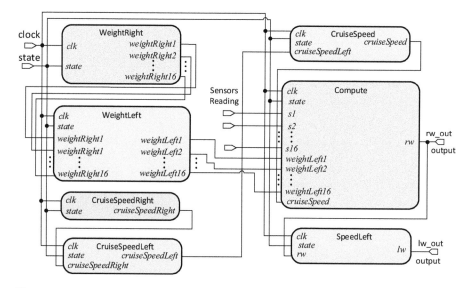

Fig. 8.4 Register transfer level (RTL) model of NPS1. It consists of 7 modules, although NPS1 has 69 membranes. There is a one-to-one correspondence between membranes and programs. Programs can be synchronized in one module with parallel constructs of Verilog. This is the reason why the number of modules can be reduced substantially. Also, a *state* port was added to NPS1; hence the system is able to report idle and busy conditions. From [43]

First, a testbench of NPS1 implementation was designed to verify whether it performs correctly. Figure 8.5 shows the behavioral simulation waveform obtained in Vivado 2018.2. In the first three cycles, the value of *rw-out* (corresponding to *rw*) holds 0, 310.6953125 and 289.3046875, thus behaving exactly as the computing process of NPS1.

The Post implementation timing simulation and PeP simulation results of NPS1 are shown in Figs. 8.6 and 8.7 respectively. The speedup of FPGA implementation of NPS1 comparing CPU simulation (in PeP) is calculated in Eq. (8.3). By comparing these results obtained on FPGA with those obtained by PeP, we observe small differences due to the different representation and precision of real numbers. The error is given in Eq. (8.4), and its order of magnitude is 10^{-5}, which is small for engineering applications like robot control. Data accuracy can be improved by assigning more bits to fractional part of a real number variable.

$$\frac{1.1703 \times 10^7}{1.2334 \times 10^2} = 9.49 \times 10^4 \tag{8.3}$$

$$\begin{cases} e_{rw} = |\frac{289.3 - 289.3046875}{289.3}| = 1.6203 \times 10^{-5} \\ e_{lw} = \frac{310.7 - 310.6953125}{310.7} = 1.5087 \times 10^{-5} \end{cases} \tag{8.4}$$

Name	Value
clk	0
counter[1:0]	0
weightLeft1[23:0]	0.0999755859
weightLeft2[23:0]	0.4000244140
weightLeft3[23:0]	0.5999755859
weightLeft4[23:0]	0.8000488281
weightLeft5[23:0]	-0.8000488281
weightLeft6[23:0]	-0.5999755859
weightLeft7[23:0]	-0.4000244140
weightLeft8[23:0]	-0.0999755859
weightLeft9[23:0]	-0.0999755859
weightLeft10[23:0]	0
weightLeft11[23:0]	0
weightLeft12[23:0]	0
weightLeft13[23:0]	0
weightLeft14[23:0]	0
weightLeft15[23:0]	0
weightLeft16[23:0]	0.0999755859
rw_out[23:0]	0.0
lw_out[23:0]	289.3046875

Fig. 8.5 Waveform of the behavioral simulation of NPS1. The values of $weightLeft_i$ alternate as expected. Sensors' readings s_i take the value in the last row of Table 8.1, and they are not shown on this screenshot. The computing results are *rw-out* and *lw-out*. From [43]

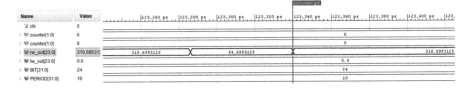

Fig. 8.6 Post implementation timing simulation waveform of NPS1. From [43]

```
WARNING:Maximum number of simulation steps exceeded; Simulation stopped
INFO:Simulation finished succesfully after 3 steps and 0.011703 seconds; End state below:
num_ps = {
  SpeedLeft:
    var = { lw: 310.70, }
    E = {}
  SpeedRight:
    var = { rw: 289.30, }
    E = {}
```

Fig. 8.7 Results of simulation of NPS1 using PeP simulator. Computation results together with computing steps and time costs are printed on screen to show users. (E)NPS should be described in a particular format that meets the requirements of PeP before running simulation. From [43]

8.2.2   Enzymatic Numerical P Systems (ENPS)-Based Membrane Controllers on FPGA

ENPS work in all-parallel mode, so multiple programs are executed concurrently in one membrane. This allows to greatly simplify the membrane structure. ENPS1 from Fig. 8.8 has the same function as NPS1 illustrated from Fig. 8.2, but is composed of a considerably smaller number membranes: 17 vs 69 in NPS1. More

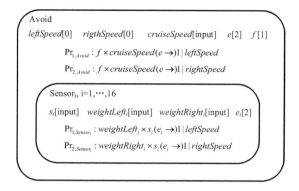

Fig. 8.8 Target enzymatic numerical P system ENPS1. The value of variable e is larger than that of f in membrane **Avoid**, so these two programs can take place. Variables e_i have greater values than s_i so the 16 programs in membrane **Sensor$_i$** can execute in parallel. From [43]

importantly, ENPS1 needs only one step to get the result, improving performance by three times comparing to NPS1, which calculates three steps. Performance improvement is achieved by getting rid of delivery membranes, and the speed of the left wheel and right wheel is calculated at the same time, not sequentially as in NPS1 case.

ENPS1 Verilog RTL model contains one module named **Enps** to perform the behavior of ENPS1. The behavioral simulation waveform of **Enps** is depicted in Fig. 8.9. PeP simulation results of ENPS1 are given in Fig. 8.10.

The post implementation timing simulation results of ENPS1 are shown in Fig. 8.11. The speedup of FPGA implementation of ENPS1 comparing CPU simulation (in PeP) is calculated in Eq. (8.5). Because ENPS1 is a simple model, CPU performs its computation also fast. So the speedup declines contrasting to that of NPS1.

$$\frac{2.993 \times 10^6}{1.07025 \times 10^2} = 2.8 \times 10^4 \tag{8.5}$$

8.2.3   GNPS-Based Membrane Controllers on FPGA

The control law given in Eqs. (8.1) and (8.2) is targeting the e-puck robot that has a small size (its diameter is 70 mm) and low velocity (its max speed is 0.129 m/s) [2]. Using it for Pioneer 3 DX that has the dimension of 510×380 mm and cruise speed of 0.4 m/s [32] does not fit quite well this new platform. More precisely, control law 1 neglects the dimension of robot and supposes that its angular velocity is constant, which gives rise to a high chance to bump on obstacles when the robot is close to obstacles.

Based on kinetics analysis, control law 1 was extended to control law 2 [42] (see Eq. (8.6)), originating from [15]. In this equation, x_i are the readings of sonar

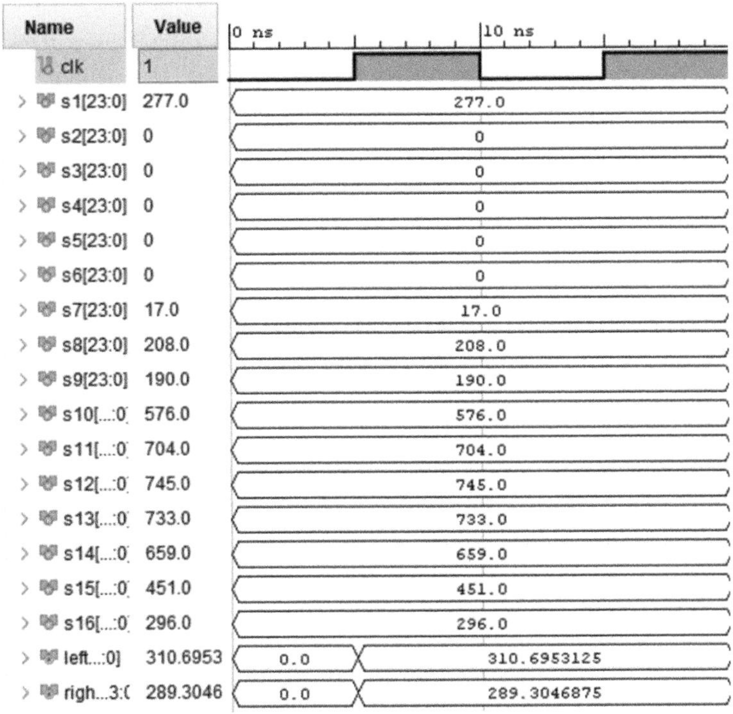

Name	Value	0 ns	10 ns
clk	1		
> s1[23:0]	277.0	277.0	
> s2[23:0]	0	0	
> s3[23:0]	0	0	
> s4[23:0]	0	0	
> s5[23:0]	0	0	
> s6[23:0]	0	0	
> s7[23:0]	17.0	17.0	
> s8[23:0]	208.0	208.0	
> s9[23:0]	190.0	190.0	
> s10[...:0]	576.0	576.0	
> s11[...:0]	704.0	704.0	
> s12[...:0]	745.0	745.0	
> s13[...:0]	733.0	733.0	
> s14[...:0]	659.0	659.0	
> s15[...:0]	451.0	451.0	
> s16[...:0]	296.0	296.0	
> left...:0]	310.6953	0.0	310.6953125
> righ...3:0	289.3046	0.0	289.3046875

Fig. 8.9 Waveform of behavioral simulation of ENPS1. The left and right wheel speed variables gain their expected values after the first rising edge. From [43]

```
WARNING:Maximum number of simulation steps exceeded; Simulation stopped
INFO:Simulation finished succesfully after 1 steps and 0.002993 seconds; End state below:
num_ps = {
  Avoid:
    var = { Spl: 310.70,  Spr: 289.30,  cruiseSpeedLeft: 0.00,  cruiseSpeedRight: 0.00,  f: 0.00, }
    E = { e: 2.00, }
```

Fig. 8.10 PeP simulation results of ENPS1. From [43]

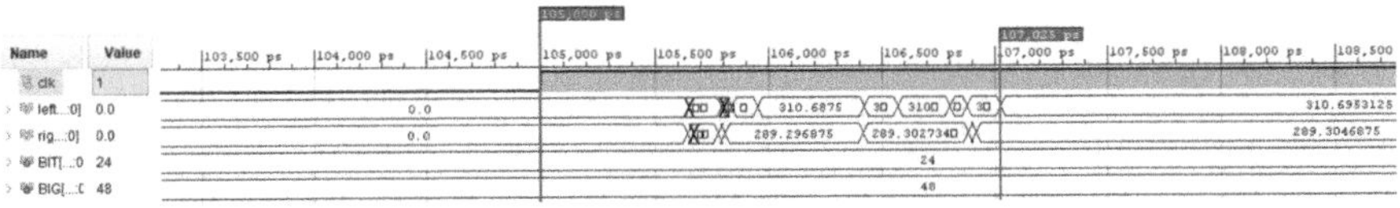

Name	Value	103,500 ps	104,000 ps	104,500 ps	105,000 ps	105,500 ps	106,000 ps	106,500 ps	107,000 ps	107,500 ps	108,000 ps	108,500
clk	1											
> left...0]	0.0		0.0			310.6875	3100				310.6953125	
> rig...0]	0.0		0.0			289.296875	289.302704D				289.3046875	
> BIT[...0	24						24					
> BIG[...C	48						48					

Fig. 8.11 Post implementation timing simulation waveform of ENPS1. From [43]

sensor, $i = 2, 3, 4, 5$, r_1 is the robot gyration radius, d_i are the concerned distances detected by sensors, min selects the nearest distance, $H \in (0, 1)$ is a safety factor, ω is the angular velocity of robot, and θ_i are the angles between symmetric line of robot and the connecting line of robot and obstacles. Other variables have the same meaning as that of control law 1. GNPS3 is devised to accommodate control law 2, as illustrated in Fig. 8.12.

$$
\begin{cases}
d_i = (x_i + r_1) \cos \theta_i \, (i = 2, 3, 4, 5) \\
d = min(d_2, d_3, d_4, d_5) \\
cruisespeed = H * \frac{|\omega|(d^2 - r_1^2)}{2r_1} \\
lw = CruiseSpeedLeft + \sum_{i=1}^{16} s_i * weithtLeft_i \\
rw = CruiseSpeedRight + \sum_{i=1}^{16} s_i * weithtRight_i \\
s_i = -x_i + M
\end{cases}
\tag{8.6}
$$

This GNPS is implemented in FPGA using the method described in Sect. 7.4. Post implementation timing simulation and PeP software simulation are given in Figs. 8.13 and 8.14, respectively. The speedup is calculated in Eq. (8.7). Hardware resource and power consumption are shown in Fig. 8.15.

$$
\frac{2.0997 \times 10^7}{2.60657 \times 10^2} \approx 8.06 \times 10^4
\tag{8.7}
$$

Comparing to software simulation of P systems, FPGA implementation of P systems can achieve a remarkable speedup which can be as high as 10^4 in the case of (E)NPS and GNPS in which non-determinism does not exist. A NPS, ENPS and GNPS which are used as robot controllers are implemented in FPGA. NPS with universal asynchronous receiver/transmitter (UART) communication ability which has the potential to substitute on-board computer of Pioneer 3 robot was designed and implemented as well. As a consequence, the host FPGA has the potential to substitute the on-board computer of Pioneer 3 DX robot to perform computational tasks.

8.3   Robot Path Planning with FPGA Implementation

Besides robot motion control, path planning is another domain which can benefit from the parallelism of NPS (regarding all variants as a whole) with respect to the computation-intensive tasks involved to produce an obstacle-free path. Comparing to applications of NPS accomplished in control area, few works had been done. In this section, a path planning algorithm called rapid-exploring random tree (RRT) is selected as the object, which will be arranged in the framework of ENPS to speedup its procedures that can be executed in parallel. Then the ENPS-RRT model will be implemented in FPGA, achieving a considerable speedup in contrast with software simulation [44].

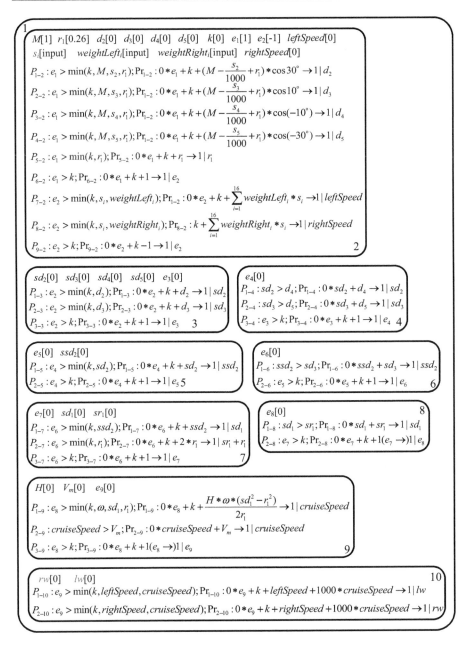

Fig. 8.12 GNPS3 implementing control law 2. From [42]

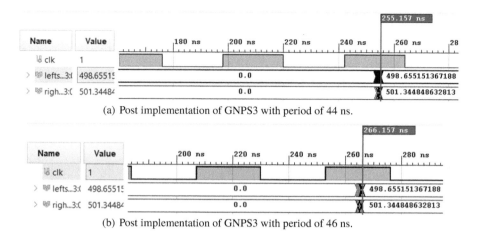

(a) Post implementation of GNPS3 with period of 44 ns.

(b) Post implementation of GNPS3 with period of 46 ns.

Fig. 8.13 Post implementation of GNPS3. From [42]

```
WARNING:Maximum number of simulation steps exceeded; Simulation stopped
INFO:Simulation finished succesfully after 10 steps and 0.020997 seconds; End state below:
num_ps = {
  Calculate_Speed:
    var = { Spl: 498.65,  Spr: 501.35,  SWL: 0.00,  SWR: 0.00, }
    E = { e10: 0.00,  cruiseSpeed: 0.00, }
  CruiseSpeed:
    var = { w: 0.00,  Vmax: 0.50,  H: 0.00, }
    E = { e8: 0.00,  e9: -1.00, }
  Calculate_dmin:
    var = {}
    E = {}
  Calculate1:
    var = { T: 0.00,  r1: 0.00,  d2: 865.50,  d3: 984.08,  d4: 984.08,  d5: 865.38,  f: 0.00, }
    E = { e1: 0.00, }
```

Fig. 8.14 PeP simulation of GNPS3. It takes 0.020997 s to output the result. From [42].

The first attempt to arrange RRT in ENPS is presented in [38], where a variant of ENPS named random enzymatic numerical P systems with proteins and shared memory is designed to organize RRT. This model is simulated with an extended P-Lingua software [12]. On the other side, FPGA implementation of RRT algorithm is also a new topic. There are not many researches reported before. A hierarchical FPGA architecture for RRT algorithm is given in [27], while a hybrid architecture composed of combinatorial and hierarchical architectures is proposed in [26, 28]. In [53], a FPGA parallel architecture is devised for RRT star (RRT^*) achieving speedups from 30~90 times comparing embedded/desktop software simulation.

8.3.1 RRT Algorithm

As a randomized planning technique, rapidly exploring random tree (RRT) has several good qualities such as it is biased to unexplored state space, the vertices (referred to as RRT points in this paper) are nearly uniformly distributed, and only

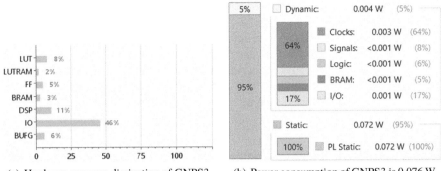

(a) Hardware resource dissipation of GNPS3.   (b) Power consumption of GNPS3 is 0.076 W.

Fig. 8.15 Hardware resource dissipation and power consumption of hardened GNPS3. From [42]

nearest-neighbor queries are needed [22,23]. RRT has had been increasingly applied in path planning since its establishment in 1998. There are many researches on this topic; refer to [1,9,18,37,47]. RRT algorithm can be explained as follows.

Assume that the map is a rectangle whose two legs have the length of p and q, respectively. There are m obstacle points in this map. The duty of RRT algorithm is to produce an obstacle free path generated by linking n path nodes which should be calculated at first. The path node generated by RRT algorithm is called RRT point. The distance between two neighboring RRT points is a predefined value τ. The rotation radius of robot is ξ. The lower left intersection point of two legs is deemed as the original point O, and the robot initial position I is the root RRT point. The first random point R_1 whose two coordinates are the products of p and q multiplying two random numbers in the range of [0, 1] respectively. Compute a point RT_{p1}, so that the distance of point I and RT_{p1} equals to τ, i.e., $|IRT_{p1}| = \tau$. Before claiming that RT_{p1} is the first RRT point, it should be confirmed. The verification procedures are composed of computing all the distances between m obstacle points to the line segment IRT_{p1}. If the minimum distance of these m distances is larger than ξ, the RT_{p1} is saved as RT_1, the first RRT point. Otherwise, discard RT_{p1} and re-begin by feeding two new random numbers to produce a new R_1, until RT_1 is obtained.

At the beginning of computing the second RRT point RT_2, there are two path node now (I and RT_1). Generate a random number denoted as R_2 in the same way stated, and calculate the distances $|IR_2|$ and $|RT_1R_2|$. Choose the RRT point which is closer to R_2 as starting point; then compute RT_{p2} in the line segment SR_2 where $S \in \{I, RT_1\}$ (note that $|SRT_{p2}| = \tau$). Next perform verification procedures to validate RT_{p2}. After RT_2 is produced, proceed to compute RT_3. So, to generate the n-th RRT point RT_n (I is excluded), n distances ($|IR_n|, |RT_1R_n|, \ldots, |RT_{n-1}R_n|$) should be calculated and the smallest one should be selected. Keep in mind that in the verification procedures, there are m distances that will be computed, then find out the minimum one, the computation amount of RRT algorithm is huge, especially when m and n are large numbers. Although RRT points are computed in serial order, these distance calculations can be done in parallel. Obviously, by the parallelization, RRT can be accelerated to a large extent.

The main body of RRT algorithm is given in Algorithm 5, where x_{init} is robot initial point and $Sample()$ gives the random points. $Extend(G, x_{rand})$ is the verification procedure which is described in Algorithm 6, where $Nearest(G, x)$ returns the nearest RRT point in G to x and $Steer(x_{nearest}, x_{new})$ runs a simulated motion from x to y in consideration of robot rotation radius ξ. If trajectory is obstacle free, then $ObstacleFree(x_{nearest}, x_{new})$ returns true, otherwise false.

Algorithm 5: RRT algorithm

Input: x_{init}, N
Output: $G' = (V', E')$
1 $E = \emptyset; i = 0$;
2 **while** $i < N$ **do**
3 $\quad$ $G \leftarrow (V, E)$;
4 $\quad$ $x_{rand} \leftarrow Sample()$;
5 $\quad$ $i \leftarrow i + 1$;
6 $\quad$ $(V, E) \leftarrow Extend(G, x_{rand})$;
7 **end**

Algorithm 6: $Extend(G, x_{rand})$ of RRT algorithm

Input: V, E
Output: G'
1 $V' \leftarrow V; E' \leftarrow E$;
2 $x_{nearest} \leftarrow Nearest(G, x)$;
3 $x_{new} \leftarrow Steer(x_{nearest}, x_{new})$;
4 **if** $ObstacleFree(x_{nearest}, x_{new})$ **then**
5 $\quad$ $V' \leftarrow V' \cup \{x_{new}\}$;
6 $\quad$ $E' \leftarrow E' \cup \{(x_{nearest}, x_{new})\}$;
7 **end**
8 **return** $G' = (V', E)$;

This research arranges RRT algorithm into a bio-inspired parallel model—enzymatic numerical P system (ENPS), and implement this model on the FPGA which is a prototyping platform supporting sequential/parallel processing. IEEE 754 floating point (FP) number is selected as the real number format for its large dynamic range and high precision. This format allows the future application of RRT into a large-scale map with an amount of obstacle points. Taking into account of the complexity of RRT algorithm and IEEE 754 format, and the capacity of the target FPGA chip, the RRT procedure generating 2 RRT points in an environment with 8 obstacles points is considered. In spite of the simplicity of the RRT considered, the method proposed is easy to scale to incorporate more obstacle points and generate more RRT points, provided that target FPGA has enough hardware resources. On the other hand, as an incremental algorithm, it is impractical to implement an RRT generating a great number of RRT points in FPGA for it requires substantial amount of resources. The designed ezymatic numerical P system rapid-exploring random tree (ENPS-RRT) model is depicted in Fig. 8.16.

8.3.2   Arithmetic Units Design

In the IEEE 754 single precision floating point format, 32 bits are assigned to a FP number. Bits 0–22 store mantissa and bits 23–30 represent the exponent. The last bit denotes the sign, 0 for positive and 1 for negative. The exponent is an 8-bit unsigned number, so it cannot represent negative exponent. To resolve this problem, exponent is biased by the constant 127. But it does not mean the exponent range is $[-127, 128]$ since several special cases called exceptions utilize the range endpoint.

We cannot write arithmetical expressions in Verilog *always* blocks because these expressions are described by a series of instantiated adders, multipliers, and other arithmetical units, other than those fixed point format formulas represented explicitly by Verilog operators. If all the arithmetical units are triggered only by clock rising edge, they will always be active, and the timing is tremendously chaotic. In this research, these floating point arithmetical units are designed in such a way that they are sequentially triggered instead of synchronous triggered. To be specific, the adder and multiplier are designed to output results one clock period later (this latency can only be observed in behavioral simulations; their actual latencies are larger than one clock period). A counter is added to count the clock cycle, and a flag signal generated by rising edge detection bears a rising edge at the clock rising edge. At the next rising edge of clock, the flag has a falling edge and keeps low. This flag signal holds value one only for one clock period so it can be used to fire the unit whose trigger signal port connects to this flag just once.

Addition and subtraction are closely related so that $a + b$ does not always mean an addition; it can be a subtraction as well. The ultimate action is determined not only by the operator but also by the signs and magnitudes of both operands. As a consequence, an adder can be a subtractor at the same time. We design adders in line with this thought. So the adder must have a port to input desired operator, $+$ (binary 1) or $-$ (binary 0). The final operation is the XOR of the sign of two operands and the input operator. The main procedures of the multiplier are illustrated in Fig. 8.17.

The design of floating point multiplier is relatively easy compared to the design of a floating point adder. Add the exponents of two operands and multiply their mantissas; then extract specific 23-bit according to the first bit of the mantissa product. The main procedures of the multiplier is illustrated in Fig. 8.18.

It is trivial to compare magnitude of two fixed point numbers for we can use Verilog $\geq$ and $\leq$ operator. However, to compare two floating point numbers is not such intuitive because we have to design comparator, no operators to use. There are three parts in a floating point number: sign, exponent, and mantissa. At first the sign bit is compared then comparing exponent and mantissa successively. Two FP numbers are equal only when these three parts are equal correspondingly. Absolute value comparison which combines exponent and mantissa compare can simplify

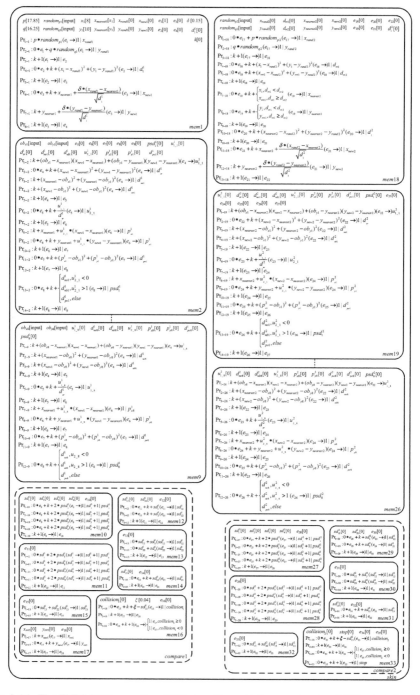

Fig. 8.16 The ENPS-RRT executing RRT algorithm which generates two RRT points in eight obstacle points. From [44]

Fig. 8.17 Procedure diagram of the adder. This is a composite unit which can perform addition and subtraction. From [44]

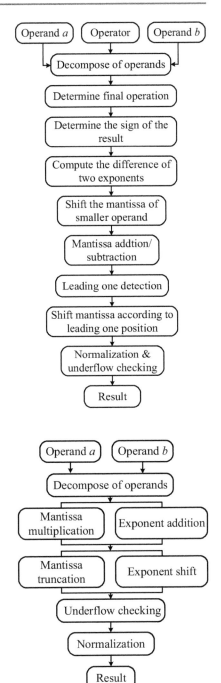

Fig. 8.18 Procedure diagram of the multiplier. From [44]

this process to some extent. This is the trick adopted to design the comparator that compares two input FP numbers and output the smaller one.

RRT algorithm involves inverse square root calculation in new RRT point generation. The hardware resources/power consumption and time latency are too expensive to afford if it is tackled in frontal attack. A method based on Newton approximation that arose in the source code of *Quake3* 3D game [41] launched in the 1990s presents an incredible solution to this intractable problem. A deduction of this approach is detailed in [24].

Solving an arithmetical expression is a serial process for the precedence of operators are different. Even for operators with the same priority, they should be executed in sequential. The intrinsic serialism of arithmetic is the origin why adders and multipliers are triggered at distinct time. For the difficulty of designing high-performance FP divider, we use Xilinx FP IP core to do divisions instead of developing it from scratch. The latency of FP divider is customized to one clock cycle, in accordance with devised FP adder and multiplier. However, this divider is triggered at rising edge of clock; we cannot change this because it is a packed IP core. To make divider triggers by flag generated by preceding unit, assign zero to dividend and one to divisor so the result is zero before the flag is one. When at the clock rising edge and flag has value one, assign actual dividend and divisor value to the divider. By this way, the divider timing is ordered.

There are two types of random number generator which can be implemented in FPGA: true random number generator (TRNG) and pseudo random number generator (PRNG) [21, 25, 46]. In consideration of the difficulty to design a TRNG, this research designs a PRNG producing IEEE 754 FP number in the range of $(0, 1)$ basing on linear feedback shift register (LFSR). XOR is utilized as the operation among certain bits of the register to jumble up the order of pseudo numbers. The penalty of LFSR-based PRNG is that the sequence of generated pseudo number is invariant if the seed is constant. To address this problem, two LFSRs are concatenated so that the output of the first LFSR is input to the other as seeds, making the seed always in dynamic to augment randomness. The LFSR-based PRNG is triggered only by clock rising edge so is always active.

RRT algorithm requires the random number range to be $[0, 1]$ instead of $(0, 1)$. However, 0 is an exception FP number with unique bit representation. The exponent of any IEEE 754 real number in $(0, 1)$ is "0111_1110," while 1's exponent is "0111_1111' (its mantissa is all-zero). Thereby, it is more pragmatic to sacrifices 0 and 1 because of their uniqueness. In the first attempt, we try to produce the 23-bit pseudo random number by giving a 23-bit number as the static seed for the first LFSR and input the pseudo random number to the second LFSR as its dynamic seed. Then, concatenate "0_0111_1110" to the output of the second LFSR to constitute a 32-bit FP number. However, the final pseudo random number tends to be very small. This method is modified by generating 27-bit pseudo random number, setting the exponent to "0111_1110" if it is larger, and concatenating "0_0111" to the 27-bit number. By this way, a more uniform distributed FP random number sequence is obtained.

8.3.3 Enzymatic Numerical P System Rapid-Exploring Random Tree Register Transfer Level (ENPS-RRT RTL) Model Design

IEEE 754 single precision FP standard is resource/power hungry for its long bit width [45]. As stated above, considering the complexity of RRT algorithm and the capacity of our target FPGA, we contrive an ENPS-arranged RRT model generates two RRT points in an environment with merely eight obstacle points. Despite its simplicity in terms of the quite limit RRT points and obstacles, the methodology presented takes effect to generate more RRT points in an environment with large-scale obstacle points for it is scalable. Verilog is employed as the HDL to design RTL model of ENPS-RRT. The "module" hereafter refers to Verilog module.

On account of the interaction between enzymatic variables and conditional rules, the computational process of an ENPS is deterministic. Meanwhile, the introduction of flag signal sequences the processing order of ENPS-RRT. Under this circumstance, the function of enzymes is substituted by flag signals. The root cause of this replacement is that we cannot instantiate a module (e.g., a FP unit) in the *if-else* construct of HDL, while fixed point arithmetic can be contained for the using of operators, where the quantitative relations of enzymatic variables and variables in the production functions are expressed in the condition of *if*.

As computing arithmetic by instantiating FP units correspondingly, the RTL model of ENPS-RRT illustrated in Fig. 8.19 is designed in accordance with arithmetic operations in it. Figure 8.19 presents the RTL model generating one RRT point in an environment with two obstacle points. Due to the conspicuous structural complicity, it is unfeasible to present a legible panorama RTL model block diagram of ENPS-RRT so only this part is given (in effect, Vivado indeed draws an exhaustive schematic. Nevertheless, because of the sophistication, the connections are too small to read when expanding modules to FP unit level). Robot initial point (x_1, y_1) is the root of all RRT point. When computing the first potential RRT point, it is the only RRT point and regarded as the nearest point to the first random point. So there is no comparison module to determine the nearest RRT point to the random point.

Two LFSR-based PRNG modules `random` keep working all the time to produce FP number sequence, and their random number output ports are connected to module `co_rand1` which generates the first random point $(x_{rand}1, y_{rand}1)$. The RTL model of ENPS-RRT begins to work after the port *begin* of `co_rand1` receiving a rising edge. This is done by connecting port *begin* to the pin of a button in the FPGA developing board. `co_rand1` contains two *Fp_mul_Eg* multipliers to execute rule Pr_{1-1} and Pr_{2-1} of ENPS-RRT concurrently. After random point $(x_{rand}1, y_{rand}1)$ is obtained, the *control* port of `co_rand1` emits a flag signal to the *state* port of module `d1_1` to stimulate it, which begins to calculate the square distance between (x_1, y_1) and $(x_{rand}1, y_{rand}1)$ (Pr_{4-1}). `d1_1` is composed of two *Fp_add_Egs* which compute the coordinate differences between initial point and the random point, two *Fp_mul_Es* that calculates the squares of two differences, and one *Fp_add_Egsc* that gives the square sum.

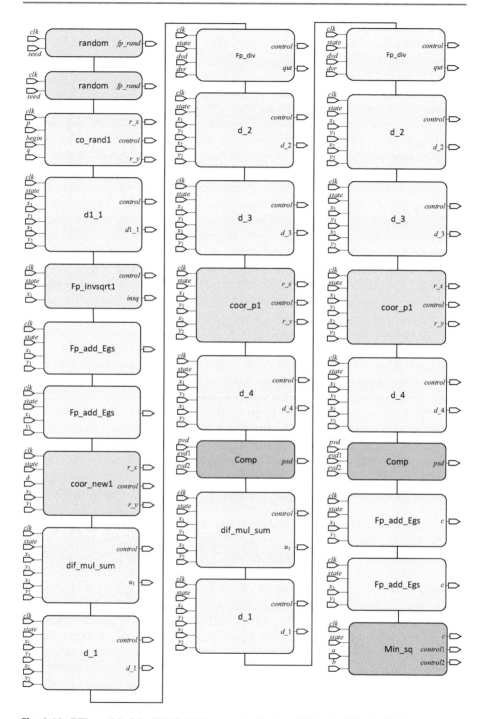

Fig. 8.19 RTL model of the ENPS-RRT generating the first RRT point. The detailed interconnections of modules are omitted for they are excessively complicated. From [44]

Module `Fp_invsqrt1` calculates inverse square root of d_1^1. Alongside the processing of `Fp_invsqrt1`, compute coordinate difference of $(x_{rand}1, y_{rand}1)$ and (x_1, y_1) with two *Fp_add_Egs*. Then, flag signal from `Fp_invsqrt1` activates module `coor_new1` comprising four *Fp_mul_Ess* and two *Fp_add_Egsc* to calculate the first potential RRT point (x_{new1}, y_{new1}) (Pr_{6-1} and Pr_{7-1}).

After the potential RRT point is derived, if the line segment taking (x_1, y_1) and (x_{new1}, y_{new1}) as the two endpoints is obstacle free, i.e., all the distances from obstacle points to this segment are larger than robot rotation radius (ξ), then this potential point is indeed a RRT point. This verification begins with the simultaneous computation of Pr_{1-2}, Pr_{2-2}, Pr_{3-2}, and Pr_{4-2} by module `dif_mul_sum`, `d_1`, `d_2`, and `d_3`, respectively. Module `coor_p1` deals with rule Pr_{8-2} and Pr_{9-2}. Pr_{11-2} is coped with `d_4`. The distance selection rule Pr_{13-2} is determined by `Comp`. All these modules are packed in a higher level module `pdist`.

Distances between eight obstacle points and the line segment (x_1, y_1) − (x_{new1}, y_{new1}) are computed in parallel so the performance will be improved to a large extent, especially for large amount of obstacle points. When the eight distances are obtained, seven `Min_sq`s in total are needed to figure out the smallest distance. Execute $\xi - distance$ to the two smallest distances, and utilize another `Min_sq` to output the minimal distance. If it is negative, the segment is obstacle free, and the potential point is a valid RRT point. Then the first RRT point is stored as (x_{rrt1}, y_{rrt1}), sending a flag signal from port *control2* of `Min_sq` to activate the computation of the second potential RRT point. Otherwise discard this point; transmit a flag signal from port *control1* of `Min_sq` to port *state* of `co_rand1` to resume the calculation of (x_{new1}, y_{new1}) until it is a RRT point. Membranes included in a dashed block called *compare1/2* in Fig. 8.16 carries out the work of the eight `Min_sq`s.

In order to compute the second potential RRT point, the nearest point to the second random point (x_{rand2}, y_{rand2}) should be chosen from (x_1, y_1) and (x_{rrt1}, y_{rrt1}). This process corresponds to rules Pr_{1-18} to Pr_{8-18} in ENPS-RRT, and module `nearest2` performs this work. After the second potential point (x_{new2}, y_{new2}) is obtained, carry out the verification stated above to confirm whether it is a RRT point. To scale the module to incorporate more obstacle points, one can instantiate more `pdist` modules and enlarge the comparison logic for selecting the minimum distance.

NPS and ENPS can be simulated by a software named PeP. PeP can also offer elapsed time (in seconds) used to compute some predefined steps. From a hardware point of view, the software simulation is a CPU implementation of an algorithm. As a result, this returns time reflecting the performance of the CPU in host computer. Furthermore, this CPU implementation time is indispensable to compute the speedup of FPGA implementation of NPS. The PeP simulation results of ENPS-RRT are given in Fig. 8.20.

```
WARNING:Maximum number of simulation steps exceeded: Simulation stopped
INFO:Simulation finished succesfully after 34 steps and 0.097948 seconds  End state below:
num_ps = {
  skin:
    var = {}
    E = {}
  mem1:
    var = { p: 0.00,  q: 0.00,  random_p1: 0.00,  random_q1: 0.00,  x1: 8.00,  y1: 10.00,  x_nearest1: 8.00,  y_nearest1
  : 10.00,  x_rand1: 10.00,  y_rand1: 5.00,  x_new1: 8.06,  y_new1: 9.86,  k: 0.00,  delta: 0.15,  one_d1: 0.00,  two_p: 0
  .00,  two_q: 0.00,  two_x_nearest1: 0.00,  two_y_nearest1: 0.00,  two_delta: 0.00,  two_x_rand1: 0.00,  two_y_rand1: 0.0
  0,  two_x1: 0.00,  two_y1: 0.00, }
    E = { e1: 0.00,  e2: 0.00,  e3: 0.00,  e4: 0.00, }
  mem2:
    var = { ob_x1: 4.00,  ob_y1: 10.00,  one_u1_1: 0.00,  one_d_sr: 0.00,  one_d_no1: 0.00,  one_d_nb1: 16.47,  one_u2_1
  : 0.00,  one_p_x1: 0.00,  one_p_y1: 0.00,  one_d_po1: 13.79,  one_psd1: 16.00,  three_x_nearest1: 0.00,  three_y_nearest
  1: 0.00,  two_x_new1: 0.00,  two_y_new1: 0.00,  two_ob_x1: 0.00,  two_ob_y1: 0.00,  three_ob_x1: 0.00,  three_ob_y1: 0.0
  0,  ob_x2: 12.00,  ob_y2: 10.00,  one_u1_2: 0.00,  one_d_no2: 16.00,  one_d_nb2: 0.00,  one_u2_2: 0.00,  one_p_x2: 0.00,
  one_p_y2: 0.00,  one_d_po2: 13.79,  one_psd2: 15.58,  two_ob_x2: 0.00,  two_ob_y2: 0.00,  three_ob_x2: 0.00,  three_ob
  _y2: 0.00,  ob_x3: 8.00,  ob_y3: 6.00,  one_u1_3: 0.00,  one_d_no3: 16.00,  one_d_nb3: 0.00,  one_u2_3: 0.00,  one_p_x3:
  0.00,  one_p_y3: 0.00,  one_d_po3: 2.21,  one_psd3: 14.91,  two_ob_x3: 0.00,  two_ob_y3: 0.00,  three_ob_x3: 0.00,  thr
  ee_ob_y3: 0.00,  ob_x4: 8.00,  ob_y4: 14.00,  one_u1_4: 0.00,  one_d_no4: 0.00,  one_d_nb4: 17.14,  one_u2_4: 0.00,  one
  _p_x4: 0.00,  one_p_y4: 0.00,  one_d_po4: 2.21,  one_psd4: 16.00,  two_ob_x4: 0.00,  two_ob_y4: 0.00,  three_ob_x4: 0.00
  ,  three_ob_y4: 0.00,  ob_x5: 5.50,  ob_y5: 7.50,  one_u1_5: 0.00,  one_d_no5: 12.50,  one_d_nb5: 0.00,  one_u2_5: 0.00,
  one_p_x5: 0.00,  one_p_y5: 0.00,  one_d_po5: 10.56,  one_psd5: 12.10,  two_ob_x5: 0.00,  two_ob_y5: 0.00,  three_ob_x5
  : 0.00,  three_ob_y5: 0.00,  ob_x6: 11.50,  ob_y6: 12.50,  one_u1_6: 0.00,  one_d_no6: 0.00,  one_d_nb6: 18.83,  one_u2_
  6: 0.00,  one_p_x6: 0.00,  one_p_y6: 0.00,  one_d_po6: 17.46,  one_psd6: 18.50,  two_ob_x6: 0.00,  two_ob_y6: 0.00,  thr
  ee_ob_x6: 0.00,  three_ob_y6: 0.00,  ob_x7: 5.50,  ob_y7: 12.50,  one_u1_7: 0.00,  one_d_no7: 0.00,  one_d_nb7: 13.50,
  one_u2_7: 0.00,  one_p_x7: 0.00,  one_p_y7: 0.00,  one_d_po7: 1.94,  one_psd7: 12.50,  two_ob_x7: 0.00,  two_ob_y7: 0.00
  ,  three_ob_x7: 0.00,  three_ob_y7: 0.00,  ob_x8: 11.50,  ob_y8: 7.50,  one_u1_8: 0.00,  one_d_no8: 18.50,  one_d_nb8: 0
  .00,  one_u2_8: 0.00,  one_p_x8: 0.00,  one_p_y8: 0.00,  one_d_po8: 5.39,  one_psd8: 17.44,  two_ob_x8: 0.00,  two_ob_y8
  : 0.00,  three_ob_x8: 0.00,  three_ob_y8: 0.00, }
    E = { e5: 0.00,  e6: 0.00,  e7: 0.00,  e8: 0.00,  e9: 0.00, }
```

(a) ENPS-RRT membrane 1 simulation results which contains the first RRT point $(8.06, 9.86)$.

```
  mem18:
    var = { random_p2: 0.00,  random_q2: 0.00,  x_rand2: 13.00,  y_rand2: 6.50,  d_rt1: 37.25,  d_rt2: 35.74,  x_nearest
  2: 8.06,  y_nearest2: 9.86,  x_new2: 8.18,  y_new2: 9.78,  two_x_rrt1: 0.00,  two_y_rrt1: 0.00,  two_d1: 0.00,  two_x_ne
  arest1: 0.00,  two_y_nearest1: 0.00,  two_x_rand2: 0.00,  two_y_rand2: 0.00,  two_x_nearest2: 0.00,  two_y_nearest2: 0.0
  0,  three_x_nearest2: 0.00,  three_y_nearest2: 0.00,  three_x_rand2: 0.00,  three_y_rand2: 0.00, }
    E = { e18: 0.00,  e19: 0.00,  e20: 0.00,  e21: 0.00,  e22: 0.00, }
```

(b) ENPS-RRT membrane 18 simulation results which contains the second RRT point $(8.18, 9.78)$.

Fig. 8.20 PeP simulation of ENPS-RRT which performs 34 steps and costs 0.097948 s to get results. The results of PeP save two significant digits. From [44]

8.3.4 ENPS-RRT on FPGA

The hardware facilities involved in FPGA implementation are a host computer equipped with an Intel Core i7-7820HQ and 16 GB RAM; a Xilinx VC707 evaluation board featured a Virtex-7 XC7VX485T-2FFG1761 FPGA [49]. The FPGA integrated developing environment employed is Xilinx Vivado 2019.1.

For the sake of ensuring that RTL model behaves as expected, a testbench should be designed to validate it. An ENPS-RRT RTL model is instantiated in the testbench, together with the clock cycle declaration and initial value setup of input variables. Then, perform RTL model behavioral simulation which presents the model behavior by drawing waveforms of variables. The RTL model turned out to function well if waveforms and values meet design objectives. Set clock period as 10 ns; the behavioral simulation waveform of ENPS-RRT is given in Fig. 8.21. Note, the length of clock period is not important for behavioral simulation because it is a software simulation conducted by host computer CPU, and all the gate latencies and datapath latencies are neglected. As a consequence, behavioral simulation can verify the functionality of a RTL model but void of timing analysis.

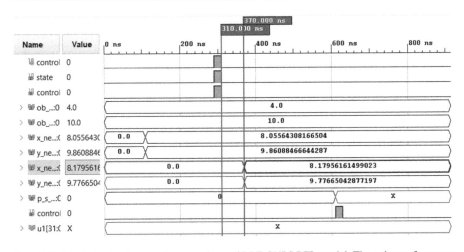

Fig. 8.21 The behavioral simulation waveform of RRT-GNPS RTL model. The red waveforms are caused by the lack of initial values of variables. This phenomenon can be eliminated by assigning initial values to *reg* variables. From [44]

If the behavior of RTL model meets requirements, the subsequent action is to synthesize design which is done automatically after clicking synthesis icon in Vivado. Once synthesis completes, two important procedures should be performed: set constraints and hardware debug cores. Constraints include physical constants and timing constraints. Physical constants define the correspondence relationship between RTL model input/output ports and FPGA input/out pins. Timing constraints set clock cycle and input/output delays and other constraints related to clock. Obstacle points are assigned to corresponding variables via Verilog system task "$readmemh" from a .txt file stored in host computer, instead of accessing these data through pins. So the input ports are clock input and co_rand1's *begin* port. The computational results of FPGA cannot be observed directly but can be checked by performing hardware debug in the integrated logic analyzer (ILA). To observe a variable, a debug core should be set in the synthesized model to probe values obtained in FPGA. Perform debug core setting after synthesizing model at least once.

Target FPGA has two differential clock pins. To generate a clock from these two pins, a global clock input buffer IBUFGDS whose input ports are the two pins should be instantiated to output a clock with period defined by timing constraints. The second RRT point's y-coordinate (y_3) is selected to output so pins should be allocated to y_3 port. This is a vector port with 32-bit; hence it needs 32pins. With respect to the complicity of ENPS-RRT, the clock period is set to 40 ns, which means the FPGA harden ENPS-RRT computes 2.5×10^7 times per second (the frequency is 25 MHz). This set may be modified after implementation if it fails to meet timing closure.

$$9.7948 \times 10^7 \div 3.05901 \times 10^3 = 3.20195 \times 10^4 \qquad (8.8)$$

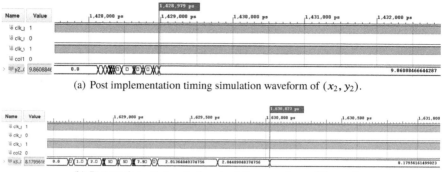

(a) Post implementation timing simulation waveform of (x_2, y_2).

(b) Post implementation timing simulation waveform of (x_3, y_3).

Fig. 8.22 The stable value of first RRT point (x_2, y_2) appears at 1428979 ps (1428.979 ns), while the second RRT point (x_3, y_3) arises at 1630027 ps (1630.027 ns). The total elapsed time is $1428.979 + 1630.027 = 3059.01$ ns. From [44]

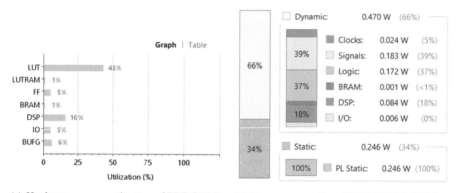

(a) Hardware resource utilization of RRT-GNPS.   (b) Power consumption of RRT-GNPS is 0.716 w.

Fig. 8.23 The resource utilization and power consumption of ENPS-RRT. From [44]

After RTL model is synthesized successfully, carry on implementation in which conducts netlist/power optimization, reports timing together with hardware resource/power consumption, and completes *Place & Route*. Gate delay and datapath delay are taken into account during implementation to evaluate timing situation so post implementation timing simulation can reflect the real performance of the implemented model. Post implementation timing simulation of ENPS-RRT is shown in Fig. 8.22. FPGA costs nearly 3059.01 ns to obtain two RRT points, while host computer CPU costs 0.097948 s to get them. So the speedup is computed in Eq. (8.8).

The resource utilization and power consumption of ENPS-RRT are shown in Fig. 8.23. ENPS-RRT costs 43% of look-up table (LUT) because of the long bit width of IEEE 754 representation. If narrow bit width FP format, e.g., 16-bit FP, or floating point representation is used, the LUT utilization can be reduced by almost

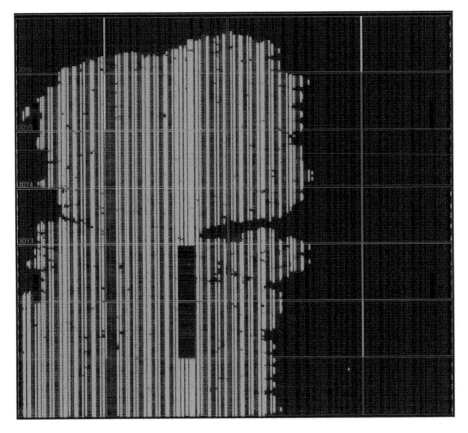

Fig. 8.24 The *Place* & *Route* of ENPS-RRT

half. 16% of DSP resource is utilized by arithmetic operations. Narrow bit width FP or fixed point format will decrease this amount as well. The consumptions of other resources make up small percentages. The *Place* & *Route* of ENPS-RRT is given in Fig. 8.24.

This research organizes RRT algorithm into the formal framework of ENPS and resorts to the parallel architecture of FPGA to speedup this computation-intensive algorithm. An ENPS-RRT FPGA implementation method working on IEEE 754 floating point arithmetic units is proposed. Since the fact that carries out arithmetic operations by instantiating a serial of FP units, the function of enzymatic variables is replaced by flag signals signifying the completion of FP units. A tandem LFSR-based FP number generator producing IEEE 754 compliant FP numbers in the range of $(0, 1)$ is devised to provide random numbers for ENPS-RRT. Compared to CPU simulation of ENPS-RRT, the FPGA hardened counterpart achieves a speedup of 10^4 order of magnitude. If narrow bit width FP units or fixed point arithmetic are used to represent arithmetical expressions, the potential speedup could be an order of 10^5.

8.4   Conclusion

This chapter concentrated on two examples of concrete applications using P systems and implemented using FPGA hardware. The applications discussed in Sects. 8.2 and 8.3 target the area of robotic control that already has many successful applications using variants of numerical P systems. Traditional approaches in robotics use on-board computers or remote control to perform many computationally intensive tasks, as the power of robot microcontroller driving actuators and analyzing sensors is not sufficient for most of them.

The approach presented in this chapter is different. It aims to create a specialized FPGA-based hardware unit that would quickly carry out the needed computations and that would communicate directly with the robot microcontroller. This allows to conceive autonomous robots that do not require a computer for operation. The applications described earlier in this chapter show that it is possible to design a chip that would control the robot movement at a local (PID with obstacle avoidance) and global (path-planning to a goal) level.

Moreover, it is also possible to replace the robot microcontroller by FPGA either by integrating a soft or hard microprocessor in the FPGA design or by writing appropriate drivers that would allow the FPGA to interact directly with the sensors and actuators. This opens the possibility for a very fast reaction time, 3–4 magnitudes faster than traditional approaches. As pointed out in Chap. 7, at the moment data acquisition speed from sensors is relatively low with respect to the FPGA speed, so there are no immediate gains using the proposed approach. However, with the advent of faster sensors, the gains will be consequent. We remark that the traditional architecture hits its limits because the communication between the robot microcontroller and the external computing device is usually performed using a serial port (either directly, or via WiFi or Bluetooth bridges), which features relatively low communication speeds. Hence, at the moment, there is a bottleneck that does not allow to use high-speed data acquisition directly on the device. This problem can be easily solved by using FPGA-based designs, as they allow to incorporate faster communication channels. In our opinion, this is a very promising research direction.

As discussed in Chap. 7, the translation of GNPS to a hardware design is not very complex, and it is quite well investigated (see the PhD [42]). So, the main challenge is to encode algorithms in a parallel manner using the formalism of GNPS. As shown in Sect. 8.3, complex algorithms like RRT can be parallelized and expressed in GNPS, so it is reasonable to admit that more applications of such type would appear in the nearest future.

The hardware implementation of tissue P systems [29], SN P systems [7, 19, 20] and their variants [40, 50, 51] to real-life applications is also promising future direction.

References

1. I. Aguinaga, D. Borro, L. Matey, Parallel RRT-based path planning for selective disassembly planning. Int. J. Adv. Manuf. Technol. **36**(11–12), 1221–1233 (2008). https://doi.org/10.1007/s00170-007-0930-2
2. C. Buiu, C. I. Vasile, O. Arsene, Development of membrane controllers for mobile robots. Inf. Sci. **187**, 33–51 (2012). https://doi.org//10.1016/j.ins.2011.10.007
3. C. Buiu, A. George. Membrane Computing models and robot controller design, current results and challenges. J. Membr. Comput. **1**(4), 262–269 (2019). https://doi.org/10.1007/s41965-019-00029-8
4. F.G.C. Cabarle, H.N. Adorna, M.A. Martínez-del-Amor, A Spiking neural P system simulator based on CUDA, in *Membrane Computing. CMC 2011*, ed. by M. Gheorghe, Gh. Păun, G. Rozenberg, A. Salomaa, S. Verlan. Lecture Notes in Computer Science, vol. 7184 (2012), pp. 87–103. https://doi.org/10.1007/978-3-642-28024-5_8
5. J.M. Cecilia, J.M. García, G.D. Guerrero, M.A. Martínez-del-Amor, I. Pérez-Hurtado, M.J. Pérez-Jiménez, Implementing P systems parallelism by means of GPUs, *Membrane Computing. WMC 2009*, ed. by in Gh. Păun, M.J. Pérez-Jiménez, A. Riscos, G. Rozenberg, A. Salomaa. Lecture Notes in Computer Science, vol. 5957 (2010), pp. 227–241. https://doi.org/10.1007/978-3-642-11467-0_17
6. J.M. Cecilia, J.M. García, G.D. Guerrero, M.A. Martínez-del-Amor, M.J. Pérez-Jiménez, M. Ujaldón, The GPU on the simulation of cellular computing models. Soft Comput. **16**(2), 231–246 (2012). https://doi.org/10.1007/s00500-011-0716-1
7. R.T.A. de la Cruz, F.G.C. Cabarle, H.N. Adorna, Generating context-free languages using spiking neural P systems with structural plasticity. J. Membr. Comput. **1**(3), 161–177 (2019). https://doi.org/10.1007/s41965-019-00021-2
8. E. Csuhaj-Varjú, M. Gheorghe, R. Lefticaru, P colonies and kernel P systems. Int. J. Adv. Eng. Sci. Appl. Math. **10** (3), 181–192 (2018). https://doi.org/10.1007/s12572-018-0224-y
9. D. Devaurs, T. Siméon, J. Cortés, A multi-tree extension of the transition-based RRT: application to ordering-and-pathfinding problems in continuous cost spaces, in *2014 Proceedings of IEEE/RSJ International Conference on Intelligent Robots and Systems (IROS)* (2014), pp. 2991–2996. https://doi.org/10.13140/RG.2.1.1210.3523
10. N. Elkhani, R. C. Muniyandi, G. Zhang, Multi-Objective Binary PSO with kernel P system on GPU. Int. J. Comput. Commun. Control **13**(3), 323–336 (2018). https://doi.org/10.15837/ijccc.2018.3.3282
11. S. Fan, Y. Gong, G. Zhang, Y. Xiao, H. Rong, P. Paul, X. Ma, H. Huang, M. Gheorghe, Implementation of kernel P systems in CUDA for solving NP-hard problems. Int. J. Unconv. Comput. 16(2/3), 259–278 (2021)
12. M. García-Quismondo, R. Gutiérrez-Escudero, M.A. Martínez-del-Amor, E. Orejuela-Pinedo, I. Pérez-Hurtado, P-Lingua 2.0: a software framework for cell-like P systems. Int. J. Comput. Commun. Control **4**(3), 234–243 (2009). https://doi.org/10.15837/ijccc.2009.3.2431
13. M. Gheorghe, F. Ipate, R. Lefticaru, M.J. Pérez-Jiménez, A. Turcanu, L. Valencia-Cabrera, M. García-Quismondo, L. Mierla, 3-COL problem modelling using simple kernel P systems. Int. J. Comput. Math. **90**(4), 816–830 (2013). https://doi.org/10.1080/00207160.2012.743712
14. M. Gheorghe, R. Ceterchi, F. Ipate, S. Konur, R. Lefticaru. Kernel P systems: from modelling to verification and testing. Theor. Comput. Sci. **724**, 45–60 (2018). https://doi.org/10.1016/j.tcs.2017.12.010
15. Z. Huang, J. Dong, Y. Duan, G. Zhang, Mobile robot membrane controller design with enzymatic numerical P systems for obstacle avoidance behavior. Comput. Syst. Appl. **28**(7), 17–25 (2019) (in Chinese). https://doi.org/10.15888/j.cnki.csa.006976
16. F. Ipate, C. Dragomir, R. Lefticaru, L. Mierla, M.J. Pérez-Jiménez, Using a kernel P system to solve the 3-COL problem, in *Pre-Proceedings of the 13th International Conference on Membrane Computing, CMC13* (2012), pp. 243–258

17. F. Ipate, R. Lefticaru, L. Mierla, L. Valencia-Cabrera, H. Han, G. Zhang, C. Dragomir, M.J. Pérez-Jiménez, M. Gheorghe, Kernel P systems: applications and implementations, in *Proceedings of The Eighth International Conference on Bio-Inspired Computing: Theories and Applications (BIC-TA), 2013*, ed. by Z. Yin, L. Pan, X. Fang. Advances in Intelligent Systems and Computing (2013), pp.1081–1089. https://doi.org/10.1007/978-3-642-37502-6_126

18. L. Jaillet, J. Cortés, T. Simeon, Transition-based RRT for path planning in continuous cost spaces, in *2008 Proceedings of IEEE/RSJ International Conference on Intelligent Robots and Systems (IROS)* (2008), pp. 2145–2150. https://doi.org/10.1109/IROS.2008.4650993

19. Y. Jiang, Y. Su, F. Luo, An improved universal spiking neural P system with generalized use of rules. J. Membr. Comput. **1**(4), 270–278 (2019). https://doi.org/10.1007/s41965-019-00025-y.

20. Z.B. Jiménez, F.G.C. Cabarle, R.T.A. de la Cruz, K.C. Buño, H.N. Adorna, N.H.S. Hernandez, X. Zeng, Matrix representation and simulation algorithm of spiking neural P systems with structural plasticity. J. Membr. Comput. **1**(3), 145–160 (2019). https://doi.org/10.1007/s41965-019-00020-3

21. P. Kohlbrenner, K. Gaj, An embedded true random number generator for FPGAs, in *Proceedings of the ACM/SIGDA 12th International Symposium on Field Programmable Gate Arrays.* Monterey, California, USA, February 22–24 (2004), pp. 71–78 https://doi.org/10.1145/968280.968292

22. S.M. LaValle, Rapidly-Exploring Random Trees: A New Tool for Path Planning. TR 98-11, Computer Science Dept., Iowa State University, October 1998. http://lavalle.pl/papers/Lav98c.pdf

23. S.M. LaValle, J.J. Kuffner, Rapidly-exploring random trees: progress and prospects, in *2000 Proceedings of IEEE International Conference on Robotics and Automation*, (2000), pp. 995–1001

24. C. Lomont, Fast Inverse Square Root. Technical Report, Department of Mathematics, Purdue University (2003)

25. M. Majzoobi, F. Koushanfar, S. Devadas, FPGA-based true random number generation using circuit metastability with adaptive feedback control, in *Cryptographic Hardware and Embedded Systems—CHES 2011. CHES 2011*, ed. by B. Preneel, T. Takagi. Lecture Notes in Computer Science, vol. 6917 (2011), pp. 17–32. https://doi.org/10.1007/978-3-642-23951-9_2

26. G.S. Malik, *FPGA Based Massively Parallel Architectures for Super Fast Path Planning via Rapidly Exploring Random Trees (RRT).* Master Thesis, International Institute of Information Technology, Hyderabad, 2016

27. G.S. Malik, K. Gupta, K.M. Krishna, S.R. Chowdhury, FPGA based hierarchical architecture for parallelizing RRT, in *Proceedings of the 2015 Conference on Advances in Robotics.* AIR 2015, Goa, India, July 2–4 (2015), pp. 121–126

28. G. Malik, K. Gupta, R. Dharani, K.M. Krishna, FPGA based hybrid architecture for parallelizing RRT. Comput. Res. Rep. (2015). abs/1607.05704

29. C. Martín-Vide, Gh. Păun, J. Pazos, A. Rodriguez-Patón, Tissue P systems. Theor. Comput. Sci. **296**(2), 295–326 (2003). https://doi.org/10.1016/S0304-3975(02)00659-X

30. M.A. Martínez-del-Amor, *Accelerating Membrane Systems Simulators using High Performance Computing with GPU*, Ph.D. Thesis, Universidad de Sevilla, 2013. http://hdl.handle.net/11441/15644

31. C. Nvidia, NVIDIA CUDA programming guide. http://docs.nvidia.com/cuda/cuda-c-best-practices-guide/

32. Omron Co. Ltd., Pioneer 3 Operations Manual (2017)

33. D. Orellana-Martín, L. Valencia-Cabrera, A. Riscos-Núñez, M.J. Pérez-Jiménez, P systems with proteins: a new frontier when membrane division disappears. J. Membr. Comput. **1**(1), 29–39 (2019). https://doi.org/10.1007/s41965-018-00003-w

34. Gh. Păun, G. Rozenberg, A. Salomaa (eds.), *The Oxford Handbook of Membrane Computing* (Oxford University Press, Oxford, 2010)

35. A.B. Pavel, C. Buiu, Using enzymatic numerical P systems for modeling mobile robot controllers. Nat. Comput. **11**(3), 387–393 (2012). https://doi.org/10.1007/s11047-011-9286-5

36. A.B. Pavel, C.I. Vasile, I. Dumitrache, Robot localization implemented with enzymatic numerical P systems, in *Biomimetic and Biohybrid Systems. Living Machines 2012*, ed. by T.J. Prescott, N.F. Lepora, A. Mura, P.F.M.J. Verschure. Lecture Notes in Computer Science, vol. 7375 (2012), pp. 204–215. https://doi.org/10.1007/978-3-642-31525-1_18

37. R. Pepy, A. Lambert, Safe path planning in an uncertain-configuration space using RRT, in *2006 Proceedings of IEEE/RSJ International Conference on Intelligent Robots and Systems (IROS)* (2006), pp. 5376–5381. https://doi.org/10.1109/IROS.2006.282101

38. I. Pérez-Hurtado, M.J. Pérez-Jiménez, G. Zhang, D. Orellana-Martín, Simulation of rapidly-exploring random trees in membrane computing with P-lingua and automatic programming. Int. J. Comput. Commun. Control **13**(6), 1007–1031 (2018). https://doi.org/10.15837/ijccc.2018.6.3370

39. M.J. Pérez-Jiménez, A. Riscos-Núñez, Solving the subset-sum problem by P systems with active membranes. N. Gener. Comput. **23**(4), 339–356 (2005). https://doi.org/10.1007/BF03037637

40. H. Rong, K. Yi, G. Zhang, J. Dong, P. Paul, Z. Huang, Automatic implementation of fuzzy reasoning spiking neural P systems for diagnosing faults in complex power systems. Complexity **2019**, 2635714 (2019). https://doi.org/10.1155/2019/2635714

41. Ryszard. Origin of Quake3's Fast InvSqrt(). https://www.beyond3d.com/content/articles/8/

42. Z. Shang, *Hardware Implementation of Cell-inspired Computational Models*. Ph.D. Thesis, University Paris-Est Créteil Val de Marne, 2020

43. Z. Shang, S. Verlan, G. Zhang, I. Pérez-Hurtado, FPGA Implementation of robot obstacle avoidance controller based on enzymatic numerical P systems, in *Pre-proceedings of the 8th Asian Branch of International Conference on Membrane Computing*, November 14–17, 2019, Xiamen, China, 184–214

44. Z. Shang, S. Verlan, G. Zhang, I. Pérez-Hurtado. FPGA Architecture for generalized numerical P system arranged rapid-exploring random tree algorithm, in *Pre-Proceedings of the 2020 International Conference on Membrane Computing*. September 14–18, 2020, Ulaanbaatar, Mongolia

45. J.Y.F. Tong, D. Nagle, R.A. Rutenbar, Reducing power by optimizing the necessary precision/range of floating-point arithmetic. IEEE Trans. Very Large Scale Integr. Syst. **8**(3), 273–286 (2000). https://doi.org/10.1109/92.845894

46. K.H. Tsoi, K.H. Leung, P.H.W. Leong, Compact FPGA-based true and pseudo random number generators, in *11th Annual IEEE Symposium on Field-Programmable Custom Computing Machines, FCCM 2003*, Napa, CA, USA, 2003, pp. 51–61. https://doi.org/10.1109/FPGA.2003.1227241

47. H. Umari, S. Mukhopadhyay, Autonomous robotic exploration based on multiple rapidly-exploring randomized trees, in *2017 IEEE/RSJ International Conference on Intelligent Robots and Systems (IROS)*, Vancouver, BC, 2017, pp. 1396–1402. https://doi.org/10.1109/IROS.2017.8202319

48. C.I. Vasile, A.B. Pavel, I. Dumitrache, J. Kelemen, Implementing obstacle avoidance and follower behaviors on Koala robots using numerical P systems, in *Proceedings of the Tenth Brainstorming Week on Membrane Computing*, ed. by M. García-Quismondo, L.F. Macías-Ramos, Gh. Păun, L. Valencia-Cabrera, vol. II (Fénix Editora, 2012), pp. 215–228

49. Virtex-7 FPGA VC707 Evaluation Kit. https://www.xilinx.com/products/boards-and-kits/ek-v7-vc707-g.html#overview

50. T. Wang, G. Zhang, H. Rong, M.J. Pérez-Jiménez, Application of fuzzy reasoning spiking neural P systems to fault diagnosis. Int. J. Comput. Commun. Control **9**(6), 786–799 (2014). https://doi.org/10.15837/ijccc.2014.6.1485

51. T. Wang, G. Zhang, J. Zhao, Z. He, J. Wang, M. Pérez-Jiménez, Fault diagnosis of electric power systems based on fuzzy reasoning spiking neural P systems. IEEE Trans. Power Syst. **30**(3), 1182–1194 (2015). https://doi.org/10.1109/TPWRS.2014.2347699

52. X. Wang, G. Zhang, F. Neri, T. Jiang, J. Zhao, M. Gheorghe, F. Ipate, R. Lefticaru, Design and implementation of membrane controllers for trajectory tracking of nonholonomic wheeled mobile robots. Integr. Comput. Aided Eng. **23**(1), 15–30 (2016). https://doi.org/10.3233/ICA-150503
53. S. Xiao, N. Bergmann, A. Postula, Parallel RRT star architecture design for motion planning, in *2017 27th International Conference on Field Programmable Logic and Applications (FPL)*, Ghent, 2017, pp. 1–4. https://doi.org/10.23919/FPL.2017.8056773

Index

© The Author(s), under exclusive license to Springer Nature Singapore Pte Ltd. 2021   277
G. Zhang et al., *Membrane Computing Models: Implementations*,
https://doi.org/10.1007/978-981-16-1566-5